The Royal Musical Association

Music in Britain, 1600–2000

ISSN 2053-3217

Series Editors:
BYRON ADAMS, RACHEL COWGILL AND PETER HOLMAN

This series provides a forum for the best new work in the field of British music studies, placing music from the early seventeenth to the late twentieth centuries in its social, cultural, and historical contexts. Its approach is deliberately inclusive, covering immigrants and emigrants as well as native musicians, and explores Britain's musical links both within and beyond Europe. The series celebrates the vitality and diversity of music-making across Britain in whatever form it took and wherever it was found, exploring its aesthetic dimensions alongside its meaning for contemporaries, its place in the global market, and its use in the promotion of political and social agendas.

Proposals or queries should be sent in the first instance to Professors Byron Adams, Rachel Cowgill, Peter Holman or Boydell & Brewer at the addresses shown below. All submissions will receive prompt and informed consideration.

Professor Byron Adams
Department of Music – 061, University of California, Riverside, CA 92521–0325
email: byronadams@earthlink.net

Professor Rachel Cowgill MBE
Department of Music, University of York
Heslington, York, YO10 5DD
email: rachel.cowgill@york.ac.uk

Emeritus Professor Peter Holman MBE
119 Maldon Road, Colchester, Essex, CO3 3AX
email: peter@parley.org.uk

Boydell & Brewer, PO Box 9, Woodbridge, Suffolk, IP12 3DF
email: editorial@boydell.co.uk

Previously published volumes in this series are listed on our website, https://boydellandbrewer.com.

The Royal Musical Association

Creating Scholars, Advancing Research

Leanne Langley

THE BOYDELL PRESS

© Leanne Langley 2024

All rights reserved. Except as permitted under current legislation
no part of this work may be photocopied, stored in a retrieval system,
published, performed in public, adapted, broadcast,
transmitted, recorded or reproduced in any form or by any means,
without the prior permission of the copyright owner

The right of Leanne Langley to be identified as
the author of this work has been asserted in accordance with
sections 77 and 78 of the Copyright, Designs and Patents Act 1988

First published 2024
The Boydell Press, Woodbridge

ISBN 978 1 83765 038 5 (hardback); 978 1 83765 230 3 (paperback)

The Boydell Press is an imprint of Boydell & Brewer Ltd
PO Box 9, Woodbridge, Suffolk IP12 3DF, UK
and of Boydell & Brewer Inc.
668 Mt Hope Avenue, Rochester, NY 14620–2731, USA
website: www.boydellandbrewer.com

The publisher has no responsibility for the continued existence or accuracy of URLs for
external or third-party internet websites referred to in this book, and does not guarantee
that any content on such websites is, or will remain, accurate or appropriate

A CIP catalogue record for this book is available
from the British Library

Contents

	List of Illustrations	vii
	Preface	xi
	Acknowledgements	xvii
	List of Abbreviations	xxi
1	Before the Musical Association: The Weight of Performance Culture, 1800–1874	1
2	Developing Purpose, 1874–1924	31
3	Fresh Challenges, 1924–1944	95
4	Towards UK Musicology, 1945–1960	139
5	Coming of Age, 1960–1980	171
6	Widening Directions, Shifting Ground, 1980–2024	203
	Coda	231
	Appendix I: Presidents	239
	Appendix II: Secretaries, Treasurers, Editors, Librarian	241
	Appendix III: Honorary Foreign Members and Honorary Members	245
	Appendix IV: Dent Medallists and Other Award Holders	247
	Bibliography	251
	Index	259

List of Illustrations

❧ Figures

1. Musical Antiquarian Society, leaflet showing Council, 1846; BL shelfmark 816.l.47.(173) (by permission of the British Library Board) — 11
2. John Pyke Hullah, president of the Musical Institute, 1851–53; albumen carte-de-visite by Elliott & Fry, 1860s (© National Portrait Gallery, London) — 18
3. *Charles Kensington Salaman*, Honorary Secretary of the Musical Society of London, 1858–64, and of the Musical Association, 1874–78; oil on canvas by Sidney Starr, c. 1890, Ferens Art Gallery, Hull Museums (© Ferens Art Gallery/Bridgeman Images) — 20
4. Marylebone Literary and Scientific Institution, 17 Edwards Street, Portman Square, later a rehearsal and meetings base for the Musical Society of London, 1862–67; lithograph by T.M. Baynes of the Institution's opening, Lord Brougham in the chair, 4 March 1835 (© Westminter City Archives) — 22
5. 'British Museum, Plan of New Reading Room in Quadrangle', on ticket to a private view of the new building, 5 May 1857 (© Trustees of the British Museum) — 25
6. Officers and Original Members of the Musical Association, from *PMA*, 1 (1874–75), pp. vii–ix (courtesy of JSTOR) — 38
7. Fourth Congress of the International Musical Society, London, 1911, group portrait outside the entrance to the Imperial Institute, South Kensington, 3 June 1911; photograph by Bedford Lemere & Co. (Historic England Archive) — 60
8. Notice card for the twenty-seventh Musical Association AGM, 12 November 1901, with synopsis of J.E. Borland's paper, BL Add. MS 71033, fol. 40 (RMA Papers, British Library, by permission) — 75
9. 'The Greatest Library in the World – The Reading-Room of the British Museum', from the *Sphere*, 13 April 1907; illustration by Fortunino Matania, detail (© Illustrated London News Ltd/ Mary Evans Picture Library) — 81

viii LIST OF ILLUSTRATIONS

10	Guillaume Dufay, 'C'est bien raison de devoir essaucier', ballade for three voices, Bodleian Library MS. Canon. Misc. 213, fol. 55v: https://digital.bodleian.ox.ac.uk/objects/a4120d22-b62f-4b57-861d-43c839c790a0/ (photograph © Bodleian Libraries, University of Oxford, used by Creative Commons licence CC-BY-NC 4.0)	87
11	*Professor E.J. Dent*, drawing by Edmond X. Kapp, 1941 (photograph © The Fitzwilliam Museum, University of Cambridge; reproduced courtesy of Chris Beetles Gallery, St James's, London)	108
12	Parry Room Library, Royal College of Music, photograph by *Daily Herald*, c. 1933 (© Royal College of Music/ArenaPAL)	123
13	Rupert Erlebach to Dr Fellowes, 23 May 1938, on behalf of the Musical Association Research Subcommittee, BL Add. MS 56236, fol. 32 (RMA Papers, British Library, by permission)	125
14	Sylvia Townsend Warner, photograph, London, late 1920s, D-TWA/STW/alone/5, from the Sylvia Townsend Warner collection (used by permission of the Dorset History Centre)	129
15	Edmund Horace Fellowes, photograph by Walter Stoneman, February 1944 (© National Portrait Gallery, London)	135
16	Cover designs for *PRMA* 79 (1952–53) and 80 (1953–54) (courtesy of JSTOR)	145
17	Festival of Britain, 1951, South Bank Exhibition, postcard photograph of an artist's impression, aerial view (private collection, by permission)	151
18	R.T. Dart to Rupert Erlebach [October 1951], with printing instructions for Musica Britannica titling, BL Add. MS 71044, fol. 30 (RMA Papers, British Library, by permission)	163
19	*Sir Anthony Lewis*, oil on canvas by Pamela Thalben-Ball, 1976 (photograph © Royal Academy of Music; reproduced as an orphan work after a diligent search for the artist's estate owner)	167
20	Nigel Fortune, photograph by John Casken, late 1990s (courtesy of John Casken)	174
21	Anonymous correspondent to RMA [March 1964], BL Add. MS 71037, fol. 1 (RMA Papers, British Library, by permission)	179
22	'Geographical Distribution of RMA members', c. 1972, by Nigel Fortune; redrawn from a map pasted in RMA Papers, Manchester, M MS 2, fol. 123 (by permission of the RMA)	189

23	Thurston Dart and the Faculty of Music at King's College London, photograph, 1968, KCL photographer unknown; Cambridge University Library, Thurston Dart Archive, GBR/0012/MS Dart 5/17 (image © Cambridge University Library; reproduced by permission of Cambridge University Library and King's College London)	200
24	Stanley Sadie, Leanne Langley and Christina Bashford with *The New Grove Dictionary of Opera*, 1992, at Macmillan Publishers, London; photograph, *Opera* magazine, November 1992, photographer unknown (reproduced by permission of *Opera* magazine, courtesy of John Allison)	206
25	Cover designs for *JRMA* 112, pt 2 (1987) and 145, pt 1 (2020) (private collection, by permission)	217
26	London blue plaque at 20 Frith Street, Soho, London, commemorating the location of a house where Mozart 'lived, played and composed' in 1764–65, placed by the RMA in 1991; photograph by Spudgun67 (used by Creative Commons Attribution-Share Alike 4.0 International: https://creativecommons.org/licenses/by-sa/4.0/)	221
27	Simon McVeigh, Mieko Kanno, Warwick Edwards and Barbara Kelly at a conference celebrating the 150th anniversary of the Royal Society for Music History of the Netherlands, Paushuize, Utrecht, 2018 (by permission of the RMA)	230

Tables

1	Selected individual scholars, 1800–75	5
2	Musical Association papers on scientific subjects, 1874–1924	76
3	Musica Britannica, 1951–61: the first sixteen volumes	161
4	Comparative contents of *PRMA* 100 (1973–74) and *Modern Musical Scholarship* (1980), both edited by Edward Olleson	192

The author and publisher are grateful to all the institutions and individuals listed for permission to reproduce the materials in which they hold copyright. Every effort has been made to trace the copyright holders; apologies are offered for any omission, and the publisher will be pleased to add any necessary acknowledgement in subsequent editions.

Preface

By any measure, the Royal Musical Association is an odd sort of music club. Not a professional guild, elite society or lobbyists' group, a trade union, music teachers' body or hobbyists' circle, it was founded as a learned society in the English tradition, akin to the venerable Royal Society for scientists begun in 1660. Embracing members from more than one branch of musical practice and aural experience, including several contemporary Royal Society fellows, the Association was broad in coverage and high-minded from the start, but, unlike its seventeenth-century counterpart, it was not selective according to musical eminence or achievement. Instead it was a mixed body for intending investigators – a starter group with prominent scientists providing the yeast. All its early joiners, regardless of their musical level, social status, occupation or sex (women were included), came by choice and were relatively new to music scholarship, interested in probing music intellectually by whatever angle or means.

Though hardly revolutionary in 1874, research involving music had never gained enough purchase in Britain, or enough practitioners, to last as a collective enterprise until then. Indeed coherence was still not certain, given that there was not yet any recognized field of dedicated music study in Britain with its own protocols, certainly not one called 'musicology' close to the emerging Austro-German *Musikwissenschaft* in central Europe. Nor, crucially, was any British university open to music as a serious academic study, as against composing. The founders' idea was to create such a field. In establishing its procedures and building up a fund of published papers, they hoped to secure the desired academic opening, and with it higher social standing, through 'investigating' and 'discussing' music rather than performing it – no small feat in a market-driven Victorian culture alive with composers and performers, many gaining enormous popular attention, cash and critical commentary. By contrast, recognition for music scholars would be an uphill journey for decades.

In a further oddity, although deemed 'royal' by a decree of George VI in 1944, the Association never sought to have its objectives and constitution incorporated by royal charter; after seventy years, it welcomed the king's personal accolade and found it useful in attracting external support. But the RMA has never enjoyed direct royal patronage or government funding and still has no premises of its own or institutional affiliation. Like other educational charities, it receives favourable tax status for giving public benefit through its activities but remains fully self-determining, relying on voluntary support through memberships, donations and income from its publications. Manifestly, the Association has survived and excelled, facilitating some of the best music research in the world along with effective public communication of that work and its value. In 2024 the Royal Musical Association celebrates its 150th anniversary, offering a prime moment to take stock of its history and appraise its achievements. This book is the outcome of that study.

My emphasis has been on the people who came together to form the Musical Association in 1874, and on those in later generations who sustained it. By publishing their papers and discussions as other learned societies had done, the founders also hoped to render their subject genuinely useful in the national discourse, lifting music's public relevance and making its scholarly pursuit worthy of state support through university acceptance – which did come, if surprisingly late in the day. All along, in creating a viable community around both practical and speculative research, members benefited from the camaraderie and intellectual exchanges inherent in associating with each other, often across class, gender, subject and professional divides. Gradually expanding their activities through connection with parallel advances in library organization, commercial publishing, education, sound recording and public broadcasting, university growth and, not least, cooperation with colleagues abroad and the arrival of European émigrés in the 1930s, the RMA succeeded in making musicology in Great Britain an international force by the mid-twentieth century.

The aim of my narrative is twofold: first, to reveal new findings from the Association's extensive archive and publications, never before studied as a whole, about how the founders, Council and evolving membership saw their identity and fashioned it, gaining ground, sometimes losing it, in debates about the purpose and objects of music research – with implications for how research might be funded; and second, to highlight particular research outcomes by scholars affiliated with or recognized by the RMA, contributing to new understanding of music and its benefits and cultures worldwide. In this way, the Association's development, together with changes in the UK music profession including academic affiliation for scholars, can be seen as a backdrop for a range of identifiable research achievements – from important discoveries of previously unknown early musical works, how they sounded and how they were used, to percipient analyses of sonic expression in a range of cultures, whether in flights of aesthetic beauty, as tools of education and intellectual development, or by co-option for social and political purposes.

The text weaves together these strands in a single chronological account, itself divided into six broad chapters reflecting successive changes: from new-member drives, joint activity with the International Musical Society (later the International Musicological Society) and the contexts of world war – twice, including some resistance to German methods through privileging a broad, critically orientated English form of 'musical research' over the perceived limitations of a more doctrinaire central European 'musicology' – towards expansion in university music professorships, Arts Council support for Musica Britannica, the BBC Third Programme, curricular innovations at King's College London, *New Grove* lexicography initiatives at Macmillan Publishers and deepening government involvement in the organization of university research. This dual focus on the developing Association and on individual scholars and their work, increasingly exemplary by the highest international standards, opens a much-needed new perspective. At root, I hope it's more empathetic, lively and human-centred than is evoked by outdated stereotypes of gentlemen's clubs, as well as more attentive to the distinctive character and development of British music scholarship than has often been the norm, especially over such an extended period.

Long assumed to be inferior, or at least subsidiary, to Austrian, German, Dutch, Belgian, French and, later, American musicology – notably by some British scholars themselves, whether in crises of confidence or in frustration at local limits – British work emerges instead as more broadly conceived, variegated and prescient than many readers may expect, treating music predominantly as an art. My discussion of research preoccupations and favoured source material encompasses three large areas: (1) early song, music manuscript study, transcription and editing (for performing, recording or publication, fuelling a range of period and national interpretations); (2) global instruments, acoustics and the study of sonic attributes, with ethnographic methods applied to both world and local musics and cultural contexts (exploring music's social and communal values, often through scientific or mathematical means); and (3) continual integration and reinterpretation of composers, composition, performers and listeners, embracing the traditional life-and-works study but also analysis, performance studies, perception (listening, psychology, expression) and reception issues, all within the broad, holistic spheres of performance, theory and history. Aspects of all these interest areas, including extra-musical influences, can be shown to resonate with some of the earliest work of Musical Association founders.

This historical reframing from a British perspective of the 'job musicologists do', with reference to what the RMA founders first imagined and attempted, how they proceeded and how and why conditions changed, is timely not only for celebrating one organization's special anniversary. It also sheds light on current social and ideological tensions globally, reflecting stark recognition of embedded wrongs in many human societies. Recent widespread critiques of nineteenth- and twentieth-century British colonial history around race, gender and patronage, for example, are valid and necessary, often revelatory when close evidence is provided. But sometimes they may also target a little too readily all national bodies, people and published monuments from earlier days as easy prey, essentializing them as imperialistic or patriarchal by definition with little thought for evidence of overt complicity in specific wrongs. The narrative offered here provides a deeper context for such debates, enriching and complicating any simplistic ideological assumptions of the present about the past, or of one nation about another, besides bringing forward some principled scholars and hard-won achievements otherwise ignored or forgotten in wider commentary about British musical culture. Far from invoking 'English exceptionalism', chauvinism or any pride in the totality of British music or musical thought, moreover, this story charts a rather slow dawning that Britain in fact possessed substantial stores of all kinds of earlier music and popular music including its own creations, and that serious researchers needed to push ahead in studying and learning from this richness.

My primary source material rests in the Association's own archive, currently held in two locations. The first, main, portion comprises fifty-five manuscript volumes known as the Royal Musical Association Papers, held at the British Library. Consisting of Council and other committee minute books, official papers and correspondence, 1874–1971, this material is preserved as BL Add. MSS 71010–64, and relates also to two earlier deposited volumes, BL Add. MSS 56236 (1938) and 59670 (1936–51). The second, smaller portion, still in the Association's possession, comprises eight boxes of uncatalogued papers, chiefly bound committee minutes, loose additional papers, leaflets and some correspondence, 1950–97, currently held in Manchester as part of a working archive used by the former RMA Executive Officer Dr Jeffrey Dean. These last materials, an early portion of which were discovered at Durham University in 2006 and transferred to Manchester, are intended by agreement for deposit in the British Library in due course. Like most archives, both these period collections are themselves 'constructed' rather than completely objective or whole. But they offer the fullest look yet possible into this complex organization and how it developed over several generations.

Besides the official archive, I've also consulted related source material in the New York Public Library, a wide range of secondary sources including articles, essays, books and encyclopaedias, and complete files of the RMA's own publications or associated ones: *Proceedings of the Musical Association* (*PMA*, 1875–1944); *Proceedings of the Royal Musical Association* (*PRMA*, 1945–85); *Journal of the Royal Musical Association* (*JRMA*, from 1986); *Royal Musical Association Research Chronicle* (*RMARC*, from 1961); and Musica Britannica (MB, from 1951, a national collection of British music). For the earlier years in particular I've consulted publications of the International Musical Society in which the Musical Association participated: *Sammelbände der Internationalen Musikgesellschaft* (*SIMG*), *Zeitschrift der Internationalen Musikgesellschaft* (*ZIMG*) and later *Acta musicologica* (from 1931). To facilitate my own and others' research, I compiled my own chronological listing, with an author index, of all articles appearing in the last sixty years of the *Proceedings/Journal of the Royal Musical Association*. A reference tool of this nature, succeeding earlier *PMA/PRMA* article listings that came to an end in 1965, was intended for publication by the Association in the late twentieth century but was never completed.

Despite, or perhaps because of, such abundant material and this project's potential scope, I've naturally had to step back and select, weighing what seemed to me most important in shaping a meaningful story. Otherwise there would be no history, only chronology. By extension my chosen narrative is not value-free; I have my own biases, which are clear enough, although I've tried to be fair. The greatest challenge has been finding a balance between the Associational group at any one time and its individual members, including many who were never on the Council or who left no obvious trail in the minutes but were still active as key researchers, or similarly, others who were once active then dropped out, or moved in and out of RMA range at different periods according to circumstances, a familiar pattern. In a similar way, while not wishing to produce a circumscribed company history, I've chosen to focus squarely on the Association and its activities rather than to explore the whole of British music scholarship across wider contexts and debates, from the role of Darwinism in some English readings of music history to the challenges of music editing and publishing as a central musicological activity leading to performance; from the place of textual criticism and palaeography in canon formation to the shift from nineteenth-century historicism to post-war modernism using musicological science to replace romantic accretions with an ideal musical Urtext; and from fruitful discussions over 'text versus context' to the centrality of British research in the historical performance movement of the 1960s and onwards. These are all focused areas in which solid historiographical accounts have already registered, with further detailed treatments still in the making.

By contrast, the RMA as a subject itself has seemed not only less relevant to current music studies, perhaps less compelling in worldwide intellectual history, but also, presumably, dull and uninviting, requiring a great trawl through dusty records. I happen to like (proverbial) dust because layers of discovery might lie underneath – which perhaps explains why I accepted the challenge. Another reason could be that I've been working on the relevant background for some time, starting with the seventeenth-century English press, musical writing and intersections in eighteenth-century literary and music publishing, and the developing of reading audiences for serious music literature, including dictionaries in the nineteenth century, while also tracking the labyrinthine networks of London concert-giving and conservatory training, the context in which organizing a dedicated music scholarly group was first advocated. At all events, I see my task less as providing a conspectus of progress on specific research topics or methods – what have we learned in Purcell, Mozart or Verdi research? how have gender studies developed? which practices in music analysis have been most productive? – than as painting the social and intellectual world in which they could all flourish, and did. Forging that place in the UK national landscape was a great achievement, and it remains an ongoing challenge even now. Welcome to the Royal Musical Association.

Acknowledgements

It is a pleasure to record my thanks to the organizations and people who've encouraged my interests, aided my research and supplied answers to particular queries. As I always hoped, this book has benefited from the contributions of many hands and voices.

My first debt is to the RMA itself, whose current president Simon Keefe, as Editor of RMA Monographs in 2014, first asked if I would write a book on the Association's history for the sesquicentenary. He has been unfailingly supportive since that time, even when the dimensions of my study exceeded an RMA Monograph's extent. Together with Mark Everist, our indefatigable president, and Chris Banks, of the RMA Publications Committee and formerly the British Library where as Music Curator she catalogued the original RMA Papers, Simon and all the Council officers have stood behind the project. Most recently Simon McVeigh and Barbara Kelly, successor presidents to Mark, have given generous practical help. I hasten to add that, at my own request, the Association never officially commissioned me to produce a history, although they willingly covered a portion of my travel costs to visit collections. At all times I was unencumbered, enjoying the freedom to range widely, probe meaning and seek answers or advice. Through sharing specific memories, Julian Rushton, a former RMA president of wide scholarly experience, and Jeffrey Dean, recently retired Executive Officer, have been particularly helpful. I would also like to thank the eight 'expert witnesses' who responded to my request for their RMA reflections: H. Diack Johnstone, Elizabeth Wells, John Irving, Rachel Segal, Fiona M. Palmer, Graham Dixon, John Deathridge and Natasha Loges. From the 1950s to the 2020s, in and beyond music academic life, this group offers ample evidence of the Association's wide reach and good effects.

My second debt is to the library collections I consulted, chiefly that of the British Library with its unmatched breadth and depth, expert librarians and public-facing staff in the Rare Books and Music Reading Room, all of whom provide constant care for important materials. They gave me ready access in sometimes difficult circumstances. While I was hopping buses, dodging train strikes, queuing for entry to time-limited sessions and navigating one-way systems during the COVID-19 pandemic, they were coping with similar restrictions; the cyber-attack on the Library in autumn 2023 proved still more disruptive for everyone. At the best and worst of times, BL Reading Room staff were ready with good suggestions, manuscripts, Reader Pass assistance, friendly smiles, helpful emails and even – beyond the call of duty – eyeglass repairs. My thanks go to all, starting with Richard Chesser, Rupert Ridgewell and Chris Scobie of British Library Music Collections. Between the Association and the BL, as it were, sits a remaining portion of RMA manuscript material in the Manchester home office of Jeffrey Dean. I spent two very pleasant weeks in Manchester, studying those minute books and other papers, enjoying the generous advice and hospitality of Jeff and his wife Penelope Gouk; I thank them most warmly. A further heroic information service was provided in Covid lockdowns by the staff of the London Library, St James's Square, who not only sent requested books by post to my Southampton address, but offered immediate access to an unrivalled set of research databases and reference publications though remote membership. I couldn't have managed without them (and Thomas Carlyle's founding of the Library). Another fillip was provided by the New York Public Library for the Performing Arts, Lincoln Center, where in 2019 I found unique papers of the Musical Society of London among Edward Rimbault's materials; I'm grateful to Jessica Wood for helping me gain access to them. Finally, the richness of the online Georgian Papers Programme was crucial to my earliest work on the original Royal Academy of Music and its proposed research plans in 1813. I thankfully acknowledge this publicly available catalogue created by the Royal Archives at Windsor Castle.

And third, I must heartily acknowledge Boydell & Brewer, above all Michael Middeke, Editorial Director, Modern History and Music, for his encouragement and guidance in collecting my ideas, preparing a proposal and executing the task of writing – though I also have to thank him for his patience when my progress was slow. With a shrewd eye and careful language, Crispin Peet was exemplary as editorial assistant. Julia Cook and Demi Wormgoor kept things moving while Fiona Little and Tanya Izzard completed the most exacting editorial work with skill and precision, for which I'm particularly grateful. I'd also like to thank Boydell's 'Music in Britain, 1600–2000' series editors, Byron Adams, Rachel Cowgill and Peter Holman, for their support of this project in the first place. For discussion of my thoughts as work began or proceeded and for helpful replies to requests, I'm delighted to thank Karen Arrandale, Amanda Babington, Christina Bashford, Michael Byde, Sarah Collins, Hugh Cobbe, Rachel Cowgill, Jeremy Dibble, Warwick Edwards, David Fallows, Annegret Fauser, Rebecca Herissone, Sarah Hibberd, Sir Roland Jackson, Tamara Levitz, Simon McVeigh, Fiona M. Palmer and Jan Smaczny. In addition, Julian Rushton, Paul Scruton and David C.H. Wright generously read the text and offered perceptive advice, not only correcting errors and misunderstanding but also making me sound better.

I also extend my thanks to the galleries, museums and libraries whose archivists and licensing managers helped me secure permission to use images of material in their collections: The British Library (Cerys Savinkins); National Portrait Gallery, London (Mark Lynch); Ferens Art Galley, Hull (Kerri Offord), and Bridgeman Images; Westminster City Archives (Oliver Jones); The British Museum (Elizabeth Bray and Francesca Hillier); JSTOR; Historic England Archive (Leah Prior); Mary Evans Picture Library (Lucinda Gosling); Bodleian Libraries, University of Oxford; The Fitzwilliam Museum, Cambridge (Emma Darbyshire), and Chris Beetles Gallery, London (Pascale Oakley-Birch); Royal College of Music and ArenaPAL (Mike Markiewicz); Dorset History Centre (Luke Dady); Royal Academy of Music, London (Ian Brearey); John Casken; Cambridge University Library (Johanna Ward) and King's College London (Gemma Hollman); *Opera* magazine (John Allison); Wikimedia Commons;

Royal Institute of British Architects (Jonathan Makepeace); and the Royal Musical Association.

Further, I'd particularly like to thank my family members who lent a hand throughout the most intense work periods, above all my husband Paul Scruton for his technical expertise and good sense, and my sons William and Michael Scruton for their irrepressible mood-lifting skills. Michael has been a key assistant providing linguistic and editorial support I couldn't have found elsewhere; he compiled several of the book's appendices and contributed enormously to the supplementary material available at www.leannelangley.com/projects/the-royal-musical-association. This comprises current listings of Musica Britannica volumes and RMA Monographs, as well as *PRMA/JRMA* articles, volumes 91 (1964–65) to 149 (2024), with an author index. In a text dense with so many names, dates and events, there will naturally be errors of fact and interpretation too: these are my responsibility alone, and I would value receiving corrections or comments from readers.

Lastly, I'd like to pay tribute to the memory of six significant friends – mentors and RMA colleagues from my earliest days in the UK – without whose abiding influence I could never have undertaken this study: Alec Hyatt King, Tim Neighbour, Arthur Searle, Nigel Fortune, Stanley Sadie and Cyril Ehrlich. Their intellectual stimulation, friendly support and legacy of scholarly commitment years before I ever contemplated the Association's history have remained purposeful and inspiring throughout my work. Their impact goes on for all of us.

> I am a part of all that I have met;
> Yet all experience is an arch wherethrough
> Gleams that untravelled world, whose margin fades
> For ever and for ever when I move.
>
> —Alfred Tennyson, *Ulysses*

Leanne Langley
Southampton, April 2024

List of Abbreviations

❧ *General*

Add.	Additional (Manuscript)
AGM	Annual General Meeting
AMS	American Musicological Society
BBC	British Broadcasting Corporation
BFE	British Forum for Ethnomusicology
BIRS	British Institute of Recorded Sound
BL	British Library
BM	British Museum
B.Mus.	Bachelor of Music
fol.(s)	folio(s)
IAML	International Association of Music Libraries
IGMw/SIM/ISMR	Internationale Gesellschaft für Musikwissenschaft/Société Internationale de Musicologie/International Society for Musical Research (founded 1927), from 1949 International Musicological Society
IMG	Internationale Musikgesellschaft/International Musical Society (1899–1914)
IMS	International Musicological Society (used only from 1949)
ISCM	International Society for Contemporary Music
ISMR	International Society for Musical Research
KCL	King's College, University of London
KVNM	Koninklijke Vereniging voor Nederlandse Muziekgeschiedenis/Royal Society for Music History of the Netherlands
M.Mus.	Master of Music
MSL	Musical Society of London
Mus.Doc.	Doctor of Music

xxii LIST OF ABBREVIATIONS

NPS	New Philharmonic Society
NYPL	New York Public Library
OUP	Oxford University Press
r	recto
RAE	Research Assessment Exercise
RAM	Royal Academy of Music, London
RCM	Royal College of Music, London
REF	Research Excellence Framework
RILM	Répertoire International de Littérature Musicale/International Repertory of Music Literature
RISM	Répertoire International des Sources Musicales/International Inventory of Musical Sources
RMA	Royal Musical Association
Univ.	University
v	verso
V&A	Victoria and Albert Museum, London

❧ Bibliographical

BOOKS, MUSIC EDITION

Grove 1 – Grove 5	George Grove, ed., *A Dictionary of Music and Musicians* (London: Macmillan, 1879-89); 2nd edn, ed. J.A. Fuller Maitland, 1904–10; 3rd edn, ed. H.C. Colles, 1927; 4th edn, ed. H.C. Colles, 1940; 5th edn, ed. Eric Blom, 1954, with supplementary vol., 1961
MB	Musica Britannica
New Grove	Stanley Sadie, ed., *The New Grove Dictionary of Music and Musicians* (London: Macmillan, 1980)
New Grove 2	Stanley Sadie, ed., with executive ed. John Tyrrell, *The New Grove Dictionary of Music and Musicians*, 2nd edn (London: Macmillan, 2001)

ODNB	*Oxford Dictionary of National Biography*, ed. Brian Harrison (Oxford: Oxford University Press, 2004), http://www.oxforddnb.com
Report of the Fourth Congress	*Report of the Fourth Congress of the International Musical Society: London 29 May – 3 June 1911* (London: Novello & Co., 1912)

PERIODICALS

JAMS	*Journal of the American Musicological Society*
JRMA	*Journal of the Royal Musical Association*
ML	*Music & Letters*
MQ	*Musical Quarterly*
MT	*Musical Times*
Notes	*Notes, the Quarterly Journal of the Music Library Association*
PMA	*Proceedings of the Musical Association*
PRMA	*Proceedings of the Royal Musical Association*
RMARC	*R.M.A. Research Chronicle*; from 1978, *Royal Musical Association Research Chronicle*
SIMG	*Sammelbände der Internationalen Musikgesellschaft*
TLS	*Times Literary Supplement*
ZIMG	*Zeitschrift der Internationalen Musikgesellschaft*

Allow me to state, with all the formality due to an official communication, that the Musical Institute is not, nor is it consistent with any of its present plans that it should become, a *performing* or *concert-giving* Society. We come together – to borrow from our prospectus a long word, which I believe has no synonyme – for the 'intercommunication' of musical knowledge amongst Professors and Amateurs; and the *principal* means proposed for such intercommunication are, of course, the reading of papers, or essays, or articles (called by whatever name), and conversation afterwards on the subjects treated therein. Without doubt musical *performance* of some kind will generally form part of our 'transactions'; but it will be incidental to, and having immediate reference to[,] the subject under discussion.

—John Hullah, President
Inaugural Address to the Musical Institute of London, 14 February 1852
[emphasis original]

1

Before the Musical Association: The Weight of Performance Culture, 1800–1874

'Musical research' was a challenging idea in nineteenth-century Britain. Even as late as the 1930s its definition and purposes were debated in both Britain and the USA as its practice edged closer to *Musikwissenschaft, musicologie* or musicology.[1] The mystique around what such a pursuit involved, how it might be undertaken and why its results might be useful or important evoked for many an image of *un*musical digging, scientific exactitude and tedious explanation apt to squeeze the life out of music itself, threatening a pleasure millions of listeners valued. Why bother? British readers, in particular, more than American ones, already had access to an impressive range and quantity of printed information on music, whether historical writing about musicians and society, critical responses to heard music, news of music events at home and abroad, discussions of composers and their works, or philosophical explorations of music's nature. By the late nineteenth century, these topics had been treated for more than a century in general magazines, specialist music journals, higher literary reviews, dictionaries and books, much of it at a sophisticated level designed to cultivate even more readers (and sell more print). So how a deeper investigation of specific aspects of music might enhance the conversation, and what could conceivably be gained by examining physical sound, musical genres, performance styles, instruments, historical periods and exotic cultures, all in forensic detail, remained doubtful even to some early Musical Association members. This hesitancy – call it a healthy British caution – suggests that in 1874 the Association's founding must have rested on still tentative ground. Indeed, far from emerging fully formed as the result of a thrusting Victorian demand for knowledge and status, the Musical Association was neither inevitable nor bound to last. It began quietly on the initiative of a small group of people from mostly middle-class backgrounds with diverse musical and, importantly, non-musical interests. What they shared, beyond intellectual

---

[1] See, for example, Waldo S. Pratt, 'On Behalf of Musicology', *MQ*, 1 (1915), 1–16; Louis Harap, 'On the Nature of Musicology', *MQ*, 23 (1937), 18–25; and three articles by Edward J. Dent, describing the English attitude and academic background for international readers: 'The Scientific Study of Music in England', *Acta musicologica*, 2 (1930), 83–92; 'Music and Musical Research', *Acta musicologica*, 3 (1931), 5–8; and 'The Historical Approach to Music', *MQ*, 23 (1937), 1–17.

curiosity and a willingness to learn from each other, was a determination to cohere as a learned society. Several previous attempts at something similar had faltered.

In this chapter I explore key precedents and feeder lines for the network of interests surrounding the early Musical Association. While it would be wrong to think that together these led inexorably to the founding in 1874, or that the Association set out to preside over music-scholarly output for Britain, it's still useful to trace how priorities in music research and its professionalization developed in tandem. From the early nineteenth century, scholars' personal experiences, economic status, time and place, together with the practical, intellectual, national or societal conditions likely to have stimulated their work, show distinct patterns. A number of people acted alone, driven by their own passions and opportunities; others acted in concert, as members of music or publishing clubs. Music societies that tried to include research aims or lectures along with other activities rarely made a serious mark on scholarship, however; their research forums tended to fade quickly, overshadowed by more immediately appealing choices for subscribers such as concerts, choir practices and conversaziones. Low interest from lack of member confidence in how to begin an investigation, how to share one's findings, even how to form questions or listen to reports of other people's work, emerges from the story of these groups. As things turned out, the all-inclusive music society was not conducive for developing scholars or scholarship, and instead underscored a divide between music lovers and music investigators rather than bridging it, despite good intentions. Yet when seen over a seventy-year continuum, with particular scholars' names recurring across more than one research endeavour, club or society, and many of these publishing work of genuine quality for the period, it's clear that the Musical Association did not arise in a vacuum. The diversity of experience and occupation in its early members, moreover, whether source collectors and music executants, literary professionals or noted scientists, laid the foundation for what were seen as the Association's early strengths, including public credibility, social openness and methodological flexibility.

I'll divide the discussion into three parts, covering individuals, publishing schemes and music clubs with research aims, before going on to compare contemporary parallels in the development of Science and History as professional disciplines.

Individuals

A bit like the old narrative of music composition in Victorian Britain, nineteenth-century British music scholarship has long been viewed pathologically, backwards from a simple Modernist-derived value opposition between 'antiquarian' or 'arm-chair' practices and those of more advanced mid-twentieth-century musicology.[2] Even as a fair attempt to celebrate post-1945 scholarly achievements, though, this reductive strategy disappoints for ignoring myriad dissimilarities in context, audience and intent between the two cultural periods. To cite one example, reference to the prevalence in Victorian research of English clerics, organists and music journalists as if those occupations essentialized some inherent weakness badly miscalculates who held educated professional interest in research activity, access to musical sources and the means of their literate public discussion. The tenor of twentieth-century writing, too, can be problematic. Noting with regret the absence of a single towering figure like a Forkel, Fétis or Eitner, this line of critique typically salutes British editors, scientists, folksong collectors and instrument-builders for their busyness, but traces no ultimate outcomes or significance. The tone may rise again at the mention of E.H. Fellowes and Francis Galpin, then soar when Edward J. Dent and Robert Thurston Dart come into view, but readers of this kind of commentary are left with the unmistakable impression that not much of scholarly consequence happened beforehand, in nineteenth-century Britain. That cannot possibly be true.

Part of the problem lies with a genuine gap in our knowledge of disparate, individual projects not usually viewed together, as well as in ignorance of potential sources – private papers, lecture notes, library and sale catalogues, company archives and distinguished literary and music journals including foreign ones. Another part of the problem lies with two limits in viewpoint – unguarded acceptance of the progressive model of history, and the use of loaded, or at least ambiguous, terms of personal reference – amateur versus professional, antiquarian versus musicologist, musician versus scholar, researcher versus 'expert'. To some extent, the trope of progress is apt for the age of Robert Stephenson and Charles Darwin, useful in classifying who did what and how successfully or otherwise. But by forcing us to look for bigger and better published monuments, themselves adhering to quasi-modern standards, the progressive model works too easily like an industrial template. It sets the pattern before all the evidence is in, may yield a false (or falsely negative) image and certainly misses significant and subtle details. Labels carrying class distinctions are probably inevitable but no less blind. Social class for musicians and scholars ran the gamut across the century, whereas modern judgements of intellectual class depend on subject matter as well as methodology, and in any case can reveal more about current intellectual preoccupations than about Victorian ones.

---

[2] See, for example, Vincent Duckles, 'Musicology, III, §3. Great Britain and the Commonwealth Countries', *New Grove* (1980), in which repeated references to oldness, the church and the 'amateur tradition' work to convey a constricted stereotype for British musicology, an account little revised in *New Grove 2* (2001); and Christian Kennett, 'Criticism and Theory', in *The Twentieth Century*, ed. Stephen Banfield, Blackwell History of Music in Britain, vol. 6 (Oxford: Blackwell, 1995), 503–18, in which 'the gentleman amateur' is used both structurally and thematically with little qualification.

More important, and surely more reliable, is the simple test of solid work whatever the topic or personal status – work that was careful, thorough, well informed for the period and enquiring, intellectually honest. Table 1 presents a selected listing of eighteen individuals who can be associated with serious music-scholarly activity and publication at some time between about 1800 and 1875 – much of it original, substantially better than had existed before, and providing a stimulus to further research.[3] Their names appear here under the first, second or third quarter of the century according to their earliest scholarly engagement, marking less an age band than their music research in a career perhaps crowded with other activities. Not one of these people was a musicologist, and few were trained in research techniques. Only two were independently wealthy (Ouseley, Dannreuther); most earned their living in middle-class professions, as teachers, lecturers, writers, solicitors, politicians, administrators or businessmen, much like intellectuals in other scientific fields. All were born before 1850 (seven before 1800); only five were born and educated outside the UK (Schoelcher, Engel, Dannreuther, Pauer and Hueffer), so that fundamentally the list represents British work.

Very broadly, research interests in this period coalesced around three subject areas: indigenous song collected from all four UK vernacular traditions, Welsh (Jones), Irish (Bunting), Scots (Dauney) and English (Chappell), as well as early vocal music from cultivated European traditions (Novello, Rimbault, Ouseley, Hueffer); undervalued 'classical' composers, notably Bach, Purcell, Mozart, Handel and Wagner (Dannreuther, Pauer, Hueffer); and sound phenomena, including instrument construction and pitch systems. The changing temper of the times is revealing when these themes are tracked.

Edward Jones, a Welsh harpist, tune collector and historian of Welsh literature active in London, was harpist to the Prince of Wales from about 1788, and by 1820, when the prince became king, was known as Bardd y Brenin ('the king's bard') to George IV. Besides preserving more than 200 traditional melodies, he published important books, *The Musical and Poetical Relicks of the Welsh Bards* (1784), *The Bardic Museum* (1802) and *Hên ganiadau Cymru* (1820), which helped to open up Welsh history and culture for other antiquarians. Edward Bunting's work in Irish music was similarly pivotal, alike redemptive and investigative. From the 1790s he transcribed hundreds of traditional harp tunes collected on tours and festival visits from Belfast to Connacht and Dublin, publishing three volumes of the 'ancient music of Ireland' and writing in some depth about it (1797, 1809, 1840). The first, *A General Collection of the*

---

[3] This selection is deliberately tight for the purposes of discussion, omitting many other 'scholarly' people known from their press and dictionary contributions, lecturing or important music collecting in this period, such as James Bartleman, William Ayrton, Joseph Warren, Edward Taylor and W.H. Husk. Although shrewd and knowledgeable, they didn't make a distinctive intellectual contribution using the collections they owned. See A. Hyatt King, *Some British Collectors of Music, c. 1600–1960* (Cambridge: Cambridge Univ. Press, 1963).

Table 1. Selected individual scholars, 1800–1875

1800–25	1825–50	1850–75
Edward Jones	Vincent Novello	F.A. Gore Ouseley
Edward Bunting	William Dauney	Victor Schoelcher
William Crotch	William Chappell	Carl Engel
Samuel Wesley (with C.F. Horn)	John Hullah	Edward Dannreuther
John Stafford Smith	Edward F. Rimbault	Ernst Pauer
	Edward Holmes	Francis Hueffer
		William Pole

Ancient Irish Music, is now recognized as 'the most seminal and influential publication in the history of Irish music'.[4]

In contrast to preserving national heritage, a lot of early British editorial work on old, 'lost' or inaccessible sources of European and English music was meant to foster discovery and fresh performance in new times. Samuel Wesley's pathbreaking edition, with C.F. Horn, of J.S. Bach's forty-eight preludes and fugues for keyboard (Book 1, 1810) and Vincent Novello's editions of seventeenth-century Italian church music (*The Fitzwilliam Music*, 1825–27) and of Purcell's sacred music (1828–32) are representative. The immediate practical aim was to put unfamiliar but exemplary music into wider circulation, improving or seeding solid repertories for home and church. Around the same period, still older music was transcribed for teaching and learning purposes, as with William Crotch's *Specimens of Various Styles of Music* (London, 1808–15), linked to a series of well-received public lectures he gave in Oxford and London at the Royal Institution, with illustrations played at the keyboard;[5] and John Stafford Smith's remarkable *Musica antiqua: A Selection of Music of This and Other Countries, from the Commencement of the Twelfth to the Beginning of the Eighteenth Century* (1812), a collection of some 190 pieces

---

[4] Harry White, 'Bunting, Edward', *Dictionary of Irish Biography: From the Earliest Times to the Year 2002*, ed. James McGuire and James Quinn, 9 vols. (Cambridge: Cambridge Univ. Press, 2009), https://www.dib.ie/biography/bunting-edward-a1117 [accessed 26 Oct 2022]. On Edward Jones, see Trevor Herbert, 'Jones, Edward [called Bardd y Brenin]', *ODNB*.

[5] Jamie Croy Kassler, 'The Royal Institution Music Lectures, 1800–1831: A Preliminary Study', *RMARC*, 19 (1983–85), 1–30, includes information on Crotch's series (1805–07, 1820–25, 1829) and Wesley's too (1808–09, 1826–28), noting that Crotch's success made a welcome contribution to the Institution's balance sheet. Crotch's stature as Heather Professor at Oxford from 1797 assisted his appointment as the first conservatory director in the UK, Principal of the Royal Academy of Music (RAM), London, in 1822–32. He published an abstract of his Royal Institution lectures in 1831. Other venues for public music lectures at this period included the Surrey Institution and the London Institution.

including his proposed renderings of trouvère notation, the whole intended for use in the home, study or library.

A little later, at the other end of the kingdom, the Scottish solicitor William Dauney shed new light with his *Ancient Scottish Melodies from a Manuscript of the Reign of James VI* (Edinburgh, 1838). In this partial transcription of the seventeenth-century Scottish Skene MS, prefaced by a history of music in Scotland, Dauney restored early, simple versions of popular Scottish tunes that had been over-elaborated in eighteenth-century arrangements, so that the tradition of Scottish national song could be interpreted afresh. William Chappell's *A Collection of National English Airs, Consisting of Ancient Song, Ballad and Dance Tunes* (1838–40) did much the same for some 245 English tunes at a time when English popular music had never been taken seriously before, let alone studied in depth. Chappell's book in particular, with commentary and essay, was revelatory.

By the 1840s, 50s and 60s, scholars stood on more familiar musical ground but had to dig deeper for satisfying answers. Especially notable are two documentary biographies of well-known but underexamined composers, tracing style, chronology and social context for the first time. Edward Holmes's *The Life of Mozart* (1845) and Victor Schoelcher's *The Life of Handel* (1857) both ranged well beyond conventional storytelling, using correspondence, press reports, music manuscripts and early printed editions to raise new questions. Holmes's book, the first English biography of Mozart, was later praised by the German scholar Otto Jahn in his own Mozart research. Schoelcher, the French politician, friend and collaborator of Friedrich Chrysander and outspoken abolitionist exiled in England, amassed more than 3,000 primary sources in his quest for understanding a wider culture around eighteenth-century music; his impressive Handel collection now rests in the Bibliothèque Nationale, Paris.[6]

Also in critical vein but provoking wide political debate, the leading essayist Thomas Carlyle had prodded the nation's conscience with his pamphlet *Chartism* (1839), questioning England's underlying 'condition' after its rapid industrial shift had created deplorable factory and labour problems. Music scholars joined the discussion and some sought to address social issues. In what might be termed an early exemplar of practice-led research, John Hullah made three trips to Paris to observe continental methods of teaching vocal music to the untutored while developing his own sight-singing system for large groups of English school teachers, male and female. Though later eclipsed by the more flexible tonic sol-fa method of John Curwen, Hullah's system caught on in the early 1840s, winning him national repute, a teaching post at King's College London (KCL), a

---

[6] See Richard G. King, 'The Fonds Schoelcher: History and Contents', *Notes*, 53 (1997), 687–721. Schoelcher's research assistant, tracking newspaper and periodical references in the British Museum, was Michael Rophino Lacy. On Schoelcher's collaboration with Chrysander, see Friedrich Chrysander, 'Victor Schoelcher: Eine Erinnerung', *Die Zukunft*, 6 (20 Jan 1894), 117–23; and Richard G. King, 'New Light on Handel's Musical Library', *MQ*, 81 (1997), 109–38.

purpose-built hall and later a government inspectorship; his growing authority as a music educator, meanwhile, placed him in a unique position to extol the benefits of research. Thousands of new sight-singers formed choirs, some even tackling J.S. Bach's B minor Mass *Credo* with orchestral accompaniment in 1851, while publishers devised a range of materials to support music learners.[7]

Beginning in the century's third quarter, the arrival of new German immigrants, technological improvements seen in instruments displayed at the Great Exhibition, and the founding of the South Kensington Museum (later the Victoria and Albert Museum, or V&A) accelerated interest in modern and primitive instruments alike, as well as in the physics of pitch. The German émigré Carl Engel became the Museum's organological adviser; he produced detailed publications about its large instrument holdings, and by 1870 a systematic classification system for them, soon extending this work to the study of folk music cultures. Three miles away, William Pole, professor of civil engineering at University College London who was also interested in instrument design (besides Bach and Mozart), worked to assimilate the meaning of Hermann von Helmholtz's *Lehre von den Tonempfindungen* ('Sensations of Tone', 1863). Pole leaned heavily on Helmholtz to form his own understanding of acoustics as a physiological basis for music theory, which he explicated in lectures and publications. With later researchers, notably A.J. Ellis and A.J. Hipkins, Pole eventually helped to lower the high concert pitch in England, while further research by others in the study of sound led to work in music perception, aesthetics and psychology.

From the mid- and late 1870s, the number of individuals working on these and other topics began to rise noticeably, not from any sudden opening in training or employment for music researchers, but from the greater intellectual heft and attention brought to music investigation by 'amateurs', that is, by respected non-music-performing professionals, educated or experienced at a level higher than technical training often in an altogether different field who, sensibly, had something to contribute.[8] Already in mid-1874, eight of the names in Table 1 were among the founding members of the Musical Association, freely crossing social and occupational boundaries. In music society lists of the 1860s, for example, William Chappell, Carl Engel and Francis Hueffer appear as 'amateurs', meaning non-music executants, whereas John Hullah, Frederick Ouseley (a wealthy baronet, Mus.Doc., and by profession a clergyman),

---

[7] See [Edward Holmes], 'Our Musical Spring', *Fraser's Magazine*, 43 (1851), 586–95, esp. 590, where the reviewer applauds John Hullah's conducting of his best singers in the B-minor Mass *Credo* on 19 March 1851 at St Martin's Hall, 'an event of the utmost importance in the musical history of London'. Holmes's article embeds a survey of the English Bach awakening to date, with special reference to Wesley's work. Later in 1851, Ewer & Co. published Bach's *Six Motetts*, with English text adapted by William Bartholomew.

[8] See William Pole, 'Professional Musicians and Musical Amateurs', *MT*, 24 (1883), 432–33, an illuminating discussion of 'the different classes of people who have to do with music' (432) and how they related to one another.

Edward Dannreuther and Ernst Pauer (both trained pianists),[9] and William Pole (a paid organist, Mus.Doc., by profession a civil engineer) are given as music 'professionals'. Clearly in this context, such labels were used as membership categories, not restrictive social or intellectual indicators: in musical knowledge and regular music activity, none of these people was amateurish, and professional definitions were changing. Meanwhile, well-known scientists who were engaged in physical sound study, notably John Tyndall, a colleague of Pole's, opened another fruitful avenue of intellectual crossover in the early 1870s (more of Tyndall later).

Publishing Schemes

In contrast to individuals following a personal quest, some music scholars joined societies dedicated to publishing unfamiliar sources of a defined historical topic or repertory. These paralleled the work of clerical antiquarians and ecclesiological devotees who from the 1840s worked in local and county chapters across the country to excavate and collect ancient building remains or compile community histories; more than fifty such societies were founded between 1838 and 1886, mobilizing popular enthusiasm for recovering a material past by linking it with local pride. Even more closely, music publishing societies shadowed special-interest publishing clubs devoted to issuing previously unedited or inaccessible manuscripts relating to the history or literatures of England. With thousands of local subscribers, such textually focused clubs readily found the finance for handsome publications issued in series.[10] Among the first and most successful of these was the Camden Society, which from 1838 attracted the musically literate too. The Camden's particular influence continues today through the Camden Series of the Royal Historical Society, with which it merged in 1897.

For music scholars, a targeted publishing society could remedy gaps in public familiarity with much old music of known repute, national or sacred, that was otherwise hard to find. The time seemed ripe. Not only was the period of Carlyle's condition-of-England question suggestive for a resetting of national priorities – many people felt that uncovering a distant aesthetic or spiritual past might offer fresh perspective on the present – but access to such sources was also acknowledged to be extremely limited. Music collecting by the British Museum (BM), for example, founded in 1753, had started late in its history and remained haphazard for decades; its small music stock, soon enlarged by the enforcement of copyright deposit law in the early nineteenth

---

[9] Pauer was advanced in his approach to performing earlier music, from 1862 giving concerts of J.S. Bach on a harpsichord and editing anthologies of early English keyboard music; see Peter Holman, 'The Harpsichord in 19th-Century Britain', *Harpsichord & Fortepiano*, 24 (2020), 4–14.

[10] See Philippa Levine, *The Amateur and the Professional: Antiquarians, Historians and Archaeologists in Victorian England, 1838–1886* (Cambridge: Cambridge Univ. Press, 1986), esp. 40–69.

century, then fell prey to belated cataloguing and inadequate storage, so that drawing on private music collections, some of them owned by people willing to share their treasures, became crucial for stimulating new knowledge. In turn, a dedicated publishing society operating as an editing club offered a way for knowledgeable members to help select and present key monuments, exchanging information with each other and developing good practice. It was not a perfect laboratory for editorial training: all members were learners, and the committee approach was only as good as its weakest member (or controlling leader). But the process opened up music and ideas, notably of the Tudor period, that otherwise would not have been available for public use and discussion for many more decades.

Five schemes of musical interest were started in the 1840s. The Percy Society (1840–52), of which William Chappell was a founding member, dedicated itself to literary publication, including rare poems and song texts. Chappell edited part of one volume, and Edward Francis Rimbault, an eager young antiquarian, acted as secretary for a time. The club issued thirty volumes over twelve years before dissolving itself. Within months of that group's inauguration, Chappell then set up what became the most important music scheme of the decade, the Musical Antiquarian Society (1840–48), 'for the publication of scarce and valuable works by the early English composers' (see Fig. 1).[11] His aim was to complement his own recently published *Collection of National English Airs* by giving specimens of the English school of harmony, in and after the madrigalian era, as exemplified in mass, motet, madrigal, ballett, opera and fantasia. The first council included the composers William Sterndale Bennett, G.A. Macfarren, William Horsley and Charles Lucas, besides Rimbault as secretary, Chappell as treasurer and publication manager, and the organist E.J. Hopkins. Rimbault remained particularly active after Chappell withdrew around 1843, with annual reports confirming that before the release of each publication, council members had trialled them by singing through the music themselves. Across seven years, the Society issued nineteen editions from Byrd to Purcell, all in open vocal scores compiled from separate parts, printed in large folio format by Chappell & Co., a visibly 'scholarly' presentation. Only latterly were sixteen additional volumes with reduced piano accompaniments supplied by Chappell's in a belated attempt to increase subscriptions by ordinary home users. Clearly the Society's early success at enrolling members – 640 at first, rising quickly to 950 nationwide – did not last. What had sounded good in the prospectus apparently misfired in practice, given that subscribers, mostly families, had expected to sing from conveniently held choral scores around the parlour piano. In 1843, member numbers dropped substantially, and by 1846

---

[11] Musical Antiquarian Society, preliminary prospectus, BL 816.l.47.(179). 'The experiment has been tried, in reference to Historical Literature and early Poetry, with extraordinary success; and it is now proposed to adopt the plan of the Camden and Percy Societies with reference to Music' (1).

the whole scheme fell into crisis; it fizzled out in 1847 with only 400 members.[12] Rimbault admitted that many people had had 'very mistaken views of [the Society's] design and intent' when they joined, flagging the problem of confused expectations, itself rooted in a distance between music's widely accepted social role in Britain at that date and its yet unimagined potential as an object of serious study.

In like fashion but at a lower level of success, the Motett Society (1841–42) was founded by the Scottish painter William Dyce to promote ancient church music for use in English worship. Dyce, better known for his association with the Pre-Raphaelites and with art education in London, was an able organist and probably edited some of the texts; for the music editorial work he relied on, again, E.F. Rimbault. Their resulting collection amounted to seventy-nine (unattributed) pieces in three series, mostly Latin motets by Renaissance or early Baroque continental composers including Victoria, Palestrina and Lassus, fitted with English texts unrelated to the originals; only some of the music was by English church composers, such as Blow, Byrd, Gibbons and Sheppard. The whole collection, printed originally by the Society, was republished in 1847 by Novello.[13] An estimate of club membership is unknown, but the degree of adapting evident throughout – 'disarranging' might be more apt – shows that the project fell far short of anything like modern scholarly principles.[14]

Finally, the Handel Society, originated by George Macfarren senior in 1843 with his son G.A. Macfarren as secretary, began with 1,000 members subscribing one guinea each. Its large folio full scores, sixteen in number covering anthems, oratorios and chamber duets, did include piano accompaniments and an editor's preface, all issued gradually by Cramer, Beale & Co. between 1843 and 1858, but the Society had been officially dissolved as early as 1848 for lack of subscribers. Although editors included William Crotch, Sterndale Bennett, Felix Mendelssohn, G.A. Macfarren and the ubiquitous E.F. Rimbault, the group's presumed market fell away owing to yet another mismatch between product format and subscribers' needs. Apparently the intent behind a monumental edition, however musically or nationally important its content, did not square with what most British purchasers wanted to own – music set out on the page for everyday performance. Any ideological attempt to claim Handel as English property seems to have carried little weight with

---

[12] Richard Turbet, 'The Musical Antiquarian Society, 1840–48', *Brio*, 29 (1992), 13–20, gives detailed member numbers across the Society's history, and a complete list of its publications, 1841–48.

[13] Richard Turbet, 'Ancient Church Music published by the Motett Society: A List with the Original Sources', *Brio*, 53 (2016), 31–41, identifies all seventy-nine works, tracing most of the original musical sources.

[14] For a pointed critique of Rimbault's collecting methods in an extraordinary if notorious career, see Richard Andrewes, 'Edward Francis Rimbault, 1816–1876', *Fontes artis musicae*, 30 (1983), 30–34. 'It has always been the fashion to ridicule the failures of our predecessors; those of Edward Francis Rimbault do seem to deserve some censure' (33).

The Musical Antiquarian Society,

For the Publication of Scarce and Valuable Works by the Early English Composers.

Council, 1846.

John Blackbourn, Organist, Clapham.
George W. Budd, Hon. Sec. to the Western Madrigal Society.
Thomas P. Chappell, Treasurer.
William Chappell, F.S.A.
George Cooper, Sub-Organist of St. Paul's Cathedral.
E. Hawkins, Gentleman of Westminster Abbey.
Edward J. Hopkins, Organist of the Temple Church.
William Horsley, Mus. Bac., Oxon.
G. A. Macfarren.
James Turle, Organist of Westminster Abbey.
Edward Taylor, Professor of Music in Gresham College.
Joseph Warren, Organist of St. Mary's, Chelsea.
Edward F. Rimbault, LL.D. F.S.A., Secretary.

Figure 1. Musical Antiquarian Society, leaflet showing Council, 1846; BL shelfmark 816.l.47.(173).

ordinary consumers in this instance. It's important to note, too, that by the late 1840s J.S. Bach had begun to rise in English public estimation against Handel. Further, within a few more decades, as Oscar Sonneck would observe in 1906, people were 'slowly awakening to the fact that [Handel's] music, after all, is German music made in England with Italian trimmings and not so genuinely English as that by Arne, Shield, Storace, and others who have been unduly underestimated in our quest for the monumental'.[15]

Beyond clubs focused on specific repertories, a completely different kind of publishing scheme also deserves mention here. Literary and much broader in scope, it was also set in train before the Musical Association was founded: Macmillan & Co.'s *Dictionary of Music and Musicians* edited by George Grove. Looking back from the twenty-first century, it's important to recall the enormous risk entailed by this project, with no subscribers enrolled at the start but heavy internal investment required for years; and similarly, to note that against expectations, given the difficulties encountered in creating it, the *Dictionary* made an astonishing impact, surprising no one more than Grove himself.[16] According to the prospectus in early 1874, he had envisioned a two-volume reference work in 'untechnical language' for the 'intelligent inquirer', by which he meant concert-goers; the whole project was to be completed in seven years by a roster of some thirty-two contributors and a small advisory group. Across its eventual fifteen years of planning and production, however, using 118 contributors, 80 per cent of them British (and 100 per cent of them signing their work, a novelty), the book mushroomed to four volumes. Grove and his team became enthralled with the process as new findings rolled in and a kind of mission creep took hold. Issued like a periodical, affordable in bits over time, the *Dictionary* appeared in twenty-five alphabetical fascicles between January 1878 and May 1889. Oddly, the instalments appeared more and more encyclopaedic in period, place and subject coverage, embracing material much earlier than the limit of AD 1450 Grove had first set, and broader geographically and more technically inclusive than he or his publisher had originally wanted. Indeed, the text in places looked wildly uneven across the alphabet, as Grove's own research deepened and his pleasure at discovery grew: Julian Marshall's 'Handel' had covered ten pages, Grove's 'Mendelssohn' took fifty-eight; Alfred Maczewski's 'J.S. Bach' received five pages, Grove's 'Schubert', *sixty-three*. The bumps were noticed.

Despite imbalances, incessant corrections, trouble with contributors and other problems, however, including the publisher's threat to pull out completely, Grove worked many years beyond his contract, proving that music

---

[15] 'European Musical Associations', *Papers and Proceedings of the Music Teachers' National Association*, 28 (1906), 115–37 at 122. The first Library of Congress music head (1902–17), Sonneck created the M, ML, MT classification scheme for music.

[16] For the *Dictionary*'s intellectual background, practical execution, authorship, sale and critical reception, see Leanne Langley, 'Roots of a Tradition: The First *Dictionary of Music and Musicians*', in *George Grove, Music and Victorian Culture*, ed. Michael Musgrave (Basingstoke: Palgrave Macmillan, 2003), 168–215.

scholarship, much of it fresh, could both fascinate and sell profitably, at home and abroad. The company sold some 14,000 four-volume sets by 1900, and a further six editions to the twenty-first century (not all of the same standard, it must be said). Far from intending to promulgate fixed musical knowledge or a deliberately national or imperial agenda, moreover, as later critics have sometimes charged, the first *Dictionary of Music and Musicians* (Grove 1) exposed striking change in real-time research internationally over the period of production. Closer to home, it stimulated a vast leap in public appreciation for music investigators and their work, sowing the seeds for an enlarged UK market in music information and discourse by bridging specialist interests and those of general readers – exactly what Alexander Macmillan had banked on. The *Dictionary* formed a landmark in English publishing, and set a new standard for musical writing that could be trustworthy but also readable, broadly appealing but also stimulating to further research and open to correction. Its success proved a good omen for the Musical Association, undergirding its members' early commitment to discussion and public communication about all aspects of music.

Music Clubs with Research Aims

For most of the nineteenth century, the immense difference in status and economic power between Britain's developed music industry and its nascent music research community was clear: any intellectual work on sources, practices and meanings, when it happened, was peripheral in a nationwide musical culture dominated by singing, playing, teaching, concerts and theatre performances, all of it supported by an ecosystem of private and commercial music businesses – printers, publishers, instrument-makers and sellers, hall and theatre managers, promoters and agents, church bodies and the exploding print industry. Once tapped, the British hunger for music was insatiable. By contrast, official support for music research in the form of government subsidy, national document and artefact collection, or even university posts for academic study and expertise (as opposed to organ playing, a bit of composing or theory teaching and the odd lecture) was almost non-existent. Scholars were on their own. Alone, that is, unless they could exploit a link to music performance by creating and selling an edition, playing its accompaniment or conducting; to literary media by reviewing, writing a book or editing a journal; or later, to education by instituting a new training system or organizing a library. The importance of connecting to live music-making was obvious, even when history or science infused one's research.

This characteristic dilemma for all musicologists, and the added economic reality behind it in this place and time, go a long way towards explaining why music clubs devoted to concert-giving would seem to have provided the ideal environment in which research work in the UK could grow and, eventually, be seen as relevant and worthwhile on its own. Indeed, at least four such nineteenth-century groups broached music investigation as part of their club identity, although their reasons for encouraging research varied. One was to enhance the intellectual standing of select members in a group who were really aiming to control entry to the music profession, like an ancient guild. Another was to educate audiences in experiencing fine music, helping to expand and differentiate markets for listening and reading. Still another was to build status for music itself, attracting enough public attention to convince government that music and its cultivation were worthy of national subsidy – an uphill battle in Britain before 1945. Whatever the reason or rationale, club members stood to gain social or intellectual prestige beyond traditional class markers. The following four group examples show a mix of these motives: the Royal Academy of Music (1813), the Musical Institute (1851–53), the Musical Society of London (1858–67) and the Musical Union Institute (1860–64). None lasted for long, but a few recurring members would go on to join the early Musical Association, and it was their understanding of previous obstacles that would prove salutary.

The 'Royal Academy of Music', in its earliest usage, was not Britain's first conservatory founded in 1822, but the name proposed in mid-1813 for what was intended to be much more, the highest board of professional musicians in Great Britain, chartered by the Prince Regent on the explicit model of the Royal Academy of Arts founded in 1768. Like that older body, approved by his father George III, the Royal Academy of Music was meant to oversee a training institute for students, many of whom would one day be elected full Academicians; but it was also meant to support teaching and music development through other activities. A closely linked group of players, for example, giving concerts of the 'most approved' modern music under the Regent's patronage, the Philharmonic Society of London, had already been established in February 1813; in effect it formed the pool of artist-practitioners giving regular 'exhibitions' at the incipient Academy. The group's preferred location for a space to house both the Philharmonic concerts and other Academy activities had also been identified and agreed by the Crown, together with the Regent's architect John Nash, by January 1813 – the Argyll Rooms on what by 1819 would be called 'Regent Street'. There was every hope that the full Academy concept could be realized there. As a quasi-political project, however, requiring official agreement as well as government cash, the Academy idea fell into abeyance: negotiating, building work on the site and the annual Philharmonic concert series inevitably proceeded at different rates. In fact the building was completed to great acclaim in 1820 and the concerts flourished for nearly two centuries at succeeding venues, but the Academy itself never came to fruition in its originally conceived form. The name was used instead for the London conservatory that grew out of further, more complex and conflicted discussions a few years later, in 1822–23.[17]

---

[17] For Nash and the founding of the Philharmonic Society, see Leanne Langley, 'A Place for Music: John Nash, Regent Street and the Philharmonic Society of London', *Electronic British Library Journal* (2013), art. 12, pp. 1–50, http://www.bl.uk/eblj/2013 articles/article12.html. For the conservatory origins, see Leanne Langley, 'Sainsbury's *Dictionary*, the Royal Academy of Music, and the Rhetoric of Patriotism', in *Music and*

The first 'Royal Academy of Music', then, only ever existed as a proposal, a written Plan; its concept nevertheless prompted the articulation of research aims and some action.[18] Like a guild, this select group was to contain 'the most ingenious and the most respectable' music professors in London, an intellectual elite: forty names including ten resident 'foreigners' were envisaged, with the 87-year-old Charles Burney as president.[19] The plan's framers, J.P Salomon and William Ayrton, with input from G.B. Viotti, Muzio Clementi and J.B. Cramer, hoped that through training, lecturing and collaborative committees, the Academy would establish and oversee the highest standards for the British music profession. Its full backstory, including an earlier drive for a British music school linked partly to Burney, is less important here than that some of this body's desiderata actually began to be taken up by Philharmonic members, notably William Ayrton through two music journals he edited, the *English Musical Gazette* (1819) and the *Harmonicon* (1823–33). His and others' research aims in the 1813 plan were three: to clarify music terminology, to define tempo meanings by use of a mechanical device, noting the speed at which composers wanted their music performed (many members had witnessed historic performances or dealt with composers directly, not least Haydn and Beethoven) and to compile a music dictionary 'from the best authorities'. All were practical, not speculative, tasks relating to performance and music education. But the full Academy plan also called for more: three annual lecture series in music history, theory and poetry, a library of 'ancient and modern' music with a place to consult it, regular meetings at which to hear 'such papers relating to the history, theory, or practice of music as may be communicated', and regular prizes for new composition. The whole vision was comprehensive and ambitious, in many ways prophetic.

Skip ahead a few decades to the Musical Institute. Although lasting only two years, 1851–53, and later seen, when noted at all, as mysteriously sudden, brief

---

British Culture, 1785–1914: Essays in Honour of Cyril Ehrlich, ed. Christina Bashford and Leanne Langley (Oxford: Oxford Univ. Press, 2000), 65–97.

[18] Royal Archives, Windsor, RA GEO/MAIN/21589–21594, 'Outline of a Plan, for the establishment of A Royal Academy of Music', in the hand of J.P. Salomon [1813]. Successive details in this paragraph come from this nine-page document, accessed through the online archive of the Georgian Papers Programme (http://gpp.rct.uk, Feb 2021). See also the printed two-page 'Abstract of a Plan for establishing A Royal Academy of Music', 19 July 1813, preserved by Sir George Smart with annotations in his hand made at a General Meeting of the Philharmonic Society on 24 July 1813, BL Add. MS 41771, fols. 6v–7r.

[19] Royal Archives, Windsor, RA GEO/MAIN/21595, 'List of such Professors of Music, as are intended to form the Academy', in the hand of J.P. Salomon [1813]. The names are: Asioli, Ashe, Th. Attwood, Wm Ayrton, Jas. Bartleman, H. Bishop, J. Braham, Dr Chs Burney (president), Dr Callcott, J. Crosdill, Muz. Clementi, R. Cooke, A. Corri, Dr Crotch, J. Cramer, F. Cramer, Wm Dance, J. Graeff, Th. Greatorex, G.E. Griffin, Wm Horsley, Chs Knyvett Sen., Chs Knyvett jun., Wm Knyvett, A. Kollmann, Robt Lindley, Naldi, Chs Neate, V. Novello, J. Potter, J.P. Salomon, Wm Shield, Sir G. Smart, Rd Stevens, B. Viotti, S. Webbe jun., Weichsell, Chs Wesley, S. Wesley, Yaniewicz.

and opaque in nature, it emerges as the Musical Association's closest relation in aims and activity. In addition, predating by nearly two decades the Netherlands music society Koninklijke Vereniging voor Nederlandse Muziekgeschiedenis (KVNM; 'Royal Society for Music History of the Netherlands', founded 1868), the Musical Institute turns out to be the earliest body anywhere devoted to the wider aspects of musical research rather than to its own nation's music in the first instance. It deserves a careful look.[20]

The Institute began life in November 1851 as the 'art and science' component of an imminent – as yet unannounced – new concert-giving body in London, the New Philharmonic Society (NPS). That initiative grew from the energetic forces behind the Great Exhibition just ended, for which the French composer Hector Berlioz had served as an instrument juror, attending the Crystal Palace in Hyde Park throughout summer 1851. A group of wealthy Exhibition sponsors were naturally eager to extend the event's warm glow and utilize its wonderful modern building; these included Charles Fox, the principal structural engineer of the Palace whose firm Fox Henderson built it to Joseph Paxton's design and technically owned the structure, and Morton Peto, the wealthy railway contractor who personally guaranteed the Exhibition, together with the music publisher Frederick Beale, Berlioz's keenest London supporter. In late 1851 they fairly jumped on the French conductor's magnetic connection with the British capital to initiate a new concert series, hiring him, with a magnificent orchestra and chorus, for a first season in spring 1852, held in the vast Exeter Hall on the Strand. As expected, Berlioz, his forces and his programmes made a spectacular success in six concerts, widely noticed in the press. Beale's particular hope of using the series to expand opportunity for modern British composers and audiences, thus for publishers too, moved a step closer to fulfilment.

Meanwhile with less fanfare, the Musical Institute had organized itself along separate lines but stemming from the same energy and financial backing as that for the NPS, now enhanced by William Chappell, who happened to be Beale's business partner at the publishing firm Cramer, Beale & Chappell. The Institute's original prospectus, excerpted in February 1852 in the *Musical World*, stated its aims:

> The Musical Institute of London is founded for the cultivation of the science and art of music, and the intercommunication of musical knowledge among professors and amateurs. Its operation will consist principally in the provision of a reading-room, the formation of a library of music and musical literature for the use of members, the holding of *conversazioni* in conjunction with the

---

[20] Alec Hyatt King, 'The Musical Institute of London and its Successors', *MT*, 117 (1976), 221–23, offered the first modern assessment of the Institute and its make-up, using contemporary press reports in the *Musical World* and a microfilm copy of its President's Inaugural Address. King's supposition that the Institute was somehow related to the Great Exhibition held more truth than he knew. The present description relies on his article but also incorporates more recent research linking the Institute to the NPS (see n. 23 below).

performance of music, and the reading of papers on musical subjects, and the publication of transactions.[21]

In fact Chappell had agreed with Beale to allow their company's Regent Street premises to serve as the NPS headquarters, while taking separate premises for the Institute's rooms down Regent Street and around the corner at 34 Sackville Street. Both arrangements were deliberately temporary for one year because, remarkably, the planners had all along hoped to base the conjoined body – new orchestral society and musical institute – at the Crystal Palace in Hyde Park once the Exhibition had been cleared away and the Palace was refitted, in mid-1852. As if by magic, not unlike the quick rise of Fox's prefabricated glass building, they would soon move in, they hoped, to a stunningly modern music centre in South Kensington, with meeting and teaching rooms, performance spaces, the Institute with its library (to 'rival the Bodleian'), an instrument museum, paper sessions and soirees.[22]

For a time, it was truly an exciting idea backed by big names and big hopes, including for music research. The Institute's first president was none other than John Hullah (see Fig. 2), Professor of Vocal Music at KCL and at Queen's College (Harley Street) and Bedford College (Bedford Square), both pioneering institutions for girls affiliated with London University. Hullah gave an inspiring address in early 1852, with the original vice-presidents named as William Sterndale Bennett, Charles Lucas and Frederick Gore Ouseley. Representing several interests and occupations, the Institute's membership eventually included 180 Fellows, all men, and forty-two Associates, all women, besides eight Honorary Fellows – Auber, Berlioz, Ernst, Joachim, Meyerbeer, Moscheles, Rossini and Spohr. Edward Holmes was on the members' list, as was Charles Neate, one of the originally mooted Royal Academicians from 1813 and friend and teacher of Charles Salaman, also an Institute member. So were professional instrumentalists and singers, music businessmen, distinguished amateurs and antiquarians. The Sackville Street premises encompassed a convenient reading room and fine library; several papers were given there in 1852–53, on the character of keys, on Thomas Moore's lyrical works (by Henry Chorley), on continental organs (Ouseley), musical ratios, music and the structure of English verse, and on acoustic vibrations. 'Intercommunication of musical knowledge' and follow-up conversations between members, whatever their station, were encouraged. Music was performed in illustration after each paper, although not yet a sample of what Hullah had named as his personal

---

[21] 'The Musical Institute of London', *Musical World*, 30 (28 Feb 1852), 129–31 at 129. The wording varied in several iterations of this statement, latterly reversing the original precedence of 'science' and 'art', adding a museum of instruments, and allowing for the performance of music in illustration to papers.

[22] John Hullah, *Musical Institute of London: Inaugural Address, Saturday, February 14th, 1852* (London: John W. Parker & Son, 1852), BL Mic.A.5941 (a microfilm including NYPL Drexel 2214.11).

Figure 2. John Pyke Hullah, president of the Musical Institute, 1851–53; albumen carte-de-visite by Elliott & Fry, 1860s.

desires – to hear a John Jenkins fantasia on period viols, or something from a Haydn symphony.

The real trouble began in spring 1852 after Parliament had voted unequivocally to dismantle the Crystal Palace (30 April), later re-erected at Sydenham. Overnight, funding fell as Charles Fox pulled out of the NPS. A domineering New Philharmonic council member claiming to have originated the whole NPS scheme, Henry Wylde, saw his own chance, put himself in charge of the concerts and refused to rehire Berlioz. Beale was outraged, but also disheartened by the loss of momentum, as he saw it, for an adequate, new, central-London concert venue. He split from Wylde and the New Philharmonic, dissolved the Musical Institute by September 1853, sold its music library in December and redirected his energies, together with Chappell & Co.'s, towards building the publishing partners' own new concert hall between Regent Street and Piccadilly, originally to be called 'New Philharmonic Hall' but in the event christened St James's Hall.[23] The Musical Institute thus vanished as quickly as

---

[23] Leanne Langley, '"Unequalled music": Berlioz, 1851 and the New Philharmonic Society', *Berlioz Society Bulletin*, no. 208 (2019), 5–17. Sources include NPS concert

it had arisen, without public explanation. No papers or meeting transactions other than Hullah's *Inaugural Address* were ever published, and no cache of original letters or planning documents seems to have survived. No museum was ever established.

Now skip ahead five more years to the new space, St James's Hall, which opened in early 1858. Wylde had kept the NPS going, haltingly and with little attempt to cultivate an academic subgroup. When he took residency at the new hall, ex-Musical Institute members, notably Salaman, tried to re-connect with him in the friendly hope of building back a library and a new joint body for orchestral-choral-academic association. Wylde rejected the idea outright and went on to expand his own empire under the New Philharmonic name, instituting simplified classes for learners as the 'London Academy of Music' at St James's Hall from 1861. Having married into money, he then erected in 1867 yet another building, St George's Hall in Upper Regent Street, and developed his practical system there very successfully; this institution was known later as the London Academy of Music and Dramatic Art (LAMDA). Salaman and colleagues, meanwhile, made their own separate arrangements at St James's Hall, hiring excellent players and the experienced conductor Alfred Mellon, another ex-Musical Institute fellow. By mid-1858 (actually on 30 April, exactly six years after the Palace plan was scuppered), a hundred founder members formed a completely new association for musically interested subscribers, professional and amateur, women and men, as the Musical Society of London (MSL). They eventually attracted a membership of 1,500; 1,600 people applied, but a ceiling was set for Hall safety. Salaman worked tirelessly as Honorary Secretary for seven years, 1858–64, and it is his collection of original MSL materials, passed to E.F. Rimbault as succeeding librarian, which now comprises the Society's papers held by the New York Public Library.[24] In every essential way, the Musical Society of London directly succeeded the Musical Institute-cum-NPS (while Henry Wylde's 'New Philharmonic Concerts' carried on concurrently).

In its original form, the MSL aimed to produce orchestral and chamber concerts, illustrated lectures, a periodical, conversaziones, academic meetings for paper-reading and trials of new compositions. Subscribers each paid a guinea, with an extra 10s.6d. for the annual set of four concerts. For a time C.E. Horsley, son of William Horsley (another of the proposed Academicians

---

programmes held by the RCM and the BL, Willert Beale's memoir *The Light of Other Days* (London, 1890), and papers in the Archive of the Royal Commission for the Exhibition of 1851, housed at Imperial College London.

[24] Musical Society of London Papers, NYPL Drexel 663. This material consists of some 130 items, 1858–64, mostly printed correspondence and announcements, annual reports, byelaws, library holdings, concert and conversazione programmes and members' lists bound in a single volume. It went to New York through purchase by the American banker Joseph W. Drexel of the major part of E.F. Rimbault's impressive private library at a Sotheby's auction in London in 1877, and thence through donation to the Lenox Library, forerunner of the NYPL – a Rimbault legacy perhaps more important than his editorial work.

Figure 3. *Charles Kensington Salaman*, Honorary Secretary of the Musical Society of London, 1858–64, and of the Musical Association, 1874–78; oil on canvas by Sidney Starr, c. 1890.

of 1813 who'd edited Byrd for the Musical Antiquarian Society), placed his valuable library of scores, history and theory books on loan for the Society's use at St James's Hall, supplemented by publishers' donations. After Horsley sold his books and emigrated to Australia, the residual library, catalogued by Rimbault, was moved to the Marylebone Literary and Scientific Institution, the MSL's subsequent office and meetings base at 17 Edwards Street, Portman Square, from 1862. Dozens of former Musical Institute members like Salaman and Horsley joined the MSL, including Willert Beale (Frederick's son), Jules Benedict, William Chappell, J.W. Davison, G.A. Macfarren, Bernhard Molique, G.A. Osborne and Frederick Ouseley. Newer members too, hundreds of them, joined the club or became Fellows or Associates, including Francesco Berger, George Grove, William Pole, Charles Santley and a very young John Stainer.

In the end, MSL orchestral concerts at St James's Hall proved a great draw, with a mix of familiar and adventurous new music well played: the concerts enjoyed notable critical success as well, from January 1859 to March 1867. All along, a choral body for Society members directed by Henry Smart met regularly at the Marylebone Institution (see Fig. 4), while interesting material objects – manuscripts, paintings, sculptures, musical portraits and exotic instruments, some shown by Victor Schoelcher – were displayed at evening conversaziones in St James's Hall, interspersed by choral and instrumental selections and coffee. The Society never produced a journal, however, and only five papers were given in three years (1860, 1862, 1863), including two on pitch by Pole, one in laryngology by an eminent doctor and one by Salaman on 'Music and Dancing in Ancient Times'. This slim record of focused intellectual exchange, and the low attendance at academic sessions ('Special Meetings of Fellows'), disappointed Salaman, prompting his ever more urgent pleas for speakers to come forward. The Annual Report of 1863 put it plainly:

> The object of these [academic] meetings does not appear to be sufficiently understood, nor their utility to be recognised. It was originally supposed that opportunities for social intercourse, and for the discussion of matters interesting to musicians as a body, would be welcomed by Members desirous of raising the professional *status* and of promoting the interests of art. That the Fellows of the Society, professional and non-professional, should meet, and avail themselves of such opportunities of communication, for the friendly interchange of thought and experience, is manifestly desirable.[25]

Desirable, but not taken up. By 1865 even Salaman's patience had waned. The MSL schedule slowed and membership decreased. Mellon became ill. It was his death in March 1867 that drew a final curtain over the Musical Society of London, proving how reliant on music-making and concert-giving the group had always been.

A fourth and final example of a London music club embracing wider purpose comes from 1860, when the violinist, concert organizer and promulgator of fine chamber music John Ella made an additional foray into the business of institutionalizing. Part of his intent was to address the lack of government support for a serious, accessible music library in the UK, but he was also seeking to consolidate his position as a taste leader. In essence he chose to use personal wealth networks among his elevated Musical Union contacts to fund a physical base for chamber music in London, called the Musical Union Institute, located at 18 Hanover Square.[26] Ella, also an ex-member of the 1851 Musical Institute, was a shareholder in St James's Hall, to which he transferred the Musical Union's concerts in 1859; he first planned to base his club there too, starting with a library, which was followed by lectures and a journal of transactions. It soon became apparent that he needed more space. With cash donations and member fees, he then hoped to run his institute away from the

---

[25] Musical Society of London Papers, NYPL Drexel 663, Annual Report 1863 [for 1862], 12 (emphasis original).

[26] See Christina Bashford, *The Pursuit of High Culture: John Ella and Chamber Music in Victorian London* (Woodbridge: Boydell Press, 2007), 243–62, tracing Ella's idea for the Institute, his initial plans to base it at St James's Hall and his fundraising methods. Key supporters included Frederick Ouseley.

Figure 4. Marylebone Literary and Scientific Institution, 17 Edwards Street, Portman Square, later a rehearsal and meetings base for the Musical Society of London, 1862–67; lithograph by T.M. Baynes of the Institution's opening, Lord Brougham in the chair, 4 March 1835.

Hall in a space large enough for library, instrument storage and chamber music classes, all for the socially elite who were his targeted funders. In the event, Ella raised enough money to lease the rooms, gather a library, mount receptions and give a few lectures. But the educational aspect dwindled rapidly, or never took off; by 1864 the Musical Union Institute had more or less finished. In 1865 he decided to give its library to the South Kensington Museum. In deliberately avoiding middle-class involvement and, crucially, not appreciating how little his chosen elite constituency cared about supporting music-intellectual endeavour, whether for their own or others' benefit, Ella failed in his attempt at this species of club-making. All the while, Musical Union concerts went on much as before, surviving to the 1880s.

❧ *Disconnecting from Performance Culture*

Despite time gaps between them and slight design differences in each of the clubs discussed above, it's clear that when one ceased to exist or its objects could not be realized, a few members carried the ideas forward, starting or joining a later club with similar aims. London's competitive music industry, churning relentlessly as artists reinvented themselves, accounts for much of the concert activity pursued by these groups; in that sense, new versions of the same kind of society are hardly surprising. What is striking is that their commitment to music-investigative possibilities including a music library, though faint, was strong enough to be passed on as well, together with hopes for social and intellectual interchange among like-minded investigators. To be sure, active music-making and listening remained the *raison d'être* of these clubs, the main activity attracting member numbers and finance, whereas a research function through an 'institute', however formulated, persisted as a kind of add-on into the bargain. By the early 1870s researchers finally realized that this imbalance, once assumed to have been helpful or economically necessary, was in fact counterproductive: hitching research to a commercial concert operation created more of a distraction, even an impasse, than an opening. The next step had to be disconnecting from UK performance culture altogether – a crucial decision that in 1874 would help define the Musical Association as a learned society.

At the same time, the logic of that uncoupling was decidedly encouraged by government and university moves hinting at newer professional paths for antiquarian and scientific researchers, including some in music. These offer context for a time when neither 'scientists' (a new word from the 1830s) nor historians, still less music scholars, were fully recognized as belonging to distinct professional disciplines. Early nineteenth-century antiquarians, whether engaged in archaeological digs or the publishing of music or other documents, had been a large mixed group up to the 1850s but then gradually differentiated themselves through amateur and professional pursuits. Historians began to pull away through the practice of literary narrative-writing and, later, studying and interpreting documents. Archaeologists pulled away, partly through religious challenges, towards more scientific approaches to material objects. Both types of antiquarian scholar as well as others in scientific fields had often relied on public lecturing at many of the private literary, philosophical and scientific institutions for middle-class communities early in the century, from the celebrated Royal Institution, London Institution, Surrey Institution and (from 1596) Gresham College in the City of London, to smaller bodies in, for example, Highgate, Bath, Leeds, Leicester, Manchester, Liverpool and Newcastle. Some of that lecturing – wonderfully performative when a speaker mixed chemicals, demonstrated electricity or unrolled a mummy in front of an enthralled audience[27] – must have been as engaging as William Crotch when he 'illustrated' his *Specimens* at the keyboard in the early 1800s. Like people in music, furthermore, archaeologists, historians and scientists published articles and books for pay, mounted conversaziones and formed their own societies, including ones that competed with each other, then ceased, re-formed or split into more specialized groups.

---

[27] For the popular spectacle, locations and meanings of one such practice, see Gabriel Moshenska, 'Unrolling Egyptian Mummies in Nineteenth-Century Britain', *British Journal for the History of Science*, 47 (2014), 451–77.

A turning point for emergent historians came with the Public Record Office Act of 1838. Through government funding it created a central repository for the nation's scattered public records, ensuring proper care and cataloguing for the first time ever, and eventually making the records publicly accessible. A building was started on Chancery Lane in 1851; curators, archivists and assistants were hired, and across the 1850s and 60s, long series of State Paper *Calendars* as well as *Chronicles and Memorials* (the Rolls) followed by indexes began to be compiled, edited and published, all of which required highly skilled and trained specialists. These were arguably the first full-time professional historians in Britain, years before History became a widespread professional academic discipline in the UK.[28] Private manuscript collections, too, were brought to public attention more gradually through the Historical Manuscripts Commission, first appointed in 1869.

In a similar way, waves of restructuring at the BM, notably in its departments of Antiquities and of Printed Books, brought incremental improvements to the collections besides rare employment opportunity for scholars. As Keeper of Printed Books from 1837, Anthony Panizzi forged ahead, aiming to increase parliamentary grants to the Museum through a series of detailed reports; these succeeded in nearly tripling the annual grant from £3,600 to £10,000 by 1846.[29] In 1841–50, Panizzi was able to hire the music antiquarian Thomas Oliphant to catalogue a huge backlog of music material, manuscript and printed items alike, which, with Panizzi's input, laid the basis for what would become the British Library music catalogue as it is today. But in reality Panizzi's attitude to music was ambiguous. Oliphant resigned when his own careful suggestions for the future development of music in the BM were rejected; in 1851 he joined the Musical Institute council as Honorary Librarian. Thereafter music languished at the Museum for thirty years, fuelling frustrations felt by scholars and clubs who then prioritized their own formations of an accessible music library. It was in the mid-1850s that accumulation of new Museum purchases and copyright deposits caused an accommodation crisis. Panizzi devised a plan for a new circular reading room surrounded by bookstacks, sited in the building's interior quadrangle (see Fig. 5); its opening in 1857 created wide public interest, and soon afterwards, one of the old rooms vacated became the Music Room. Music deposits and acquisitions rose but the Museum's capacity to list them coherently fell behind. Not until 1885, with the appointment of William Barclay Squire as an Assistant Keeper in charge of music, would the Museum begin to redress its lack of specialist attention to music through his cataloguing and acquisitions work. Squire, who had also worked as a subeditor for Grove, soon gained an international reputation as a William Byrd scholar and a music collections expert, making him one of Britain's earliest musicologists.[30]

---

[28] Levine, *The Amateur and the Professional*, 101–34.
[29] Philip R. Harris, 'Panizzi, Sir Anthony', *ODNB*; see further P.R. Harris, *A History of the British Museum Library, 1753–1973* (London: British Library, 1998).
[30] In 1884 Grove actively supported Squire's application for a BM post, admitting that in Britain 'we want a good music archaeologist of the rank of Jahn or Nottebohm or

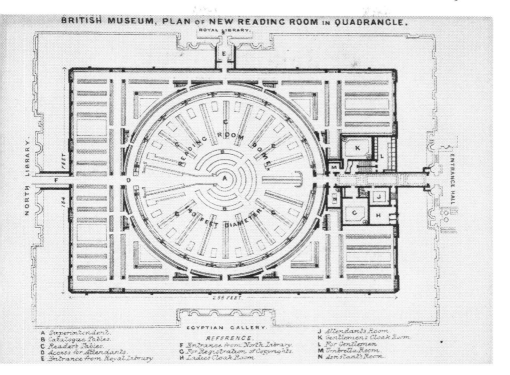

Figure 5. 'British Museum, Plan of New Reading Room in Quadrangle', on ticket to a private view of the new building, 5 May 1857.

A main force in the nation's recognition of science, meanwhile, and the government's reliance on scientific advice for a range of technical projects, had long been the Royal Society, founded in 1660 and still influential as the nation's oldest learned society.[31] Music papers figured importantly in its *Transactions* from the 1670s, on the nature of sound, the construction of musical instruments and the theory of music, but also, in the eighteenth century, on musical 'phenomena' observed in nature, from birds to child prodigies including Mozart and Crotch. In the early nineteenth century, besides frequently consulting the Royal Society, the government also employed 'men of science' in various civil service or advisory roles. And

---

Ambros – and why should you not be he (and a great deal better?)'; Grove to Squire, 30 Dec [1884], BL Add. MS 39679, fol. 108. If anyone could win Grove over to the benefits of a home-grown 'musicology', it was William Barclay Squire.

[31] On music and the Royal Society, see Penelope Gouk, *Music, Science and Natural Magic in Seventeenth-Century England* (New Haven: Yale Univ. Press, 1999); Katherine Butler, 'Myth, Science and the Power of Music in the Early Decades of the Royal Society', *Journal of the History of Ideas*, 76 (2015), 47–68; and Marie Boas Hall, 'Public Science in Britain: The Role of the Royal Society', *Isis*, 72 (1981), 627–29.

already for more than a century, the ancient universities had appointed professors in scientific fields such as geometry, medicine, chemistry, botany and music, although the role of professor in most of these was generally a part-time or occasional one, not residential and in music often a sinecure. After all, the traditional idea of an English university, given that Oxford and Cambridge served as part-Anglican seminary, part-finishing school for young members of the governing elite, was that it should provide a liberal education for the few through classics and mathematics. Music was for the very few, most of whom, in truth, were church organists.

Not until after 1850 did significant changes begin to unfold, largely as a result of Royal Commission investigations and the social, political and intellectual reforms they signalled. Law, modern history and more natural science came into Oxbridge curricula, college fellowships were freed from certain old restrictions (limitation to 'founder's kin'), and more dissenters were admitted. Some university reformers tried to go further, promoting subsidized or endowed scientific research on the German model, and with it, the idea that the ancient English universities ought to move towards a greater research orientation. At the same time, civic pride and a desire to extend higher education in the applied sciences led to the founding of what would later be known as the 'red-brick' universities, in Manchester, Birmingham, Liverpool, Leeds and other regional cities. The University of London was unique: though nominally the largest university in Europe as a federated body of distinguished, autonomous colleges including University College (1826), King's College (1829) and Imperial College (1907), it largely remained, until the 1930s, an examining body. All the while, pressure from the advance of experimental science, and from scientists themselves anxious to separate natural science from religious commitments, fed debates affecting university structures. Not surprisingly, the ways and means of suggested reforms were not easily agreed or implemented, including lines of work, payment and division of responsibility between a university and its colleges, and between professors and tutors. In History, especially, internal wrangling left a vacuum, so that disciplinary coherence and a sense of agreed academic community came instead independently, through the founding in 1886 of the *English Historical Review*, a quarterly published by the firm of Longmans. It was this journal which, by traditional consent, established original research, evidence-based argument and reviewing by specialists as central to the new professionalism in History.[32]

In Science, meanwhile, the important Devonshire Commission of 1871–75 had declared in 1873 that Oxford and Cambridge ought to be centres of research as well as education.[33] Its findings were debated but generally accepted, with

---

[32] On History and the universities, see Levine, *The Amateur and the Professional*, 135–63, and on the *English Historical Review*, 164–68. For more detail on the founding and customary interpretation of this journal, see Doris S. Goldstein's centenary article, 'The Origins and Early Years of the *English Historical Review*', *English Historical Review*, 101 (1986), 6–19.

[33] T.W. Heyck. 'From Men of Letters to Intellectuals: The Transformation of Intellectual Life in Nineteenth-Century England', *Journal of British Studies*, 20 (1980), 158–83

structural revisions beginning to be put in place from the late 1870s; these tended to crystallize scientific disciplines and identify their scholars as experts through professional academic affiliation and scholarly publications, although substantial support for research was still a long way off. Scientists' careers certainly benefited. All together, the number of scientific posts in English and Welsh universities grew from about sixty in 1850 to more than 400 in 1900.[34]

Throughout this period, the treatment of Music as a university degree subject moved from torpor and disagreement to, well, a bit less torpor and some agreed disagreement. At issue were questions around the dual nature of music as technical skill and intellectual activity; the purpose of a university and its constituents, including social class and the acceptable uses of music; and the practical arrangements for student attendance, teaching and assessment that would achieve Music's integration into existing academic structures.[35] All these issues presented challenges to the status quo of UK university organization. But their troublesomeness also suggests a limited understanding of music's potential and a lack of respect for it as a subject worthy of intellectual effort and academic status. Musicians felt the slight. Frederick Ouseley as music professor at Oxford (1855–89), together with his younger protégé and successor John Stainer, and later C.V. Stanford as professor at Cambridge (from 1887), made the greatest impact by seeking changes in the residential requirement for music professors and in the content and delivery of music degrees. The high reputations and personal commitment of these three also helped to raise public awareness of university music, although at this stage the highest outcome, a new doctoral music degree at Cambridge by 1893, still applied only to composition, not to any wider humanistic or scientific consideration of music or its cultures. At the same time, Edinburgh and London universities continued to struggle over what a music degree was for, who needed one, and how much theoretical or scientific content (acoustics) or practical skill in harmony and counterpoint should be required. No single resolution was found. If to some parties an element of science offered a way forward, as in the University of London, to others practical skills were paramount, such as at the Royal College of Music (RCM), a conservatory granting qualifications and even degrees to aspiring performers and music teachers.

---

at 178, citing the *Royal Commission on Scientific Instruction and the Advancement of Science* ('Devonshire Commission'), Third Report (1873). For background on the Commission, chaired by William Cavendish, the 7th Duke of Devonshire, and access to all eight of its detailed reports, see http://www.educationengland.org.uk/documents/devonshire/index.html [accessed 21 Nov 2022].

[34] Heyck, 'From Men of Letters to Intellectuals', 180. Despite the improvements noted by Heyck, however, the success of advocacy for university research and its endowment in this period should not be exaggerated. Discussions of the 1870s failed to effect lasting change, while new arguments had little impetus until after 1918.

[35] See Rosemary Golding, *Music and Academia in Victorian Britain* (Aldershot: Ashgate, 2013), which helpfully compares the universities of Edinburgh, Oxford, Cambridge and London to draw out these issues.

This picture of the tensions among music academics mirrors what had happened on a larger scale, earlier, with historians and scientists, each group aiming to define its discipline and garner new status through routes supported by government and the universities. It all makes sense when seen as a professionalizing shift from the 1860s and 70s into the twentieth century. But we would be mistaken to assume that an urge for self-definition applied only to elite intellectuals, or to university teachers and students; or that the move towards specialization by historians and scientists necessarily created a hard and fast boundary between the new professional discourse exemplified by the *English Historical Review* and more popular ways of writing about history or science – or music. For all along, despite the rhetoric of professionalization, there was an alternative, middle way for scholars and serious readers outside the academy. Its impetus came from commercial publishing.

Many publishers saw the implications of the Education Acts of 1870 and 1880, which established new Board schools for children and gradually made schooling compulsory. Naturally they responded to the demand for basic primers, tutors, subject histories and reference works, equipping new generations of young middle- and lower middle-class learners. The music publisher Novello, Ewer & Co. commissioned John Stainer for just this purpose, securing him to edit its Music Primers series between the late 1870s and 1890s. A few publishers sensed the disciplinary changes at higher education level too, but chose to respond by widening the general market for intellectual discussion rather than dividing it into academic and non-academic strands. Through dedicated periodicals and books presenting ideas by writers of high expertise yet expressed in language everyone could understand, they succeeded in cultivating a bigger reading public for 'scholarly' material than the academic specialists could attract, in turn developing the capacities of many more general readers.

Of all such publishers, none was more assiduous than Alexander Macmillan. Both Macmillan and C.J. Longman were worried by the implications of a scholarly discourse catering for a miniscule academic readership. But it was Macmillan in particular who pursued the alternative – expanding the potential market for science, history and music. With the astronomer Norman Lockyer, he launched *Nature* magazine in 1869 for the public discussion of scientific topics. In the 1870s he nudged Grove, the experienced civil engineer, to write geography primers for schools when his music dictionary project began to slow – but then agreed to let the dictionary resume once Grove knuckled down and the public response to the dictionary became so positive. And it was Macmillan who encouraged Grove's integration of music essays into *Macmillan's Magazine*, with sophisticated articles by Dannreuther, Edmund Gurney and Henry Leslie appearing alongside work by historians, anthropologists and linguists.[36] In the period of Grove's editorship of *Macmillan's*,

---

[36] *Macmillan's* was a literary monthly started in 1859, the first shilling periodical in Britain. Grove's tenure as editor from 1868 was the first in its history to include music articles, essentially testing the market for music books. Partly to accommodate those

1868–83, his contributors included Octavia Hill, Millicent Garrett Fawcett, the Cambridge historians Mandell Creighton and J.R. Seeley, Lockyer, the biologist T.H. Huxley, the experimental physicist John Tyndall, the Oxford historian E.A. Freeman and the independent historian J.R. Green. All were identified by name and paid professionally for their work, which was shaped ultimately by a literary editor, Grove himself, addressing a general audience. By contrast, Longmans' *English Historical Review*, edited by Creighton, would have to stop paying contributors after its first year, so small was the journal's readership.[37] A future for serious music writing, historical or critical, was still possible in the literary sphere, then, as long as publishers, editors and writers were willing to collaborate.

All these new pathways must have sent positive signals to music investigators wary of affiliation with concert-giving. The hope of improved access to original sources through the BM, Public Record Office, South Kensington Museum and private collections like that of Ouseley; a slightly greater hope of academic acceptance for music as more than a religious or occasional social activity, with widened possibilities for its theoretical and historical substance in some institutions; and strong interest from literary publishers cultivating informed reading audiences: such developments surely encouraged intending Musical Association founders in their decision to cut ties with concert promotion. Any career scientists wishing to join them would have been very welcome too, able to advocate the benefits of music research to practising musicians as well as to wider networks of academic colleagues and the public. Signs of a new form of association, intellectual as well as musical, were on the horizon.

---

articles, and articles on historical and religious topics besides, Grove reduced the magazine's purely literary content, above all serialized novels – an extraordinary innovation at the time. See Ann Parry, 'The Grove Years, 1868–1883: A "New Look" for *Macmillan's Magazine*?', *Victorian Periodicals Review*, 19 (1986), 149–57.

[37] In her 'Academic Discipline or Literary Genre? The Establishment of Boundaries in Historical Writing', *Victorian Literature and Culture*, 32 (2004), 525–45, Leslie Howsam argues that emphasis on the *English Historical Review* as a landmark in professionalizing History too neatly privileges a certain kind of academic writing over more literary approaches to writing and publishing scholarly work, which were cultivated specifically by Alexander Macmillan to attract and educate a broader reading audience.

2

Developing Purpose, 1874–1924

In June 1906, conferees at the twenty-eighth Annual Meeting of the (American) Music Teachers' National Association in Oberlin, Ohio, heard an illuminating paper on 'European Musical Associations' by Oscar G. Sonneck, head of the Music Division of the Library of Congress, the USA's national library in Washington, DC. Sonneck, a New Jerseyan educated in Germany, had done his homework. After differentiating four classes of musical association by particular interest – performing, pedagogic, protective and learned – and citing familiar American counterparts of the first three, he went on to advocate the less familiar fourth type, lacking in the USA, a learned music society. Using 'general', 'special' and 'elastic' in his category descriptions, he then surveyed a number of European learned groups ranging from the seventeenth-century Accademia dei Filarmonici in Bologna and Lorenz Mizler's eighteenth-century Societät der musikalischen Wissenschaften in Leipzig to the nineteenth-century Musical Antiquarian Society and Plainsong and Mediaeval Music Society in England; and from the Deutsche Händel Gesellschaft, Gesellschaft zur Herausgabe der Denkmäler der Tonkunst in Oesterreich and Robert Eitner's Gesellschaft für Musikforschung (1868–1905) to the Musical Association in London, besides Dutch, Scandinavian and more Prussian and Bavarian bodies along the way. The full scope is informative, the ordering and comparisons logical, including the following:

> The Gesellschaft für Musikforschung did not pay much attention to acoustics, aesthetics, psychology, theory and kindred subjects, whereas the annual Proceedings of the Musical Association in London abound in such papers. On the other hand, this most important of English associations, founded in 1874 and incorporated in 1904, does not include the publication of music in its program, as appears from the full title of the society, 'Musical Association for the investigation and discussion of subjects connected with the art and science of music'.[1]

After noting some of the Association's rules and regulations, Sonneck continued:

> The list of members, deceased or living, came to include practically every English musician and musical scholar of renown and speaks well not only for the vitality of the Musical Association and its splendid organization, but also explains to a certain extent why the prominent English musicians possess such an enviable

---

[1] Sonneck, 'European Musical Associations', 134.

grasp on the theoretical, historical, aesthetic, in short, scientific problems of their art. If you have ever glanced over the complete index of the papers read and discussed at the meetings – in 1899 they numbered already 217 papers – this fact will no longer surprise you.

He then exemplified the range of 'these generally excellent papers and discussions' by selecting twenty subjects encompassed in the Association's *Proceedings* to 1899: 'new notations, copyright, Wagner, pitch, criticism, music-recorders, women musicians, Russian operas, thematic coincidences, aesthetics, music-printing, carillons, Sullivan, formation of libraries, the viola da gamba, music in schools, metronomes, form, Irish music, [and] exotic music'.[2]

What impressed Sonneck about the Musical Association, setting it apart from both earlier and contemporary groups, was its emphasis on musical science, the wide topical coverage in its papers and its waiving of music publication as part of its mission. A further distinction was the group's cooperative spirit, shown by its decision to work closely with the new Internationale Musikgesellschaft (IMG, 'International Musical Society') centred at Berlin in 1899 – a 'unique compliment paid by a venerable body of learned men [*sic*] to an infant organization'.[3] Coming from a knowledgeable outsider – one, too, seeking models for American music scholarship – this positive report is striking. What Sonneck doesn't say is how the British group came to be constituted as it was, why those particular emphases pertained and how the Association achieved its vitality and 'splendid organization'. I will consider those questions here, looking at the body's founding and earliest members, its rules and routines, the group's aims for growth and development, its international outreach, including cooperation with the IMG, and some of its members' research themes across the first fifty years, 1874–1924. In the absence of any government or academic support for UK music scholarship at this period, an essential step was to develop and refine the Association's purpose. Regular meetings would foster individual work, and the society's structure would provide a laboratory in which a range of researchers could experiment.

ࣽ Founding

Since the beginning of the twentieth century, credit for the idea of starting a musical body along the lines of a British learned society has gone to the well-known organist and composer John Stainer, who was twenty-seven at the time he first discussed it with William Pole. Pole, as we have seen, a civil engineer and academic, was a

---

[2] Ibid., 135.
[3] Ibid. The IMG had been founded by Oskar Fleischer (Berlin) in connection with Breitkopf & Härtel (Leipzig), with its legal headquarters in Leipzig. Sonneck would go on to co-found the *Musical Quarterly* with Rudolph Schirmer at G. Schirmer's in New York in 1915. See Claude V. Palisca, 'American Scholarship in Western Music', in Frank Ll. Harrison, Claude Palisca and Mantle Hood, *Musicology* (Englewood Cliffs, NJ: Prentice Hall, 1963), 87–213, esp. 122–49.

mature music student, aged fifty-three, whose Oxford Mus.Doc. exercise Stainer had examined (along with F.A.G. Ouseley and C.W. Corfe). Stainer's recollection, after Pole died in late 1900, was that their conversation had occurred at Oxford in 1867 on the occasion of Pole's taking the degree. Stainer further confirms that Pole attended the new group's first organizational meeting on 16 April 1874, and that Charles Salaman, who did not attend but, as we know, had ably managed the Musical Society of London in 1858–67, soon 'took up the matter warmly, and by his work, and tact, and knowledge of musicians, backed by W. Spottiswoode, [...] really placed the Association on the sound basis on which it now stands'. Stainer concludes of Salaman: 'The idea was mine, but the construction was his.'[4] This skeletal founding story, amplified by details gathered in the early 1980s by Hugh Cobbe through recovery of the Association's earliest minute books, now in the British Library, still stands as reliable in outline.[5] Its depiction of the original forces behind the Association, however, invites fresh thought involving William Spottiswoode, Pole and their colleagues outside music. For there was clearly something different in this mix of 1874, the people and their rationale for joining together, that did not exist in earlier musical groupings and went beyond a basic separation from concert-giving. That something was science, alike the involvement of scientists in modern sound research, public esteem for scientists' intellectual stature, and scientists' practical experience in managing learned societies, including care over scholarly infrastructure (libraries, journals, indexes, equipment) and a penchant for promoting their own work.

Stainer explains the seven-year gap between his conversation with Pole in Oxford and the initial meeting of the new society in April 1874 as relating to his arrival in the capital to take up his new post at St Paul's Cathedral. The unstated assumption was that, to be viable, any such member organization had to be based in metropolitan London, not in a university setting; Stainer couldn't begin to raise support for it until he himself was there, and his new job didn't start until March 1872. Yet as we know, there were other, senior actors behind the scene in the capital already, above all Pole and Salaman, who'd been associated with the MSL lecture sessions, now defunct since 1867, and who would also value a new formation. The fact that wider developments in sound research had been proceeding, while both commercial publishing and official investigations into

---

[4] 'Occasional Notes', *MT*, 42 (1901), 91. For an earlier version of the same narrative, see John Stainer, 'Inaugural Address to the Twenty-First Session', *PMA*, 21 (1894–95), xiii–xvi. Here Stainer's memory is particularly imaginative. Of those he claims attended the first meeting, Ellis, Goss, Griesbach and Helmore were not invited and Wheatstone did not attend. Reporting Stainer's death in the annual 'Report' for 1900–01, the secretary Percy Baker referred to him as 'virtually founder of the Association' (reflecting *Grove 1*). In 1912 *Report of the Fourth Congress*, 394, Baker described the Association as 'projected in Oxford' by Stainer. By 1924, in his fifty-year overview of the Association, Baker stated simply, 'The founder of the Musical Association was John Stainer' (*PMA*, 50 (1923–24), 129). In fact Stainer attended Council meetings only rarely even as president, though he did give five papers, 1874–1901, including his important description of Bodleian MS. Canon. Misc. in November 1895.

[5] Hugh Cobbe, 'The Royal Musical Association, 1874–1901', *PRMA*, 110 (1983–84), 111–17.

science education in the late 1860s and early 70s were creating new possibilities for music, only pressed the issue further, independently of Stainer's career move. In truth, Pole emerges as the likely networker in all these worlds, centred in London, who almost certainly brought the elements together, catalyzed finally by John Stainer's appointment to St Paul's.[6]

William Pole had written his first concert programme notes in the early 1850s for the NPS, as had George Grove, while his scientific work as physicist and engineer won him a Fellowship of the Royal Society in 1861, the same year Hermann von Helmholtz, on one of many London visits, lectured on sound at the Royal Institution. Pole followed Helmholtz's work closely for his own investigations into the acoustical basis of music theory, expressed in lectures at the MSL in the early 1860s and later reworked for the Royal Institution in 1877 (published as *The Philosophy of Music*, 1879). Indeed Pole and Helmholtz became personally acquainted, not least when Pole, who happened to be colour-blind, served as a subject for Helmholtz's and James Clerk Maxwell's experiments in colour perception, held at Maxwell's Kensington home in mid-April 1864, followed by, according to Helmholtz, 'a splendid lunch with champagne'.[7]

Meanwhile the Irish physicist John Tyndall belonged to the same circle of eminent scientists interested in sound. A Royal Society fellow from 1852, professor at the Royal Institution from 1853, then its superintendent from 1867, Tyndall was known for his brilliant lecture-demonstrations and outspoken advocacy of experimental science. His work in sound, first through his evening working men's lectures at the School of Mines in 1866, then in lectures for the Royal Institution published as *Sound* in 1867, culminated in the study of how sound travels through the atmosphere under various conditions.[8] Though not a musician, Tyndall responded to heard music and enjoyed the opera; his knowledge of acoustics, whether through foghorn experiments for the government or advice on how structural shapes and materials affect sound,

---

[6] The belated tradition crediting Stainer as prime mover was strong enough to elicit surprise in Gerald Abraham by the 1970s, in 'Our First Hundred Years', *PRMA*, 100 (1973–74), pp. vii–xiii. On reading an early *Illustrated London News* report of the society that omits Stainer (31 Oct 1874), Abraham assumed that Stainer had drafted it himself, his own modesty preventing self-mention. An alternative view might be that in 1874, Stainer's role was broadly unknown at the time or thought subsidiary, his scholarly and organizing activity far less prominent than that of others mentioned, and that the paragraph, probably written by Salaman, was meant to promote the Association, not chronicle its origins. In 1874, in any event, success was far from certain; Stainer himself never claimed credit for the idea of the Association until 1894, still less the 'founding'.

[7] Quoted in David Cahan, 'Helmholtz and the British Scientific Elite: From Force Conservation to Energy Conservation', *Notes & Records of the Royal Society*, 66 (2012), 55–68 at 63.

[8] For Tyndall's early work on sonorous vibrations in 1867, including coastal sound signalling, see Roland Jackson, *The Ascent of John Tyndall: Victorian Scientist, Mountaineer, and Public Intellectual* (Oxford: Oxford Univ. Press, 2018), 202–03; for Tyndall's Christmas Lectures, 1873–74, on 'The Motion and Sensation of Sound', written up for the Royal Society and for *Nature*, see pp. 327–28.

placed him on the Organ Committee for the Royal Albert Hall in 1868.[9] More important, he became one of three Gas Referees for the Board of Trade in 1872 alongside William Pole, who'd held a parallel role there since 1870 (both served until the 1890s and they knew each other well). By 1878 Tyndall would be associated with the first UK demonstration of the loud-speaking telephone, or 'phonograph', at the Royal Institution.[10]

Until recently, John Tyndall was largely forgotten except for his discovery of why the sky is blue and of the physical basis for the greenhouse effect, now understood as crucial to climate science. In the period under discussion, however, he was a celebrated public figure, sometimes controversial, and by 1874 president of the British Association for the Advancement of Science. For present purposes, it was his closeness to Pole from the 1860s and 70s, and their joint friendship with the Oxford-trained mathematician William Spottiswoode, a wealthy amateur scientist who was Queen's Printer and Treasurer of the Royal Society from 1870, that gave such a distinctive impetus to the launching of the Musical Association: no fewer than six of the twenty-two people invited to the first meeting were Royal Society fellows, including one past president (George Airy, the Astronomer Royal) and two future presidents (Spottiswoode and Lord Rayleigh), one of whom would be a Nobel prize winner (Rayleigh); a further invitee was a distinguished medical doctor (W.H. Stone).[11] Spottiswoode's firm, Eyre & Spottiswoode, was in fact printing all the Devonshire Commission Reports, including that of 1873 recommending that Oxford and Cambridge be centres of research. More immediately, Spottiswoode had executive experience in multiple learned societies, making him the ideal spokesperson to propose, with Pole and Stainer's approval, the first meeting of a new kind of music society at his home in Grosvenor Place – a home that had hosted many a friendly musical evening with singing, as well as dinners for elite scientists and government ministers.[12] If one event potentially set the final ball rolling, it may have been Macmillan & Co.'s contracting of George Grove as their literary editor in late 1873, followed by circulation in March 1874 of the firm's music

---

[9] Jackson, *The Ascent of John Tyndall*, 282. Tyndall's colleagues on the committee included, among others, the conductor Michael Costa and R.K. Bowley of the Sacred Harmonic Society.

[10] 'The Phonograph at the Royal Institution', *Graphic* (16 Mar 1878), 259, 262, describes a lecture by W.H. Preece on the 'telephone', with an image of Tyndall assisting the experiment on p. 268. See also Jackson, *The Ascent of John Tyndall*, 378–80.

[11] For a fascinating study of relationships behind the Royal Society involving Spottiswoode, Tyndall, Airy and others at this period, some of them suggestive of principles transferred to the Musical Association, see Ruth Barton, '"An Influential Set of Chaps": The X-Club and Royal Society Politics, 1864–85', *British Journal for the History of Science*, 23 (1990), 53–81.

[12] Dr W.H. Stone, who gave the Association's first paper on 2 November 1874, singled out Spottiswoode as the body's 'earliest promoter' ('On Extending the Compass and Increasing the Tone of Stringed Instruments, with especial reference to the Author's and Mr. Meeson's Elliptical Tension-bars', *PMA*, 1 (1874–75), 1–3 at 1). After his death in June 1883, the Association's Annual General Meeting (AGM) recognized Spottiswoode as 'an ornament to science [who] had been very useful to the Association' (BL Add. MS 71011, fol. 12v).

dictionary prospectus; Pole's name appeared among its thirty-two contributors already signed up.[13]

Here is Spottiswoode's letter of invitation, making the case for an exploratory meeting:

50 Grosvenor Place
8th April, 1874

Dear Sir, – It has been suggested by several leading persons interested both in the theory and practice of Music, that the formation of a Society, similar in the main features of its organisation to existing Learned Societies, would be a great public benefit. Such a Musical Society might comprise among its members the foremost Musicians, theoretical as well as practical, of the day; the principal Patrons of Art [music and literary publishers, church and university representatives]; and also those Scientific men whose researches have been directed to the science of Acoustics and to kindred inquiries. Its periodical meetings might be devoted partly to the reading of Papers upon the history, the principles, and the criticism of Music; partly to the illustration of such Papers by actual performance; and partly to the exhibition and discussion of experiments relating to theory and construction of musical instruments, or to the principles and combination of musical sounds.

With a view to ascertain the opinions of persons interested in these subjects, and to attempt a more precise definition of the objects and constitution of such a Society, it is proposed to hold a meeting here, at which your presence is requested, on Thursday, April 16th, at 2.30 p.m.

I am, Dear Sir, yours faithfully,
W. Spottiswoode

The following Gentlemen have been invited to attend this meeting.

Dr. Pole	Professor H.S. Oakeley, Edinburgh
Sedley Taylor, Esq., M.A.	Sir R.P. Stewart, Dublin
Wm. Chappell, Esq., F.S.A.	The Astronomer Royal [Sir George Airy]
George Grove, Esq.	Sir C. Wheatstone
Rev. R. Haweis, M.A.	G.A. Macfarren, Esq.
Professor Tyndall	E.J. Hopkins, Esq.
Carl Engel, Esq.	John Bishop, Esq., Cheltenham
Arthur Sullivan, Esq.	Lord Rayleigh
Sir F. Ouseley, Bart.	W. Spottiswoode, Esq.
Sir W.S. Bennett	Dr. Stone
Dr. Stainer	J. Hullah, Esq.[14]

---

[13] 'Preparing for Publication: The Dictionary of Music (A.D. 1450–1874)', London: Macmillan & Co., Mar 1874; bound with 'General Directions for Contributors' and several headword lists (RCM Library XXII.E.24 (4), copy of A.J. Hipkins).

[14] BL Add. MS 71010, fol. 8.

According to the Association's Minutes, nine people attended – Spottiswoode, Tyndall, Sedley Taylor (Trinity College, Cambridge; author of *Sound and Music*, 1873; grandson of the Norwich musical writer Richard Mackenzie Bacon), Chappell, Grove, Hullah, Pole, Macfarren and Stainer. Apologies for absence with messages of approval were received from Stone, Oakeley, John Bishop and Hopkins.[15] Haweis agreed to join but never paid his subscription; Sterndale Bennett never responded. All the others did, Rayleigh belatedly, besides by 2 November 1874 another 122 people including eleven women. Their names are recorded in the front matter of the first *Proceedings* volume (1874–75), pages vii–ix, in a format that would reappear for each year's membership in succeeding years to volume 79 (1952–53), after which a streamlined list began to appear at the back of each volume (see Fig. 6).

At that very first meeting, Spottiswoode had been in the chair to begin the business but had to leave to attend a meeting of the Royal Society; Pole then took over for the discussion, which included mention of the Musical Institute and the Musical Society of London as precedents. Macfarren recalled that several times an important paper had been given to only a very small audience despite the large membership of those groups. Chappell pointed out that comparison with the present proposal wasn't fair since those earlier bodies had operated chiefly as concert societies, with the 'scientific element' not properly represented. Pole agreed (twice disappointed by scant attendance at his papers). Taylor suggested that two levels of participation might help, members and Associates, since some people would like to attend and ask questions but without the responsibility of reading a paper; Grove agreed but countered that learned society membership did not necessarily carry the obligation of reading a paper, with which Tyndall concurred. Hullah, who had once led the Musical Institute but never participated in the MSL, urged extreme care in selecting original members: he believed the first twenty or thirty names would stamp the character of the organization (perhaps revealing his frustration over the Musical Institute and New Philharmonic episode). Grove suggested that a small committee should form to consider possible rules and potential Members; Tyndall then made that formal proposal. Those elected to the committee were Chappell, Pole, Spottiswoode, Hullah and Stainer, who met again a few days later with Stainer acting as secretary.

The ten rules they in turn proposed were approved at a second general meeting on 29 May, at the South Kensington Museum with Hullah in the chair. The nineteen people attending formed a first group of Original Members: W. Chappell, J. Barnby, M. Garcia, W.H. Stone, R.H.M. Bosanquet, A.J. Ellis, W.H. Monk, Salaman, T. Helmore, C.E. Stephens, E.J. Hopkins, S. Taylor, E. Dannreuther, J. Goss, E.H. Thorne, J.H. Griesbach (died January 1875),

---

[15] Ibid., fol. 9v. John Tyndall sent a brief note to Spottiswoode just after 2 pm on 16 April [1874], indicating that he could not attend the meeting but would be 'glad to belong to the Musical Society' (Royal Institution, MS JT/1/T/1351). Somehow, though, he changed his plan and went, arriving in time to participate and commenting in the discussion. I am grateful to Roland Jackson for alerting me to Tyndall's letter.

OFFICERS, &c.

PRESIDENT.
The Rev. Sir FREDERICK A. GORE OUSELEY, Bart., M.A., Mus. Doc. Oxon,
Prof. Mus. Univ. Oxon.

VICE-PRESIDENTS.
GROVE, GEORGE, Esq., D.C.L.
HULLAH, JOHN, Esq.
MACFARREN, GEORGE ALEXANDER, Esq., Mus. Doc. Cantab., Prof. Univ. Camb.
SPOTTISWOODE, WILLIAM, Esq., M.A., F.R.S., LL.D.
TYNDALL, Professor JOHN, F.R.S., LL.D., &c. &c.

COMMITTEE.
CHAPPELL, WILLIAM, Esq., F.S.A.
HULLAH, JOHN, Esq.
OSBORNE, GEORGE ALEXANDER, Esq.
POLE, WILLIAM, Esq., F.R.S., Mus. Doc. Oxon.
PRENDERGAST, ARTHUR H. D., Esq., M.A.

SALAMAN, CHARLES KENSINGTON, Esq., Hon. Mem. Acad. St. Cecilia, Rome.
SPOTTISWOODE, WILLIAM, Esq., M.A., F.R.S., LL.D.
STAINER, Dr. JOHN, M.A., Mus. Doc. Oxon.
STONE, Dr. W. H., M.A., F.R.C.P.

ORIGINAL MEMBERS.
Adams, William Grylls, Esq., M.A., F.R.S., Professor King's College.
Airy, Sir George Biddell, K.C.B., D.C.L., M.A., P.R.S., Astronomer-Royal, &c.
Alloway, J. A., Esq., S.C.F. (*Lond.*)
Banister, Henry Charles, Esq.
Barnby, Joseph, Esq.
Barnett, John Francis, Esq.
Barrett, W. A., Esq., Mus. Bac.
Barry, C. A., Esq., M.A.
Bassett, H., Esq., F.C.S.
Beddome, Leonard W., Esq.
Bellamy, The Rev. J., D.D., President St. John's College, Oxon.
Benedict, Sir Julius, Knt.
Benson, Lionel S., Esq.
Berger, Francesco, Esq.
Best, W. T., Esq. (*Liverpool*)
Bishop, John, Esq. (*Cheltenham*)
Bliss, The Rev. W. H., M.A., Mus. Bac. Oxon. (*Windsor*)
Bosanquet, R. H. M., Esq., M.A., F.R.A.S., F.C.S., Fellow of St. John's College, Oxon.
Bridge, J. Fredk., Esq., Mus. Doc., Oxon., Professor Owens College, Organist Manchester Cathedral.
Browne, Lennox, Esq., F.R.C.S. Edin.
Case, G. E., Esq.
Champneys, Frank, Esq., B.A.
Chappell, William, Esq., F.S.A.
Chappell, Arthur S., Esq. (Treasurer)
Clarke, Somers, Esq., Junr.
Clay, Frederick, Esq.

Cobb, Gerard F., Esq., M.A., Trin. Coll. Camb.
Coleridge, Arthur Duke, Esq., M.A.
Cooper, Alexander S., Esq., F.C.O.
Crawford, Major George A., M.A.
Crow, E. J., Esq., Mus. Bac. Cantab., Organist Ripon Cathedral.
Cummings, W. H., Esq.
Cusins, W. G., Esq.
Dannreuther, Edward, Esq.
Davison, J. W., Esq.
Deacon, H. C., Esq.
Deane, The Rev. H., B.D., St. John's College, Oxon.
Dick, Cotsford, Esq.
Drew, Miss Catherine.
Dunn, Mrs., of Inglewood.
Eastlake, Lady.
Ellis, Alex.J., Esq., B.A., F.R.S., F.S.A.
Elvey, Sir George, Knt., Mus. Doc. Oxon. (*Windsor*)
Engel, Carl, Esq.
Fitzgerald, Lord Gerald.
Frost, H. F., Esq., Organist Savoy Chapel Royal.
Gadsby, Henry, Esq.
Garcia, Manuel, Esq.
Gladstone, W. H., Esq., M.P.
Goldschmidt, Otto, Esq.
Goodeve-Erskine,Rev.John Francis E., M.A.
Goolden, W., Esq., M.A.
Hamilton-Gordon, The Hon. Lady.
Goss, Sir John, Knt.
Green, Joseph, Esq.

Figure 6. Officers and Original Members (*PMA*, 1, 1874–75), continues on next two pages.

ORIGINAL MEMBERS—*continued*.

Grove, George, Esq., D.C.L. (*Vice-President*)
Baillie-Hamilton, J., Esq.
Helmore, The Rev. T., M.A.
Hermann, L., Esq.
Hiles, Henry, Esq., Mus. Doc. Oxon. (*Manchester*)
Hill, Arthur, Esq., B.E. (*Cork*)
Hopkins, Edward J., Esq., Org. Temple.
Holmes, Henry, Esq.
Hueffer, Dr., Ph.D.
Hullah, John, Esq. (*Vice-President*)
Hullett, Capt. C. H., Organist of St. Peter's, Vere Street.
Janion, Miss.
Joule, Benjamin St. J. B., Esq., Hon. Organist St. Peter's, Manchester.
Kingston, Alfred, Esq.
Leslie, Henry, Esq.
Littleton, Alfred, Esq.
Linton, Robert P., Esq., F.R.C.S.
Lloyd, Charles H., Esq., B.A., Mus. Bac. Oxon.
Lunn, Henry C., Esq.
Macfarren, George Alexander, Esq., Mus. Doc. Cantab., Prof. Univ. Camb. (*Vice-President*).
Mackeson, Charles, Esq., F.S.S.
McCreagh, Major.
Martin, G. C., Esq., Mus. Bac. Oxon.
Marshall, Julian, Esq.
Marshall, Mrs. Julian.
Metzler, George T., Esq.
Monk, W. H., Esq., Prof. King's Coll.
Monk, Edwin George, Esq., Mus. Doc. Oxon., F.R.A.S., Org. York Minster.
Monro, D. Benning, Esq., M.A., Oriel Coll. Oxon.
Montgomery, Hugh, Esq., M.A.
Morant, John, Esq.
Newdegate, The Hon. Mrs.
Oakeley, H. S., Esq., M.A., Mus. Doc. Cantuar., Prof. Univ. Edin.
Osborne, George Alexr., Esq.
Ouseley, The Rev. Sir Fredk. A. Gore, Bart., M.A., Mus. Doc. Oxon., Prof. Univ. Oxon. (*President*)
Parkinson, W. W., Esq.
Parratt, Walter, Esq., Mus. Bac. Oxon.
Pauer, Ernst, Esq.
Phasey, Alfred, Esq.
Pole, Wm., Esq., F.R.S., Mus.Doc.Oxon.
Pontigny, Victor De, Esq.
Prendergast, A. H. D., Esq., M.A.
Prescott, Miss Oliveria.
Prout, Ebenezer, Esq., B.A.
Pye, Kellow J., Esq.
Randegger, Alberto, Esq.

Romano, Giuseppe, Esq., Hon. Mem. Acad. dei Quiriti, Rome; Hon. Mem. Cir. Bonamici, Naples.
Reynell, V. C. Reynell, Esq., M.A., King's Coll.
Ringrose, William W., Esq., Mus. Bac. Oxon. (*Great Marlow*)
Rosa, Carl, Esq.
Rougier, Henry, Esq.
Rudall, H. A., Esq.
Salaman, Charles K., Esq., Hon. Mem. Acad. St. Cecilia, Rome (*Hon. Sec.*)
Sargood, Mr. Serjeant.
Schira, F., Esq.
Sinclair, Arthur J., Esq.
Smith, Miss Flora M.
Smith, H. Ambrose, Esq.
Spottiswoode, William, Esq., M.A., LL.D., F.R.S. (*Vice-President*)
Stainer, John, Esq., M.A., Mus. Doc. Oxon., Org. St. Paul's Cathedral.
Stanford, C. Villiers, Esq., B.A., Organist Trinity College, Cambridge.
Statham, The Rev. Wm., B.A. (*Ellesmere-Port, Cheshire*)
Southgate, Thomas Lea, Esq.
Steggall, C., Esq., Mus. Doc. Cantab.
Stephens, Charles Edward, Esq.
Stephens, Samuel Jno., Esq.
Stewart, Sir Robert Prescott, Knt., Mus. Doc. Dublin, Prof. Univ. Dublin.
Stone, Dr. W. H., M.A., F.R.C.P.
Sullivan, Arthur S., Esq.
Sylvester, Professor J. J., F.R.S.
Taylor, Sedley, Esq., M.A., Trin. Coll. Camb.
Taylor, James, Esq., Mus. Bac. Oxon, Organist New College, Oxon.
Thorne, E. H., Esq.
Tilleard, James, Esq.
Trotter, The Rev. C., M.A., Trin. Coll. Camb.
Troutbeck, The Rev. John, M.A.
Turle, James, Esq., Org. Westminster Abbey.
Tyndall, Professor John, F.R.S., LL.D. (*Vice-President*).
Verrinder, C.G., Esq., Mus.Doc.Cantuar.
Walker, The Rev. H. Aston, M.A., Oriel Coll. Oxon.
West, Robert G., Esq.
Wheatstone, Sir Charles, Knt., F.R.S., LL.D., D.C.L.
Meadows-White, Mrs. F.
Wilkinson, Richard, Esq., M.D.
Wylde, Henry, Esq., Mus. Doc. Cantab., Gresham Professor.
Zimmermann, Miss Agnes.

—(*continued*)

MEMBERS ELECTED SINCE NOVEMBER 2, 1874.

Astley, Miss Constance.
Ball, Henry, Esq.
Beevor, Mrs.
Bell, J. M., Esq.
Bennett, Joseph, Esq.
Bishop, C. K. K., Esq.
Boulton, Captain, R.N.
Buttery, Horace, Esq.
Cardew, A., Esq., Magd. Coll. Oxon.
Courtenay, Miss.
Fowler, W. W., Esq., M.A., Lincoln Coll. Oxon.
Gill, William Henry, Esq.
Hall, C. G., Esq.
Halpin, Col. George.
Higgs, James, Esq., Mus. Bac.
Hunt, H. J. B., Esq., Ch. Ch. Oxon.
Kempe, R. A., Esq.
Kennedy, T. S., Esq.
McNaught, W. G., Esq.

Mallock, H. R. A., Esq., Hertford Coll. Oxon.
Miller, The Rev. H. Walter, Mus. Bac. Oxon.
Ramsbotham, Dr. S. H.
Rhodes, Alfred, Esq.
Rivington, Septimus, Esq., M.A.
Rutt, Arthur, Esq.
Smiley, George, Esq.
Tatton, —, Esq., M.A., Balliol Coll. Oxon.
Tunstall, John, Esq.
Verney, Mrs. Frederick.
Wilton, Right Hon. Earl of, P.C.
Ward, Miss.
Ward, Miss S.
Watson, Michael, Esq.
Welch, W., Esq., M.A.
Willis, Mrs. Armine.

Figure 6—*concluded*

C. Wheatstone (died October 1875), W.A. Barrett and Hullah. This meeting further decided to begin regular paper sessions in November 1874, and to welcome women as members, a previously well-accepted principle at both the Musical Institute and MSL, though not in English learned societies generally.[16] Among the first to be approached were Elizabeth, Lady Eastlake, the prominent journalist and writer on art, and Agnes Zimmermann, a noted pianist and composer, both of whom joined quickly. Stone and Salaman were added to the committee.

In summer 1874, further meetings of this small committee, later called the Council, attempted to arrange a regular venue for meetings: several suggestions proved impractical, including the South Kensington Museum, KCL and Willis's Rooms. Two possible names for the organization were proposed – 'The Musical Society of Great Britain' and 'The Musical Scientific Society' – while ideas for new member recruitment yielded lists of people to invite (Carl Rosa and Edmund Chipp were suggested but soon declined, though Rosa joined

---

[16] In his *Inaugural Address* to the Musical Institute in February 1852, Hullah had been pleased to note this difference from other artistic and scientific societies, and thought the rationale was obvious: 'It would be monstrous at this day to set on foot a *Musical Institute* with which artists like Mrs Anderson or Madame Viardot Garcia could by no possibility be connected' (*Musical Institute of London, Inaugural Address*, 11, emphasis original). His personal experience of working with many women school teachers, singers and pianists would have confirmed that view. Women had also long been members of the Philharmonic Society.

later). Plans for a promotional press campaign embraced the *Academy, Athenaeum, Choir* and *Musical World*. Accordingly as the secretarial load increased, Salaman agreed to relieve Stainer of that duty, staying on as secretary until 1877. At a third general meeting on 4 August 1874, at Salaman's house with A.J. Ellis in the chair, the body's name was discussed at length, with final agreement on 'MUSICAL ASSOCIATION', adding a carefully worded strapline in small capitals: 'FOR THE INVESTIGATION AND DISCUSSION OF SUBJECTS CONNECTED WITH THE ART AND SCIENCE OF MUSIC'. By avoiding 'Society' and its connotations, using instead the more liberal 'Association' to suggest a bridging of intellectual interests and social levels, the organization sealed its identity as a broad-church body, and one, too, unrelated to the enterprise of giving concerts. Prof. Ouseley, Stainer's mentor, was unanimously elected president. At last, by the time of a fifth committee meeting in October, the venue had been settled as the Beethoven Rooms, 27 Harley Street, Cavendish Square, and the Treasurer as S. Arthur Chappell, William's younger brother. Spottiswoode and Tyndall were both pleased be invited to serve as vice-presidents, two among five, and Tyndall wrote to thank the Association for that honour. The first papers to be given, back-to-back on 2 November 1874, were by Stone and Bosanquet, Macfarren taking the chair. With fifty-one signing members and seventeen guests in attendance, the opening meeting made a solid start.[17]

❧ *Rules and Protocols: Establishing Discipline*

Those first ten rules agreed in May 1874 laid the groundwork for how the Association would operate. Apparently simple, they in fact embodied more meaning and challenge than a first reading might have conveyed to Original Members. Here's the list:

1. This Association is intended to be similar in its organisation to existing Learned Societies.

2. The Members will consist of practical and theoretical Musicians, as well as those whose researches have been directed to the science of Acoustics, the history of Music, or other kindred subjects.

3. The Association will hold its meetings on the first Monday of every month, from November to June, at five o'clock p.m., when papers will be read and discussed as at other Learned Societies. These papers may treat of any subject connected with the Art or Science of Music.

4. Experiments and performances may be introduced, when strictly limited to the illustration of the Papers read.

5. Papers and Communications will be received from, or through, any Member of the Association.

---

[17] BL Add. MS 71019, fol. 1.

6. Reports of the Proceedings will be distributed to the Members, and will be published.

7. It is not intended that the Association shall give Concerts, or undertake any publications other than those of their own Proceedings, and the Papers read at their meetings.

8. The Election of Members will be by Ballot.

9. The management will be vested in a Committee, to be annually elected by the Members of the Association.

10. The annual subscription to the Association is One Guinea.[18]

The emphasis on 'learned societies', 'researches', 'papers' and 'experiments' was intentional. So was the wide approach to membership, joined to a narrow description of purpose: every interest or expertise would be welcomed, including from non-musicians, but paper reading and discussion would replace concerts and extraneous publication. For people in UK music circles, this combination was completely new. At the Musical Society of London, for example, all members had been required to possess practical music knowledge whether joining in professional or non-professional categories: rank and class mattered but social differences would be overcome positively through the commonality of everyone simply being 'Musicians'.[19] Now, being musical or musically active was not what the Musical Association founders sought, nor was a member's occupation or employment particularly significant. Instead, this new plan drawing on English learned society custom provided for procedures, as in rules 5, 6 and 7, that would probably have been unfamiliar to members of earlier music clubs. 'Papers and Communications will be received', rule 5, alludes to an established scholarly practice in which dated communications sent in to a learned society, or to colleagues who were members, could advance knowledge and help establish priority in discovery or thought just like formal papers delivered in person. Given that other researchers might be working on related questions, conveying information in this way was seen as critical for building up reliable new knowledge; by extension, oral reading to a learned society, even of brief reports, constituted a form of publication. No case was more salient around this time than that of Charles Darwin, who in early July 1858 had used a series of letters about his work and communications

---

[18] 'Musical Association for the Investigation and Discussion of Subjects Connected with the Art and Science of Music, 1874: Rules', *PMA*, 1 (1874–75), pp. iii–iv at iv. A slightly earlier form of the Rules appears in BL Add. MS 71010, fol. 44.

[19] Musical Society of London, Prospectus of First Season, 'code of laws' [p. 3, point 2]: 'The members consist of Fellows, and Associates; who, whether Professional or Non-Professional, must be Musicians' (Musical Society of London Papers, NYPL Drexel 663, items unnumbered).

with friends to demonstrate to the distinguished Linnean Society (founded 1788) his priority in theorizing natural selection.[20]

Next to follow in the Musical Association rules, 'Reports of the Proceedings will be distributed [...] and [...] published', rule 6, signals accountability, encouraging both personal and intellectual discipline. Whatever transpired at the Association's ordinary meetings, that is, including papers read out, would be listened to, discussed, and a summary shared with all members; the need for everyone to keep up, whether attending or not, was presumed to be integral to the scholarly life. Publication of the 'Papers read', specified in rule 7 finally, was the most obvious mark of learned society custom and easy to grasp on the face of it. Here, however, publication implied a more complex set of actions – regular, systematic and costly, subject to member subscriptions – than anything undertaken by previous music clubs, including those who'd issued music editions or an evanescent music journal: the goal was to produce an original multi-author volume of record, annually and quickly. As with the venerable Royal Society itself after 1752, this rule in effect committed the Musical Association to becoming its own publisher, with all the interlocking tasks and financial risk such a role entailed. Although the inclusion of after-paper discussions was not stipulated until 1876, the practice of taking down and printing such commentary, in readable form, began as early as January 1875 when Spottiswoode chaired a paper by J. Baillie-Hamilton.[21] This aspect of the new regimen might have seemed inconsequential to a few members, or overly expensive to others, requiring the continual hire of a professional shorthand reporter. But discussion was central to the Association's name and intent from the start, and, as Pole and Spottiswoode surely knew, something concrete had to be done to stimulate members' serious engagement with research, putting everyone on their toes. A paid reporter in the room fitted the bill, and at the same time helped to create a permanent record of 'live' questions and comment by named contributors who were present, from the 1870s to 1945, after which the practice ceased in this form.[22] The printed 'Discussion' sections are indeed

---

[20] Derek Partridge, 'The Famous Linnean Society Meeting: From Old Errors to New Insights', *Biological Journal of the Linnean Society*, 137 (2022), 556–67. Joseph Hooker and Charles Lyell acted for Darwin on the occasion, 1 July 1858, to ensure timeliness. Darwin's rival theorist was Alfred Russel Wallace, who conceived his own version of natural selection independently.

[21] 'On the Application of Wind to String Instruments', *PMA*, 1 (1874–75), 42–50. Of its nine-page extent in *PMA*, half the article's length is taken up by after-paper discussion, a good sign of listener interest as well as apparent skill in Spottiswoode's chairing and the reporter's ability to capture detailed comments.

[22] Cobbe, 'The Royal Musical Association', 115, notes frequent Council complaints about the 'inaccuracy and even incompetence' of shorthand writers. But he also stresses the reports' value in giving modern readers a 'very clear idea of the savour of the meetings', essential for modern contextual reading. The last session to include full printed discussions was 1945–46 (*PRMA* 72). After a hiatus of five sessions (1946–47 to 1950–51), shorter summary discussions were introduced in *Proceedings* from 1951–52 (*PRMA* 78) to 1956–57 (*PRMA* 83) and thereafter discontinued altogether.

a remarkable feature of early *Proceedings* volumes, portraying the meetings almost like modern seminars. In the absence of any formalized research training in music, moreover, they were specially valued by students as well as by regional and foreign subscribers unable to attend.

After a year and a half of operating this way, with eight paper meetings a year from November to June (an annual 'session'), three or four separate Council meetings, a first Annual Report and re-election of Officers at an AGM in late October, a few points needed amplifying or adding. Thus the ten rules of 1874 became eight paragraphs of 'Rules and Regulations' in early 1876.[23] Most were codifications of practices already in use, and they included the following:

- The history of music is made explicit as a foundational object ('[…] formed for the investigation and discussion of subjects connected with the Art, Science, and History of Music').[24]
- Any intending member has to be proposed by two standing members.
- Subscriptions are due on 1 November, and anyone withdrawing must give notice before 31 October.
- Special general meetings may be called when necessary, with due notice.
- Every member may invite a guest to ordinary meetings.
- An annual report of each year's activity, including the papers read or abstracts of them and of the discussions, all edited by the Honorary Secretary, will be sent to every member.

The size and make-up of the Council, and the election and length of service of its members, changed slowly over the years. As the Association's governing committee, this group comprised, besides a treasurer and an Honorary Secretary, the president, several vice-presidents, and seven to ten Ordinary Members who nominally stood for re-election every year; they were usually re-elected. Unsurprisingly, such an inward approach to leadership, accepted as honourable and efficient in the early days,[25] soon contributed to periods of stasis and a Council top-heavy with vice-presidents (*eighteen* by 1898, including Grove, Parry, Pole, Rayleigh, Stanford and Sullivan), all of them distinguished but serving little purpose other than as figureheads. It was not until October 1901 that open balloting for all Council members was formally

---

[23] 'Rules and Regulations, Passed at Two Special Meetings of the Members, held at 27 Harley Street, W., on February 7 and April 3, 1876', *PMA*, 2 (1875–76), pp. v–vii.

[24] 'History of Music' was never consistently added to the strapline, however, whether because the Association's formal name could not be changed, historical approaches were already implied in both 'Art' and 'Science' or through Council disagreement. The phrase did appear in the group's advertising matter more frequently from 1890 in an effort to widen public appeal and attract new members.

[25] The Honorary Secretary James Higgs pointed this out as a weakness in October 1883. He recommended getting more fresh names on the Council 'instead of continually re-electing the same gentlemen' (Council meeting, 29 Oct 1883, BL Add. MS 71011, fol. 13), an observation suggesting that the routine of election already signalled a lack of engagement.

agreed, and much later, restrictions on length of service and the number of vice-presidents.

A problem more pressing for day-to-day administration, especially in record-keeping, storage of *Proceedings* back volumes and knowledge of Association procedures, was the migratory nature of the meetings. It is a settled fact that the Musical Association never had – and still does not have – an institutional base, nor even an office space to call its own. Before each annual session, the venue of every meeting had to be negotiated and booked for rental in advance (sometimes *gratis* or at favourable rates) according to the numbers expected, physical convenience, timing and equipment needed – mainly chairs for group seating (rented separately from Harrod's at one point), but also a piano and occasionally limelight or a magic lantern. Hence from the Beethoven Rooms in Harley Street in 1874, with Council meetings in private homes or, in the 1880s at Stanley Lucas, Weber & Co.'s premises in New Bond Street, paper meetings moved in 1890 to the Royal Academy of Music (RAM), Tenterden Street, and thence to the Royal College of Organists, Hart Street, Bloomsbury, in autumn 1894, while the Council began meeting in 1904 at Broadwood & Co. in Conduit Street, the piano makers, through a business link with Hugh Spottiswoode (William Spottiswoode's son). Broadwood's kindly offered free use of a piano, so the paper meetings moved there too in 1904. In 1913 both sets of meetings transferred to the new premises of the music publishers Novello & Co. in Wardour Street, Soho (Alfred Littleton, head of the firm, had been a Council member since 1907 and Novello then printed the *Proceedings*). By 1921, with Hugh Allen as RCM Director and new president of the Musical Association, Council meetings took place at the College, where paper sessions would soon follow. (Many other venues had been approached, from the Royal Society of Chemistry in Burlington House and the Medical Society of London, Chandos Street, to the London Academy of Music, Princes Street, Cavendish Square, and the College of Preceptors, Bloomsbury Square: in all cases, the answer was 'no' or the result unsatisfactory.)

With all this movement multiplying the chances for clerical error and miscommunication, someone in June 1901 raised the thought of collating the previous quarter-century of Association resolutions into one easily transportable and accessible place, a short-form record book with dates and cross-references to the Minutes, a sensible idea. Not only was there a danger of losing documents and muddling previous decisions, whether on bank orders, meeting arrangements or *Proceedings* volumes; the group also needed to clarify its election procedures before taking any steps towards legal incorporation, a hope long mooted on the Council. A further spur to running a tighter ship, if one were needed, was the growing aim of closer cooperation with music scholars abroad; the Association's finances and communications needed to be in good order for that to work smoothly. All these matters came together through the far-sighted and tenacious – some would say fussy and tiresome – Dr Charles Maclean, the vice-president who suggested the record book. A former Eton College music director who'd studied in Germany, Maclean had latterly joined the civil service in India for twenty-two years; his perceptiveness when returning to England around 1897 was exceeded only by his eagerness to ensure transparency and fairness, protecting the Association's reputation. The record book he envisioned, itself reflecting the group's expanding importance, became known as the 'Standing Instruction Book'. Begun in 1901, it eventually spanned the period from August 1874 to January 1933 and is now preserved in the British Library as Additional MS 71018.[26] For a bird's-eye view of decisions taken over those nearly sixty years, here's a small selection of entries to 1924:

19 Oct 1874	Lady members may take part in business proceedings and may vote
19 Apr 1875	*Proceedings* volume saleable to the public
4 Dec 1876	Papers may be read by non-members
5 Mar 1888	Papers previously read elsewhere cannot be read here [suggested by W.H. Cummings]
10 June 1888	The following institutions to receive volumes of the *Proceedings* gratis:– Royal Institution; Royal Academy of Music; Royal College of Music; The Conservatoriums at Paris, Brussels, Cologne and Leipzig; Berlin Hochschule; Vienna Gesellschaft der Musikfreunde; Guildhall School of Music; Universities of Cambridge, Oxford, Edinburgh & Dublin
14 Oct 1889	Secretary to employ legal assistance when debts amount to £3.3.0 [chasing overdue subscriptions]
27 Nov 1894	Arrangements for a refreshment contract [tea, coffee at meetings]
7 Dec 1897	New York Public Library to receive *Proceedings* volumes at 10/6 [a modest discount], with same rate for back numbers
3 July 1898	Secretary to send a complete printed Agenda when summoning each Council Meeting
11 Apr 1899	*Proceedings* volumes to be indexed
22 Jan 1900	Breitkopf & Härtel of Great Marlborough Street to undertake the distribution in Great Britain of I.M.G. publications, at the charge of the I.M.G.
13 Feb 1900	'In connection with the International Musical Society' to be added to all publications

---

[26] Maclean's proposal appears in the Council minutes of 7 June 1901, when a subcommittee to oversee the project was elected: Otto Goldschmidt, Maclean himself and W.W. Cobbett, with paid help from the secretary, Percy Baker (BL Add. MS 71012, fol. 94r–v). On 31 July the subcommittee reported back, proposing eleven resolutions for how to embed systematic record-keeping, improve communication with members and prepare for changes to governance, including fair balloting of the membership for Council elections (fols. 97v–100v). Variously referred to as the 'Standard' or 'Standing' Instruction Book, Add. MS 71018 contains thirteen openings and shows at least three different hands.

20 Nov 1900	Brief account of each monthly meeting to be sent to the Central Press Agency
31 July 1901	Secretary to keep an account of the total number of members on the books as at 30 June in each year
24 Oct 1902	Extempore lectures to be taken down in shorthand
29 May 1903	Papers may be reprinted by the I.M.G.
28 July 1903	Send *Proceedings* volume for review to certain papers
21 July 1904	'Incorporated 1904' to be used in all printed matter
23 July 1907	Abstracts of papers to be previously obtained from Lecturers
21 July 1910	Autumn circulars to be sent to Union of Graduates, Plainsong Socy., St Paul's Ecclesiological Socy., Church Music Socy., Folk Song Socy., Musicians' Company, Philharmonic Socy., Oxford & Cambridge Music Club, & Incorporated Socy. of Musicians
4 Oct 1917	The meetings this Session begin at 3.30 pm & terminate not later than 5 pm [wartime measure]
28 Jan 1919	Council is of opinion that in future the Presidency should not be held for more than three years consecutively
8 July 1919	Secretary to ask for MSS of papers to be sent in not later than July; if not sent by then, the volume of *Proceedings* to be made up without them
14 Oct 1919	Number of meetings reduced from eight to six
19 Apr 1920	Remove 'in connection with the International Musical Society' from the Association's publications[27]
15 Feb 1921	Back volumes offered to members @ 5/- & to Universities @ half price

Finally, the decision to incorporate as a legal entity, enacted in June 1904, marked a new point of arrival for the Association and its status after thirty years. Originally suggested in 1897 as a protection for Council members, the idea was put aside as not yet critical given the organization's modest size and turnover. Mentioned again in 1900 after membership reached 200 and agreements with the IMG in Berlin began to be made, the idea stalled, came up again in 1902, then was put off again. At last in July 1903, incorporation was formally considered and by November had been agreed at a Special General Meeting. Acting as their Honorary Solicitor, Arthur T. Cummings (son of W.H. Cummings) applied to the Board of Trade and helped members draw up their Memorandum and Articles of Association, which then replaced all previous versions of the rules and regulations.[28] Like a Declaration of Trust,

---

[27] This decision, proposed by Alexander Mackenzie, was in fact recorded not in the Standing Instruction Book but in the Council minutes of 8 June 1920, BL Add. MS 71013, fol. 178. It is inserted here for chronological clarity.

[28] For the Licence (17 June 1904), Certificate of Incorporation, Memorandum of Association and Articles of Association, see *PMA*, 30 (1903–04), pp. iii–xiv. These

incorporation protected Council members from personal liability for any Association debts or failure costs.[29] It also allowed them, safely, to engage in trade, invest, give out money for their objects (grants) and pay salaries, as long as all the Association's income and property were used for the objects they declared and none of it was paid by dividend or bonus as 'profit' to any member personally; accounts were subject to inspection.

As the new century opened out, then, with more members, a new president, Hubert Parry, and a direct connection with European scholars, the Musical Association could assert itself afresh, less as an 'institution' than as a private limited company. Oscar Sonneck's impression of 'splendid organization' had been spot on.

❦ Membership and Development

Structure and rules are one thing, real people and their musical work something else. Yet the link between them was tangible: what the Association could actually do for scholarship was dependent on memberships, or a number of paid subscriptions, at least in the years before any sales of *Proceedings* to libraries and the public produced significant income, and decades before any music research imperative from UK universities encouraged participation. Getting people in the door and getting them to join were crucial. At first glance, the trajectory of member numbers looks impressive. From a solid 176 members in the first session, 1874–75, to 244 members in mid-1924 ('the highest in the history of the Association'),[30] it's clear that the society expanded by almost 39 per cent over its first fifty years. Growth did not occur in a single steady rise, however, or even a sudden one, but seems to have fluctuated with confidence in the leadership, interest in the papers, expenditure on advertising and promotion, and world events affecting international relations. Indeed, member numbers hovered fairly consistently around 170 until the late 1890s, going up to 224 only in 1901. This strong level remained steady until 1912. Member numbers then fell to a low of 159 in 1916, a 29 per cent drop from 1901 owing largely to the Great War. By 1919, with post-war printing costs much increased, a deliberate rebuilding was needed so that the Association's numbers could recover, first to 198 (1920), then 232 (1923), then 244 (1924), enabling the publishing programme to move back into balance with income from subscriptions.

---

documents were routinely reprinted, with minor changes, at the front of subsequent *PMA* volumes until 1937. They would be largely rewritten in 1945.

[29] Hard financial liability had been a painful reality in the 1820s for the Regent's/Royal Harmonic Institution, the property and publishing arm of the early Philharmonic Society. Not being legally constituted cost individual members thousands of pounds when the Institution business broke up in late 1822, though the group had operated successfully under difficult conditions and its work continued under new management. See Langley, 'A Place for Music: John Nash', 42–44.

[30] 'The Musical Association: Report', *PMA*, 51 (1924–25), pp viii–xi at ix.

This degree of vulnerability, especially in a relatively small special-interest group, meant that the Association's existence and reputation had to be cultivated, promoted, even fought for, often with missional fervour by the long-serving secretary J. Percy Baker.[31] Council meetings gave regular attention not only to the problem of chasing late subscribers and convincing members to stay who'd thought of resigning, but also to authorizing circulars for more and more potentially interested cognate societies and press outlets. Journal reporters were invited to review meetings as well as copies of *Proceedings*. Members were frequently reminded – implored – to invite a friend along. Persuasive letter-writing raised the model of other learned societies such as the Royal Geographical Society, in which every subscription supported both worldwide exploration and other members' research regardless of one's physical location or ability to attend meetings; Musical Association members from as far afield as Greenock, Scotland (1877), or Wellington, New Zealand (1886), were held up as exemplary. A later tack urged simple loyalty to the group's work when wartime conditions were especially stringent. All these efforts produced results. Most effective was each autumn's sessional circular listing forthcoming paper meetings: copies were sent out in the early 1900s to a thousand addresses of members, prospects and the press, and again in the early 1920s ('direct mailing' in modern terms). Membership drives under Baker could sometimes add thirty or forty new names a year.

Already in the late 1870s, Council members were suggesting additional forms of membership. One was to honour distinguished foreign scholars, reflecting well on the Association's stature and at the same time spreading knowledge of its work. Another, Life Membership with its one-off higher fee of ten guineas, was meant to encourage long commitment to the Association while building its investment funds. The 'Honorary Foreign' idea was held back until 1888, when Hermann von Helmholtz and Philipp Spitta, both of Berlin, and François-Auguste Gevaert of Brussels were approached and gladly accepted, Gevaert in particular being keen to acquire all the back issues of *Proceedings* for the Brussels Conservatoire, which he directed; his enthusiastic request, in turn, prompted the Council to send *gratis* copies to thirteen more institutions in hopes of furthering the Association's European reputation (see the 'Standing Instruction Book' entry for 10 June 1888 above). In 1900 Guido Adler himself, a key founder of European musicology, wrote to ask if the Musikhistorisches Institut, Vienna, might also have a set of *Proceedings*; the Association promptly made him an Honorary Foreign Member whereby he would receive his own copy free and could order back numbers on the usual terms.[32] Further Honorary Foreign Members before 1924 included Hugo

---

[31] Baker (1859–1930) was the Association's first paid officer, Assistant Secretary, in 1887–91, and thereafter the paid secretary, 1892–1930, serving for a total of forty-three years.

[32] In February 1901 Adler wrote again to London, asking about his diploma: he had expected to receive a certificate of honorary membership. Baker replied, reassuring him that his name would appear in all printed lists of Musical Association members

Riemann, Arrigo Boito, Vincent d'Indy, Hermann Kretzschmar, Camille Saint-Saëns, Charles van den Borren and, in 1922, Oscar Sonneck. Meanwhile the Life Member proposal, agreed swiftly, began building a nest egg in 1879; by 1882 enough cash had been accumulated to purchase government stock, which was held in trust for the group by Otto Goldschmidt and William Pole in the first instance. Those funds grew. By mid-1924 an investment of £850 was yielding steady income and the Association had twenty-five Life Members, including David James Blaikley (of Boosey's), Adrian Boult, Capt. Evelyn Broadwood, Percy Buck, Sir Henry Hadow, Morton Latham, both Edward and J.F.R Stainer (John Stainer's sons) and A.H. Fox Strangways.

But what of the ordinary members? These names of selected Honorary and Life Members beg the question of how the whole Association's make-up might be characterized and how it changed over its first fifty years. Were they all middle- and upper-middle-class English men, educated, white, privileged, with 'Victorian' or 'Edwardian' attitudes? A broad-brush comparison based on members' sex, national identity, education and geographical location, comparing the information contained in published membership lists for 1874–75 and 1923–24, suggests that the Association's profile was not that simple. It shows instead both more diversity than modern scholars might expect and a clear movement from science backgrounds towards more musical ones, including composing and performing careers, by the 1920s. At the outset, for example, some 10 per cent of Association members were women (including Alice Mary Smith/Mrs Meadows White), rising to c. 16 per cent by 1924, with two women holding Mus.Doc. degrees (Mary Davies, Emily Daymond). Among other traits, the 1874–75 group had one leading member who was blind (G.A. Macfarren), at least two of same-sex or bisexual orientation (Constance Astley, Agnes Zimmermann), many of Jewish heritage including the senior mathematician who'd experienced discrimination at Cambridge, James Joseph Sylvester,[33] a few Irish members and more of continental European background (E. Dannreuther, C. Engel, F. Hueffer, F. Niecks, Victor de Pontigny, A. Randegger, G. Romano). Perhaps only about 50 per cent in this early period possessed earned university degrees; two members had hereditary titles (Ouseley and Rayleigh), three were knights (Julius Benedict, John Goss, R.P. Stewart), and one was an MP (W.H. Gladstone). Around 9 per cent of the earliest members were qualified scientists or could be considered musical science researchers.

(BL Add. MS 71012, fol. 83v). Certificates for the Association's Honorary Foreign Members were provided in due course.

[33] As a non-Anglican at Cambridge, Sylvester could neither take his degree nor compete for prizes or fellowships. He later taught at University College London and the University of Virginia, but disappointments on social and religious grounds led him into the London insurance business, then mathematical research at the highest level by the 1870s and 80s, including professorships at Johns Hopkins (Baltimore) and Oxford universities. He was a devoted student of music and a friend of John Tyndall's. See Karen Hunger Parshall, 'Sylvester, James Joseph', *ODNB*.

By 1924, Association members included a distinguished Japanese, several Scots, many Americans, some Canadians, a small number of members in Australia and New Zealand and the Russian-British pianist Mark Hambourg. Again, at least two members in the later group were of same-sex or bisexual orientation (Edward J. Dent, Rosa Newmarch). From one-third of the originally targeted club of 1874 being working scientists – though only one-eleventh of actual members in 1874–75 – the 1924 list had many fewer of these and only one Fellow of the Royal Society (James Swinburne).[34] Like that of 1874, the later group also had some lawyers, historians, engineers, businesspeople, educators and a few clergy. But many more members were musically trained, had degrees, or were still in training, working as organists, music technicians, teachers, composer-performers or administrators; Elgar and Mackenzie were there, besides Edward German, Henry J. Wood and Adrian Boult. Probably closer to 60 per cent of the Association in 1924 possessed earned university degrees or other qualifications. There were two titled members, seven knights, two people with honorific titles, a number of military rank, several working mothers (including Mrs J. Murray MacBain, Mrs Reginald Lane Poole) and some outspoken feminists (Jane M.E. Brownlow). As ever, music-literary types including well-known critics, editors and other professional writers, male and female, were present and actively involved. As for geographical spread, a rough tally suggests that in both periods, only some 11 per cent of the total Association membership resided or worked out of London, in the regions or abroad, from Cork, Dublin and Enniscorthy to Dundee, Glasgow and St Andrews; from Eton, Oxford and Cambridge to Manchester, Ripon and York – not forgetting Ellesmere Port, Weymouth, Malta, North America and many other places.[35] Without fuller information and deeper study of separate individuals, it is impossible, and unfair, to generalize about attitudes. Two things are clear: the reductive binary of 'amateur' and 'professional' is inadequate to convey the spectrum of skills, education and working experience in these two groups; and, as many *Proceedings* discussions show, variable attitudes and divergent opinions, including political ones, were common among even a single-subject interest group. In a learned society like the Association, moreover, reasoned questioning was expected, almost an article of faith. In that context, shorthand period descriptors used pejoratively, such as 'Victorian' or 'Edwardian', are meaningless.

More revealing for member development is how the Association fostered social relationships, a facet of learned society culture that was always seen as

---

[34] The relatively small number of 'science' members throughout the first fifty years belies that group's strong influence in early decades, since they were among the earliest members happy to step forward and give papers. For a list of PMA papers investigating scientific subjects, 1874–1924, see Table 2 below, pp. 76–79.

[35] As early as 1883, Stephen S. Stratton had suggested the Association should do more to attract members outside London, possibly establishing branches in large centres such as Birmingham and Manchester ('it would materially strengthen the position of the Society', 29 Oct 1883, BL Add. MS 71011, fol. 15r–v). In fact regional chapters would not be set up for another ninety years.

one of the advantages in starting such a group. Everyone knows that positive social relations can smooth a path for intellectual exchange, as it did across geographical and language boundaries for the physicist Helmholtz, his wife Anna and their British colleagues, furthering the acceptance of new scientific ideas in both Britain and Germany.[36] In the simplest of Musical Association efforts, tea and coffee encouraged half an hour's conviviality before late-afternoon paper meetings, notably from autumn 1895, when hot drinks were provided to promote social mixing and conversation (sherry would be the social lubricant in the 1960s). A more complex step had been the planning of an extra Association event in mid-July 1895, welcoming a hundred visiting American musicians and music teachers. The exchange of spoken papers by John Stainer and Waldo Selden Pratt, the distinguished American hymnologist and music historian, confirmed a mutual respect for each country's musical heritage and opened the way for future linkage, although the British hosts had to apologize for their small attendance at a July meeting.[37] Such initiatives, small and large, grew partly from a boost to the Association's confidence on reaching its twentieth anniversary in 1894, that warm glow radiating through Stainer's address at the start of the 1894–95 session, 3 November 1894, further enhanced by the presence of a large audience including Baker's new recruits: a total of eighty-two members attended on the day, a record number.[38] In fact attendances for each paper meeting in the six sessions from 1891–92 to 1896–97 show a near 100 per cent increase between the first three of those sessions and the last three, from an average of twenty-seven at each meeting in the early 1890s, to fifty-three from 1894–95 to 1896–97. Time and venue changes also played a role, along with successful targeting of music professionals as members, and a lift in interest towards newer paper subjects, many of them more historically framed for both Western and global musics than had previously been the case.

[36] Cahan, 'Helmholtz and the British Scientific Elite', 55, credits the sense of trust engendered by social relationships. Anna von Helmholtz (1834–99), a well-known salonnière in Berlin and the translator of many scientific works, accompanied her husband on extended visits to London and shared in social exchanges. The pianist Anton Rubinstein, among other musicians, frequented her salons.

[37] Waldo Selden Pratt, 'The Isolation of Music', *PMA*, 21 (1894–95), 153–68, chaired by Stainer, with a discussion led by Randegger. After a fulsome introduction, Pratt developed the theme of music's separateness in American society and how music education might encourage change. Attendance was noted as 120, which included only about twenty members of the Association (see n. 38 below). Later, Pratt became president of the Music Teachers National Association and worked with Macmillan & Co. to produce the American supplement to *Grove 2* (New York, 1920). His article 'On Behalf of Musicology' (the first in *Musical Quarterly*, 1915) was required reading in some American musicology programmes to the 1970s.

[38] BL Add. MS 71011, fol. 179v, facing inside back cover, gives scratch attendance figures for each meeting of the six sessions, 1891–92 to 1896–97. Stainer's 'Inaugural Address to the Twenty-First Session', *PMA*, 21 (1894–95), pp. xiii–xvi, preceded a paper by F.G. Edwards on the Mendelssohn organ sonatas, a double bill which may have encouraged the healthy attendance.

A third example of how the Association expanded sociability, perhaps the most important, concerns the unwitting invention of the Annual Dinner, a key gathering, almost every year, from the late 1890s to the mid-1930s. The concept started with a fondness for national celebration. But rather than simply enacting an empty formality, sharing a meal together became an affirming way to develop the Association's group identity. In early 1897, the year of Queen Victoria's Diamond Jubilee, Thomas Lea Southgate proposed that the Association should have a paper 'reviewing the progress of music in England'; members could attend a special meeting for the purpose and then dine together in the evening.[39] The idea pleased, and at once wheels started turning. W.H. Cummings agreed to speak on 'Music during the Queen's Reign' with Stainer presiding, and a date was set for 8 June 1897 (the official jubilee was observed on 22 June). Baker booked a venue, the large, grand Holborn Restaurant on Kingsway, opposite what would soon be Holborn Underground station. Popular with clubs, societies and the socially aspirant as a kind of fine-dining destination, the Holborn could easily seat more than a hundred at long tables (its large corner site is now a glass-fronted Sainsbury's grocery). In the event, Cummings's paper offered a 'lucid and comprehensive review' to a large audience, and the meal was a great success. Indeed the whole occasion delighted and gratified especially 'country members', who enjoyed coming to London and meeting their fellow Association members and friends, doubtless sharing musical and personal interests; some ninety-five people attended. The Council then decided that such a positive occasion should be repeated regularly, and so it was, every year in November or early December, by 1901 becoming the 'Annual Dinner' accompanied by five or six short speeches (toasts) and a light musical programme.[40]

Besides returning to the Holborn, Baker found other alluring restaurants – the Monico on Shaftesbury Avenue, the Criterion at Piccadilly Circus, the Trocadero, the Hotel Great Central on Marylebone Road and Frascati's in Oxford Street. Attendance occasionally disappointed, and in wartime the event had to be dropped completely. A strong revival of the tradition occurred only in January 1924, when the dinner was billed as a banquet to celebrate the Association's fiftieth birthday (Connaught Rooms, 125 people attending). Further dinners in the late 1920s and 30s took place at the Café Royal, Regent Street, or at Pagani's, the well-known artists' retreat in Great Portland Street, near Queen's Hall. But in retrospect, place is less important than precedent and pattern. The habit of gathering everyone together for one big event a year, with a paper, food, some reflection and social exchange, offered a model for what in 1966 would become a weekend spring conference highlighting scholarship,

---

[39] Council meeting, 9 Feb 1897, BL Add. MS 71012, fol. 6. The programme and dinner menu for 1897 have not survived; Cummings's paper appeared in *PMA*, 23 (1896–97), 133–51.

[40] See Baker's comment on the dinner's success and on Cummings's paper in the 'Report' for 1896–97, in *PMA*, 24 (1897–98), p. xiv. For later dinner menus and programmes, see BL Add. MS 71033, fols. 11–26 and 175–87.

including that of younger members: it quickly developed into what is now the flagship Annual Conference. On the way to this development, and alongside it, would be more receptions for visiting guests, occasional concerts, book or music launches and the hosting of large international music conferences. None was more challenging than the London Congress of the IMG planned for May 1911, partly hosted by members of the Musical Association. Enter again Dr Charles Maclean, the efficient procedural expert who could organize anything.

International Connections

In February 1899, coincidentally after twenty-five years of Musical Association papers, printed *Proceedings* and social exchange, the German scholar Oskar Fleischer launched the Internationale Musikgesellschaft (IMG), hoping to encompass Britain and Ireland, among other places, as a National Section within a larger federated body of music researchers internationally. In effect Fleischer in Berlin, together with colleagues in Leipzig at Breitkopf & Härtel, wanted to create one or more local branches, or Ortsgruppen, in the UK and Ireland, which would hold periodic meetings for reading papers and, with a central committee and its polyglot publications, promote the vitality of the larger society. An approach to the Association for cooperation in this plan, facilitating a local group, raised interest but also a few eyebrows. Since the Musical Association had already successfully engaged in the same sort of endeavour for years, they considered it 'both undesirable and impracticable to attempt to hold rival meetings in London for discussing identically the same class of subjects'.[41] Instead, they negotiated a compromise whereby members of the Association who joined the IMG – receiving its publications, facilitating and sharing in international music research – could do so at a reduced rate, while anyone outside the Association could join the IMG on the usual terms, all pre-agreed with the founding publishers Breitkopf & Härtel. On 20 February 1900, an 'English Committee' of the IMG representing the National Section, led by its original officers Hubert Parry, Otto Goldschmidt, William Barclay Squire and Charles Maclean, agreed that the Musical Association would act as 'an Ortsgruppe for the City and County of London', with Messrs Breitkopf & Härtel, London, as treasurers. As noted above, the Association added the words 'in connection with the International Musical Society' on its publications and prospectuses. The effect was salutary for both organizations. In each of the years 1900–11, about half of all Association members joined the IMG, while IMG British members outside the Association grew by a factor of six, from seventeen in 1900 to 102 in 1911. The total IMG membership by mid-1911 was 1,028, spread among seventeen national sections. Separate Ortsgruppen were eventually set up in Dublin and Edinburgh, and the English Committee was

---

[41] 'Report on the National Section, Great Britain and Ireland', *Report of the Fourth Congress*, 391–94 at 392.

able to intervene with central management so that IMG publications became 'really, and not nominally, international'.[42]

Of its two periodicals, the monthly *Zeitschrift der Internationalen Musikgesellschaft* (*ZIMG*), called the 'Monthly Journal' in IMG descriptions, published short items of contemporary news including book and music reviews, notes and queries, and branch reports, while the quarterly *Sammelbände der Internationalen Musikgesellschaft* (*SIMG*), the 'Quarterly Magazine', carried fewer but more substantial research articles, around twenty to twenty-five a year, including some read as papers at the Musical Association. Both titles included material in German, French, English and Italian as needed (Russian, Polish, Romanian and Spanish authors adopted French or English), and both titles eventually ran across the period 1899–1914.[43] But it was the English Committee, chiefly Maclean, who ensured oversight of the four-language balance, so that UK readers could more readily benefit from the content in the periodicals and contribute to them. He argued for more space for English-language contributions, for example, raising the original proportion of 3 per cent of extent in 1900, across both publications, to 25 per cent from 1901 onwards. Maclean also established the precedent of using a local editor to oversee local contributions, namely himself for Great Britain and Ireland, inserting extra 'English Sheets' with each issue of *ZIMG* from October 1903 (Jahrgang 5). Further, the English Committee upheld the IMG's cooperative spirit by calling out the unfairness of allowing the French section in 1907 to issue their own fully French combination of magazine and journal: unavailable to non-French members, it simultaneously inhibited French contributions to *ZIMG*.[44]

Going still further, Great Britain and Ireland's English Committee (president from 1906, Alexander Mackenzie) undertook an especially important commitment at the IMG Vienna Congress in 1909, offering to conduct the 1911 Congress in London, following on from earlier congresses in Leipzig (1904) and Basel (1906) and the Vienna event. Its organization, financing and flair, placing English-language and international scholarship against a backdrop of British music-making, astonished everyone ('by general consent admitted to

---

[42] Ibid., 393, where the growing member numbers are also recorded.

[43] Content listings for both IMG titles were provided to Musical Association members in a periodic 'Appendix' at the back of *Proceedings* volumes: for the first to fifth years of *ZIMG* and *SIMG*, see *PMA*, 30 (1903–04), 155–66; for the sixth to tenth years, *PMA*, 35 (1908–09), 135–50; for the eleventh year, *PMA*, 36 (1909–10), 125–28, and *PMA*, 37 (1910–11), 151–54 (reprinted); and for the twelfth full year, *PMA*, 41 (1914–15), 163–76.

[44] Maclean raised the matter with the Musical Association Council in October 1907, and secured their support for a complaint against the IMG governing body (BL Add. MS 71013, fols. 27v–28). The French journal had grown out of the *Mercure musical* (1905), adding '*et bulletin français de la SIM: Société Internationale de Musique (Section de Paris)*' to its head title. For debates among French scholars and critics about musicology's role in public discourse in France at this time, see Michel Duchesneau, 'French Musicology and the Musical Press (1900–14): The Case of *La revue musicale*, *Le mercure musical* and *La revue musicale SIM*', trans. Kimberly White, *JRMA*, 140 (2015), 243–72.

be [...] brilliant').[45] London would not see the like for another eighty years, until the International London Mozart Conference of 1991 and the Sixteenth Congress of the IMS of 1997. Because this week-long IMG Congress is barely mentioned in surviving Minutes, other papers or discussions of the RMA, or in histories of the IMS, one of its successors,[46] its achievement is worth revisiting here.

The Congress took place from Monday 29 May to Saturday 3 June 1911. Its official setting was the Imperial Institute, University of London, in South Kensington (now Imperial College, founded 1907), where since 1887 science, industry and culture had joined in celebration of internationalism; recalling the Great Exhibition of 1851, the Institute also promoted modern trade and manufactures. Planning for the Congress from October 1909 had involved two main challenges – how to balance festivity and concert-making with the reading of papers (no one wanted a musical congress without music), and how to pay for everything, given that IMG member fees and ticket sales would be insufficient and in Britain no court or government grants could be expected.[47] The only possible course was to raise most of what was needed from private individuals and institutions, a year-long quest. As the final *Report of the Fourth Congress of the International Musical Society: London 29 May – 3 June 1911* (London: Novello & Co., 1912) shows, some 205 guarantors pledged a total of £10,000 to cover expenses. Among those pledges were a large amount, £500, from Messrs Novello & Co., who happened to be preparing for their own hundredth anniversary in 1911 (including the opening of impressive new premises in Wardour Street), and a smaller but still substantial sum, £50, from the Musical Association.[48] In fact it was the coordinated leadership between the Association and Novello's, the printer of *Proceedings*, that steered the Congress

---

[45] Anon., 'The International Musical Congress: London, May 29 to June 3', MT, 52 (July 1911), 441–54 at 441.

[46] Percy A. Scholes, *The Mirror of Music, 1844–1944: A Century of Musical Life in Britain as Reflected in the Pages of the Musical Times*, 2 vols. (London: Novello & Co. and OUP, 1947), 763–64, discussed the Congress briefly. He was a member of both organizations in 1911. Abraham, 'Our First Hundred Years', gives a guarded nod to the IMG, noting its two journals with English wrappers and affirming that during this period 'our Association markedly widened its outlook' (p. xi). In his summary of the IMG in 'A "Prelude" to the IMS', in *The History of the IMS (1927–2017)*, ed. Dorothea Baumann and Dinko Fabris (Basel: Bärenreiter, 2017), 11–19, Martin Kirnbauer touches on Maclean's role in rejecting the Germans' unilateral dissolution of the IMG in September 1914, but never mentions the London Congress.

[47] [C. Maclean], 'Redaktioneller Teil: Informal Notes on the Congress', ZIMG, 12 (1911–12), 271–76.

[48] 'List of Guarantors', *Report of the Fourth Congress*, 5–6, itself a fascinating index to music and science patronage in Edwardian Britain, from the industrialist and science benefactor Otto Beit's enormous £1,000, to the pianist J.F. Barnett's guinea. According to the website measuringworth.com, the total £10,000 in 1911 would equate to around £1.2 million in 2022. Although the Congress was held 'under the patronage of His Majesty the King', the king never appeared nor gave any financial support. The Lord

to success: the chair and deputy chair of the Congress Executive were, respectively, Alexander Mackenzie and Alfred H. Littleton (head of Novello's), while its efficient joint secretaries were Charles Maclean and W.G. McNaught (editor of Novello's *Musical Times*).

Taking a step back, the name 'Imperial Institute' will raise many modern eyebrows. The dark cloud of imperialism hangs over nearly everything about late nineteenth- and early twentieth-century Britain; its practices are inescapable, and at some level all of us are complicit. But however we now interpret the British Empire as a concept, historically and critically, including its deep wrongs and far-reaching, long-lasting harms for millions of people around the globe, it is a fact that in the period 1909–11 metropolitan London was at a peak of its imperial strength and self-confidence. There was no question, no doubt at all, that foreign visitors should be welcomed with humility and open arms but also shown solid evidence of Britain's industrial, economic and political strength, as well as fresh evidence of a newer, softer power less appreciated abroad – the stable and flourishing state of British music and musical culture. In 1909 Mackenzie, Maclean and their team could not have known that a coronation would take place in late June 1911, the formal crowning of King George V and Queen Mary with all its imperial pomp. But the preparations for that event surely added extra lustre to the Congress, not least through cleaner streets and a warmer patriotic fervour than might otherwise have prevailed. On the musical side, the decision that Congress concerts should be almost wholly devoted to 'English' music, past and present, was taken early in the planning, alike to please the guarantors, preserve consistency with former IMG practice and avoid uncertain eclectic experiments; a British emphasis in the music was certainly expected, even if it also reflected the coronation mood a little more closely than some planners might have wanted.[49] The only musical event a few conferees noticed as divergent, because unremarkable in itself and unrelated to the Congress, was the concluding Saturday night performance of *Rigoletto* at Covent Garden.

Before that night, the week's programme was crammed full of ceremonies, receptions, exhibitions and speeches, concerts and special church services,

---

Mayor of the City of London gave an afternoon reception at the Mansion House and presided at the banquet, but municipal authorities similarly gave no financial aid.

[49] 'Redaktioneller Teil: Informal Notes', 273. Maclean, for one, seems to have regretted that the musical offerings were not a little more international in scope, with the modern choices a bit more 'courageous' than 'goodnatured'. But to secure finance for the whole event, pitching it as 'a great and memorable festival of British music' was seen as 'the only rational course for the committee to adopt'; see 'The International Musical Congress, London, May 29 to June 3: Meeting at the Mansion House', *MT*, 52 (Mar 1911), 160–64 at 160. All the speeches on that occasion made clear that for funders, the purpose of the London Congress was to remove foreign prejudice about English music. After the fact, the most vocal critic of so much British music at an international congress was Rosa Newmarch, in her 'Chauvinism in Music', *Edinburgh Review*, 216 (July 1912), 95–116, which Maclean answered in his 'Chauvinism and British Music', *MT*, 53 (Aug 1912), 520.

English and Latin, besides paper presentations.[50] After a Monday night reception at Novello's with an exhibition of music printing, some 400 guests attending, the opening ceremony at the Imperial Institute the next day included a cordial welcome from A.J. Balfour, the former Prime Minister, a keen musical amateur and the designated president of the Congress. On Tuesday a historical chamber music concert at Aeolian Hall and a Ladies' Lyceum Club reception were followed by an evening orchestral concert at Queen's Hall, the Queen's Hall Orchestra presenting works by modern British composers with the composers conducting (Ralph Vaughan Williams, C.V. Stanford, Frederick Corder, A.C. Mackenzie, Parry, Walford Davies, Adam Carse and Joseph Holbrooke). Wednesday, Thursday and Friday mornings were given to the reading of five plenary and seventy-six individual papers organized in six strands – History; Ethnology; Theory, Acoustics and Aesthetics; Church Music; Instruments; Bibliography and Contemporary Questions. The Great Britain and Ireland contribution was proportionate, totalling sixteen papers out of the eighty-one (c. 20 per cent). Of these, eleven were given by Musical Association members – Parry, Cummings (by now Musical Association president), E.J. Dent, W.H. Frere, W. Barclay Squire, Herbert Antcliffe, J.A. Fuller Maitland, W.H. Hadow, Cyril Rootham, F.W. Galpin and McNaught; nearly all were published in the *Report of the Fourth Congress* (1912). What marred this 'scientific' element of the Congress, as opposed to the festive and business elements, was the Institute's inadequate lecture-room accommodation combined with a tightly compressed schedule, requiring four or five papers to be read simultaneously in screened compartments within one large hall. The result created what Jules Écorcheville, the witty president of the Northern France section, dubbed 'musicological polyphony' – not the last time such an effect would be heard at a large musicology conference.[51]

After the papers each day, the committee put on another smorgasbord of music events - a military band concert by the Coldstream Guards ('probably [...] superior in tone to that of any Belgian or Prussian band', according to Maclean); a special service at St Paul's Cathedral with English words and old English music, conducted by George Martin; an afternoon reception at the Mansion House given by the Lord Mayor and Lady Mayoress, with light music by the (amateur) Westminster Orchestral Society; a Wednesday evening

---

[50] The week's events are listed, then described individually with full texts of speeches and musical programme details in *Report of the Fourth Congress*, which also contains lists of the 154 foreign visitors, all the paper-givers and their abstracts in English.

[51] 'Banquet at the Savoy Hotel', *Report of the Fourth Congress*, 49. For Maclean's description of the paper call in July 1910, and of how lecture offers were pragmatically accepted, organized, abstracted and scheduled, see "Redaktioneller Teil: Informal Notes', 273–75. He admitted that the result could hardly be anything other than 'a *literary picnic*' and maintained the impracticality of allocating speakers to hours 'with the precision of a railway-timetable or the turns at a music-hall' (274, emphasis original). He explained the space problem by reference to the University of London as an examining, not a lecturing, body, comparing it unfavourably in this respect with the University of Vienna.

reception at Grocer's Hall, Prince's Street, with a selection of seventeenth-, eighteenth- and nineteenth-century English instrumental music and song; an afternoon choral concert at Queen's Hall by the Huddersfield Choral Society, including Bach and Handel among Gibbons, two Wesleys, Wilbye, Sullivan, R.J.S. Stevens, Purcell and Morley; another evening orchestral concert at Queen's Hall, by the London Symphony Orchestra, with more works by living British composers conducted by themselves or by Dan Godfrey (W.H. Bell, Frederic Cowen, Edward Elgar, Samuel Coleridge-Taylor, Ethel Smyth, Edward German, William Wallace); a second chamber music concert at Aeolian Hall with modern British works, featuring the Wesseley Quartet, Myra Hess and Lionel Tertis; a special performance of early English church music, with Latin words, at Westminster Catholic Cathedral, conducted by R.R. Terry; and a closing Friday night banquet at the Savoy Hotel in the Strand, with light music.

Two final offerings stand out in particular: a midnight reception on Thursday 1 June at the offices of the *Daily Telegraph* in Fleet Street, where delegates were conducted through the building to see all the editorial and machine processes involved in producing a 24-page edition of the newspaper, each visitor departing with a copy of the next morning's paper;[52] and a Saturday luncheon, on 3 June, at the House of Commons, extended to all the foreign visitors and the Congress executive (men only), followed by a tour through both Houses of Parliament. Maclean proudly highlighted this occasion in the Preface to the *Report of the Fourth Congress* as 'the first time when a body of musicians, as such, has been entertained by the British Government'.[53] Though only symbolic, the event made a strong impact on Maclean and his local colleagues, buoyed as they were by the presence of so many distinguished foreign musicologists more familiar with state support for music. Just before the luncheon and after a closing business meeting at the Institute, a large group portrait was arranged by Novello's to mark the occasion of the Congress. Taken by Bedford Lemere & Co., one of the foremost architectural photographers in Britain, it appeared first in the *Musical Times* of July 1911 and subsequently in Percy Scholes's *Mirror of Music* (1944); see Figure 7. Now part of a collection belonging to the archive of Historic England,[54] this image captures a moment in time when many international music scholars now known only by name and their published writings come alive as real people, standing (or sitting)

---

[52] For a description of the event and the people attending, see coverage in the newspaper itself, 'Musical Congress: Reception at "The Daily Telegraph" Office', *Daily Telegraph* (2 June 1911), 15.

[53] Charles Maclean, 'Preface', *Report of the Fourth Congress*, p. iii.

[54] 'Portrait of the Musical Congress outside the entrance to the Imperial Institute' (Historic England Archive, Bedford Lemere Collection BL21220/002), taken on Saturday, 3 June 1911. No individual identifications accompany the picture. I have tentatively identified some 73 sitters out of 111, using the Congress's published attendance lists and as many independent images of potential subjects as possible, noting their putative ages at June 1911. Situated on the new Imperial Institute Road, the building was eventually demolished in the 1950s, leaving the Queen's column of Imperial College as the only visible landmark.

Figure 7. IMG Congress members, Imperial Institute, London, 3 June 1911 (see next three pages for key).

1. Max Friedländer	11. Carl Hennerberg	21. Amalie Arnheim
2. Jules Écorcheville	12. Richard Andersson	22. ? Frederic Cowen
3. Oscar G. Sonneck	13. Erwin Felber	23. ? Frau Ludwig
4. D.F. Scheurleer	14. J.G. Prod'homme	24. Betti Volkmar-Arnheim
5. Julián Carillo	15. M.-D. Calvocoressi	25. Edward J. Dent
6. Cecilio de Roda	16. Emil Hertzka	26. Hugo Leichtentritt
7. Adolf Sandberger	17. Angel Menchaca	27. Charles van den Borren
8. W.G. McNaught	18. ? Madame Launis	28. Max Seiffert
9. Armas Launis	19. Lionel de La Laurencie	
10. Tobias Norlind	20. Friedrich Ludwig	

29. Hermann Kretzschmar
30. Alexander Mackenzie
31. Hubert Parry
32. Guido Adler
33. ? Franz Pazdírek
34. Angul Hammerich
35. Alfred Littleton
36. ? Madame Calvocoressi
37. W.W. Cobbett
38. J.A. Fuller Maitland
39. Thomas Lea Southgate
40. Charles Maclean
41. W. Barclay Squire
42. ? Kathleen Schlesinger
43. ? Clifford B. Edgar
44. ? J. Percy Baker
45. Fausto Torrefranca
46. ? Fritz Stein
47. Egon Wellesz
48. Assia Spiro-Rombro
49. Eugénie Lineff
50. ? T. Wesley Mills
51. Albert A. Stanley
52. Curt Sachs
53. Baron Alexander Kraus, Jun.
54. ? Henri Quittard
55. Frau Dr Egon Wellesz
    (Emmy Stross)
56. Friedrich Spiro
57. Otto Kinkeldey
58. Canon F.W. Galpin
59. Albert Visetti

60. ? Henry Prunières
61. C.V. Stanford
62. W.H. Cummings
63. ? Gustav Schreck
64. Vito Fedeli
65. Oskar von Hase
66. Frederick Bridge
67. Johannes Wolf
68. Alicja Simon
69. Henryk Opienski
70. Otto Andersson
71. Georg Schünemann
72. ? Karol Szymanowski
73. Rudolf Chrysander

together as a united body before the Great War. We can only imagine the procedure for placing everyone in position – note Mackenzie and Parry front and centre, between Hermann Kretzschmar and Guido Adler on either side, with other senior national representatives along the front – and then the mixed conversations and reflections as everyone dispersed for the luncheon and a final afternoon in the British capital.

Last impressions had been conveyed in speeches at the banquet of the previous evening, and would follow in print after the Congress had concluded. Even allowing for pleasantries, these were positive and generous. Kretzschmar (Berlin), already an Honorary Member of the Association, mentioned 'the greatness and the majesty of the British Empire', the 'whole-souled English life', the character of London with its splendid contrasts from the 'enormous traffic in the streets' to the 'parks with their wonderful trees'. Adler (Vienna) appreciated the warm welcome visitors had received, and the charming artistic and social gatherings provided; he noted that any dissonances in the scientific discussions had all been 'resolved into sweet consonances'.[55] Michel-Dmitri Calvocoressi (Paris) thought the Congress had been 'uncommonly successful' at creating musical acquaintanceships, the kind that often end in cordial relations and enlightenment. He was especially pleased with the survey of British music from its beginnings to the present day, admitting that 'we know too little of British music abroad'. He gave his special compliments to the London Symphony Orchestra and the Huddersfield Choral Society. Albert Stanley (Ann Arbor, Michigan, USA) singled out the unbounded yet unassuming hospitality, the service at St Paul's and, again, the inspiring performance of the Huddersfield singers. Prof. Adler, who like Calvocoressi and Stanley wrote at the request of the *Musical Times*, admitted that the artistic and social side had somewhat overshadowed the Congress's scientific part; he felt the freedom of choice in theme for papers, though helpful in producing new ideas, did not tend towards concentration or good discussions. But he was full of admiration for the choristers from St John's College, Cambridge, who illustrated Cyril Rootham's paper on choral training, as well as for the tonic sol-fa exercises presented in McNaught's paper. He was positively 'astonished' at the Huddersfield Choral Society, even more so when told by Mackenzie that England possessed 'several choral societies quite as good'. On the scientific side, too, Adler confirmed his esteem for the scholars whose work he had witnessed: 'We stand shoulder to shoulder with our English colleagues, who can point to a long line of pioneers.' He went on: 'And here I must draw attention to a quality which is not always to be found among us Continentals: modesty, in which lies a powerful factor for future development.'[56]

One aspect of that modesty, mixed with gentle humour, had first shown itself in Parry's speech at the opening ceremony. In a light-hearted talk laced with English self-deprecation, Parry thanked the foreign visitors for

---

[55] *Report of the Fourth Congress*, 48.
[56] The Calvocoressi, Stanley and later Adler comments in this paragraph come from 'Impressions of the International Musical Congress', *MT*, 52 (July 1911), 452–54.

their 'wonderful hardihood' in coming in 'the spirit of generous enterprise to inquire if it is really true that at last there is some music in this country. (Laughter.).' After all, he continued tongue-in-cheek, they must know how awful, dreadful and sad everything is in a country where the weather is 'always in a fog', where the inconveniences of daily life, the glum approach to art and culture, the social crudeness and the music must all follow suit.[57] Five days later at the Friday banquet, as if in a double-act, Mackenzie mirrored Parry's bluff congeniality, making a toast to 'The health of foreign visitors' after first enquiring sympathetically about how well they had held up during the week: 'It is very gratifying to me that all this British music with which they have been regaled has had no more serious effect upon them than of producing in a few of the least robust a mild attack of home-sickness. (Laughter.).' He predicted a strong future for more British music, some of it 'difficult to classify. (Renewed laughter.)', and then affirmed the unbroken good humour of the Congress and the sincerity of welcome to all. 'Old friendships have been cemented and many new ones have been found and formed, and surely mutual understanding, reciprocity, and what is still better, good-will, will be the inevitable and natural result of this happy Congress.'[58] For his part, Maclean in true modesty affirmed that the Congress had given 'a vast deal of pleasure to a great many persons'.[59]

The next Congress, held at Paris in June 1914, was reported briefly to the Association by Percy Baker.[60] Within weeks war broke out. On 30 September the Leipzig base of Breitkopf & Härtel, more specifically Oskar von Hase as IMG treasurer, unilaterally announced the IMG to be at an end – a nationalistic move that incensed Charles Maclean, who knew that the society's members, two-thirds of whom were not German, had not voted constitutionally for any such dissolution. In a long memo of 22 May 1915, Maclean, by then General Secretary of the whole organization (as he saw it) and sole member of the surviving executive, asserted that the IMG was still in existence; he put forward a plan to maintain and even build connections, with a hope that the society could be reconstituted as a fully international body after the war, an idea supported

---

[57] Parry's opening speech is reprinted in *MT*, 52 (July 1911), 445–46. His reference to fog echoed an idea in Mackenzie's appeal to potential funders in February: 'I think the occasion might go very far to dispel the residue of a gradually disappearing mist. It might afford a somewhat clearer and brighter view, and bring about a fairer recognition of much worthy and honest endeavour which has been put forth in this country in every department in the art of music (Applause). We must all sing in unison' (*MT*, 52 (Mar 1911), 161).

[58] 'International Musical Congress', *MT*, 52 (July 1911), 448.

[59] 'Redaktioneller Teil: Informal Notes', 276. For further impressions appearing in the *Neue freie Presse* and the *Signale für die musikalische Welt*, see 'International Musical Congress', *MT*, 52 (Aug 1911), 517–18, including comments by Adler, Hugo Leichtentritt and Johannes Wolf.

[60] J. Percy Baker, 'The Congress of the International Musical Society', *PMA*, 40 (1913–14), 173–75.

by France and Denmark as well as Great Britain and Ireland.[61] However, it was a counter-proposal by the Dutch musicologist D.F. Scheurleer in 1915 which eventually prevailed, involving only neutral countries and a neutral staff organization from 1921. Operating as the Société Union Musicologique and publishing from The Hague, 1921–26, this group later emerged as direct predecessor to the Internationale Gesellschaft für Musikwissenschaft (IGMw) of 1927, styled from 1949 the International Musicological Society (IMS), which still flourishes.[62] Charles Maclean had died in June 1916, much lamented by the Musical Association.[63] Alexander Mackenzie and the remaining Committee for Great Britain and Ireland finally resigned their connection with the IMG in April 1920.[64] They never acknowledged the legality of any dissolution of the IMG by Hase and his colleague Kretzschmar in September 1914.[65]

❧ *Sessions, Proceedings, Research*

Without doubt, the London Congress of 1911 had raised the profile of British music, especially among foreign visitors who'd had little idea of its depth and quality across centuries, let alone its contemporary vigour. Local conferees, too, some traditionally biased against the home article in favour of anything and everything from the Continent, had their ears opened, their attention engaged through a strong increase in foreign interest. In that sense alone, the Congress did good work by widening everyone's purview. But the benefit went further. The Musical Association began looking for opportunities to expand foreign contact. Already by spring 1912, they'd received a paper from Albert Stanley about graduate work in music in the USA.[66] Closer to the UK under wartime

---

[61] For a three-page printed document containing this explanation, including Baker's 'The Position of the International Musical Society' and a copy of Maclean's Circular Memorandum to all IMG members (22 May 1915), both of which appeared in the *Musical News* (24 July 2015), see BL Add. MS 71034, fols. 50–51. Maclean's earliest published reaction, of late November 1914, appeared in a Letter to the Editor of the *Musical Times* for January 1915, 29–30. See also Chapter 3, pp. 115–16, and nn. 55–56.

[62] Kirnbauer, 'A "Prelude to the IMS"', 14–19.

[63] In the Association's Report for 1915–16, Percy Baker wrote: 'He was always ready to forward the best interests of the Musical Association to the utmost of his power. The services that he rendered to it were not always public, and their full extent is never likely to be widely known. His work for the International Musical Society, with which the Association has been in connection since its foundation in 1899, was no less whole-hearted and much more arduous' ('Report', *PMA*, 43 (1916–17), pp. xix–xxiii at xxi).

[64] BL Add. MS 71013, fol. 178.

[65] For more on the German background, including Kretzschmar's role in the IMG dissolution, see Annegret Fauser, 'Guido Adler and the Founding of the International Musicological Society (IMS): A View from the Archives', *Vremennik Zubovskogo instituta* [Annals of the Zubov Institute], 7, no. 4 (2019), 97–113.

[66] Albert Stanley's contribution was read in May 1912 in his absence by the Association secretary Percy Baker ('Graduate Work in Music in America, with a Survey of the

DEVELOPING PURPOSE, 1874–1924   67

or post-war stringencies, they sought, then welcomed, in-person papers by Dutch and Swiss scholars able to travel – the bibliophile Prosper Verheyden on Peter Benoit and the modern Flemish school (1914), and the educator Emile Jaques-Dalcroze on the influence of eurhythmics on musical movement (1918). Most impressive was a study sent by the Belgian musicologist Charles van den Borren on 'The Genius of Dunstable' (1921, read by Barclay Squire). Van den Borren had attended the London Congress in 1911. Like Hugo Leichtentritt, near whom he stands in the large group portrait taken on 3 June (Fig. 7), Van den Borren must have sensed that beyond all the warm compliments to British music, there remained room for scholarly improvement, and not only among British researchers. Leichtentritt had observed after the Congress that too many papers had been given by second- and third-rate speakers: 'We were too often reminded that there are some people who confuse scientific ability with a diligent study of the dictionary.'[67] His implication is well taken. The qualities of original thought, scholarly rigour and analytical insight were not automatic in any nation's incipient musicologists; such skills had to be modelled, taught, developed and practiced just like musical ones. To gain some idea of how they were fostered in the UK, or not, it helps to look back and trace the Association's work in encouraging papers, planning annual sessions and establishing publishing routines.

Given the lack of formal music research training in Britain, it comes as no surprise to find that filling each year's programme with eight speakers, or even six in the post-Great War period, was a struggle. Beyond experienced scientists who at the start were eager to share their findings in acoustics or sound phenomena, exactly where were the bulk of British papers to come from that treated wider music-historical and aesthetic ideas, manuscript and printed sources, or contemporary social and technical questions? Answer: from people already exploring their own, or publicly available, book, music and instrument collections, their own performing, composing or teaching practices and their own experiences as listeners, travellers and consumers. This distance from established music research culture or any codification of research method surely helps to account for the eclecticism of Association topics noticed by Oscar Sonneck (and sometimes later dismissed prematurely by others as amateur); it may also explain any literal 'diligent study of the dictionary' heard by

---

Conditions on which it Rests', *PMA*, 38 (1911–12), 117–39). Having already given two papers at the London Congress, on the value of an instrument collection to students and on American music festivals, he became increasingly involved as a long-distance correspondent, furthering the Association's cause in the USA. In 1923–24 the Association made Stanley a vice-president, a role he filled until his death in 1932.

[67] Leichtentritt's remarks are translated from the *Signale für die musikalische Welt* in *MT*, 52 (Aug 1911), 518. Ten years later, Van den Borren's Dunstable paper and its discussion, notably by R.R. Terry (*PMA*, 47 (1921), 79–92), echoed the idea that modern British scholars had to be roused by continental admiration for English music and its study before they themselves discerned their prejudices against their own music.

Leichtentritt, since every would-be scholar has to start somewhere. Yet still, for years there was persistent hesitation to come forward. It was not a lack of private study, curiosity or knowledge that held people back, but rather a lack of self-confidence in the relative importance of what they knew, and of how to write and present their material for public delivery.[68] Members continually had to be reminded that the Association relied for its existence on their proposing of 'papers', that term's novelty highlighted by C.K. Salaman's repeated use of scare quotes in the mid-1870s. In late 1877 he admitted that for the third session, 1876–77, all the Association papers had depended on his exertions: not one had been offered spontaneously.[69] His secretarial procedure, at the Council's behest, had been to write several letters of invitation, receive refusals or hesitant replies, then either coax his prospects or approach different ones with alternative topics. The constant thinking, time and anxiety involved in this process was arduous, and it only increased when he also had to shepherd a year's *Proceedings* through the press; after three rounds of so much responsibility, he needed to step down.

This state of affairs continued off and on for fifty years. It was not until the early twentieth century that occasional surplus proposals meant the Council had more choice in selecting and shaping paper ideas, and even, with more experience of weak or inarticulate ones, rejecting some.[70] Before that, to help focus planning while increasing the flow of suggestions, Stainer as president had proposed in 1892 that a Council subgroup be set up for the purpose, helping the secretary, now Percy Baker. This idea was not actioned formally until late 1897, when a five-person Papers Committee came into being. Within a year, though, the concept was strongly opposed by (guess who) Charles Maclean.

---

[68] John Hullah recognized this problem in 1852 in his *Inuagural Address* to the Musical Institute: 'We have the good fortune to number among our Members many who, over and above their general musical accomplishments, have given *special* attention to certain subjects on which others must be less informed; nay, I would even risk the assertion, that *every* individual Member knows something about his Art which others either do not know at all, or at all events are unfamiliar with. To the former of these parties we look confidently for help; to the latter I would say, do not hesitate to come forward with your discovery, fact, suggestion, or inquiry […] in the fear that it be small in itself or relate to "trifles". Many a truth has lain for ages incomplete and useless for want of some one small fact' (10–11, emphasis original).

[69] AGM minutes for session 3, 1876–77 (29 Oct 1877), Add. MS 71010, fol. 129. From the same meeting, even 'short papers […] provocative of discussion' were encouraged (fol. 124v). A general reminder that anyone could propose a paper appeared in prospectuses and Annual Reports. The modern notion of a 'call for papers' on a particular subject remained decades away.

[70] Among rejected proposals were these: 'Orthography in its Relation to the Singing and Speaking Voice' and 'Accompaniments in their Relation to Part Writing', 1902; a second paper on the physiognomy of musicians' ears (the first one had not been well received), and a study of Strauss's *Symphonia Domestica*, 1905; 'The Congregation's Part in Church Music', 1913; a study of great Victorian singers, 1914; 'The Unimportance of the Classic', 1915; and 'The First Principles of Harmony', 1919.

Ever eagle-eyed about procedure and fair representation, Maclean felt that this subcommittee had usurped a role rightly belonging to the whole Council – that is, suggesting and discussing potential papers and speakers – and was therefore illegal by the Association's own regulations.[71] The Council broadly agreed, saw his point and went back to considering proposals collectively, responding to Baker's planning year by year as needed. Never passive in any event, Council members periodically named speakers or topics they wanted to encourage, imagining how to stimulate new interest or connect with an earlier paper. In the enthusiasm around folk and national musics of the early 1900s, for example, someone suggested a talk on Spanish idioms, which led to the notion of approaching the violinist and RCM professor Enrique Fernándes Arbós as an authority, and then, failing him, John Singer Sargent, the portrait artist, well known in London as a *flamenco* song aficionado. Neither prospect came through in the manner envisaged, but Arbós indeed assisted the speaker who in 1906 eventually covered the subject ably from his own researches, the Rev. Henry Cart de LaFontaine.[72] This *ad hoc* method of commissioning – for that is what it was – broadened the secretary's scope of enquiry; in making multiple personal contacts or asking a prospective speaker for more information, the Council together achieved a balance and a wider topical spread than many sessions might otherwise have had. In such a way, history did not entirely replace science, educational research and psychology were as welcome as musical biography and organology, and ethnology stood alongside theory and criticism. Planning came to a head every spring so that the next session's prospectus could be printed and circulated in advance.

In retrospect, a few creative solutions to the problem of short supply deserve notice. One was the entrusting of several lectures to a single strong speaker. Rosa Newmarch, for example, presented convincingly five times on 'The Development of National Opera in Russia', a succession of stimulating papers between 1900 and 1905, all with new information acquired at first hand and illustrated by a singer and accompanist (on one occasion, Mr and Mrs Henry J. Wood). Likewise, Henry Hadow gave a three-lecture series across 1923–24, at Hugh Allen's suggestion, on 'The Balance of Expression and Design in Music', though his topic drew less animated discussion than Newmarch's material.[73] Another idea, a wartime stopgap in 1915 offered by W.W. Cobbett, was to hold a debate between two speakers; it never materialized for practical reasons. Then there was the leavening of textual study with substantial music demonstration, notably of early instruments and repertories. In a shape akin to

---

[71] Council minutes, 25 Oct 1898, BL Add. MS 71012, fol. 29.
[72] Rev. Henry Cart de Lafontaine, 'Spanish Music', *PMA*, 33 (1906–07), 27–43; Rev. Henry Cart de Lafontaine, 'Spanish Music (Second Paper)', *PMA*, 34 (1907–08), 25–45. Cart acknowledged the work of Frederick Ouseley and latterly Pierre Aubry.
[73] Two-paper series were more common, for example, George Ashdown Audsley's 'What is Sound? Or the Substantial Theory *versus* the Wave Theory of Acoustics' *(PMA* 16 and 17); Jeffrey Pulver's 'The Ancient Dance-Forms' (*PMA* 39 and 40); and H.B. Collins's 'Latin Church Music by Early English Composers' (*PMA* 39 and 43).

a lecture-recital, this format was increasingly welcomed, as with, for example, Alfred Hipkins and his range of early keyboards in 1886, a highly valued lecture that surprised listeners with new possibilities for old music (with Anton Rubinstein graciously turning pages for Hipkins);[74] and Richard Runciman Terry, his small choir and string quartet giving 'Sidelights on Tallis' in May 1902 (one wonders if Ralph Vaughan Williams was in the audience). Unfortunately Terry's spontaneous presentation, though undoubtedly fascinating, was never committed to paper despite assiduous chasing, and therefore never appeared in *Proceedings* – a downside to using him again.[75] A final trend that helped fill the sessional diary, reflecting the period's wider public interest, was an appeal from around 1908 to noted figures in English musical life, whether orchestral player, conductor, composer or writer, such as the harpist Alfred Kastner, the timpanist Gordon Cleather, Eugene Goossens, Adrian Boult, Philip Heseltine, Arthur Bliss and George Bernard Shaw. In all, while some of these examples might smack of talks for a lightweight music club rather than scholarly explications of original research, such a dichotomy distorts the position. Meeting dates were available, members, and potential new members, were interested, teaching and learning took place, and discussions sparked further questions and ideas; all these formats, barring the debate, yielded successful gatherings if not published articles (Terry was allowed to return as a presenter under the strict condition that he submit a full draft a week in advance). The point is that in shaping its programme, the Association remained flexible and pragmatic. Council members learned to steer a course between accepting freely offered research papers and actively requesting other presentations, all to stimulate a mix of member interests and build engagement with the new discipline.

The development of social and scholarly management followed a similar path of gradual change, which can be seen in three areas - the question of fees and expenses, the still-novel role of women as presenters and the procedures of publishing. The default stance on fees was of course that no speaker got one, nor did, at this period, their music-performing illustrators, at least not from the Association's purse; performers' travel expenses could be reimbursed, and any cost of equipment or its carriage within reason. Yet default positions can be calibrated. The celebrity organist Edwin Lemare rejected the Council's speaking request outright when a large fee was not automatically attached, a response they accepted easily, whereas with Bernard Shaw they chose a more nuanced approach in 1910: an outspokenly professional author, he agreed to

---

[74] 'The Old Clavier or Keyboard Instruments: Their Use by Composers, and Technique', *PMA*, 12 (1885–86), 139–48. The identity of Hipkins's assistant is disclosed in his own entry in James D. Brown and Stephen S. Stratton, *British Musical Biography* (Birmingham: S.S. Stratton, 1897), 200, as well as in [F.G. Edwards], 'Alfred James Hipkins', *MT*, 39 (1898), 581–86 at 585.

[75] Council minutes, 24 Oct 1902, BL Add. MS 71012, fol. 125v. As a result of the shortfall of articles for *PMA*, 28 (1901–02) caused by Terry's inaction, the Council voted that in future where a lecture was not read from a script, the reporter be instructed 'to take down the discourse in short hand'.

speak without fee but as a matter of principle advised that he wouldn't supply a text. At some cost but with little hesitation, the Council asked their shorthand reporter to take down his talk and Shaw agreed; on the day, though, the talk's improvisatory nature defied verbatim reporting, so Shaw finally sent a shortened text. This positive persistence on the Council's part was a direct result of their 1902 experience with Richard Terry, whose talk had been completely lost. Another, slightly earlier concession had been the Council's reply to the working folksong collector Frank Kidson, who agreed to give a paper on melody in 1908 if the Association would pay his travel expenses from Leeds. The answer was 'yes', setting a precedent for encouraging more regional scholars to contribute actively. Both examples show the Council's readiness to make allowances where scholarship and the larger group stood to gain.

On women's appearances, similarly, the Council by 1900 wanted to encourage more 'lady members' to step forward; not only was attendance thought to improve when women took the platform, but their ideas and expertise were welcomed as refreshing. Eighteen women, two of them speaking more than once, provided twenty-three of the 408 papers in the Association's first fifty years, some 6 per cent of the total.[76] Not all of them read publicly, however, whether from modesty, inexperience or a belief that their papers would be taken more seriously if delivered by a man, especially one in sympathy with the subject. Both Margaret Watts Hughes, a Welsh singer and philanthropist who was the first woman to offer her research, in June 1887 ('Voice Figures'), and Janet Dodge ('Lute Music of the XVIth and XVIIth Centuries', May 1908), who at the time had a related but different article already accepted in the 'Quarterly Journal' of the IMG,[77] chose to have male proxies read for them; odd as it may seem now, both women were present in the room and joined the discussion at the end. The first woman to actually read her own paper, in May 1892, was Oliveria Prescott, a founding member, composer and harmony teacher who was a regular attender and participant in many discussions.[78] Of all the women presenting in this period, Rosa Newmarch seems to have commanded the highest confidence; in 1906 she became the first woman to chair an Association meeting, with a paper by Frederick Shinn on the study of music history. Usefully, an important disciplinary rule came to be articulated soon after Mrs Hughes's paper, namely, that any paper already read elsewhere could not be presented to the Association. It was not known at the time when Hughes

---

[76] By 1900, the proportion of women members had already risen to 16 per cent, but women's papers accounted for only 2 per cent of the total by that date. Charles Maclean, when chairing Rosa Newmarch's first paper in January 1900, encouraged more women to follow her example in 'readiness to address an audience' (*PMA*, 26 (1899–1900), 57–77 at 72).

[77] Janet Dodge, 'Ornamentation as Indicated by Signs in Lute Tablature', *SIMG*, 9 (1908), 318–36. Dodge's Musical Association paper was read by T.L. Southgate.

[78] Oliveria Prescott, 'Musical Design, a Help to Poetic Intention', *PMA*, 18 (1891–92), 121–34. For more on Prescott's background, experience and output, see her entry in Brown and Stratton, *British Musical Biography*, 327.

applied to the Council (she was not a member and never joined) that she had previously presented her findings, on the visual patterns her voice could make by singing into a resonator with an elastic membrane, to other groups including the Royal Society; this background was later discovered and she published her results in more than one outlet, including, besides *Proceedings*, the American *Century Magazine*.[79] While there was no suggestion of deliberate impropriety on Hughes's part, the Council felt it essential to clarify their procedures more rigorously, aligning themselves with other learned societies.

For a scholar, nothing focuses the mind more than having to commit one's ideas to print. Likewise for the Musical Association, issuing its regular *Proceedings* forced processes that defined the group's value in print: a copy of its annual journal was the Association's calling card and could be given away or sold at the Council's discretion, raising both capital and cultural esteem. Yet for author and society alike, the path to print had to be continually adjusted, scholarly conventions agreed and the accounts balanced. Across this first period, and even up to the early 1950s, no one with professional publishing expertise held editorial responsibility. Honorary, then paid executive secretaries accepted the task as a kind of combined desk-and-managing-editor role, all the while consulting authors or Council members as necessary (no dedicated editorial correspondence survives from this period); the job was an extension of sessional planning and just as accountable, though not yet technically burdensome. Scripts were collected for submission to the printer – Spottiswoode & Co. for the first four volumes (a bit expensive), then Novello & Co. until 1920 (excellent music examples), then, under post-war economies, the competitively priced Whitehead & Miller of Leeds (suggested by Percy Scholes when printing costs were seen to have doubled since 1914). This printing path alone shows the Association taking ever bigger steps away from its early science and music-commercial partners and towards becoming a more savvy self-publisher. At the start, the final copy deadline was set in a leisurely way for July each year, leaving time to chase any late contributors, resolve queries and cost examples or illustrations. As individual papers grew in length and complexity, and especially after one or two close calls including the Richard Terry fiasco, the approach tightened, in 1906, to a deadline of one week after oral presentation. The aim was to publish and deliver each volume before the AGM in late October or early November, just before the start of a new session – a step that naturally required cross-checking of every member's name, address

---

[79] See Margaret Watts Hughes, 'Visible Sound: I. Voice-Figures', *Century Magazine*, 42 (1891), 37–40; here she mentions having 'exhibited' at the 'Musical Association, the Royal Institution, The Royal Society, and elsewhere', but without any detail or reference to her *PMA* article, 'Voice Figures, with Illustrations', *PMA*, 13 (1886–87), 133–44 (originally read by D.J. Blaikley). *Century*'s 'Comment' on Hughes's findings, by the American science writer Sophie B. Herrick, is illuminating, referring to the Musical Association members John Tyndall, Sedley Taylor and Emil Behnke and their work on sound; see Sophie B. Herrick, 'Visible Sound: II. Comment', *Century Magazine*, 42 (1891), 40–44.

and membership status before mailing, an exercise in itself. In size, the print order varied between 250 and 500 copies, depending on member numbers and finance but also on any planned special distribution to libraries, foreign institutions, other societies or prospective members; the order generally hovered around 300–400, and always included fifty *gratis* offprints for each author, besides at least twelve to twenty reserve copies for future sale of back numbers. When stocks accumulated too rapidly through over-printing or loss of members, creating a storage problem, copies were sometimes sold for half price, notably in 1920 to American universities eager to acquire or complete their journal sets.

As pointers to the Association's growing awareness of its scholarly identity, footnotes, music examples, abstracts and indexes show how the rigours of communicating research developed on the page. For the bulk of this period, footnotes of any kind were rare in *Proceedings*; most papers appeared as traditional essays or formal talks, giving any necessary name, title or evidentiary material in prose (as did early *Grove* articles). Where footnotes do appear for a source or clarification, as occasionally in a paper by John Stainer, E.J. Dent or, especially, Charles van den Borren, they are not numbered but carry distinctive superscript signs at the bottom of the page – asterisk, dagger, double dagger and double vertical line, in that order (* † ‡ ‖). A particular exception occurs in Charles Sanford Terry's article of 1918 on J.S. Bach's cantata librettos, which was heavily footnoted on every page so that small superscript numbers were the obvious solution – up to nine or ten per page keyed to Terry's substantial thirty-five-page Appendix, 'Bach's Cantatas Arranged Chronologically'. In fact this paper and its Appendix, laid out in a five-column landscape table, made up one of the most complex units, and certainly the most expensive to produce, in the Association's first fifty years. The author's fastidious research as well as his laborious checking of title and source details were gratefully acknowledged by the chair, W.G. McNaught: 'We have reason to believe that it is the most complete and authoritative thing of the kind that has been put together.'[80] Less well known is that C.S. Terry, a distinguished historian of Scotland at the University of Aberdeen (no relation to Richard Terry), required such extensive proof corrections throughout his article, costing the Association heavily in a stringent period, that he was politely asked to help pay something towards them, but refused.[81] More readily accommodated were type-printed music examples, unnumbered, brief and usually placed within text near the relevant discussion. Occasionally an author required something longer, such as Janet Dodge's lute pieces for her article in 1908; again for cost

---

[80] 'Discussion', in C. Sanford Terry, 'Bach's Cantata Libretti', *PMA*, 44 (1917–18), 71–125 at 125. Percy Baker read the paper because Terry was in France on an educational assignment with the army.

[81] See the Council minutes for 8 July and 14 Oct 1919 (BL Add. MS 71013, fols. 164, 166). The expensive setting of Terry's Appendix (£76) and his corrections (nearly £20), when printing costs generally had skyrocketed, precipitated a threatened rise in the Association's subscription. That was avoided only by reducing the number of meetings a year from eight to six.

reasons, these had to be limited to two pieces across five full pages and so were especially carefully selected.

The notion of paper abstracts first arose through the need from 1899 to summarize Musical Association presentations for the *Sammelbände* and *Zeitschrift* of the IMG. Supplied either by lecturers themselves or the secretary, these were then vetted by Charles Maclean and sent to Berlin, ensuring news of British research was reported in an international forum (seven decades before the founding of Répertoire International de Littérature Musicale, or RILM). The efficacy of abstracts as advance local communication became clear as well; from around 1901, brief descriptions or synopses of scheduled London papers began to appear in the Association's promotional material to attract listeners. See Figure 8, a notice card for the twenty-seventh AGM before the start of the twenty-eighth session on 12 November 1901, on which John Borland's 'Orchestral and Choral Balance', the paper given that afternoon, is advertised by a short synopsis. Meanwhile the idea of creating a retrospective index to all the Association's published papers, a sure sign of scholarly confidence, had already been suggested in the late 1890s by F.G. Edwards, then the new editor of the *Musical Times*. By 'index' he meant simply an alphabetical listing of all articles to date by title or subject, together with an attached alphabetical list of linked authors, with the aim of providing ready access to the content of the first twenty-five volumes of *Proceedings* (the Royal Society chose a similar format). Not only would such listings be useful for current Association members and serve as a recruiting tool for new ones, but they might also spark ideas externally, helping all kinds of scholars to find valuable material they would otherwise miss.

The first such index duly appeared in volume 25 of the *Proceedings* (1898–99), after which three cumulative updates, from 1874, were published quinquennially in two parts, 'Subjects' and 'Writers', in volumes 30 (1903–04), 35 (1908–09) and 40 (1913–14).[82] The last of these revealed an interesting pattern of nine broad subject areas, according to Percy Baker. Of the 339 papers given over those first forty years (by 197 lecturers), he grouped them as follows: Instruments, 35; Philosophy and Aesthetics, 64; Acoustics and Science, 29; National Music and History, 74; Physiology, 7; Practical Music and Analysis, 48; Biography and Personal Notices, 36; Harmony and Notation, 31; and Miscellaneous, 15.[83] For the Association's fiftieth anniversary, Baker produced another cumulative version, this time a 'List of Papers read from 1874 to 1924 inclusive', presented chronologically by session in volume 50 (1923–24), accompanied by an alphabetical list of authors keyed to the sessions. Although

---

[82] Enhancing Baker's effort, the Association produced an impressive publicity brochure in mid-1913: a 5″ × 8″ oblong booklet, twenty-four pages, listing all Musical Association articles published to the end of the thirty-ninth session (preserved in BL Add. MS 71034, fols. 27–38). It was probably used to attract new members, sell overstocked *PMA* back copies and assist in the preparation of Baker's next index, for vol. 40.

[83] 'Report' of the fortieth session, *PMA*, 41 (1914–15), p. xx.

> **MUSICAL ASSOCIATION.**
> 27TH SESSION, 1900-1901.
>
> Notice is hereby given that the ANNUAL GENERAL MEETING will be held at the Royal College of Organists, Hart Street, w.c., on Tuesday, 12th November, 1901, at 4.15 p.m., in order to receive the Report of the Council, to pass the Balance Sheet, and to elect officers for the ensuing year. J. PERCY BAKER, *Secretary*.
>
> 28TH SESSION, 1901-1902.
>
> The FIRST MEETING will be held on Tuesday, 12th November, 1901, when a paper will be read on
>
> **"ORCHESTRAL AND CHORAL BALANCE,"**
> By J. E. BORLAND, Esq., Mus. B.
>
> SYNOPSIS.—Internal balance of parts in (*a*) Chorus, (*b*) Orchestra.—Mutual balance of instrumental and vocal forces.—Historical survey of two centuries.—Each period and each style of music demands separate consideration.—Futility of numerical rules unless (*a*) acoustics of buildings, (*b*) relative positions of performers, (*c*) style of scoring, and (*d*) the "personal equation," are taken into account.—Educated taste being the only ultimate referee, there is legitimate room for variety of opinion.—Some suggestions for conductors, upon whom lies, in practice, the whole responsibility of securing well-balanced performances.—Brief summary.
>
> Tea and Coffee at 5 p.m.   The Reading will begin at 5.30 punctually.
>
> **J. PERCY BAKER,** Secretary,
> 289, High Road, Lee, S.E.
> Members can admit Visitors personally or by order.
>
> THORN, WOOLWICH.

Figure 8. Notice card for the twenty-seventh Musical Association AGM, 12 November 1901, with synopsis of J.E. Borland's paper, BL Add. MS 71033, fol. 40.

individual papers are not dated in the last version, these five indexes together open up the Association's work at a glance, even now shedding light on how the group's interests developed and their claim to learned status was built. For the particular focus on scientific subjects in the first fifty years, for example, see Table 2. The next index to be produced, the sixth, would cover the first seventy years of *Proceedings*, 1874–1944, and appear as a separate booklet in 1948. The seventh version, completely redesigned and still cumulative from 1874, would not appear until *PRMA* 90 in 1966, with no further index or list appearing in print since that time.

One additional angle on the Association's early concept of its purpose runs through its history from the beginning – concern for music researchers' access to well-stocked, properly organized libraries and accurate catalogues of their music and musical literature, printed and manuscript. To some people, then and now, this might not sound like a compelling issue, but music-bibliographical knowledge could open the door to serious research in any country; in this early period it was virtually a prerequisite for historical studies. If the UK's libraries, starting with its national collection in the BM, did not provide the means of gaining that knowledge, then members of the Association felt they should speak up and advocate for improvements. This they did as a group,

Table 2. Musical Association papers on scientific subjects, 1874–1924: a selected list.

Author	Title	Date
Adams, Prof. Wm Grylls, M.A., F.R.S.	On the musical inventions and discoveries of the late Sir Charles Wheatstone, F.R.S.	1 May 1876
Audsley, George Ashdown, F.R.I.B.A.	Matters, chiefly architectural, relating to the accommodation of the organ in churches and other buildings	4 February 1889
	What is sound? The substantial theory *versus* the wave theory of acoustics	7 April 1890
	Again, what is sound? The substantial theory *versus* the wave theory of acoustics (2nd paper)	13 January 1891
Baillie-Hamilton, J.	On the application of wind to string instruments *William Spottiswoode, Esq., M.A., F.R.S., LL.D., Vice-President, in the Chair*	4 January 1875
	The Vocalion	5 February 1883
Bassett, Henry, F.C.S.	On improvements in the trumpet	2 July 1877
Behnke, Emil	The mechanism of the human voice	3 November 1879
	Photographs of the throat in singing	3 December 1883
	The registers of the voice	1 November 1886
Bidwell, Shelford, M.A., LL.B.	The recent inventions for reproducing the sound of the human voice	4 November 1878
Blaikley, David James	Communication respecting a point in the theory of brass instruments	4 February (paper) and 4 March 1878 (discussion)
	On quality of tone in wind instruments	1 March 1880
	On the velocity of sound in air	4 June 1883
	The development of modern wind instruments	3 May 1886
	Notes on the action of musical reeds	3 June 1889
	Notes on the trumpet scale	8 May 1894
	The French horn	15 June 1909

Bosanquet, R.H.M., M.A., F.R.G.S., F.C.S.	Temperament; or, The division of the octave (two parts)	2 November 1874 and 3 May 1875
	On some points in the harmony of perfect consonances	2 July 1877
	On a mode of producing continuous notes from resonators	1 December 1879
	Some experiments with a revolving stop-cock	
	On the arrangement of the stops, pedals, and swell in the organ	7 November 1881
	On the beats of mistuned harmonic consonances	
Browne, Lennox, M.D, F.R.C.S.Edin.	On medical science in relation to the voice as a musical instrument	5 June 1876
Casson, Thomas	Development of the resources of the organ	21 November 1905
Clarke, Somers	Further 'notes' on the organ, suggested by papers of Sir F.A.G. Ouseley and Mr. Audsley	5 May 1890
Cobb, Gerard F., M.A.	On certain principles of musical exposition considered educationally, and with special reference to current systems of musical theory (two parts)	5 May and 2 June 1884
	Musical psychics	1 June 1885
Crow, Edwin J., Mus.D.	Remarks on certain peculiarities in instruments of the clarinet family, together with an account of Mr. Wm. Rowlett's experiments with clarinets having a bassoon reed instead of their own	1 December 1884
Day, Capt. C.R., F.S.A.	Notes on Indian Music	13 February 1894
Eggar, Katharine, A.R.A.M.	The subconscious mind and the musical faculty	7 December 1920
Ellis, Alexander J., F.R.S.	Illustrations of just and tempered intonation	7 June 1875
	On the sensitiveness of the ear to pitch and change of pitch in music	6 November 1876
Galpin, Rev. F.W, M.A., F.L.S.	The whistles and reed instruments of the American Indians of the North-West Coast	10 March 1903
	The sackbut, its evolution and history, illustrated by an instrument of the sixteenth century	20 November 1906

—*(continued)*

Table 2—*concluded*

Goddard, Joseph	The philosophy of the higher beauty of music. Part I: The sources of musical charm and expressiveness	13 June 1899
	The philosophy of the higher beauty of music. Part II: Contrast in scenic effect and in music	14 November 1899
Gray, Alan, LL.M., Mus.D.	The philosophy of our tempered system	15 January 1902
Habens, Rev. WJ., B.A. Lond.	The modern organ	15 April 1913
Hughes, Mrs. Watts	On the musical scale	4 November 1889
Jones, E. Lancaster	Voice-figures, with illustrations	6 June 1887
Latte, Ludwig	Sound-ranging	14 February 1922
McNaught, W.G.	A new note system	14 February 1893
Mann, Mrs. Maud (Maud MacCarthy)	The psychology of sight-singing	12 December 1899
	Some Indian conceptions of music	16 January 1912
Monteith, E.R., L.R.A.M., A.R.C.M.	Colour – Music: experiments in the educational value of the analogy between sound and colour	18 March 1913
Piggott, F.T.	The music of Japan	12 April 1892
Pole, William, Mus.D. Oxon., F.R.SS.L.&E.	On the graphic method of representing musical intervals, with illustrations of the construction of the musical scale	6 December 1875
	On the philosophy of harmony	5 March 1877
Prentice, Ridley	Brotherhood's Technicon: the necessity of a systematic and scientific development of the muscles of the hand and arm for pianoforte players	5 November 1888
Rayleigh, Lord [John William Strutt, 3rd Baron Rayleigh], M.A., F.R.S.	On our perception of the direction of a source of sound	3 April 1876

Saunders, Cecil G.	On the determination of absolute pitch by the common harmonium	2 December 1878
	The mutual influence of two sounds nearly in unison	7 April 1879
Southgate, T.L.	The construction of buildings considered with reference to sound	Not given orally but published in *PMA* 8 (1881-82)
	On various attempts that have been made to record extemporaneous playing	
Spottiswoode, William, M.A., LL.D., P.R.S.	On beats and combination tones *John Tyndall, Esq., F.R.S., LL.D., in the Chair*	5 May 1879
Stone, W.H., M.D, M.A., F.R.C.P.	On extending the compass and increasing the tone of stringed instruments, with especial reference to the author's and Mr. Meeson's elliptical tension-bars	2 November 1874
	On standards of musical pitch	6 March 1876
	The causes of the rise in orchestral pitch	4 April 1881
Taylor, Sedley, M.A.	On a suggested simplification of the established pitch notation	7 December 1874
Turpin, James, Mus.B. Cantab.	Some practical bearings of the study of acoustics upon music as an art	5 March 1883
Warman, John W., A.R.C.O.	A clear coupler for the organ	10 April 1900
	The hydraulic organ of the Ancients	19 January 1904
Wyatt, Walter, Mus.B. Dunelm	A suggested system of chromatic harmony	13 March 1894

after a paper in December 1877 by W.H. Cummings designed to stimulate just such a reaction, called 'The Formation of a National Musical Library'.[84] Following lively discussion, a sharing of variable working experiences and further Council consideration, the Association sent a short polite letter, or 'memorial', to the BM Trustees in March 1878, requesting three actions that 'would be a great convenience to students': (1) acquire more rare music and music literature, (2) make a dedicated catalogue of music and music literature together and (3) print that catalogue for public sale or consultation.[85] In some ways these requests were naïve, even uninformed, about the Museum's methods and progress over the previous thirty years in building its collections and cataloguing music separately; a polite but defensive reply came from the Museum's Principal Librarian, J. Winter Jones, three months later.[86] Yet the memorial's thrust had been fundamentally correct, and the crucial importance of cataloguing to scholarship remained pressing; despite recent progress, the Museum's music cataloguing was indeed inadequate and uncoordinated, and no usable printed version of a catalogue was on the horizon. The beginnings of real change came seven years later through the appointment in 1885 of, at last, a music specialist at the Museum to 'take charge of the Collections of Music'.[87] Whether that forceful representation of 1878 had carried some weight in this direction is unprovable, but it seems at least possible. The eventual appointee, barely thirty, was William Barclay Squire, whose work would be essential in raising the prestige of the BM Music Room 'to the high level of that of the rest

---

[84] *PMA*, 4 (1877–78), 13–26. This was the second of Cummings's twelve papers for the Association between 1876 and 1910. Discussants were G.A. Crawford, George Grove, William Chappell, Frederick Bridge, R.H.M. Bosanquet, Edward Bond (Keeper of MSS, British Museum), Otto Goldschmidt and Ebenezer Prout.

[85] For a draft of the memorial, presented to the Council for approval on 4 March 1878, see BL Add. MS 71010, fol. 140r–v. As chair of the Cummings paper, George Grove had moderated the discussion by explaining to colleagues how little the Trustees knew or cared about music; rather than blaming them directly, he advocated a more persuasive approach, which may explain the memorial's final emphasis on 'the importance of all that appertains to the art and science of Music and how enormously that art has risen in general estimation in recent years', and on how the Museum facilities 'have not kept pace with the constant advance and interest of the general public and the pressing necessities of students'. The Council printed and circulated an extra 100 copies of Cummings's paper to elicit more signatures.

[86] J. Winter Jones to James Higgs, Esq., Honorary Secretary, Musical Association, 24 June 1878, copied into the Council minutes of 1 July 1878 (BL Add. MS 71010, fols. 144v–145). Jones shrewdly sidestepped the issue of printing a catalogue: 'the Trustees feel that they must postpone the consideration of this subject' (fol. 145). For the full text of the memorial and of Jones's reply, see 'Report of the Council', *PMA*, 5 (1878–79), pp. xiii–xiv.

[87] A. Hyatt King, 'The Music Room of the British Museum, 1753–1953: Its History and Organization', *PMA*, 79 (1952–53), 65–79 at 71. The key attitude shift, noted at a Trustees' meeting of 17 January 1885, occurred when Trustees chose to overrule their Principal Keeper's views and look instead for a music specialis.

Figure 9. 'The Greatest Library in the World – The Reading-Room of the British Museum', from the *Sphere*, 13 April 1907; illustration by Fortunino Matania, detail.

of the library'.[88] Two of his six strong references came from George Grove and Frederick Bridge, both of whom had attended Cummings's paper and helped draft the memorial.

Private libraries, in turn, besides other small music collections in churches, cathedrals, universities and music societies across Great Britain and Ireland, also engaged the attention of Squire as an Association member and an increasingly authoritative writer on international musical libraries, notably in

---

[88] Ibid. Further on Squire, see Alec Hyatt King, 'William Barclay Squire, 1855–1927: Music Librarian', in *Musical Pursuits: Selected Essays* (London: British Library, 1987), 187–99.

the second edition of *Grove's Dictionary* (Grove 2) in 1906.[89] All along, too, other Association members were consulting rare music and texts, and pooling information about a range of library holdings. James E. Matthew, a member who happened to own one of the largest private libraries of musical literature in the world (more than 5,500 distinct works, besides 1,400 volumes of music), gave a paper in 1903 that revealed just how splendid his collection was; he welcomed the Association to his home in South Hampstead, where he showed and discussed several choice items.[90] Above all, Squire's work at the Museum and liaison with European counterparts, including some connected to the IMG committee on bibliography, meant that he was able to secure wide (moral) support for the cataloguing of small library collections in Britain and Ireland: in 1911 the entire IMG leadership recognized that such a step would advance all European music scholarship. Certainly Squire had been clear in his *Grove* 2 article that Britain lagged behind much of the rest of Europe (including Italy) in this regard, and that rectifying the gap would be in every scholar's interest.[91]

After the war, in spring 1919, Squire gave a paper to the Association entitled simply 'Musical Libraries and Catalogues'.[92] Like the Cummings presentation forty-two years earlier, it had been designed to elicit Council action in the form of a subcommittee who could make a practical proposal; the appointees were Godfrey Arkwright, Dent, Fellowes, Squire and Terry. Reporting back a year later, they recommended ways to identify, preserve and catalogue valuable music in small collections, printed and manuscript; the Council then sent this report to the Carnegie United Kingdom Trust in hopes of gaining financial aid to start the survey. The Appendix to *Proceedings* for 1920–21 reveals, however, that the application was unsuccessful: the Carnegie Trustees were already giving substantial help towards the publication of Tudor Church Music, a large

---

[89] W.B.S., 'Libraries and Collections of Music – I. Europe', *Grove 2*, vol. 2 (1906), 690–717. 'Great Britain and Ireland', subdivided by city, is treated on pp. 700–11, with salient details of the holdings in each collection as well as related catalogues or bibliography.

[90] James E. Matthew, 'Some Notes on Musical Libraries, and on That of the Writer in Particular', *PMA*, 29 (1902–03), 139–68. His home was at 100 Fellows Road, London NW, near Swiss Cottage. Matthew's collection is noted in Squire's *Grove 2* article on 'Libraries and Collections of Music – I. Europe', 707. Much of the collection would be purchased in 1908 by Paul Hirsch in Frankfurt (via the Berlin dealer Leo Liepmannssohn), eventually to make its way back to Cambridge in 1936, and thence to the British Museum in 1946; a note of the sale appears in *MT*, 49 (Jan 1908), 19. See also Chapter 3 ahead, n. 62.

[91] 'Congress Resolutions Passed and International Committees Recognized', *Report of the Fourth Congress*, 386, noting that the General Meeting resolved it was 'desirable' for a thorough survey to be undertaken of the musical libraries in Great Britain and Ireland, public and private.

[92] W. Barclay Squire, 'Musical Libraries and Catalogues', *PMA*, 45 (1918–19), 97–111. The paper was given on 8 April 1919, with discussants including E.H. Fellowes and Richard Terry.

and important music edition in progress, and would do no more.[93] Squire's advocacy died with him in 1927. The work he envisaged, in part, would be taken up systematically in the 1950s through Edith B. Schnapper's *British Union-Catalogue of Early Music Printed before the Year 1801: A Record of the Holdings of over One Hundred Libraries throughout the British Isles* (2 volumes; London: Butterworths, 1957), later known as BUCEM. It too was another significant, albeit isolated, step towards the identification and cataloguing of early printed and manuscript music in UK libraries, a subject that finally rose in priority again under the joint auspices of the International Association of Music Libraries and the International Musicological Society, supported in the early 1960s by the Royal Musical Association. As Répertoire International des Sources Musicales, or RISM, that bigger project gained adherents worldwide. Taking a long view now, it is not entirely fanciful to see some of the earliest seeds of RISM UK in W.H. Cummings's paper of 1877.

Of course, advocacy for its own sake was never a foundational aim behind the Musical Association. Early members were not primarily seeking to influence social, economic or political conditions, or expecting music research to solve world or even local problems. Those possibilities evolved later as the practices of musicology, with its global reach and humanistic themes, broadened along with other disciplines and intellectual currents in and out of academia. Rather, the founders wished to establish music research as valid and important, distinct from concert culture, by seeking new knowledge that would find a useful purpose or application in society – a bit like the work of their senior science colleagues, a community in which debate over the benefits of pure research versus those of practical problem-solving was ongoing, but in which attention to sources, method, evidence and interpretation remained paramount. For that reason, the Association took great care over its scholarly priorities, and only slowly reset them. Lobbying, advocating for educational change or joining the causes of other professional bodies was far less important than building a reputable Musical Association in the first place, enabling members to get on with research. With that goal, the library and cataloguing issue of the 1870s chimed well, whereas periodic external appeals for particular investigations (the decay in sight-singing in schools), financial help (to equip a sound research laboratory), or professional support (merging with another music society) fell on deaf ears. The focus remained on attracting researchers who could present and publish their findings.

---

[93] 'Appendix: Care of Small Collections of Printed and Manuscript Music', *PMA*, 47 (1920–21), 109–12. Fellowes and Terry were also actively assisting the Tudor Church Music project. For background on the project, first suggested in 1916 in association with Henry Hadow, see Richard Turbet, 'An Affair of Honour: "Tudor Church Music", the Ousting of Richard Terry, and a Trust Vindicated', *ML*, 76 (1995), 593–600.

ꙮ Twenty Articles

To illustrate that focus and conclude this chapter, I offer the following selection of twenty articles published in *Proceedings* between 1874 and 1924. They don't all make for easy reading, but they are nevertheless exemplary in some way and have clear historiographical value, revealing how new ideas were presented, became influential or in time could be challenged. Some pieces are unexpectedly sophisticated, even elegant; others reveal by discussion how the Association challenged a speaker, or might have.[94] As a group, moreover, these articles reflect many of the central issues, methods and themes that occupied the Association before and beyond 1924, including empirical sound study as foundational to ethnomusicology, music bibliography, manuscript discovery of 'new' old music, gender study in context, possibilities for historical performance, folksong collecting and analysis, nationalism in nineteenth-century music, style change and the value of criticism, idiomatic music for an obsolete instrument, cultural differences between East and West, musical biography, promotion and analysis of modern composition, early Italian genre history, linguistic codebreaking in deciphering Tudor notation and the gradual remaking of a national music narrative for Britain.

I give them here in chronological order with brief comments on the context or scholarly achievement at the time. Together the articles give a sense of the intellectual environment the Association was providing.

1. **Alexander J. Ellis**, 'On the Sensitiveness of the Ear to Pitch and Change of Pitch in Music', 8 November 1876; *PMA*, 3 (1876–77), 1–32. In this paper Ellis first presented his concept of the 'cent', described as a hundredth of an equal-tempered semitone. The idea was to measure a listener's sensitivity to deviations from specific pitches independent of a piano, composed music, or frequency measurements. After finding that musically experienced listeners typically heard the perfect fifth, the unison and the octave as in tune with an accuracy of 1–2 cents, the major tone within 4–5 cents and most other consonant intervals within 10–18 cents, he then suggested reasons for his results, and later conducted more studies pointing to the role of human agency in constructing scale systems worldwide: systems did not emerge from acoustic principles occurring naturally, but were 'artifices fashioned diversely from place to place through direct human intervention and choice' (see Jonathan

---

[94] Two papers not on this list are notable for how their discussions revealed weakness, whether through inarticulacy and dogmatic delivery or lack of evidence. In his second paper of a series, 'Again, What is Sound? The Substantial Theory *versus* the Wave Theory of Acoustics: II', *PMA*, 17 (1890–91), 59–94, George Ashdown Audsley failed to explain his suggested replacement for the theory of sound waves, despite his critique of that theory and the paper's title (he projected a third paper, but then emigrated to the USA). James Swinburne, in 'Women and Music', *PMA*, 46 (1919–20), 21–42, though he'd had his paper printed and circulated in advance to stir interest, presented no evidence for his exaggerated claims against women, preferring to let misogyny spark discussion, which worked on the day but led nowhere.

P.J. Stock, 'Alexander J. Ellis and His Place in the History of Ethnomusicology', *Ethnomusicology*, 51 (2007), 305–24, esp. 307, 316–17). Ellis's approach as a seeker of real-world data opened a path for the development of modern ethnomusicology in both theory and practice, leading to an understanding of pitch and hearing as open to the same testing and outcomes worldwide, without bias towards Western systems.

2. **William H. Cummings**, 'The Formation of a National Musical Library', 3 December 1877; *PMA*, 4 (1877–78), 13–26. This paper, by one of the great Victorian private collectors as well as a celebrated tenor and music administrator, set out his view of what a national library should contain, and how the BM in particular, though full of great treasures, fell short in its collecting and care of music and musical literature. Cummings was shrewd in his assessment, understanding, for example, that successive editions of popular music ought to be kept for their future historical value even though they might be thought worthless at the time. He also understood research method, and the need for more efficient working tools to make collections known and accessible to the whole community, whether 'amateur or professional, upholders of old notation or apostles of a new; and on behalf of both sexes' (19). His consciousness-raising among scholars and at the BM, as noted above, formed an important part of the drive towards improving UK music research capability.

3. **Stephen S. Stratton**, 'Women in Relation to Musical Art', 7 May 1883; *PMA*, 9 (1882–83), 115–46. This article was strikingly forward-thinking for the time, even pathbreaking in examining women's achievement in music, especially in composition. It lists more than 380 names of women composers, partly as a corrective to omissions in *Grove 1*, and asks how and why they were able in their circumstances to become creative artists. Here Stratton, an organist, teacher and critic based in Birmingham, became one of the earliest writers to question a long-held belief in biological difference as explanatory of female underachievement in music composition, instead positing that acculturation and lack of training was the root problem. Stratton was also important as a gatherer of first-hand biographical information from his Musical Association colleagues and many others of both sexes for his dictionary compiled with James D. Brown, *British Musical Biography* (Birmingham, 1897), a source that remains useful in relation to early members.

4. **A.J. Hipkins**, 'The Old Clavier or Keyboard Instruments: Their Use by Composers, and Technique', 7 June 1886; *PMA*, 12 (1885–86), 139–48. Hipkins was an internationally known expert on the piano and its precursors, and long a technician at Broadwood's; his understanding of pitch, tuning and historical keyboard construction permeated this lecture, which demonstrated how five early instruments, namely, an Italian sixteenth-century spinet, a late seventeenth-century English spinet, a Flemish double keyboard harpsichord of c. 1614, an English one of 1771 and a German clavichord built in the mid-eighteenth century, differed from each other and from the pianoforte.

Linking the historical development of composing for each instrument to its corresponding technique proved a revelation, even for scholars who knew the music but had never heard it on original instruments. The works played were by Byrd, Blow, Gibbons, Lully, Purcell, Handel, Scarlatti and J.S. Bach. Hipkins gave similar talks to other societies; this one remained in his memory for the support of Anton Rubinstein as his page-turner. An extensive profile of Hipkins in *Musical Times*, 39 (1898), 581–86, includes a portrait by Edith Hipkins of her father playing a double harpsichord.

5. **John Stainer**, 'A Fifteenth Century MS. Book of Vocal Music in the Bodleian Library, Oxford', 12 November 1895; *PMA*, 22 (1895–96), 1–22. This is only one of Stainer's seven papers for the Association between 1875 and 1900, but it proved to be his most important for a developing English musicology, and revelatory for knowledge of fifteenth-century secular song, above all by Guillaume Dufay. The lecture, chaired by Cummings, attracted sixty auditors and was well devised by Stainer to make a positive impact by his careful explanation of the unfamiliar sounds listeners would detect in the illustrations, including cadential open fifths, parallel fifths and the crossing of parts. He also drew on prior Continental scholarship to establish the manuscript's importance. In all he mentioned twenty-eight Dufay songs, including 'C'est bien raison' (see Fig. 10), and listed all the other composers (including Binchois), as well as describing the manuscript's notation, transcriptions made by his two assistants (his son J.F.R. Stainer and daughter Cecie Stainer), and something of the composers' known circumstances. Six Dufay songs were played by a small group of modern violas. From the discussion, it's clear that listeners grasped the huge stride Stainer had made in revealing new information; later the manuscript was understood to encompass some 245 hitherto unknown works, filling a large gap in music history. Parry was delighted and took the news as verifying his cherished 'process of evolution' in music, while Cummings declared the lecture 'of immense value to students and writers of musical history' (22). For more on the manuscript itself, Bodleian MS. Canon. Misc. 213, its provenance, history, contents and the significance of its location in Oxford, see David Fallows, ed., *Oxford, Bodleian Library MS. Canon. Misc. 213*, Late Medieval and Early Renaissance Music in Facsimile, ed. Margaret Bent and John Nádas, vol. 1 (Chicago and London: University of Chicago Press, 1995), reviewed by Iain Fenlon in *JRMA*, 122 (1997), 289–93; and Jeremy Dibble, *John Stainer: A Life in Music* (Woodbridge: Boydell Press, 2007), 257–60, who confirms that Stainer was first made aware of the Bodleian MSS catalogue by the Bodley's Librarian E.W.B. Nicholson in late summer 1894.

6. **Rosa Newmarch**, 'The Development of National Opera in Russia', 10 January 1900; *PMA*, 26 (1899–1900), 57–77. Russian culture was a timely subject in late nineteenth-century London; unfamiliar Russian works began to be heard in the capital's concerts and seen in good stage productions. Newmarch, a professional writer and journalist, widely travelled, wanted to place this music within wider cultural history and was anxious to communicate without

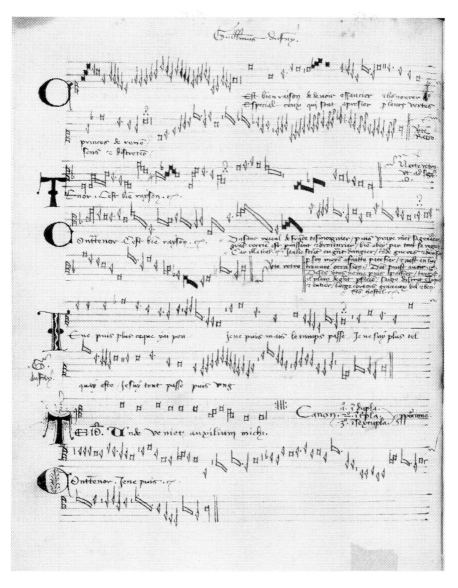

Figure 10. Guillaume Dufay, 'C'est bien raison de devoir essaucier', ballade for three voices, Bodleian Library MS. Canon. Misc. 213, fol. 55v.

jargon. The Musical Association gave her that opportunity. This paper became the first of five in a series that ran to 1905, published as separate articles in *PMA* 28, 29, 30 and 31; much of the text reappeared, often verbatim, in her book of 1914, *The Russian Opera* (London: Herbert Jenkins), where Newmarch credited the Association. Over the whole series, starting with Glinka in 1836 and running to Rimsky-Korsakov in 1899, she provided what she felt to be fresh and stimulating information, sourced to authorities she had met or studied with in Russia from 1897, notably Vladimir Stasov, who, admittedly, had helped advance the narrative of a coherent Russian 'nationalist school' thirty years earlier. Often called the 'Mighty Handful' in opposition to more elite, Western-facing composers such as Tchaikovsky, this invented image was in fact by 1900 old political dogma, not new; later Russianists considered it ill-founded and manipulative. But Newmarch used it for her real aim of offering a model for British emulation – a strong new identity for British composers within a wide international framework in the twentieth century, distinct from the domination of German music. See Philip Ross Bullock, *Rosa Newmarch and Russian Music in Nineteenth and Early Twentieth-Century England* (Farnham: Ashgate, 2009).

7. **Lucy E. Broadwood**, 'On the Collecting of English Folk-Song', 14 March 1905; *PMA*, 31 (1904–05), 89–109. By this date, Lucy Broadwood was well known as a past master in the art of folksong collecting. Careful to define her terms and the purpose of her work in trying to save a type of traditional ballad needing study, she delineated folksong from genteel English music as well as from pseudo-Scotch or pseudo-Irish music manufactured by the English. Limiting the material to her own experiences gave the lecture both authority and an original perspective. After surveying former practices, she explained the circumstances of each of her own collecting trips to ground her analysis. With two of her best vocal collaborators, James Campbell McInnes and Charles Lidgey, she performed several illustrations throughout the paper, which were admired especially for the singers' care with apt delivery. In discussion, W.H. Cummings, J.A. Fuller Maitland, T.L. Southgate and Rosa Newmarch joined in advocating the larger aims of folksong work, including a certain urgency to assist the movement ('a sort of race against time', according to Fuller Maitland). The paper's success led the Association to contact the Folk-Song Society directly. For more, including this lecture's impact on Percy Grainger, see Dorothy de Val, *In Search of Song: The Life and Times of Lucy Broadwood* (Farnham: Ashgate, 2011), which includes a photograph of Broadwood and McInnes at the piano.

8. **Frank Kidson**, 'The Vitality of Melody', 17 March 1908; *PMA*, 34 (1907–08), 81–99. Kidson was more experienced than Broadwood as a folksong collector, and distinctive also in his provincial working-class background, but both scholars were dedicated students of authentic song sources and knew each other's work. This lecture stands out for Kidson's technical discipline in looking only at tune, not anything about harmony or execution. His method was

to treat tunes as living organisms ('vital melody'), rather than past artefacts that were frozen, precious, in or out of favour by a period opinion – not composed tunes and definitely not accompanied or altered to suit a middle-class drawing-room taste; he believed that if a tune pleased at least two generations, it would survive. To focus listening, he had his examples played solo on the violin by an assistant; he then described political and national associations, words and changes in different versions as the tunes were passed on. Taking an instinctive observational approach, the paper was scholarly and honest in a way that differed from that of some other song collectors (notably Sabine Baring-Gould); it was also informed by Kidson's careful comparison of published sources to link and explain common tune factors across time and place. The chairman Fuller Maitland referred several times to 'this delightful paper'. Having first predicted there wouldn't be much discussion, though, he was wrong: the comment was considerable.

9. **Janet Dodge**, 'Lute Music of the XVIth and XVIIth Centuries', 19 May 1908; *PMA*, 34 (1907–08), 123–53. Janet Dodge's background and career remain something of a mystery but her expertise in the lute repertory of sixteenth- and seventeenth-century Europe is clear. This excellent article, together with her discussion of ornamentation signs in lute tablature, appearing in *SIMG* (vol. 9, spring 1908), suggest a mind of some sophistication. Here she presented a coherent summary of compositional schools by place, covering sources, contexts and styles for the better part of two centuries. Her six music illustrations were played on a piano rather than a lute, largely because few expert players or playable instruments were available. Some listeners regretted the fact, evidently expecting by 1908 that original-instrument playing technique would be a guide to tone and meaning. Dodge, who attended but did not read her lecture – T.L. Southgate assisted – stressed that her focus was on the music itself, not the instrument or its performance. Tablature as an unfamiliar notation raised as much interest as tone and playing tempo, but she insisted that her stress remained on the repertory. Decades later, Dodge's work would be acknowledged and built on by David Lumsden and others.

10. **George Bernard Shaw**, 'The Reminiscences of a Quinquagenarian', 6 December 1910; *PMA*, 37 (1910–11), 17–27. Shaw is perhaps surprising as a Musical Association speaker at this period: not only was he less active as a music critic than in the previous quarter-century, but he'd made his name partly on the back of mocking music academics as a negative force in British musical life. Still, he'd reported positively on Association meetings in the late 1870s and in 1892 when a topic interested him, such as Bach or Wagner, and his insights on performers, performance and wider culture were always valued. The main theme of his talk here, with acknowledged distance from those earlier days, was a sensible one of noting how time moves on: increased listening experience tempers what we once heard as outrageous. Unsurprising are the usual Shavian takedowns of favourite targets, from Parry, Stanford, and the lack of pragmatic theatrical skill in English composers, to preciousness in

academic prose about music; Elgar gets a predictable cheer. Underneath the apparent bonhomie and reflection, though, lurks a sense that Shaw doesn't quite know who the Association really is, what it does, or why deeper study of any music might be useful or interesting to anyone. His embedded reverse snobbery serves to remind modern readers why musicology in Britain had a long way to go before being accepted by both the public and cultural leaders.

11. **W.H. Frere**, 'Key-Relationship in Early Medieval Music', 20 June 1911; *PMA*, 37 (1910–11), 129–49. The Rev. Dr Frere had given this same paper very successfully a few weeks earlier at the IMG London Congress (31 May 1911), in whose eventual *Report* it would also be published (1912); thus appreciated by international scholars, it was eagerly awaited at the Association. Frere took the modern idea of key-relationship in tonal harmony and projected it backwards to show how five specific relations between pitches in a modern scale – those between the tonic and subdominant, between a major scale and its relative minor, between modes separated by a whole tone, or heard in the alternation of tonic and subtonic, or of tonic and mediant – found a constructive place in medieval music, with some of those patterns carrying forward to later art music. To demonstrate, he used thirteen music examples from a variety of sources and contexts, including plainsong (introit and antiphon), sequence, conductus, motet, carol and even English folksong. The paper's elegance and clarity captured Charles Maclean, in the chair, who spoke personally of Frere's 'finished manner' and skill in communicating: 'It is not very often that we have here words spoken with such full understanding, and put so easily and clearly' (146). To Maclean, Frere had built a convincing bridge between 'the old melodic world' and the early twentieth-century one.

12. **Mrs Maud Mann (Maud MacCarthy)**, 'Some Indian Conceptions of Music', 16 January 1912; *PMA*, 38 (1911–12), 41–65. This is a sophisticated paper, well presented, by an Irish violinist-turned-ethnographer of Indian music. After study and field work in India in 1907–09, MacCarthy gave lecture-recitals in London over the next two decades (marrying William Mann in 1911). Here she surveyed aspects of Indian classical music by first setting the scene, playing the *vînâ*, a South Indian plucked lute, in accompaniment to her own 'microtonal' singing at an imagined shrine of Sarasvati, the Hindu goddess of learning and the arts. Carefully preparing Western expectations (even making a Beethoven analogue), yet asserting that Western analysis would always render Indian music incomprehensible, she explored Indian principles including *râga* and *tâla*, or tone and time. Delivered authoritatively, the paper suggested that Western music had much to learn from Indian, a new idea in 1912. The paper was republished as a pamphlet by the Theosophical Publishing Society in 1913, revised with additional notes, a preface and acknowledgement of the Musical Association. For more on MacCarthy's work and influence, see Martin Clayton, 'Musical Renaissance and its Margins in England and India, 1874–1914', in *Music and Orientalism in the British Empire, 1780s to 1940s: Portrayal of the East*, ed. M. Clayton and B. Zon (Aldershot: Ashgate, 2007),

71–93; and Nalini Ghuman, *Resonances of the Raj: India in the English Musical Imagination* (Oxford University Press 2014), 11–52.

13. **W. Denis Browne**, 'Modern Harmonic Tendencies', 19 May 1914; *PMA*, 40 (1913–14), 139–56. A young composer, pianist and critic who'd studied at Cambridge, William Denis Browne had just given the London première of Alban Berg's Sonata, op. 1 (11 May 1914), when he delivered this paper. His playing skills must have been as impressive as the thought shown here. Unusually imaginative, the paper presents a convinced approach to contemporary uses of harmony; it touches on historical precedents, comparing present and past to defuse criticism of modern composers for their music's presumed 'ugliness'. Among other examples, Browne refers directly to recent London performances of Schoenberg's music, championing it in a way that provides meaningful, instructive criticism rather than overt promotion. Unluckily, the discussion was led by an old-school chairman, W.H. Cummings, who, though polite, was genuinely uncomprehending at Browne's material and point of view, a circumstance that now seems to place the young man all the more in a fresh light. Later readers found it especially poignant that the speaker was killed in the Gallipoli campaign little more than a year after the paper. He had helped E.J. Dent at Cambridge and learned from him, and was a close friend of Rupert Brooke's.

14. **Edmund H. Fellowes**, 'John Wilbye', 16 February 1915; *PMA*, 41 (1914–15), 55–86. Fellowes was a minor canon at St George's, Windsor, and had been working on English madrigal composers for only three years when he presented this paper, having recently published his first volumes in *The English Madrigal School* (Stainer & Bell, 1913–24). Many more volumes would follow as well as performances, and he quickly became the leading authority on English music from c. 1545 to 1645, spearheading new scholarship through revived interest in Tudor music. Although not a novel kind of study, Fellowes's life-and-works approach here offered fresh biographical information, firmly sourced, as a context for Wilbye's two books of sixty-four madrigals (of 1598 and 1609), 'scarcely any of which fall below the very highest standard of excellence' (55). After detailing how he discovered the composer's will, death date, property and family relations, connections in Suffolk and Norfolk and service to patrons, Fellowes summarized the madrigal form and its original part-book presentation, without barring, to show how previous inaccurate transcriptions had caused misunderstanding. A string quintet played two illustrations, and a six-voice ensemble sang a further selection. R.R. Terry gave his thanks for a 'Paper so excellent, and so bristling with points' (84). Fellowes's next paper, a year later, would be on Thomas Weelkes.

15. **Edward J. Dent**, 'The Laudi Spirituali in the XVIth and XVIIth Centuries', 20 March 1917; *PMA*, 43 (1916–17), 63–95. This was the third of Dent's seven papers to the Association between 1904 and 1945, following studies of Alessandro Scarlatti and Leonardo Leo. It extended his focus on Italian Baroque music,

almost unique among British scholars at the time, by tracing the words, music and cultural context of *laudi* collections – hymns and devotional songs originally compiled for a religious confraternity in fourteenth-century Florence that later fed into the oratorio in late sixteenth-century Rome. By surveying successive types of *laudi* themselves, he showed how these fervent songs in the vernacular, meant to attract and keep ordinary people coming to church, were suffused with well-known secular tunes and other folk or dance elements borrowed from popular music, some potentially from early opera. Crediting authorities including Domenico Alaleona, he suggested how a *lauda* text could convert the 'fountain of love' into the fountain of virtue, or a 'tooral-looral-loo' refrain in an English folksong could be replaced by 'Dolce Giesù'. The conclusion was obvious: despite any pure separation of sacred from secular claimed for religious music by Church fathers, it is highly probable that a mixing of secular tunes with sacred words went back to the earliest Christians in Rome. In discussion, Hubert Parry acknowledged 'the vast amount of enlightenment' the paper had given, helping to unravel the mysteries and development of music. 'In this matter we know we can trust Mr. Dent, and he has proved it, not for the first time, in tracing out the things there are to know about the *Laudi Spirituali*. […] The subject really radiates suggestively in all directions' (93).

16. **C.H. Clutsam**, 'Classicism and False Values', 16 April 1918; *PMA*, 44 (1917–18), 127–52. A London-based Australian pianist, accompanist, composer and music critic (*Observer*), Clutsam wrote this challenging paper to express his irritation with the current, too-prevalent veneration of Classical composers he saw as hindering the progress and appreciation of modern ones. He was not opposed to Classical music itself, or any music, but argued simply for less public attention towards Haydn, Mozart and Beethoven in particular, so that more space and time could be given to living composers adopting new methods and styles in the new century. The paper was read in Clutsam's absence by Edwin Evans, who broadly supported his views as they touched on taste, English criticism, concert and operatic life, modern audiences and music education. Forthright and stimulating, the paper evoked unusually extensive comment from seven commentators – Arthur Fox, H.H. Statham, Geoffrey Shaw, E.J. Dent, R.R. Terry, Parry (in the chair) and Evans – so much in fact that discussion almost outweighed the paper in length. Clutsam had hit on an issue that was to raise many residual thoughts about music's direction after the war, and about the nature of progress. As Evans reaffirmed, Clutsam had hoped to offer ways ahead for 'the new in modern music as against an indiscriminate worship of the classics' (151).

17. **S. Townsend Warner**, 'The Point of Perfection in XVI Century Notation', 11 February 1919; *PMA*, 45 (1918–19), 53–74. An imaginative piece of writing in itself, this is an early and thoughtful treatment of the meanings behind mensural notation in sixteenth-century English music. Sylvia Townsend Warner, a young, highly skilled and productive member of the Tudor Church Music editorial committee, explained her solutions when transcribing the Ludford

MS in the BM, outlining the different rhythmic functions of the small dot or stroke above affected notes in the manuscript. She would later emerge as preeminent over all the committee during that twelve-year project, 1917–29, including Richard Terry, who taught her how to read early notation, and Percy Buck, who chaired this paper and more or less admitted that Warner already understood more than he did (though inexplicably he used a back-handed compliment to foreclose any discussion). The lecture was reported in detail in the *Musical Times* for April 1919, reiterating Warner's conclusion about the freedom and subtlety of rhythm in this music. For further background, see Richard Searle, 'Sylvia Townsend Warner and *Tudor Church Music*', *Journal of the Sylvia Townsend Warner Society*, 12 (2011), 69–88.

18. **W. Barclay Squire**, 'Musical Libraries and Catalogues', 8 April 1919; *PMA*, 45 (1918–19), 97–111. Squire organized his discussion by types of collection – 'Great Public Libraries', such as the BM; and 'Smaller Libraries', both 'free' ones that lend books to the public (e.g. Birmingham and Manchester) and those connected to institutions including cathedrals and colleges. He revealed much about the historical reasons for peculiarities in the BM's operation, such as why there was never a music department (as in Berlin or Washington), so that printed music belonged to the Department of Printed Books and manuscript music formed part of the Department of Manuscripts: in neither case, until Squire's time, was there any specialist staff devoted to music, a 'survival of the old-fashioned view that music was a mere pastime' and 'not to be encouraged' (98). In describing the content and purpose of the two collections, he further explained how music entered or 'drifted into' them and how well, or not, their curators cared for it. His purpose was to offer possible remedies for how to identify and catalogue the most important music items in UK collections, comparing exemplars in pre-war Germany by Robert Eitner, and more recently in Italy by the Associazione dei Musicologi Italiani. Squire's argument led directly to the idea that the Association should take up this work. 'The foundations of Musicology are the documents, manuscripts or printed music of past times. The first step in making them accessible is that it should be known where they are to be found, and this first step consists in cataloguing – the spade-work of research' (106). E.H. Fellowes and Richard Terry supported the project, and a firm proposal was made two years later to the Carnegie Trust, but rejected.

19. **Charles van den Borren**, 'The Genius of Dunstable', 15 March 1921; *PMA*, 47 (1920–21), 79–92. Translated by William Barclay Squire and read by him, this paper began to answer Stainer's call in his 1895 article for more detailed work on Dufay as a successor to Dunstable. It remains important not only for Van den Borren's patient, scholarly method but for signalling the virtues of Dunstable and his compositions before most Britons would have understood their own early culture or known much about Dunstable's music, let alone heard any. Some documentary points had already been contributed by Charles Maclean in *SIMG* (1910), not mentioned here; much more would be done later on Dunstable's, or more correctly Dunstaple's, music by Manfred

Bukofzer, Brian Trowell and especially Margaret Bent. Although some of Van den Borren's information has long been superseded by these scholars' discoveries, the article has the merit of showing a logical and systematic way of discussing the music as well as placing an early English composer in his social and historical context. Such an approach became a model for Van den Borren's later students and for the development of English musicology generally, not least through the Belgian's mentoring of Robert Thurston Dart. The paper was illustrated by vocal examples sung by R.R. Terry's small ensemble.

20. **Gustav Holst**, 'The Tercentenary of Byrd and Weelkes', 9 January 1923; *PMA*, 49 (1922–23), 29–37. Laced with idiosyncratic observations, this paper turned on the idea that English music has had a tendency to flare up and then disappear. From Dunstable, Holst moved to the Tudor composers, hailing ever more recent discoveries from Wilbye to Morley, Weelkes, Tomkins and Ward (crediting Fellowes for much), and most recently the first volume of Tudor Church Music to show how quickly things were moving forward. After affirming the usual trope about England's slowness to appreciate her own music, then rediscovering it with great surprise and pleasure, Holst offered a set of comparisons including John Bull with Debussy in using the whole-tone scale, and other pairings in programme music, solo song and choral music, to suggest how the English came first in making great 'discoveries'. Holst elevated Weelkes above Byrd as 'the real musical embodiment of the English character in his fantastic unexpectedness'. Alighting on unexpectedness, the speaker then highlighted what modern musicians were doing to perform older English music. With a small group of singers from Morley College, described as 'ordinary people' who would present five pieces by Byrd and Weelkes, he asserted that 'England – for the first time – is really learning her own music.' The chairman, Alan Gray, responded that in the previous fifty years or so, 'I doubt if a more pleasant – there probably have been many more profound – I doubt if a more pleasant lecture has ever been delivered before the Musical Association' (35).

3

Fresh Challenges, 1924–1944

At the start of the Musical Association's fiftieth session on 4 November 1923, its president Sir Hugh Allen (1921–24), the organist and choral conductor, expressed his hope for 'a happy and fruitful' time ahead, both in papers yet to be presented and in membership growth. He admitted that although past papers had often been 'very remarkable', the Association was still 'nothing like so well known as it should be', as shown by its small membership. Enlarging the group and perhaps altering 'our manner of doing things' would be priorities for consideration over the next year. He was probably expressing Percy Baker's secretarial view and revealing his own lack of focus, noting vaguely that improvements were needed if the group were to 'keep pace with the times'. All members were invited to a discussion at the next meeting.[1] Unstated but understood was that a continual flow of new members and ideas was essential for paying the bills and stimulating research. In the lingering absence of university training programmes and research-orientated jobs or other incentives for students and professional musicians, that flow had to come from the efforts of Musical Association members themselves. As things turned out, the Council indeed deliberated in 1924 and beyond, but to little effect: small size emerged as a symptom rather than an underlying cause of difficulty. Shortly after a chirpy President Allen stepped down and Baker retired, member numbers fell slowly. Despite the fillip of some stellar new recruits between the late 1920s and the early 40s, with impressive papers and discussions by members and visitors alike, the Council could only vacillate between complacency and hand-wringing: total membership continued to fall. Even with some upward fluctuation, by 1943 it was down to 185 – a near 25 per cent drop from the high of 244 in 1924, not all of that owing to another world war.

Finding consistently good papers, maintaining publication standards and attracting listeners of skill and interest were familiar challenges. Fresh issues too arose in this period, or at least became harder to ignore. What came out of the Association's responses to these by the mid-1940s at last began to make a difference, largely through the presidential nudges and negotiations of Edward J. Dent (1928–35), Percy Buck (1935–38) and E.H. Fellowes (1942–47). Together these moves prepared the ground for what would become a post-war turnaround in public recognition of British music scholars and scholarship. Taking

---

[1] Hugh Allen, 'The Fiftieth Session', *PMA*, 50 (1923–24), p. xii; see also Percy Baker's 'Report' of the fiftieth session in *PMA*, 51 (1924–25), pp. viii–xi. No conclusions from the discussion meeting were published.

the whole twenty-year period 1924–44 as one, I will look first at the peculiar mix of challenges affecting the Association around this time, and then at laudable responses through three case studies: E.J. Dent's interactions with the Association; the arrival of European émigrés from 1932 and the Association's Research Committee of 1938; and the wartime presidencies of Francis Galpin and E.H. Fellowes.

🎵 A Culture of Complacency?

Compared with the Association's first fifty years with its solid organization and scholarly achievements, this briefer period seems in some ways a desultory one, with less drive, more perfunctoriness and more frequent turnover in leadership – six presidents in twenty years as against, formerly, six presidents in fifty years (albeit one, Hubert Parry, who returned to the role after a health alert: 1901–08, then 1915–18). One early sign of malaise was Hugh Allen's eagerness to shed his president's mantle in favour of more exciting developments at the RCM, where he was Director, and to find a quick replacement. Assuming that from autumn 1924 the Association had to have a senior figure as leader regardless of any research interest or commitment, Allen approached the new Professor of Music at Cambridge, Charles Wood, pressing him into the job (1924–26) while reassuring the Council – astonishingly, it seems now – that Wood would 'at any rate join', which he did.[2] Hardly a ringing endorsement of Allen's judgement of the situation, this episode nevertheless points to residual ambiguities around what the Association's work should be or try to achieve, and indeed around the perceived value of research in the larger nexus of British music education, training and performance. Allen himself is said to have once resigned the emoluments of a New College Oxford fellowship 'in order to avoid having to undertake research'.[3] He was never really interested.

For his part, Wood, a celebrated composition teacher, was already suffering ill health at fifty-eight when he accepted the Association's presidency; though he served as an able chair at several meetings, he died in July 1926, less than two years into the post. In turn, the Council moved swiftly to replace him with the first vice-president on their list, Joseph Cox Bridge (Frederick Bridge's younger brother), organist and former professor at Durham University, a long-time Association member, skilled antiquarian and reliable paper-giver.

---

[2] Council minutes, 9 Oct 1924 (BL Add. MS 71014, fol. 35).

[3] Brian Trowell, 'Gerald Ernest Heal Abraham, 1904–1988', *Proceedings of the British Academy*, 111 (2001), 339–93 at 369, citing Abraham's memoir of Jack Westrup by way of distinguishing the change in attitude to research between Allen and Westrup, successive holders of the Heather Chair of Music at Oxford. According to the Allen Papers in New College Archives, the work Allen was asked by Warden William Spooner in 1918 to complete for his fellowship, on 'Musical colour', was related to his paper 'Some Considerations of the Effect of Orchestral Colour upon Design and Texture in Musical Composition', *PMA*, 35 (1908–09), 109–21. Reading it suggests why his decision to abandon research was the right one.

At seventy-three and retired to London, he too was able to sustain the president's role for only two years; he asked to step down in July 1928 and died the following year. Unluckily, all this took place as Percy Baker began to lose steam. Formerly so full of energy, ideas and devotion to expanding the Musical Association's influence beyond university and conservatory, he declined in health quickly from mid-1930 and was gone before Christmas. After forty years of sterling service, this was a harder blow than losing two presidents.[4] J.B. Trend, the Hispanist and Council member, filled Baker's shoes on a temporary basis – a bright idea by the succeeding president Edward J. Dent (1928–35) – but the Annual Dinner was cancelled in the secretary's memory. The Association's 'offices' moved formally from Baker's home to that of the new secretary from January 1931, Rupert Erlebach (1894–1978), an aspiring composer-scholar and librarian at the RCM. As if to mark the change from old times to new, January 1931 also saw the first report of a Council member giving attendance apologies by 'telephone message', novel enough at the time to be minuted.[5]

Rapid shifts in officer personnel presented their own challenges to momentum and collective memory about how things were done in the organization. At the same time, that phenomenon can be seen against the backdrop of broader post-1918 generational change in which new professionalizing processes were already replacing class markers as signs of merit in many fields; new energy and determination on behalf of music scholarship might well have been expected. Indeed all manner of music-making and performance reasserted itself after the Great War, as if the war to end all wars had been only a minor blip; rapid technological development through recording, public broadcasting and new international travel routes only amplified the possibilities for more and better cultural communication. Granted that British musicology was slower than music composition and performance to come into its own, and slower locally than in some other European contexts where universities positively welcomed its practice and teaching, still the combined societal and economic climate in the UK seems to have placed a further drag on any significant changes in the way university music study was organized. In trying to re-establish 'normality' after the war, guard against too much change for its own sake, recover from loss and forestall economic slide – the country's financial state remained poor into the late 1920s and early 30s – Musical Association leaders felt that preserving the status quo was a safer course. To what extent their inward conservatism was always deliberate is unclear; it seems to have stemmed mostly from a mix of inertia, inexperience (particularly Erlebach's) and doubt about new directions. At least the door was open for anyone with vigour and specific suggestions who could step in with confidence. As events would show, reaching out strategically to new voices and models, at home and from abroad, would offer the best chances of improvement.

---

[4] See his obituary in *The Times* (15 Dec 1930), repr. as 'Mr. J.P. Baker', *PMA*, 57 (1930–31), p. xxiv.

[5] Council minutes, 8 Jan 1931 (BL Add. MS 71014, fol. 106). The phone caller was Cyril Rootham.

A closer look at the Association's accumulating problems will give some perspective. For one thing, the increasing number of specialized musical journals welcoming serious, even learned content, an aspect of the lively publishing landscape in early twentieth-century Britain, cut across the Association's efforts to maintain a clear sense of how its papers should differ from the discourse in other journals. While commercial competition was irrelevant – the Association's annual *Proceedings* was a membership organ – the tone and distinctiveness of *PMA* content and thus its issuing body's reputation now fell under closer scrutiny, occasionally coming up short. On the one hand, general observers and both internal and external critics perceived the Association as boring, stuffy and unapproachable; on the other, a few internal critics, those hoping to extend scholarly rigour, found that too many Association papers were lightweight, pretentious and 'journalistic'. Both angles were valid, even predictable given the range of member backgrounds and the variety of topics and treatments typically characterizing Association meetings. What now became pressing was how long that variety should persist in the face of better, more focused work elsewhere, whether in musicological writing abroad or in other English journals. Several of the new periodicals cultivated music interests very close to those of Association members and were indeed supplied and read by them, including the *Musical Antiquary* (1909–13, publishing an early Dent article), founded by Godfrey Arkwright at Oxford; the *Chesterian* (1915–61) issued by the London music publisher J. & W. Chester to cover modern international composition; *Music & Letters* (*ML*, 1920–), set up by A.H. Fox Strangways with a literary emphasis partly in opposition to the style of *Proceedings*;[6] *Gramophone* (1923–), established by the Scottish author Compton Mackenzie to assist recording enthusiasts and classical music collectors;[7] and the *Journal of the English Folk Dance and Song Society* (amalgamated in 1932 from two earlier titles of the separate dance and song bodies), edited by Frank Howes. Many of those founders or editors and their contributors, not least Edwin Evans, D.F. Tovey, George Dyson, Lucy Broadwood and H.C. Colles, participated at one time or another in the Musical Association and published valuable research in its *Proceedings*. A parallel medievalists' group, the Plainsong and Mediaeval Music Society founded in 1888, focused on liturgical chant and published editions rather than a journal, but it too shared some influential members with the Musical Association. All the while, older general music titles of repute – the *Musical Times*, *Musical Standard*, *Monthly Musical Record* and so on – continued to publish shorter articles of historiographical value.

In this climate, crossover by Association members was not only inevitable but healthy, while a proliferation of serious music outlets at slightly differing levels of sophistication certainly did no harm to the spread of wider public

---

[6] Sarah Collins, 'The Foundation of *Music & Letters*', *ML*, 100 (2019), 185–91.
[7] See Compton Mackenzie, 'The Gramophone: Its Past, its Present, its Future', *PMA*, 51 (1924–25), 97–119, a summary of the instrument's technological development, recorded repertory and social implications.

interest in music, all to the good.[8] The real issue was how such an abundant mix of specialization here, reportage there, may have paradoxically encouraged the Council to accept or invite journalistic talks or 'lecturettes', rather than to seek out or encourage research-based presentations positing new findings. Even assuming that an additional factor was the need to fill meeting dates after a shortage of offered papers, the long-term effect was still one of miscellany and diffuseness, often a failure to connect with previous work or to go deeper – signs of a lack of embedded research culture and, more to the point, the lack of a pipeline of younger people who might have undertaken serious music research with supervision.

From another angle, the Association's practical arrangements presented problems, too. From 1919, the number of paper meetings had necessarily been reduced to six per session to cut costs (avoiding a subscription rise that year), which pertained up to 1940; wartime conditions then caused a reduction to only four meetings a year, prolonging a trend away from the frequent seminar-style exchanges that had been so fruitful in earlier days. Meanwhile signs of individual lethargy or unease increased from the mid-1930s, including poor attendance at Council meetings (some twelve or thirteen vice-presidents regularly did not attend); a failure to follow up defaulting members, compounded by a reluctance to advertise or send flyers to other societies and the press; and a highlighting of the group's contingent status by repeated requests from an institutional host to move the Association's books and papers out of a borrowed London space (from Novello's premises in 1925 to the secretary's home, thence to the RCM in 1933, then to the RAM in 1943).

This last challenge, a kind of perpetual physical displacement, was undoubtedly inconvenient. But it was trivial compared with the existential crisis facing many central European music scholars under racial and political persecution in their own countries. Distressed but hopeful, many of them fled Europe and arrived in the UK as refugees, holding in their hands the seeds of growth and a much-needed deepening for British musicology. The chance to welcome them put British humanistic values into practice, posing another set of real-time challenges, diplomatic, economic and personal, not all straightforward. As music-loving individuals with something to give, the émigrés, for their part, happened to come at an opportune moment for the Musical Association. The stage was set for real change.

❧ E.J. Dent and the Musical Association

Edward Joseph Dent (1876–1957) is one of three Musical Association presidents to have become the subject of a modern documentary biography – significantly, the only one not also a composer; a large volume devoted to his life by Karen Arrandale now complements major books on Sir John Stainer and

---

[8] Akin to the cultivation of multiple reading audiences for serious history writing in the 1870s and 80s. See Chapter 1, pp. 28–29.

Sir C. Hubert H. Parry by Jeremy Dibble.[9] Of course none of these three subjects owes his cultural importance to a stint as Association president, so it's logical that a relatively small learned society would figure only briefly in their stories, especially when compared with the more weighty contexts of Anglican church music and Oxford University for Stainer, the RCM and Oxford for Parry, or Cambridge University, opera and internationalism for Dent. Stainer's pivotal role in the early Association and his scholarship, well known in his lifetime, receive due coverage in his biography, while Parry's music-historical interests are shown to pervade parts of his. By contrast, Dent's work through the Association is barely explored in Arrandale's expansive study. This is likewise understandable because his impact there seems less obvious than in other areas of his work, traceable neither in his letters and diaries nor in earlier biographical accounts, those by Philip Radcliffe, Winton Dean and Philip Brett, for instance.[10] Instead, evidence of Dent's activity in the Association lurks piecemeal across the group's minute books, correspondence and publications, and in publications of the IMG (1899–1914) and its reincarnation from 1927 as the International Society for Musical Research (ISMR; identical with the Internationale Gesellschaft für Musikwissenschaft, IGMw; also Société Internationale de Musicologie, SIM). Many traces lie under the radar, so to speak, or seem sufficiently linked within wider networks to be relegated as less important.

In particular, Dent's Musical Association activity has to be disentangled from his simultaneous work for two parallel international groups that have drawn far more attention for involving the fraught intersection of modern musical styles with early twentieth-century European politics, especially its ideological and geopolitical tensions. These are the new-music, annual-festival-orientated International Society for Contemporary Music (ISCM), founded in

---

[9] Jeremy Dibble, *John Stainer: A Life in Music* (Woodbridge: Boydell Press, 2007); Jeremy Dibble, *C. Hubert H. Parry: His Life and Music* (Oxford: Clarendon Press, 1992); and Karen Arrandale, *Edward J. Dent: A Life of Words and Music* (Woodbridge: Boydell Press, 2023). Dibble further explored Parry's intellectual interests in 'Parry as Historiographer', in *Nineteenth-Century British Music Studies*, vol. 1, ed. Bennett Zon (Aldershot: Ashgate, 1999), 37–51.

[10] Philip Radcliffe, 'Edward Joseph Dent, 1876–1957', *Proceedings of the British Academy*, 62 (1976), 411–18, notes only that Dent read a paper to the Musical Association in 1935. Winton Dean, 'Edward J. Dent: A Centenary Tribute', *ML*, 57 (1976), 353–61, stresses his international standing as a musicologist but never mentions any Association connection. Philip Brett, 'Musicology and Sexuality: The Example of Edward J. Dent', in *Queer Episodes in Music and Modern Identity*, ed. Sophie Fuller and Lloyd Whitesell (Urbana: Univ. of Illinois Press, 2002), 177–88, similarly never mentions the Association, presenting Dent's characteristically 'antiparochial', 'counterdisciplinary' and 'oppositional' strategies as signs of his homosexual self-fashioning in the (new) field of musicology. A recognition that the Association itself was working against the grain in British culture at this period, encouraging Dent, led by him, and equally eschewing a more mainstream form of European (German) and hence American musicology, was not yet part of the historical placing.

Salzburg in 1922 with headquarters in London; and the aforementioned research-orientated International Society for Musical Research, or ISMR (also known contemporaneously as IGMw or SIM), founded at Basel in 1927, linked directly to the Musical Association and known from 1949 as the International Musicological Society (IMS). Both organizations were set up as federated bodies of national sections; their officers and chairs in turn represented local or national societies, while private individuals and institutions could also subscribe. Occasionally the two groups' festivals and paper-reading congresses were planned to coincide in the same city, such as Liège in 1930 and Barcelona in 1936. But in activity and administration they were separate, very different entities, linked only by some common members and the broad aim of re-establishing creative and scholarly interchanges disrupted by the Great War; in this way, it was hoped, music and its study might help facilitate new international understanding alongside the more formalized systems of the League of Nations (founded in 1920).[11]

In both of these music groups Dent stood tall for years as the leading English figure, indeed the active president of both while also serving as a Musical Association Council member, vice-president and then president, thus achieving an unprecedented degree of visibility and elected responsibility among British and European composers and music scholars: in 1932–35 he was president of all three organizations at once. His practice of musical diplomacy through a clear sense of calm and fairness, great linguistic skill, personal charm and explicit avoidance of political controversy enabled musicians of all factions to trust him, at least until more overt Bolshevist- or Nazi-related confrontations occurred in Prague 1935 (ISCM) and Barcelona 1936 (ISCM and ISMR).[12] At the ISCM's founding in Salzburg in 1922, Dent had been seen as knowledgeable and well connected, tactful and usefully disinterested for not being an active composer himself, while London was perceived as a

---

[11] For the founding of the ISCM, a 'deliberately internationalist musical equivalent of the political initiative behind the League of Nations', see Annegret Fauser, 'The Scholar behind the Medal: Edward J. Dent (1876–1957) and the Politics of Music History', *JRMA*, 139 (2014), 235–60, esp. 238–39; the organization's founding was spearheaded by Rudolph Reti and Egon Wellesz with Dent. By contrast, the ISMR had the benefit of a prior history connecting European, British and North American music scholars through the IMG (1899–1915), in which many people involved in the ISMR from 1927, like Dent, had already been active.

[12] On the Prague and Barcelona confrontations, see Fauser, 'The Scholar behind the Medal'; Anne C. Shreffler, 'The International Society for Contemporary Music and its Political Context (Prague, 1935)', in *Music and International History in the Twentieth Century*, ed. Jessica C.E. Gienow-Hecht (New York: Berghahn, 2015), 58–92; and Giles Masters, 'Performing Internationalism: The ISCM as a "Musical League of Nations"', *JRMA*, 147 (2022), 560–71. Shreffler in particular describes the shift in 1935 from a perception of the ISCM as apolitical to one of being a haven of freedom in opposition to Nazism and cultural Bolshevism. For Barcelona, see further below, pp. 113–15.

world musical capital with an 'organizing faculty' not found elsewhere.[13] At the ISMR's founding in Basel in late September 1927, although not one of the original scholarly notables invited by Guido Adler and Wilhelm Merian to determine the new body's structure, Dent contributed forcefully to the main public meeting and the founding statutes. As a serving Musical Association Council member just then moving up to become a vice-president, he'd already gained his Council's full agreement to represent them at this meeting; they asked him to express sympathy with the new organization but not to commit to a periodical predominantly in one language, a clear reference to those unwelcome German efforts twenty-five years earlier to dominate *SIMG*.[14]

He took the hint and went further. As Annegret Fauser has shown, it was precisely Dent who insisted at Basel that the scholarly activity of smaller nations – all of them – be safeguarded against any dominance by what was widely perceived as 'the particular hegemony of Germany'.[15] Dent's demand for perfect equality didn't prevail, since the founding document ultimately named Germany, France, England and Italy as the four nations at the forefront of musicological research, to be represented in the ISMR Directorium with three of them in the Bureau.[16] Yet it was this very stipulation that also opened one of three founding vice-presidential positions to Dent, his quick election at Basel allowing him to become ISMR president within a few years, and thence host of the organization's 1933 Congress in Cambridge. All the while he kept the Musical Association updated and involved as an ISMR corporate member at the annual 'Benefactor' level of 40 Swiss francs.[17] For present purposes, it's important to stress that just as Dent officially represented the (more venerable) Association in all ISMR/IMS dealings, so the Association supplied the taproot of his ultimate authority there; he acted on the Association's behalf, not his own.

---

[13] Edwin Evans, 'The Salzburg Festival', *MT*, 63 (1922), 628–31. Evans became chairman of the British section, and succeeded Dent as ISCM president in 1939.

[14] Council minutes, 27 Sept 1927 (BL Add. MS 71014, fol. 67r–v). The main meeting at Basel was held on 29–30 September. The ISMR statutes committed to using German, English, French, Italian and Latin in its publications. For the earlier episode, including Maclean's insistence on a fairer language spread in IMG publications, see Chapter 2 above, pp. 54–55. *SIMG* was effectively the predecessor of *Acta musicologica*.

[15] Annegret Fauser, 'Edward J. Dent (1932–49)', in *The History of the IMS (1927–2017)*, ed. Dorothea Baumann and Dinko Fabris (Basel: Bärenreiter, 2017), 45–49 at 45–46.

[16] Ibid., 46, quoting 'Die Gründung der Internationalen Gesellschaft für Musikwissenschaft', *Mitteilungen der Internationalen Gesellschaft für Musikwissenschaft/ Bulletin de la Société Internationale de Musicologie*, 1 (1928), 1–9 at 3.

[17] Council minutes, 8 Nov 1927 (BL Add. MS 71014, fol. 69r–v). A year earlier, in November 1926, W.B. Squire had suggested a possible affiliation with the 'Union Musicologique'. The Association asked their member Herbert Antcliffe, resident in The Hague, to request more information from D.F. Scheurleer, the instigator, but Scheurleer died in early 1927 only a few weeks after Squire, so the matter rested until later that year. For more on the Société Union Musicologique, initially formed in 1921 of scholars from non-combatant countries, see Kirnbauer, 'A "Prelude" to the IMS', 11–19.

In light of that deep connection, it makes sense to look more closely at Dent's interactions within the Musical Association – what he drew from the group that might have shaped his research and philosophy, and what he gave back as a leader. This body was, after all, the main training ground for incipient British musicologists from the 1870s to the 1940s. Dent had begun as a self-starter like everyone else, with little understanding of what music research was meant to achieve, or how to form relevant questions or answer them.[18] But from 1900, once immersed in unfamiliar source material, Italian libraries and his own genuine curiosity about early opera, notably Alessandro Scarlatti's, he was hooked. He joined both the Association and the IMG in November 1901 and remained an active member of both for more than half a century.[19] Naturally he heard other people's papers at Association meetings, delivered his own – seven all together, between 1904 and 1945 – and chaired even more, often raising or replying to useful discussion points. He also gave papers in Europe, cultivated myriad contacts (musical and musicological), and by the autumn of 1923 found himself elected an Ordinary Member of Council while based in London as a writer and critic. Already by that date, besides his earlier teaching and work in opera production, he'd published two papers on Scarlatti – one in *SIMG*, one in the *Proceedings* – and a book on the composer; three more papers in *SIMG* on related topics, and two in *Proceedings*, on Leonardo Leo and on the *laudi spirituali*; and further, a Festschrift chapter, a valuable book on Mozart's operas (still useful), and articles in *Musical Antiquary*, *Musical Quarterly* and *ML*: 'productive' would be a fair description. Within another four years, in mid-1927 just after his first year back at Cambridge as Professor (following Charles Wood), he was elected a vice-president of the Association, and in the following year 1928, after J.C. Bridge's departure, president.

Barely fifty-two years old (youngish by recent Association standards), Dent was now a seasoned practitioner of an emergent kind of British musicology blending archival, historical, literary and interpretative work into a coherent and elegant whole on the page – all traits reflecting his breadth of practical experience and commitment to a common-sense application of research, rather than to a more clinical, theoretical or systematized form of German *Musikwissenschaft* (though he knew what that entailed too). Always keen to call this activity in Britain 'musical research' rather than 'musicology' and to delineate for Europeans and Americans the peculiar social and economic circumstances of music study in Britain, explaining conservatory training

---

[18] It was C.V. Stanford, his former composition instructor at Cambridge and a vice-president of the Association, who in summer 1900 first suggested to Dent he might try to find out about Leonardo Leo and other 'lesser Italian composers' as a possible dissertation topic for his fellowship application. Three decades later, in 'Music and Musical Research', 5, Dent recalled how little research training he'd had – and how little was still readily available in 1931 (see Arrandale, *Edward J. Dent*, 69–70).

[19] Dent was elected a member on 12 November 1901 (BL Add. MS 71012, fol. 112); his referees were Dr Maclean and Percy Baker. His parallel membership in the IMG was indicated with an asterisk by his name in the published members' list for 1901–02.

versus university education while stressing their joint, overriding emphasis on music as an art, Dent claimed something distinctive for British research that saw musical performance, the training of the imagination and wider cultural understanding as its desired ends.[20] In effect he asserted a logical, pragmatic basis for the discipline as he wanted to practise it.

But was he completely unique in this approach, the sole paragon of British excellence in an otherwise sluggish music-academic environment? That view grew among his adherents because Dent was indeed an international luminary, prominent in several roles and widely admired as a university teacher. A slightly wider view might allow that his intellectual success drew at least partly on engagement with a community of other scholars through the Musical Association, with its opportunities to hear, discuss, read and reflect on ideas presented in a range of papers. Many of Dent's methods and comparative strategies, for example, were neither pioneered by nor exclusive to him. Tracking a single genre through a composer's output, turning up new or unfamiliar works or tracing a genre's history in the output of diverse composers across a long time period; explaining the co-existence, even intermingling, of sacred and secular elements in traditional vocal music; interpreting the critical debate around old versus new music in modern performance culture; and exploring William Byrd's secular works as a spur to understanding social context, technique and aesthetic value in English music: all these themes resonate broadly with parallels in Association papers Dent would have known by other scholars, though he often followed a trail further than most, in an imaginative way that was unique to him. Among those other Association-related scholars were John Stainer (on fifteenth-century secular song), Frank Kidson (English folksong), Walter Frere (early medieval music), G.H. Clutsam (Classical versus contemporary works), James E. Matthew and William Barclay Squire (European libraries, catalogues), Squire and Gustav Holst (Byrd, Weelkes), Charles van den Borren (English madrigals, including songs by Byrd) and E.H. Fellowes (Dowland).[21] Moreover, Dent was not the first British scholar to apply his findings towards a useful outcome for wider society, a founding

---

[20] Dent articulated his position over a twenty-year period, developing his sense of the purposes of musical research when writing for different readerships: 'Music in University Education', *MQ*, 3 (1917), 605–19; 'The Scientific Study of Music in England' and 'Music and Musical Research', both in *Acta musicologica*; and 'The Historical Approach to Music'. The last, his lecture in September 1936 on receiving the first honorary Doctor of Music degree conferred by Harvard University, addressed musicology head-on in *MQ*, in the nation where that new discipline was beginning to make strides. While affirming the many good reasons for conducting research, he stuck to his guns on the prime aim of seeking an emotional artistic experience, studying the past 'for the intensifying and the development of the creative imagination' (17).

[21] Squire's work on Byrd first appeared in the Appendix to *Grove 1* (1889), and his exploration of 'Musical Libraries' in *Grove 2* (1906). Van den Borren, proposed as an Honorary Foreign Member by Squire, had been elected in February 1921 (Council minutes, 15 Feb 1921, BL Add. MS 71013, fols. 184v–185), five years before he gave his paper on English madrigals (in English).

hope of the Musical Association from its earliest days. In an echo of the long-running Cummings–Squire initiative to increase library provision for music researchers, first set out in Association papers of the late 1870s, then followed up in 1919–21 to effect national improvements, Dent launched a similar, long-running campaign, equally bold and demanding, asserting the importance of Italian opera to all eighteenth- and nineteenth-century music.[22] His last four Association papers, 1926–45, each about opera in one way or another, made the historical and linguistic case for opera in English, including by translation, setting out how it could and should become a viable cultural offering for all members of the British public. In turn, his practical work as a libretto translator for the Old Vic, then as a director of Sadler's Wells and of the Covent Garden Opera Trust, achieved as much as anyone to reach that goal.

Besides drawing on a fund of Association scholarship to which he also paid in, Dent naturally encouraged some of his best Cambridge students to participate in paper meetings: he knew it would sharpen their focus and stimulate their efforts. His favourite, W. Denis Browne, had already given an exemplary presentation on modern composition as early as May 1914; this was followed years later, in February and March 1931, by historical papers from Rosamond Harding on early pianofortes, and Philip Radcliffe on rhythm and tonality in sixteenth-century music, both of them chaired sensitively by their professor.[23] (Much later still, Winton Dean and Frederick Sternfeld, each of whom came under Dent's influence at Cambridge in the 1930s, would also give important papers, in both cases a prelude to writing a substantial book.)[24] In fact it was Dent's skill in teaching, care for the student and concern for the Association's

---

[22] 'Italian opera was then still [in the early nineteenth century], as it always had been for nearly two hundred years, the main source of all European musical inspiration. It is not a question of whether that Italian opera was good music or bad music in itself; it is simply the historical fact that it was the universal background of music throughout the classical epoch and throughout the epoch which preceded it' ('The Romantic Spirit in Music', *PMA*, 59 (1932–33), 85–102 at 92).

[23] See R. Harding, 'Experimental Pianofortes and the Music Written for Them', *PMA*, 57 (1930–31), 57–71, with her lantern slides turned into printed illustrations; Dent, who'd facilitated European introductions for Harding, was genuinely impressed by her research and welcomed her 'brilliant paper'. At Radcliffe's paper, 'The Relation of Rhythm and Tonality in the Sixteenth Century', *PMA*, 57 (1930–31), 73–97, Dent supported his student through further explanation, eliciting the group's interest in having more student work.

[24] Winton Dean's first paper, 'The Dramatic Element in Handel's Oratorios', *PRMA*, 79 (1952–53), 33–49, was a mature study at some distance from his Cambridge days, in which he'd participated in the Handel oratorio stagings of the 1930s. His *Handel's Dramatic Oratorios and Masques* (OUP) appeared in 1959. Similarly, Frederick Sternfeld's first paper, 'The Use of Song in Shakespeare's Tragedies', *PRMA*, 86 (1959–60), 45–59, came many years after he'd studied with Dent on long visits from Vienna in the mid-1930s, migrated to the USA, then moved back to the UK for an Oxford

direction that prompted him to lead the Council in linking these desiderata by simply opening up the Association's paper meetings, free, to students enrolled at the institution where the meetings were taking place. The idea had been prompted in the first place as thanks to Trinity College of Music for its hospitality in a new arrangement allowing the Association to use its premises, a modest *quid pro quo*.[25] How small a tweak it was to normal procedure in autumn 1931, soon after those postgraduate papers by Harding and Radcliffe, yet how significant for the Association's future, a door opened to young people as potential scholars, can hardly be overstated. Further modest actions with benefit included the president's personal letter-writing to key defaulters, kindly requesting they pay late subscriptions, which worked well in 1932; and his securing of Fox Strangways's permission to allow the *ML* contributors' list to be circularized for Association membership in 1933, another bellwether of an important future connection. Dent had a knack for setting small but significant things in motion.

Perhaps the most obvious lift at the time, however, was an improvement in the general quality of Association papers, noticeable from 1929. Dent's frequent presence in the chair helped to raise expectations and guide discussion; he had also advised the Council to steer clear of too many journalistic-style papers in their programming. Apart from his own students, he championed presenters with fresh evidence from new angles, such as his close friend J.B. Trend, who surveyed historical aspects of music in Spain from first-hand research there (January 1929, chaired by H.C. Colles), and Philip E. Vernon, who'd recently completed his PhD dissertation on the psychology of auditory perception, and came to report his findings on music cognition (February 1933). Both speakers were firm Association members.[26] They gave well-grounded presentations using compelling illustration to make an argument and open the way for further enquiry. Dent was particularly impressed by the potential in Vernon's material: 'I think I have never heard so admirably clear and lucid an exposition of a very complicated subject [...] [which] will afford many fields for discussion.' In closing remarks alluding to the possibility of his work's application to musical appreciation, meaning 'a more careful habit of self-analysis, a habit of self-examination' rather than lessons in good or bad music, Dent reaffirmed

---

lectureship in 1956, soon serving on the Association Council and as editor of *PRMA*. His *Music in Shakespearean Tragedy* (Routledge & Kegan Paul) appeared in 1963.

[25] The Council had first approached Trinity College of Music, London, for space in January 1931, received a positive reply in February, and made the decision to invite students to Association lectures that December, 'putting up a general Notice, in recognition of the College's hospitality' (Council minutes, 1 Dec 1931, BL Add. MS 71014, fol. 125).

[26] J.B. Trend, 'The Performance of Music in Spain', *PMA*, 55 (1928–29), 51–76; Philip E. Vernon, 'The Apprehension and Cognition of Music', *PMA*, 59 (1932–33), 61–84. Trend had recently published *The Music of Spanish History to 1600* (1926); in 1933 he became the first Professor of Spanish at Cambridge. Vernon studied and lectured as an educational psychologist in the USA and Canada, and at the University of London.

Vernon's study as 'of the highest value' and thanked him for his 'extremely stimulating and instructive paper'.[27]

In a different way, Dent could also offer substantive comments after papers by established researchers, including E.H. Fellowes on the songs of Dowland (November 1929) and C.B. Oldman on recent Mozart research (February 1932). Whether helping to answer wider queries about a speaker's new claims – that Dowland was, according to Fellowes, 'by far the earliest composer in the world to reach first-class rank in the realm of Art-song' – or seconding a speaker's position, Oldman's, with his own personal view – that studying the early criticism and historiography of Mozart's music was of greater value than discussing its modern-day performance[28] – Dent proved unfailingly supportive. He commended both these scholars as models for the Association, uncovering new information to challenge the old, provoking fresh ways of thinking.

After Fellowes:

> Ladies and Gentlemen, we have had to-day a paper which upholds the tradition of our Association in the highest possible way. […] We must remember that the books on musical history have given us often a very false idea of the general state of things in the sixteenth and seventeenth centuries, and we owe a very great debt to Dr. Fellowes and some other researchers for bringing us down to the real facts, which are a very different matter.

After Oldman:

> I rejoice to see that any member of our Association is doing work of that kind, and working, as I think we all ought to work, in what Mr. Oldman calls the spirit of scepticism and doubt, and of refusal to accept authority. That is what I admire in Mr. Oldman's work, and I hold it up to you all and to our younger members as an example.[29]

The improvement represented by all such papers around this time did not go unnoticed. At his own (fifth) paper on 9 March 1933, 'The Romantic Spirit in Music', chaired by H.C. Colles, Dent offered another exemplary approach. He explored the qualities of not only early nineteenth-century music, particularly by Weber and Berlioz, but also Romantic qualities found by analogy in older music including Monteverdi's. In the guise less of a research report

---

[27] Discussion in Vernon, 'The Apprehension and Cognition of Music', 78, 84.

[28] E.H. Fellowes, 'The Songs of Dowland', *PMA*, 56 (1929–30), 1–26 at 2; and C.B. Oldman, 'Mozart and Modern Research', *PMA*, 58 (1931–32), 43–66 at 63 in the discussion. Dent's steer away from discussing modern concert performance was meant to encourage more imaginative historical thinking suggested by Oldman's work. In his role at the British Museum following Barclay Squire, whom Dent much admired, Oldman was 'known already over the Continent as a learned researcher and bibliographer' (62). He had joined the Museum's Printed Books Department in 1920 and by 1948 would be Principal Keeper.

[29] Fellowes paper discussion, 'Songs of Dowland', 20, 24; Oldman paper discussion, 'Mozart and Modern Research', 64.

Figure 11. *Professor E.J. Dent*, drawing by Edmond X. Kapp, 1941 (reproduced courtesy of Chris Beetles Gallery, St James's, London).

than an interpretative historical essay, the piece concluded with one of Dent's favourite themes: 'If the study of musical history has any practical value, it is in the training of the imagination' – a tacit call for more such training in Britain, as well as for a shift in attitude to the widely presumed dominance of German music in cultural history.[30] Whether anyone in the room detected deeper meaning behind his remarks – the paper's date was less than six weeks after Adolf Hitler had become German Chancellor – listeners surely sensed the speaker's heartfelt feeling, his devotion to the primacy of Italian opera and his characteristic drive towards careful but purposeful scholarship. Studying even Romantic composers, 'the most remote in feeling from ourselves', should be conducted in a spirit of scientific analysis. For its range of insights, the paper hit home. Colles's final remarks are worth recalling:

---

[30] Dent, 'The Romantic Spirit in Music', 95. In the discussion, further: 'There is a certain orthodox attitude to the history of music which I want to combat very strongly. Some people tell us that no music matters much except that of Beethoven, Schubert, and Brahms, but I want to insist on the fact that the Italian operatic music is at the back of it all' (97).

Somehow one does not think of thanking one's President as one does other people, but we do thank him very much because he has given a great deal of time and thought to this paper, and it has been very interesting and instructive. Before you pass a vote of thanks to Professor Dent for his paper, I would like to include a word about how much we owe to him as our President. I do not suppose that all members of the Association realise as fully as the members of the Council how much time and care Professor Dent gives to the interests of the Musical Association; to interesting people in its activities and to discovering those capable of reading first-class papers such as we have had during his Presidency. So, in passing the vote of thanks to him for this paper, please pass a vote of thanks also for his presidential care of us. (Prolonged applause.)[31]

By that time in 1933, Dent had served as Association president for nearly five years, but he was not quite finished with his presidential care. In fact he was immersed in final planning for the next triennial ISMR Congress, to be held at Cambridge from 29 July to 4 August, following on from the international body's (re)founding at Basel in 1927, then its first Congress at Liège in 1930. Naturally he saw the event as an opportunity to bring to his own university the two scholarly constituencies of which he was president, harnessing alike Cambridge's town-and-gown resources, historic charm and first-rate English musical performances, while facilitating the exchange of international research including some by members of the Musical Association. Dent had first proposed his Cambridge scheme to an ISMR committee in Paris in December 1931, coincident with his election to that body's presidency.[32] He didn't officially announce the Cambridge event to the Association until October 1932, asking if the Council would now add the ISMR to their free list for *Proceedings*. They went one better and also sent a complete run of the journal from 1874, the personal set of W.W. Cobbett offered at his own suggestion.[33] Musical Association officers were fully on board with their leader.

In January 1933, the Council then began planning a London reception for ISMR members arriving from abroad for the conference. Hosted and paid for by the Association, it was held at the Royal Academy of Music on 28 July, the Friday evening before the Congress opened, and featured a welcome speech by Vice-President Percy Buck, replies by Paul Brunold of Paris and Johannes Wolf of Berlin and performances of some exquisite seventeenth-century English chamber music – three consort setts by William Lawes and the 'first performance in modern times' of a pavane for four viols by John Jenkins (exactly

---

[31] See the discussion in ibid., 101–02. As chief music critic of *The Times*, Colles was well known for his judgement, tact and humanity, displayed again here. As a respected Association vice-president and the most recent editor for Macmillan of *Grove's Dictionary* (*Grove 3*, 1927), he would soon go on to edit the fourth edition, appearing in 1940 (*Grove 4*).

[32] Arrandale, *Edward J. Dent*, 399.

[33] Council minutes, 21 Oct 1932, BL Add. MS 71014, fol. 134v.

what John Hullah, in his opening address to the Musical Institute in 1852, had dreamt of hearing one day but never did). As at the memorable IMG London Congress of May 1911, which Dent had experienced, performances were to be devoted to English music ('at the express wish of the foreign members').[34] Unlike those of that earlier event, though, the papers of 1933, too, were to be centred mainly on the subject of English music and its relation to the music of other countries – Dent's design, approved by the ISMR committee.[35] Such a focused theme, as Guido Adler had once hinted after the London Congress, could encourage discussion better than any miscellaneous approach; and good discussion would be even more likely with the smaller attendance and more intimate setting of Cambridge, despite any personal or political tensions in the air.[36] Ultimately over the four paper days, seventeen presentations were given, in German, French or English, nearly all of them concerning English music or culture running from the early medieval period up to about 1830. The roster of speakers, a remarkable mix, included Jacques Handschin, Otto Gombosi, Otto Kinkeldey, Ernst Hermann Meyer, Paul-Marie Masson and K.G. Fellerer, with four more representing the Musical Association – Anselm Hughes ('The Melodies of the Sequelae'), Percy Scholes ('Musical Life in Cambridge during the Period of the Puritan Control'), Jeffrey Pulver ('The Viols in England') and Philip Radcliffe ('John Field'). From the opening reception's hundred delighted guests to the medieval, Tudor and sacred choral performances in Cambridge colleges and a dramatic 'Historical Pageant of English Music' conducted by Boris Ord, the whole Congress proved a gratifying success for Dent, the Association and the ISMR. The Europeans had been duly impressed.[37]

To what degree, and when, Dent might have originally envisioned this Congress as a way to counter rising German nationalism among musicologists is unclear. He certainly knew by the end of 1933 that the Nazi influence inside the ISMR's publisher, Breitkopf & Härtel, was strong.[38] An earlier, more fundamental motivator behind the conception, however, well before Dent became ISMR president in December 1931, may have been the poor performances of older music he'd heard at the Liège Congress in September 1930, leading him to think that many European musicologists had missed the point of studying old music, and that England could offer an alternative. As he wrote in *Acta musicologica* early in 1931:

---

[34] Anon., 'English Music: Congress Opened at Cambridge', *The Times* (31 July 1933).
[35] See the call for papers and a draft schedule in 'Société Internationale de Musicologie (International Society for Musical Research): Congress at Cambridge, July 29 – August 4, 1933', *Acta musicologica*, 5 (1933), 1–2.
[36] See Chapter 2, p. 64 and n. 56, for Adler's statement of 1911; in 1933, Adler was honorary president of the ISMR. Arrandale, *Edward J. Dent*, 410, describes tension at the 1933 Congress arising from the presence of several strongly pro-German-identity musicologists, notably Handschin and Fellerer.
[37] See Knud Jeppesen's review, 'Der Kongreß', *Acta musicologica*, 5 (1933), 145–46.
[38] See Fauser, 'Edward J. Dent (1932–49)', 48, quoting Dent's letter to Guido Adler of 23 January 1934 about Hellmuth von Hase (a son of Oskar von Hase) and raising the need to disengage *Acta musicologica* from Breitkopf.

We must know how it sounded and do our best to understand the feelings which it was intended to express; we must also be able to read and hear old music in relation to the life of its own time. There is naturally scope for unlimited research on single points of musical history; what we badly need at the present day is a general history of music for ordinary readers. Most of the standard histories are hopelessly out of date. How out of date most of us are in the matter of performing old music was shown only too plainly at the Liège Congress. The programmes of old music were certainly interesting, but the execution of them (apart from the singing of Yves Tinayre) left much to be desired; and if we can do no better at an international congress what must our standards be in lesser centres? [...] I maintain that the practical study of old music is indispensable to the inner understanding of all music. [...] The study of old music will teach us principles of musical expression; we shall learn what is permanent and what is transitory in the art of music, not judging at haphazard as the musical journalists do, but analysing carefully and in minute detail.[39]

Dent's plan for the Cambridge Congress seems to have evolved soon after these remarks. His goal was to show not only that Cambridge was both picturesque and lively, its musicians skilled, or that early English music heard in its own setting was as beautiful as German, French or Italian, but also that in the dialect of 'Musicology' spoken in England, serious research and music performance went hand in hand to develop a 'scientific attitude of mind' – rather than, as in some other traditions, to generate 'the publication of *Denkmäler*, of dissertations and papers on apparently unimportant subjects, in which the display of learning often seems out of all proportion to the value of the facts ascertained'.[40] It was a further iteration, perhaps, of Dent's earlier riposte to a falsely drawn German conclusion about the source of finished and individual English madrigal singing, admired in Berlin when E.H. Fellowes and the English Singers visited there in 1922 – to wit, that this kind of singing was the fruit of inspiration and centuries of carefully preserved tradition. 'Their style is the fruit not of tradition, but of scholarship, of historical erudition, supplied, as every one knows, by Dr. Fellowes, and of common sense supplied by themselves.'[41] Dent was ever vigilant to scotch any easy stereotyping of English music or musical research as provincial, lazy or behind the rest of Europe for being old, different or unorthodox: in this case, orthodoxy had been displaced by study, hard work and logic.

If anything, the success of the Cambridge Congress raised Dent's standing still higher. But it's important to recall that he'd already laid the groundwork for foreign cooperation and support through his cementing of international friendships and scholarly alliances. The Musical Association helped in that pursuit and in turn benefited from it – another sign of their leader's presidential

---

[39] Dent, 'Music and Musical Research', 7.
[40] Ibid., 7–8.
[41] Edward J. Dent, 'Music: The Mozartian Tradition', *Nation and Athenaeum* (17 Mar 1923), 928, quoted by Edmund H. Fellowes, *Memoirs of an Amateur Musician* (London: Methuen & Co., 1946), 125–26.

care. Between 1930 and 1944, he, with the Council, suggested the names of seven European scholars and one American as Honorary Foreign Members – Peter Wagner, André Pirro, Johannes Wolf and Otto Kinkeldey (all 1930), Egon Wellesz (1932), Alfred Einstein (1937), and Higini Anglès and Knud Jeppesen (both 1944). Four were nominated in the first group, near the beginning of Dent's presidency, partly because the Association's Honorary Members' roster had shrunk to only three names by June 1930, partly also in anticipation of the first ISMR Congress in Liège, in September 1930, at which Dent hoped to make a strong showing for Britain's internationalism; Wagner (Freiburg), Pirro (Paris) and Wolf (Berlin) were senior ISMR officers.[42] Communications were slow, and Kinkeldey's U.S. address changes made him difficult to reach, but in the event, all four scholars warmly accepted honorary membership by early 1931, Kinkeldey 'with enthusiasm'. Wolf and Pirro agreed to visit London and read papers, although only Wolf was able to do so, arriving in December 1931 with a lecture on Italian music of the fourteenth century, in English, repeated for Dent at Cambridge. Dent's motive here surely exceeded a desire to learn ever more about the *Trecento*. In fact Peter Wagner, the ISMR's first president, had died unexpectedly in October, leading Dent to sense a possible opening for himself and the Association if he could secure Wolf's support in the imminent vote on a new ISMR president. His strategy was to show Wolf around Cambridge, to persuade him of the great potential (and reason) for holding the next ISMR congress there and thus to gain personal backing, including for himself as the next ISMR president, filling out the remainder of Wagner's second three-year term.[43] The plan worked perfectly. One might conclude that dispensing Musical Association honorary membership had been as much about political patronage as research excellence; Dent knew what he was doing. But Cambridge, and Dent for the Association, also won their ISMR places by fair vote, not diktat. That counted for something in the 1930s.

In the interim before the Cambridge Congress, Dent nominated another long-time friend for foreign membership, Egon Wellesz, the Viennese composer, musicologist and an ISCM co-founder who was set to visit Oxford in autumn 1932 to receive an honorary doctorate. The Association voted to honour him as well, and members heard with pleasure his broadly scoped

---

[42] Council minutes, 27 June 1930, BL Add. MS 71014, fol. 98v. Dent made the case for four names, then drew attention to the forthcoming Liège Congress. At Liège, Fellowes gave one of four public lectures, 'The English Madrigal of the Sixteenth Century', presented as a talk in the English way (*more anglicano*), appreciated by a large audience. Further English papers were given by Rosamond Harding and J.B. Trend, although these were not listed in the advance programme (Council minutes, 14 Oct 1930, BL Add. MS 71014, fol. 100v).

[43] Johannes Wolf, 'Italian Trecento Music', *PMA*, 58 (1931–32), 15–31. The repeat at Cambridge had been shrewdly devised by Dent (Arrandale, *Edward J. Dent*, 399); Wolf's travel expenses were paid partly by Dent and partly by Cambridge. Three-year terms for ISMR officers are specified in §14 of the founding statutes.

paper on Byzantine music chaired by Dent that November.[44] In future years, once settled in Oxford, Wellesz would remain a stalwart member of the Association. Also later, even after stepping down as the Association's president in 1935, Dent continued to suggest deserving foreign names for membership consideration. Besides the intellectual regard signified by honorary membership (which came with free access to *Proceedings* volumes), such affiliations benefited local Association members by exposing them to remarkable international scholarship, at the same time raising the Association's profile at home and abroad. As the 1930s wore on, these connections could also potentially help scholars fleeing Europe to find teaching positions in Britain or the USA. In addition to Wellesz, one important case was that of Alfred Einstein (Munich), the *Zeitschrift für Musikwissenschaft*'s first editor, whom Dent had known since the early 1920s and had already helped to attend the Cambridge Congress in 1933, appealing to the British Foreign Office.[45] Dent saw another chance to help three years later, suggesting the Council request a paper from Einstein, who was just then completing the first major revision of the Köchel Mozart catalogue and, more to the moment, had recently praised Dent's outwardly neutral political stance in preparing for what promised to be a fractious ISMR Barcelona Congress in April 1936.[46] Dent sweetened his suggestion by offering to translate any Association paper from Einstein.[47] Ultimately Fox Strangways did the translating, but the Council indeed moved quickly to offer honorary membership. When Einstein appeared in March 1937, Dent chaired his 'extremely learned' paper on Italian madrigal verse, and presented his certificate of Honorary Foreign Membership on the spot; by 1939 Einstein was safely at work at Smith College in Massachusetts.[48]

The last two nominees in this period, in February 1944, were Higini Anglès (Barcelona), suggested by Dent, and Knud Jeppesen (Copenhagen), proposed by the Council, both of them senior ISMR figures; Jeppesen edited *Acta musicologica* for more than two decades, from 1931 to 1953. Neither scholar was able to give a Musical Association paper, but in different ways they'd long supported Dent's internationalist efforts, even during a time of great stress in the ISMR from 1936 to the late 1940s. Admittedly, Anglès, the eminent Catalan

---

[44] Egon Wellesz, 'Byzantine Music', *PMA*, 59 (1932–33), 1–22. He delivered the paper on 22 November 1932 and was more than pleased by the Musical Association's recognition. Their requirement of foreign residence for Honorary Foreign Membership, however, though straightforward at the time, would soon cause difficulty once Wellesz moved permanently to Oxford.

[45] Fauser, 'Edward J. Dent (1932–49)', 47–48. Einstein had remained for a time in England in 1933, then lived mainly in Italy, near Florence; he was later offered a position at Cambridge but in 1939 chose instead to leave for the USA (Alec Hyatt King, 'Einstein, Alfred', *Grove Music Online*).

[46] See Arrandale, *Edward J. Dent*, 439–40, quoting Einstein's letter to Dent of 2 February 1936, damning ISMR Cambridge delegates who were 'pimping for Adolf Hitler'.

[47] Council minutes, 16 July 1936, BL Add. MS 71015, fol. 44v.

[48] Alfred Einstein, 'Italian Madrigal Verse', *PMA*, 63 (1936–37), 79–95. His major achievement, *The Italian Madrigal* (Princeton University Press), appeared in 1949.

priest and musicologist who'd co-arranged the Barcelona ISMR Congress with Dent, wavered sometimes, as did even Johannes Wolf under pressure from aggressive pro-Nazi colleagues, especially Heinrich Besseler.[49] The mood Besseler wished to spread inside the ISMR from 1935 was one of doubt and fear about Dent personally – that he was controlling and arrogant, didn't advance the German style of musicology, had remained supportive of Jews and other 'undesirables' and wasn't German, so shouldn't continue to head an official musicological society formed first and foremost by Germans.[50] In the end, this whispering tactic didn't succeed: too few Germans attended the Barcelona Congress (some of them prevented by Nazi restrictions), while Dent fell seriously ill just beforehand and could not attend, effectively erasing any opportunity for a vote to depose him. Together with Jeppesen, meanwhile, he had already secretly transferred *Acta* out of Germany, away from Breitkopf and straight into the competent hands of the Copenhagen publisher Levin & Munksgaard. This whole quarrelsome and dramatic backdrop to Barcelona in April 1936, a Congress of some eighty lectures, many on Spanish topics but with no British contributors,[51] which also, despite some wonderful performances of older Spanish music, had nearly broken up the ISMR, goes some way towards explaining why Jeppesen felt his English friend might need encouraging. As editor of *Acta*, now issuing from Denmark, Jeppesen paid a birthday tribute in his own English words, headed 'Edward J. Dent, on the Sixteenth of July 1936':

My dear Professor Dent,
   I think you have done your best to hide from the musicological world the fact that you have just this summer celebrated your sixtieth birthday. [...]
   I think, we may praise ourselves happy to possess, in a time so difficult to all international endeavours like this, a personality – just a personality – as yours to be at the head of our society: a man of strength, of tolerance, and of altruism.
   Since your youth you have given all your best forces to our international purpose, sparing no efforts to promote the high aim of free spiritual communication between the peoples, which is, ever has been, and ever shall be the principal cause of the welfare of art and research.
   I think you are an idealist in the clearest sense of this word, and although I know that you with your ironical fashion – known and appreciated all over the world – don't like this word, I can't help it. With your own production you have given not only very valuable contributions to both the English and the

---

[49] On the Barcelona Congress, including Dent's advance correspondence on ostensibly only practical matters with Anglès, Jeppesen, Wolf, Pirro and others from October 1935 to March 1936, see Arrandale, *Edward J. Dent*, 439–44. In the background, Besseler was simultaneously writing to Anglès and others, conducting a covert campaign to overthrow Dent as ISMR president and install a 'good German' instead (439).

[50] Ibid., 440.

[51] See Knud Jeppesen, 'Der 3. Kongress der internationalen Gesellschaft für Musikwissenschaft, Barcelona 18–25. April 1936', *Acta musicologica*, 8 (1936), 2–6. Jesús Bal y Gay, a Spanish literary scholar and friend of J.B. Trend's, was a Spanish refugee teaching at Cambridge when he spoke at the Congress.

international history of music, but also a lesson, profitable to us all, for broader and more artistic views within musical research. You have been like the salt of great seas, reanimating and refreshing, and so, we hope, you will remain.

We send you all our very best congratulations for your birthday, and we are happy to be able to add our just as heart-felt felicitations to the good news that you have just now fully recovered your health after the serious illness, by which you were attacked during our Congress in Barcelona.

We beg you to receive our most sincere thanks and wishes for the future.

> Yours faithfully
> *Knud Jeppesen.*[52]

Tragically, Spain itself was engulfed in a bitter civil war within weeks, any benefits of the Barcelona Congress soon forgotten. For his part, Dent had already grown weary of drains on his personal time, health and money as head of both the ISCM and the ISMR. He stepped down from the contemporary music society in 1938, troubled by the difficulty of maintaining a seemingly non-political, internationalist stance when real-world conditions demanded more direct intervention.[53] At the music research society, by contrast, he postponed the 1939 ISMR Congress scheduled for Copenhagen, but hung on as president until the next Congress at Basel in 1949. Helping to keep alive aspects of international scholarly communication must have seemed a more attainable goal, worth the effort.[54] Although probably unwitting at the time, this position mirrored the earlier, determined view of Charles Maclean in 1915. Exasperated by the political machinations of Oskar von Hase and Hermann Kretzschmar to control, then unilaterally cancel, the existence of the IMG in 1914 without consulting members,[55] Maclean, as its surviving General Secretary and (putative) leader, like Dent as president two decades later, held every intention of keeping the Society going; he instructed the Musical Association secretary Percy Baker to make a public explanation of the Association's difficult position in an understandable way while skirting geopolitical sensitivities: 'I am all for your mentioning the real issue; but you can put it, that practically <u>all</u> musicians and musical people in this country look equally to the historical and the present-day aspects, and there does not exist the extreme specialisation and

---

[52] *Acta musicologica*, 8 (1936), 1.
[53] See Masters, 'Performing Internationalism', esp. 569–71.
[54] *Acta musicologica* continued to appear, for example, although its content decreased to a single fascicle of some hundred pages a year, 1940–49, with material supplied by a small group of contributors.
[55] See Chapter 2 above, pp. 65–66 and n. 61. Oskar von Hase (1846–1921), IMG treasurer and part-owner of Breitkopf & Härtel in Leipzig, was the father of Hellmuth von Hase, a fervent Nazi who worked at Breitkopf from 1919; by the 1930s he was owner and general manager, deeply enmeshed in Leipzig's music and book publishing culture. But despite Maclean's understanding of Hase as source of the trouble, it was Hermann Kretschmar as IMG president who in late summer 1914 unilaterally broke up the IMG.

differentiation found in Germany.'[56] Maclean's pinpointing of a key distinction between English and German approaches to music research was not very far from Dent's philosophy, in 1915 or in the 1930s. It was a similar desire to stand up for the symbolic meaning in that distinction which fuelled the commitments of both Maclean and Dent.

After 1935 E.J. Dent participated in Musical Association events as a respected past president, seeing some of his initiatives take root. All along, the Council had periodically invited well-known foreign scholars to give papers in London without any suggestion of a link to honorary membership. Albert Smijers had come from Amsterdam to speak on Josquin in April 1927; Jaap Kunst, from Bilthoven, gave an ethnomusicological paper in February 1936 on the acoustic evidence for a probable relationship between Indonesia and Central Africa; in December 1938 Manfred Bukofzer came from Basel to speak on Dunstable, a paper that sparked a long and fascinating discussion with questions and comments from Francis Galpin (in the chair), Anselm Hughes, Frank Howes, Wellesz and Dent himself;[57] and in February 1940 Karl Geiringer, from 1938 residing in London and soon a member, gave a well-received paper on Haydn as an opera composer. Clearly the Association's understanding of what musical research could embrace expanded significantly during Dent's presidency. Its members' direct engagement with eminent foreign musicologists, including those introduced through his influence, was part of that growth.

❧ A Library, an Index and a Committee: Whither Research?

When in May 1935 Dent announced to the Association his intention of stepping down, the Council accepted his decision with great regret, thankful for the seven years he'd given. Percy Buck as King Edward Professor at London University, an established music editor, educator and vice-president, was his logical successor. Buck's energy and interests happened to range in a different direction from Dent's, towards sharpening the group's self-awareness and realizing its potential to help British students undertake research. The time was right. Several Council members had already recognized after the Cambridge Congress, and the reinstated Annual Dinner from late 1933, that the Association needed to cultivate its local members more carefully while heightening public interest in research. In addition, some felt that a greater proportion of papers should be presented by their own members: they couldn't continue to rely on

---

[56] Maclean to Baker, 30 June 1915, BL Add. MS 71036, fol. 119 (emphasis original). Maclean's persistent anger with the presumptuous German-based IMG management turned to resignation by late 1915, revealed in his last, confidential letter to Percy Baker, 2 Dec 1915 (BL Add. MS 71036, fols. 120–25).

[57] Manfred Bukofzer, 'John Dunstable and the Music of his Time', *PMA*, 65 (1938–39), 19–43. He had completed his dissertation under Jacques Handschin in 1936, and in spring 1939 left for the USA. By the early 1950s, he would be editing Dunstable's 'complete works' for MB.

European or other visiting scholars to set the pace or establish their priorities.[58] This was not a rejection of foreign influence so much as an honest admission that the Association's future depended on self-assertion, specifically a more direct seeding of younger British scholars. All these instincts gradually coalesced. Through Dent's high standards and foreign contacts, his welcome of potential émigrés to Cambridge in 1933, and now Buck's interest in providing more intellectual support for younger researchers, two new pathways opened, separately, that would begin to foster the notion of a music research *culture* inside Britain, a dedicated space in which serious musical research was seen as normative rather than odd or irrelevant. These stemmed from two events – first, the arrival in Cambridge from Frankfurt, in 1936, of a private library of music and musical literature of worldwide significance, the Paul Hirsch collection, which, initially open to users there, would be incorporated ten years later into the BM through the efforts of Musical Association members aided by magnanimous funding from the Treasury and the Pilgrim Trust; and second, the creation in 1938 of an Association Research Committee, to solicit and assess the views of research-active members on subjects and methods they thought might be productive for future work by British students. Neither event produced a transformation overnight, but both represented major steps in expanding the Association's perception of its cultural role.

As noted above, the ISMR Cambridge Congress in summer 1933 provided a chance for a number of threatened European musicologists to visit England and make connections or scout work that would aid their emigration. Otto Gombosi, Ernst Hermann Meyer and Alfred Einstein were only three: while Gombosi and Einstein eventually went to the USA, Meyer, a pupil of Hanns Eisler, remained in Britain as a composer, musicologist and teacher affiliated with London University.[59] Another scholar seeking help from Dent in particular was Dr Kathi Meyer (no relation to Ernst Hermann Meyer), a former Johannes Wolf pupil whom Dent had known since meeting her in Frankfurt in 1927. As the resident musicologist and library assistant to Paul Hirsch (1881–1951), a German industrialist and amateur violinist of Frankfurt who'd amassed 'one of the finest general collections of printed music and musical literature [...] anywhere in the twentieth century'[60] and was himself a committed ISCM supporter and personal friend of Dent's, she was in a strong position: she could offer bibliographic, editorial and research skills as well as humane musicological teaching. More relevant still, she knew the Paul Hirsch library intimately and was almost certainly aware that it was likely to

---

[58] Council minutes, 11 May 1934, BL Add. MS 71015, fol. 11r–v.
[59] E.H. Meyer joined the Musical Association, gave a paper in 1939 on form in seventeenth-century instrumental music, wrote a book on English chamber music (1946) and in 1948 moved to Humboldt University in Berlin as a professor of music sociology; he maintained his membership in the RMA, paying his subscription through Alan Bush.
[60] Alec Hyatt King, 'Paul Hirsch and his Music Library', *British Library Journal*, 7 (1981), 1–11 at 2.

be removed to England for safekeeping, possibly to Cambridge to become a working library once Hirsch and his family had also settled there. Her paper to the Cambridge Congress, 'England und Deutschland, musikalische Tradition und kulturelle Beziehungen' ('England and Germany, Musical Tradition and Cultural Relations'), programmed in German but possibly given in English, may even have served as a kind of job application, not for a university lectureship, unlikely for a woman in the 1930s in any country, but for some kind of curatorial post at the new Cambridge University Library just then being completed, scheduled to open in 1934. She and Hirsch were still working on their 'splendid' multi-volume catalogue of the collection, and she may have hoped that this work could continue under the auspices of Hirsch and/or Cambridge if the material were relocated there.[61]

In the end, no position was forthcoming. Kathi Meyer returned to Frankfurt, continued working for Hirsch until early 1936, then left for Paris in 1938 and New York in 1940. Meanwhile the Hirsch Library – nearly 1,000 linear feet – was indeed boxed up and shipped by train, probably via Strasbourg, Paris and Calais, to London. Although exact dates and details are unknown, it seems likely that Hirsch would have used a responsible agent to arrange all paperwork, fees, carriage and safe storage in advance. A similar process would have been adopted by businessmen such as German book dealers themselves relocating to the UK, as Otto Haas did, for example. Haas owned the most prestigious music and antiquarian dealer in Berlin, Leo Liepmannssohn, from whom Hirsch had purchased the James E. Matthew collection of musical literature in the first place, in 1908 – by 1936 the heart of Hirsch's collection.[62] Haas too had experienced rising antisemitism in Berlin and, around the same time as Hirsch's move, proceeded to re-establish his book and music-selling business in London with support from the antiquarian firm Maggs Bros. and the well-known dealers Percy Muir and Cecil Hopkinson.[63] It's not inconceivable

---

[61] See David Josephson, '"Why Then All the Difficulties!": A Life of Kathi Meyer-Baer', *Notes*, 65 (2008), 227–67. Meyer saw herself as a scholar, but in a letter to a friend in late July 1933 admitted that her goal was, if not to be a teacher of music history and aesthetics, then especially to work as a music librarian: 'I'd like England best, which is why I'm about to go to a conference there' (235–36 and n. 27). 'Splendid' is King's description of the Hirsch catalogues, which would only be completed in 1940 (vol. 4 appeared in 1947) with help from Edith Schnapper and Hirsch's two daughters ('Paul Hirsch and his Music Library', 2).

[62] See Chapter 2 above, n. 90, on James Matthew's paper to the Association about his collection in South Hampstead and his attempt to keep it in England. His offers to the Worshipful Company of Musicians and to Trinity College of Music, London, were refused; in late 1907 he finally sold to Leo Liepmannssohn, who in turn sold much of the collection to Hirsch in 1908. See King, *Some British Collectors of Music, c. 1600–1960*, 71, 148; and Albi Rosenthal, 'Otto Haas, Antiquarian Bookseller (1874–1955)', *Brio*, 3 (1966), 3–5.

[63] See http://www.ottohaas-music.com, where the firm's history is set out by Oliver Neighbour; and Albi Rosenthal, 'Otto Haas'. Haas's wife Kathleen Mayer, a pianist and singer who'd studied at the RAM, had formerly lived in the house where Otto

that Hirsch consulted Haas directly for advice: Haas's own transfer was completed by the end of 1935, Hirsch's by 1936. In early March 1936 it was of course Dent who facilitated Cambridge University's acceptance of Hirsch's proposal to place his collection on loan in the new CUL; that autumn Hirsch settled in Cambridge with his family, and by December his library was on the shelves, fully available to members of the university.[64]

The arrival of Hirsch's library had a long-range impact on the development of British musicology. From 1896, scholarly importance had stood first among Hirsch's collecting principles, but he was also a practical musician and a bibliophile interested in the history of music and printing. He continually built up his library, even after 1936 (with Haas's help), which now numbers more than 18,000 items ranging from incunabula and early theoretical works, some in unique or pristine copies, to original editions of operas from Peri's *Euridice* to Strauss's *Die Frau ohne Schatten*, Hindemith full scores and, especially, early editions of Mozart, Haydn and Beethoven. A broad, ideal musical library for the dedicated student rather than a specialist collection, it also contained a large number of 'complete works' sets of major composers (*Gesamtausgaben*), enhanced by music literature covering four centuries and most European countries, including library catalogues, periodicals, biography, criticism and history. The collection's educational and research utility was obvious: Dent's Cambridge students surely benefited, as did other researchers nationwide. Hirsch also made some of his most important items externally available through facsimile editions (1922–45), besides creating four catalogue volumes of the bulk of the library (published in 1928, 1930, 1936 and 1947).[65] After nearly ten years in Cambridge, a period in which both he and Haas became Musical Association members, Hirsch realized he would have to sell.[66] Concerned to

---

set up his London business in 1935–36, at 49A Belsize Park Gardens. Although Haas had disposed of most of his stock before leaving Germany, he still had knowledge of international shipping. For evidence that Haas and Hirsch were in touch in early September 1935 about the need to leave Germany soon, see Nick Chadwick, 'The Hirsch Correspondence: Some Preliminary Observations', *Brio*, 45 (2008), 60–67 at 62: at that time Haas had just received his 'blauer Brief', giving four weeks' notice of the Nazis' intention to liquidate his business.

[64] King, 'Paul Hirsch and his Music Library', 3–4.

[65] For example, Johannes Wolf edited Caza's *Tractato vulgare de canto figurato* (1492) and Alfred Einstein edited Mozart's last ten quartets; for a full list of the editions issued, see the 'Hirsch' entry in *Grove* 5. Hirsch's own four catalogue volumes provided the basis of the BM's arrangement of the collection.

[66] Hirsch joined the Musical Association in 1942, nominated by Dent. While working on his collection, he occasionally made bibliographical discoveries, communicating these in notes sent to *Acta musicologica* (on Haydn), or in articles sent to *ML* and *Music Review* (Mozart and Beethoven). Otto Haas joined the Association in 1944. Alexander Hyatt King, signing as A. Hyatt King (the name form he preferred for more than thirty years), had been nominated soon after Hirsch in 1942, recommended by Geoffrey Rendell and C.B. Oldman, both of the BM. In 1946 Cambridge University itself was unable to purchase the Hirsch Library. The other interested party was the University

preserve the collection in Britain, he sought advice from Dent and others, who initiated negotiations and a fundraising campaign, public and private. In April 1946, two Letters to the Editor of *The Times* appeared under the heading 'A Great Music Library'. The first, on 9 April, put the position plainly, asserting that Paul Hirsch was

> [...] willing to forgo part of the sum at which the collection has been valued if it can be kept intact and in Britain. That it should remain here is of the utmost permanent importance for this country; not even the British Museum has been so systematically equipped for general research in music. It is unlikely that there will ever be another chance of establishing such a library in Great Britain, since all comparable collections abroad are now in public institutions. [...]
>
> We should hesitate to ask for munificence at a time like the present if the matter were not so vitally important to the future of British music.
>
> Yours faithfully,
> ARNOLD BAX, ADRIAN C. BOULT, EDWARD J. DENT, G. DYSON, MYRA HESS, STANLEY MARCHANT, RALPH VAUGHAN WILLIAMS.

The signatories were all Musical Association members: a past president, two vice-presidents, a life member and three regular members, all of them household names in British music.

A second letter, on 20 April from Miss Seymour Whinyates, director of the British Council's music section, responded by underlining the 'grave concern' many lovers of music might feel at the threatened sale of the Hirsch Library to America, which would be 'a grievous loss to the musical prestige of this country'. She recommended the formation of a National Music Trust to coordinate the efforts of interested parties and asked them to contact Professor Dent. A third piece, this time a brief article by Dent headed 'Need for a Central Music Library: Value of the Hirsch Collection', appeared on 26 April. It described Hirsch's library in the context of other UK collections, articulating what it could offer to a range of practical researchers and why this 'most important private library in Europe' was so important to preserve, now, in a public institution in Britain.

> It must be remembered that 'musical research' is not limited to the deciphering of medieval manuscripts. Research is going on every day in all branches of music. The programmes of the B.B.C. [...] A new ballet at Covent Garden, music to a play or film, school performances all over the country may all require serious research.

And time had moved on, he noted. A 'gigantic increase in musical research studies' in America, and the destruction or dispersal of many Continental

---

of Michigan (Chadwick, 'The Hirsch Correspondence', 62), which, according to King had made a 'munificent' offer ('The Hirsch Music Library: Retrospect and Conclusion', *Notes*, 9 (1952), 381–87 at 381.).

libraries and publishing houses meant that even with unlimited resources, 'it would be utterly impossible now to create another such collection'. His plea was effective, securing public attention. But all along Dent and other distinguished voices, including Patrick Hadley (Dent's successor as professor at Cambridge), Lord Baldwin (Stanley Baldwin, former Prime Minister, from 1930 Chancellor of Cambridge University) and Lord Macmillan (Hugh Macmillan, a Law Lord, chair of the BBC Advisory Council and of the Pilgrim Trust), worked to bring about a successful conclusion to sensitive discussions. Eventually the Treasury made a special grant of £50,000, the Pilgrim Trust a very generous contribution of £60,000, and the BM Trustees pledged £10,000 (in five annual instalments), so that by July 1946 the Museum could purchase the library for £120,000 (nearly £6 million in today's terms). As Alec Hyatt King put it, looking back in 1963, 'Cambridge's loss was the nation's gain.'[67]

The Museum's acquisition of the Hirsch Library, which immediately placed the nation's music collection in a leading world position, had never officially involved the Musical Association by name, nor was the library ever mentioned in Council minutes. But the campaign surrounding it unquestionably drew on a network of expertise and trusted advice from Association members, not only Dent and Hadley but also Frank Howes, recently made chief music critic of *The Times*, and Alec Hyatt King, the new Superintendent of the Music Room at the BM, both future RMA presidents.[68] In the absence of serious state or university support for musicology, moreover, this purchase, a tangible show of government support, gave weight to the Association's effort to highlight music's intellectual value in national culture. Joy all round appears to have resulted, not least at the Hirsch garden party given for Dent's seventieth birthday in July 1946.[69] The Hirsch collection's move to the Museum was completed in January 1947, and from then on stimulated not just hopes for British research and the training of British students, but also wider understanding of musical history and its potential interpretations. Knowledge would grow of cultural

---

[67] *Some British Collectors of Music*, 75. Clearly there were some in Cambridge who grieved that the collection couldn't stay there. For details of the finance and the physical transport from Cambridge to London in late 1946 and early 1947 (three large railway vans, total weight just over 13 tons), see Alec Hyatt King, 'Quodlibet: Some Memoirs of the British Museum and its Music Room, 1934–76', in *The Library of the British Museum: Retrospective Essays on the Department of Printed Books*, ed. P.R. Harris (London: British Library, 1991), 241–98 at 272–73. See also King, 'The Hirsch Music Library', for further details of shipping, cataloguing and physical handling.

[68] Howes was appointed chief music critic of *The Times* in June 1943. King became Superintendent of the BM Music Room in late 1944 (succeeding William C. Smith, who succeeded William Barclay Squire); in 1973, under a new structure, he became Music Librarian of the British Library.

[69] King, 'Paul Hirsch and his Music Library', 1. Also see the birthday greeting from Egon Wellesz in *Acta musicologica*, 18/19 (1946–47), 1–2, suggesting that Dent's travels and intercommunication made him 'the legitimate heir and successor of Dr Burney'. Wellesz expanded: 'But you did more than this: you succeeded in changing the musical climate of England' (1).

dissemination through the study of music printing developments, and of compositional choices through careful textual comparisons; even the Museum's own music cataloguing practices were to benefit. Only from 1947, for example, was the pagination of a BM collection item, or the number of its separate vocal or instrumental parts, given in catalogue descriptions, both routine elements now.[70] Further, the four-year programme of BM cataloguing, following Hirsch's classification but also adding in a further 5,000 items not included in his original catalogues, yielded two Accessions Parts, of music (1951) and musical books (1959); this revealed the full extent of Hirsch's accumulations of first and early editions of Viennese Classical material. With some 800 Mozart entries (180 for Haydn, 579 for Beethoven and 350 for Schubert),[71] the Museum was especially well equipped to mount a Mozart exhibition in 1956, the composer's bicentenary, which in turn allowed King to attract an extraordinary loan from the London heirs of Stefan Zweig embracing their sixteen Mozart autographs; these included the composer's own thematic catalogue, a priceless document eventually donated to the British Library in 1986.[72] In such a manner, with careful stewardship, assiduous planning, and steady consultation by Readers over many decades, the Hirsch Library has continued to make its impact on musical study in Britain.

The Hirsch Library and its move to Cambridge, then London, forms a remarkable episode in the larger narrative of music collecting and research in Britain. And the important role played in its creation by an earlier Association member, James E. Matthew, deserves reiterating: Hirsch did not single-handedly collect every individual item he owned. But it's also true to say that both Matthew and Hirsch were private collectors. Their libraries lay outside the everyday workings of the Musical Association, which had meanwhile built up its own modest library of *Proceedings* volumes, besides journals of foreign societies sent in exchange, occasional gift volumes and runs of journals issued by the IMG and later the ISMR and IMS, of which the Association was a member. A slightly motley assemblage, this Association Library was nonetheless seen as an important source of reference for the membership, worth maintaining wherever a central London space could be found that allowed member and latterly student access; not every new member could afford to purchase all the *PMA* back numbers, the stock of which eventually ran down. From the early

---

[70] P.R. Harris and O.W. Neighbour, 'Alec Hyatt King (1911–1995)', *British Library Journal*, 21 (1995), 155–60 at 159.

[71] King, 'Paul Hirsch and his Music Library', 7. For details on the BM cataloguing process, see King, 'The Hirsch Music Library'.

[72] Hugh Cobbe, 'Alexander Hyatt King', *Independent* (24 Mar 1995). The Zweig heirs ultimately gave not only their Mozart autographs but Zweig's complete collection of musical and literary autographs. See Arthur Searle, *The British Library Stefan Zweig Collection: Catalogue of the Music Manuscripts* (London: British Library, 1999), tellingly reviewed by John Shepard in *Notes*, 57 (2000), 370–71.

FRESH CHALLENGES, 1924–1944   123

Figure 12. Parry Room Library, Royal College of Music, photograph by *Daily Herald*, 1933, site of the Musical Association's own library.

1930s to 1943, the Association's Library was housed in the RCM's wood-panelled Parry Room high up in the College's roof space, a particularly fitting location given that Hubert Parry, Director of the RCM in 1895–1918, had twice served as Musical Association president, in 1901–08 and 1915–18.[73]

Of course in the days before computers, using *Proceedings* efficiently required access to lists of its articles, either in publication order or grouped by topic or period and accompanied by an author index, all regularly updated in cumulative form. Such a tool had been part of the Association's scholarly apparatus since the first index appeared in volume 25 (1898–99).[74] By 1933 the most recently updated

---

[73] The Parry Room, created as a memorial to Parry, was a quiet space for reading and study. According to David C.H. Wright, *The Royal College of Music and its Contexts: An Artistic and Social History* (Cambridge: Cambridge Univ. Press, 2020), 137–38, it housed Parry's musical MSS and books left to the College, books bequeathed by Edward Dannreuther, Parry's Oxford B.Mus. hood and a copy of *Grove's Dictionary of Music and Musicians* given by George Macmillan. Hugh Allen issued the invitation to the Association, while C.B. Oldman offered a large bookcase (Council minutes, 19 Jan 1933, BL Add. MS 71014, fol. 141v).

[74] See Chapter 2, pp. 74–75, above.

version, in volume 50 (1923–24), was already ten years old. Now the broader drive to improve communication and assist students aligned with the need to resume the index. An exhaustive update for the whole sixty volumes, 1874–1934, was thus broached in Council but dropped for cost reasons and brought up again three years later, in July 1936 by Fellowes and then again that October by Percy Buck, the president. Buck offered an additional reason for spending money on a new index: beyond bibliographical tidiness or reference help, that is, he saw an emerging need to take stock of what Association members had achieved in research to date, and to suggest new avenues of work for the future. He believed that a fully updated index might stimulate a paper along those lines and perhaps lead to a group discussion on future research priorities.[75] A full consideration of costing and format, therefore, including different ways to organize the index, took place in February 1937.[76] But yet again the matter was deferred: a decision in a year's time would still be timely and could establish fifteen years between indexes as the new standard. In the meantime, Buck's underlying question about how to advise students and others in a fast-growing discipline remained unanswered. To move forward before he stepped down – Francis Galpin had been mooted to succeed Buck in mid-1938 – the Council decided to postpone the index temporarily and instead form a subcommittee to consult 'experts' directly for their thoughts on research.

Accordingly, on 17 March 1938 the Council appointed a small committee to 'investigate the conditions of research in this country' and to seek a range of views about particular areas or historical periods needing work; its four members were Marion Scott, R.O. Morris, Cecil Oldman and J.A. Westrup.[77] In the event, with Erlebach's secretarial help, they met at the RCM twice (17 May and 1 July), made a plan, took evidence in the form of written replies to a circular letter and drew up a report, all within four months. At the first meeting, they selected fourteen senior figures to approach, and devised a letter requesting the following information:

(a) Avenues of research you would recommend a student to follow.
(b) Sections of your branch which are as yet unexplored and should next be tackled.
(c) Any nearly or remotely related work that would, in your opinion, throw light on the branch or period.[78]

---

[75] Council minutes, 9 Oct 1936, BL Add. MS 71015, fols. 45v–46r.

[76] Council minutes, 26 Feb 1937, BL Add. MS 71015, fol. 54r–v.

[77] Council minutes, 17 Mar 1938, BL Add. MS 71015, fols. 70v–71r. The original agenda item had simply stated '4. – Consider possibility of advising those undertaking research' (BL Add. MS 71033, fol. 194). Council minutes record the new subcommittee's goal as twofold – to identify ways of putting intending researchers in touch with experts, and to find gaps in the work so far done 'so as to direct workers towards those gaps'. There was general agreement that the Association was 'the proper body to undertake this task'.

[78] From E.H. Fellowes's returned copy of the circular letter, dated 23 May 1938 (BL Add. MS 56236, fol. 32).

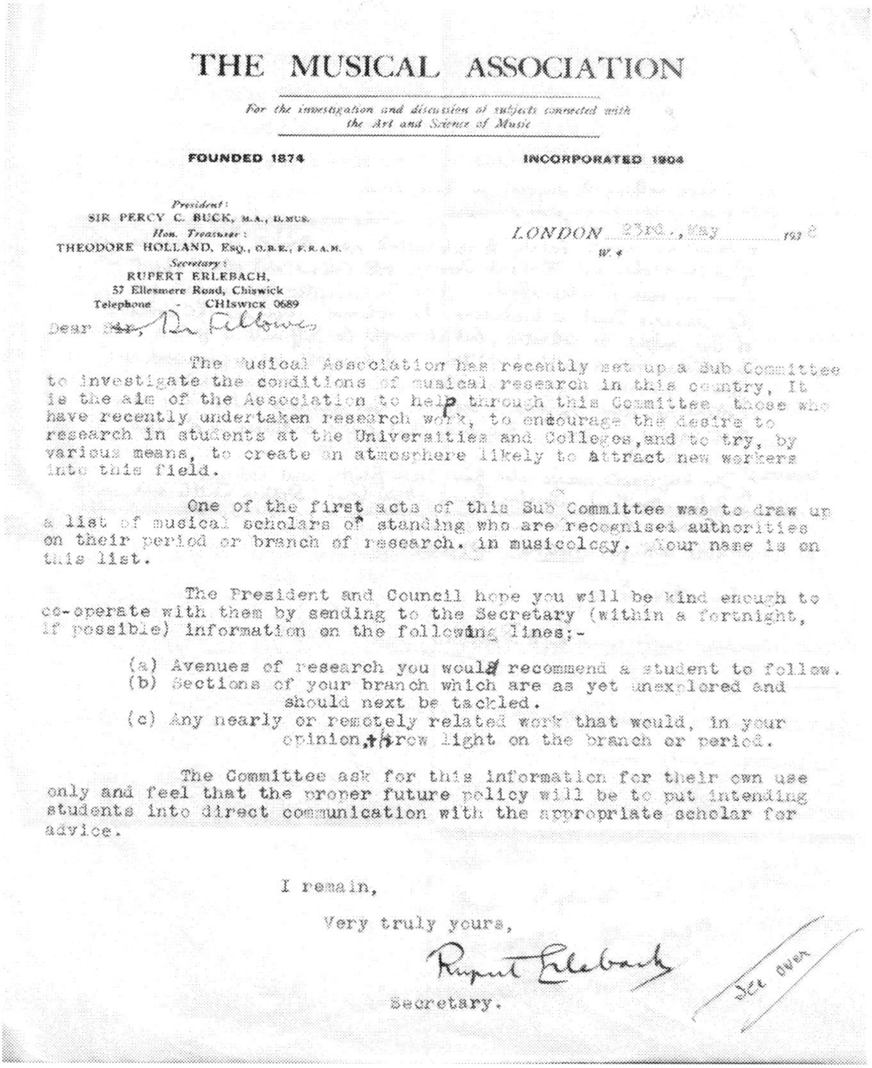

THE MUSICAL ASSOCIATION

For the investigation and discussion of subjects connected with the Art and Science of Music

FOUNDED 1874 INCORPORATED 1904

President: SIR PERCY C. BUCK, M.A., D.MUS.
Hon. Treasurer: THEODORE HOLLAND, Esq., O.B.E., F.R.A.M.
Secretary: RUPERT ERLEBACH, 57 Ellesmere Road, Chiswick
Telephone - CHIswick 0689

LONDON 23rd., May 1938
W.4

Dear ~~Sir~~, Dr Fellowes

The Musical Association has recently set up a Sub Committee to investigate the conditions of musical research in this country, It is the aim of the Association to help through this Committee those who have recently undertaken research work, to encourage the desire to research in students at the Universities and Colleges, and to try, by various means, to create an atmosphere likely to attract new workers into this field.

One of the first acts of this Sub Committee was to draw up a list of musical scholars of standing who are recognised authorities on their period or branch of research. in musicology. Your name is on this list.

The President and Council hope you will be kind enough to co-operate with them by sending to the Secretary (within a fortnight, if possible) information on the following lines;-

(a) Avenues of research you would recommend a student to follow.
(b) Sections of your branch which are as yet unexplored and should next be tackled.
(c) Any nearly or remotely related work that would, in your opinion, throw light on the branch or period.

The Committee ask for this information for their own use only and feel that the proper future policy will be to put intending students into direct communication with the appropriate scholar for advice.

I remain,

Very truly yours,

Rupert Erlebach

Secretary.

See over

Figure 13. Rupert Erlebach to Dr Fellowes, 23 May 1938, on behalf of the Musical Association Research Subcommittee, BL Add. MS 56236, fol. 32.

The experts consulted were Anselm Hughes, E.H. Fellowes, H.B. Collins, Sylvia Townsend Warner, Charles Kennedy Scott, Gerald Cooper, Ernest Walker, E.J. Dent, W.G. Whittaker, Adam Carse, Frank Howes, Canon Galpin, J.B. Trend and H.J.W. Tillyard. Ten of these replied before the deadline, many usefully, with further suggestions sent later by A.H. Fox Strangways, E.H. Meyer and H.C. Colles. Once the replies were collated, the committee then discussed them at the second meeting. The extracts below, among several others, were made by Erlebach; they represent a fair sampling of the views received.[79]

Adam Carse – 5 June 1938

My own work [...] has been centred on the investigation of the history of Wind instruments and matters relating to orchestras and orchestration. I would recommend work on the following lines:

(a) History of Wind instruments used in Orchestras and Military bands during the last four centuries.

(b) Early makers of 1) Brass and 2) Wood wind instruments in the 16th & 17th centuries. Music written for wind instruments in the 17th century.

(c) Any investigation into the period, work and lives of wind instrument makers who have not already been the subject of research.

H.B. Collins – 6 June 1938

(a) It seems to me that students must choose their own line of research. They are not likely to do much good except with subjects that interest them, and what those are they should know themselves.

(b) A very useful thing would be the translation and republication of some of the early theorists, e.g., Gafurius, Zarlino, Zacconi, etc. [...] But the most urgent thing appears to be the publication of more old English music. I have never understood why the Tudor Church Music [10 vols., published by OUP for the Carnegie United Kingdom Trust, 1922–29] was discontinued. I thought that the Editors had collected most of the material. [...] This really seems to me one of the most important projects I can think of. And such publications need not end with the Tudor period, nor be confined to Church music. It might gradually embrace a corpus of national music, like the Denkmäler series in Austria and Germany. I believe that workers would not be found wanting if the financial problem could be solved. Editions for practical use could surely be left to private enterprise on the part of existing publishers.[80]

---

[79] The original responses, together with Erlebach's typed extracts from them, are contained in BL Add. MS 56236 (96 fols.). Sources of the extracts excerpted here are: Carse (fol. 17), Collins (fol. 14), Walker (fol. 21), Kennedy Scott (fol. 22) and Cooper (fol. 20).

[80] Collins's idea for a 'corpus of national music, like the Denkmäler series in Austria and Germany', that 'need not end with the Tudor period, nor be confined to Church music', strikingly prefigured Musica Britannica, the Association's series of music editions that would be established ten years later under the leadership of Anthony Lewis. Lewis may or may not have seen Collins's letter of June 1938, but he would have been aware of the Research Committee's Report that year, recommending publication of music, whether MS facsimiles or editions of 'works not hitherto readily available'.

Ernest Walker – 20 June 1938

In the last 30 years or so much work has been done on many departments of English music that had formerly been more or less neglected: particularly on 15th- & 16th-century music – though I dare say things will still turn up for attention, particularly before 1550. In the mid 17th century Christopher Gibbons might repay research; or, in the early 18th, Croft. [...] Greene's works in general, are worth closer study. In the 19th century Loder & Pierson are worth looking into; and scholarly and detailed investigation of Parry and Stanford would, I think, be valuable.

Charles Kennedy Scott – 22 June 1938

I should suggest a very useful line of research would be the pre-Bach Cantata. I am sure there is a mass of splendid material awaiting resurrection there – from Schütz onwards.

Gerald Cooper – n.d. [late June 1938]

The one thing that is needed above all others is precise information. As I found to my horror, anyone trying to make a survey of any particular period or style is compelled to make a complete tour of Europe, not to speak of U.S.A., before he can collect anything like a complete stock of data. Hence the inaccuracy of so much musicology, which frequently inherits its information from Hawkins, via all the others who have done likewise.

I think no musicology is any good unless it leads directly or indirectly to the discovery, understanding & performance of music that is worthy of so much trouble. I have no time for the kind of theorising that goes round, round & gets nowhere.

One fearsome question needs a lot of study – ornamentation. [...] I am convinced that many, if not most, performances of 17th- & 18th-century music are ruined through lack of knowledge & understanding. [...]

There is much interesting stuff in the early German organ music, from Paumann onwards. A lot of it is tiresome, but there are good things. Also in the Italian music in the time of Frescobaldi. The French lute songs, too, are very beautiful and certainly want attention. But they need publication, not theses.

Respondents tended to comment, as requested, on their own areas of study, largely repertory- or performance-related, rather than on any larger aims, methods or critique of British research in general. The chief exception came in a letter from Sylvia Townsend Warner, by 1938 a published novelist just back from Red Cross service in the Spanish Civil War and clearly concerned with the wider meanings of musicology in an internationalist context.

Sylvia Townsend Warner – 1 June 1938

During this last week-end I took the Chair at the Commission on Musical Research at the Contemporary Music Congress.[81] [...] I will summarise the gist of our conclusions.

1. Musical Research, if it is not to become antiquarian trifling, must study the relationship of musical development to the social and economic conditions of the time; only by such means can one hope to get reliable conclusions; no branch of musicology can be adequately studied in vacuo.

2. Similarly, research into problems of musicology must take into consideration the fact that no musical development takes place exclusively within the bounds of one country. To 'nationalise' research is to set up a fence where no fence need be; involves serious risk of sterility and taking part-conclusions for the whole; and exposes musicology to the danger of non-cultural exploitation by chauvinistic or nationalistic governments. Wherever possible, musicologists should aim at working on a planned international basis, with co-operation instead of overlapping, using the facilities afforded by the International Society for Musical Research.

3. As an example of narrow-mindedness and excessive nationalism in musical research, the Commission pointed out the neglect, on the part of British musicologists, of the material for research afforded by the music of the races within the Empire. With few exceptions, such as Fox Strangways and [Percival] Kirby, this field has been neglected, and already much material has been lost to us. The Commission recommended that the B.B.C., under the guidance of musicologists, should try to include specimens of the music of the Empire in its programmes. (Incidentally, when the B.B.C. started its anti-Bari broadcasts [countering Mussolini's fascist expansionism], the 'Arabian' music included in the programme was so ludicrously a tea-shop fake as to be nothing but a laughing-stock.)

4. Finally, holding the view that musical research, if it is to be of any value, must be related to social and economic conditions, the Commission put forward a recommendation that this view should be applied to the present day; and that a good piece of musical research would be to hold an enquiry into contemporary demand and supply in music. It was felt that this might help our various teaching institutions to adapt their teaching more closely to contemporary needs, i.e. classes in music for the films, attention to recent instrumental development, recognition of the Cinema-organ at the RCO [Royal College of Organists], and so forth.[82]

---

[81] See 'Music and Life Congress: Public Attitude to Modernism', *The Times* (30 May 1938), on the two-day London conference, 28–29 May 1938, held at Queen Mary Hall, Bloomsbury, under the chairmanship of Edwin Evans. Organized by the London branch of the ISCM at a time when the European ISCM festival was being held in Nazi-controlled Stuttgart, the Congress discussions considered the problems of contemporary music from several angles – musical style, tonality, folk music and jazz, psychology, aesthetics and criticism, and contemporary musical research. Participants included Hubert Foss, Harriet Cohen, Elizabeth Maconchy, Donald Tovey, Alan Bush, Lennox Berkeley, Humphrey Searle, Erik Chisholm, Mátyás Seiber, Ernst Hermann Meyer and Frank Howes, besides Warner.

[82] For this extract of Warner's main points, see BL Add. MS 56236, fol. 12. Her original letter is at fol. 33.

Figure 14. Sylvia Townsend Warner, photograph, London, late 1920s.

130 THE ROYAL MUSICAL ASSOCIATION

Warner's observations, cogent and direct, were far ahead of their time, which makes her life's turn away from active musicology all the more regrettable. Her abilities continued to be valued; at the same ISCM meeting, for example, she was asked by a young woman for advice about a notation coach for a study of the late fifteenth-century composer William Cornysh. As an additional contribution, Warner asked one of her Congress speakers, E.H. Meyer, to share his lecture notes from the same day. These summarized his view of musicological work in Germany, Austria, France, the USA, Colombia, Mexico, Brazil and Argentina by reference to named scholars and their interests. For 'England', Meyer named no individual scholars but characterized the field revealingly:

> Musical Research in England does not yet go far enough. Government does not support big editions. University support not general. Greater study needed in: Comparative musicology (primitive and native music), Musical psychology, Acoustics, Possibilities in mechanical & electrical sound production and reproduction. In England research is done by real, practising musicians. Not by library musicologists. 'Musical Association' monthly meetings, 'Proceedings'.[83]

On the face of it, this description sounds (mostly) unarguable; on second thought, one wonders how many *Proceedings* volumes Meyer had actually read.

Erlebach's 'Report of the Sub-Committee' was presented to the Council by C.B. Oldman at their meeting of 8 July 1938, confirming that all the responses and extra submissions had been considered. For ease of reference, R.O. Morris had grouped the suggestions under three main headings: edition or publication of works hitherto not readily available; critical, technical and analytical investigation of particular composers; and research into special subjects (e.g. social and economic backgrounds, instruments and their makers, palaeography, ornamentation, oriental influence on European music, *musica ficta*).[84] The Report concluded with seven firm, if uneven, recommendations:

- That the Music Professors at Universities and Heads of Colleges and Academies be approached.
- That notice be sent to the *Acta Musicologica*, the journal of the International Society for Musical Research.
- That the publication of Facsimiles of early MSS be encouraged.
- That a reference book of Bibliography for intending students be compiled and published.
- That a handbook on Notation be written in English, or alternatively that Professor Wolf's book be translated.
- That a permanent Research Committee be set up to carry out these recommendations and to form an advisory body.
- That the existence of this permanent Committee be made public in the Press.[85]

[83] BL Add. MS 56236, fol. 25.
[84] 'Classification of suggestions received from Experts, drawn up by Mr. R.O. Morris', pasted in at Council meeting for 8 July 1938, BL Add. MS 71015, fol. 76.
[85] 'Report of the Research Sub-Committee set up at the Meeting of Council on 17th March 1938', pasted in at Council meeting for 8 July 1938, BL Add. MS 71015, fol. 74. The first draft of the 'Report' in BL Add. MS 56236, fol. 1, contains an additional

The need to spread news of this positive initiative among academic authorities, international musicologists and the British press was easily agreed and swiftly achieved: Erlebach stood ready with draft texts at the same meeting. Likewise, the recommendation to set up a 'permanent Research Committee' passed immediately: the new group would consist of an advisory body of seventeen people and a further 'executive Committee' of eight, with its own Honorary Secretary if needed.[86] Yet what those proposed *twenty-five* members were expected to do remained unclear; the Council's eagerness to progress the Report, under Buck, evidently led them to form yet another committee without weighing its tasks or practical viability. Caught up simply with moving forward, they ignored any discussion of how, or to what end. Was the new committee meant to act as editorial board for the mooted publishing projects, perhaps to execute them? Was it supposed to advise government and the universities? Was it chiefly to exude goodwill and open a communication channel for registering research topics at home and abroad? No one asked. In time, such opportunities would indeed present themselves. But already by mid-1939, top-heavy with people yet light on real leadership, the 'permanent Research Committee' tumbled into a black hole. No one produced a set of MS facsimiles, a book about bibliography or a handbook on notation. Many people who were invited agreed to join or suggested further names (H.C. Colles recommended Wellesz), but only one invitee, a young Anthony Lewis, posed a logical question: 'I should be very pleased to serve on the Executive branch of your Research Committee. What are we all going to do?'[87] The group is not known ever to have met.

Meanwhile Erlebach was at a standstill on the *Proceedings* index, while Oldman was left holding the bag for the permanent Research Committee, of which he'd consented to act as Honorary Secretary in February 1939 but which instead transformed into a leaner group organizing annual sessions, a sort of small 'Proceedings' committee, in the 1940s.[88] However, despite the lack of any evidence of life for the 'permanent' Research Committee – four years later, in June 1943, President Edmund Fellowes considered it 'dead as a doornail' and recommended burying it 'in the light of future research into our minutes'

---

recommendation that all libraries should produce catalogues of their music stock. Westrup sensibly advised Erlebach to drop this as 'a herculean labour' unrelated to the aims and powers of their committee; student needs would anyway be covered by the bibliography reference book they recommended (J. Westrup to R. Erlebach, 6 July 1938, BL Add. MS 56236, fol. 63).

[86] Permanent Research Committee: H. Allen, E. Dent, F. Galpin, D. Tovey, H.C. Colles, E.H. Fellowes, S. Marchant, E. Walker, J.B. Trend, H.J.W. Tillyard, K. Schlesinger, F.T. Arnold, G.H.P. Hewson, H.B. Collins, A. Hughes, S.T. Warner, P. Buck; Executive Committee: M. Scott, R.O. Morris, Oldman, Westrup (the original subcommittee) plus Dent, F. Howes, G. Cooper and A. Lewis (Dent was the only double entry). See Council minutes, 8 July 1938, BL Add. MS 71015, fols. 76v–77r.

[87] A. Lewis to Rupert Erlebach, 20 July 1938, BL Add. MS 56236, fol. 77.

[88] For correspondence addressed to Oldman and Erlebach regarding paper invitations, mostly of 1938–43, see BL Add. MS 59670 (38 fols.).

[89] – Oldman was wise enough to keep the letters from the original 1938 consultation. They remained in his possession until his death, separate from other Musical Association papers, to be rediscovered in late 1969 by Oldman's BM colleague Alec Hyatt King. King offered them to the RMA secretary at that time, Nigel Fortune, advising that the material would be more easily found if incorporated into the main BM manuscripts catalogue rather than isolated with RMA materials. Fortune agreed and accordingly presented Oldman's documents to the Museum in 1970, long before the bulk of other RMA Papers.[90]

As a postscript it's important to highlight the spark generated by the original Research Committee's work, collecting the views of thoughtful music scholars in Britain before World War II, some of whose ideas ignited later even if the successor committee failed. The Association's Musica Britannica (MB) series, its establishment of a UK thesis register in the 1960s and its members' many contributions to a thorough international revision of *Grove's Dictionary* in the 1970s were not the least of later achievements addressing some of the needs raised in 1938. Meetings and consultations do sometimes have lasting purpose – when they plant the seed of good ideas.

✌ *Wartime Responses*

The troubled years 1939–44 brought their own challenges to Association meetings and procedures, especially in London. To encourage potential paper-givers, Oldman's subcommittee began to assist Erlebach. Most prospects were flattered to be approached but they also declined for lack of confidence, time or access to materials ('To lecture before such a distinguished body needs more than I am capable of', wrote the organist Walter Alcock).[91] A few others said 'yes', notably the violinist May Harrison, who read a paper on Frederick Delius in March 1945. Still others said 'no' but then agreed later, including the composer Herbert Howells, who gave an address on C.V. Stanford in December 1952.[92] It was Edmund Fellowes, a skilled public communicator and by late 1942 Association president, who recommended scheduling more, shorter, papers per meeting (now reduced in number), limiting each published text to 4,000 words; his idea was to encourage more focused work yet to generate enough material to keep *Proceedings* going as normal. Not surprisingly, Dent chimed back with a reminder to seek research not journalism, especially

---

[89] E.H. Fellowes to R. Erlebach, 1 June 1943, BL Add. MS 56236, fol. 91v.
[90] A.H. King to N. Fortune, 4 Dec 1969, BL Add. MS 71052, fol. 255. This transaction explains the two outlying MS numbers for the Research Committee papers retained by Oldman, 56236 and 59670, not part of RMA Papers.
[91] Walter J. Alcock to Erlebach, 13 June 1944, BL Add. MS 59670, fol. 6.
[92] Harrison and Howells first replied to Marion Scott, who quoted Howells's comment: 'The writing of anything is a long-present worry to me in the midst of a very full timetable. And I would not like to offer my mere 2nd best to such an Association' (Scott to Oldman, 29 June 1944, BL Add. MS 59670, fol. 10).

where a proposal didn't show signs of scholarly enquiry.[93] On the problem of falling member numbers, one suggestion was to introduce new forms of subscription – an 'associate' level potentially for students, and an institutional one for universities and colleges; both ideas were earmarked for future consideration. Wider advertising was also mooted, which led to the decision in 1943 to list the Association in *Whitaker's Almanack* (it was still there as recently as 2012). More immediately effective, though, was Fellowes's method of writing to likely musicians who might join if personally invited. By the end of the 1943–44 session, fifty-one new members had been added that year, including the prominent American musicologists Gustave Reese, Glen Haydon, Gilbert Chase, Leonard Ellinwood and Richard S. Hill – a much-needed increase at a crucial time.[94]

All the same, the Association's handling of Honorary Foreign Members, in particular Wolf (1930) and Wellesz (1932), brought dissonance to the record. Once Egon Wellesz had successfully resettled in the UK in November 1938, for example, his new residence was seen to disqualify him as 'foreign', thus cancelling his honorary status too; deemed to be a regular member, he was asked to pay for his yearly membership, which he politely agreed to do. What now seems an unbelievable blunder, this action was fully corrected only much later. Worse still, without comment Johannes Wolf's name was completely erased in late 1940, treating him as an enemy though he was still active as a scholar, friendly with Dent and himself a victim of persecution in Germany; he lived to May 1947. The contrast of such officiousness with its opposite in 1914–18, when the Council voted explicitly to retain the names of all their foreign Honorary Members despite nationality, could not be stronger. Were members earlier in the century more tolerant than in later decades, or just more clear-headed?[95] A happier émigré case is that of Dr Alfred Loewenberg, who arrived in Britain from Berlin in 1935 with 'exceptional gifts for patient and accurate research' besides wide knowledge in opera and theatre studies.[96] Pursuing independent projects in the BM from 1936, he worked tirelessly to complete his now celebrated *Annals of Opera, 1597–1940* with an Introduction by Dent (Cambridge: Heffer, 1943), as well as working on other bibliographical tools including the *British Union Catalogue of Periodicals*. Loewenberg joined the Association in 1944, having also helped Rupert Erlebach refine the *Index to Papers Read*

---

[93] Council meeting minutes, 19 Apr 1945, BL Add. MS 71016, fol. 41r–v. The proposed speaker in question was Robin Hull. The number of meetings per session went back up from four to six in 1944–45.

[94] Other new members at this date included John Christie, Gerald Finzi, William Glock, Alfred Kalmus, Maud Karpeles, Malcolm Sargent, Geoffrey Sharp, Guy Warrack and Kenneth Wright.

[95] For 1918–51 as the high period of English class consciousness and the running of social and sporting clubs, the civil service, schools and the armed forces on instinctively undemocratic lines, see Ross McKibbin, *Classes and Cultures: England, 1918–1951* (Oxford: OUP, 1998; paperback edn, 2000).

[96] A. Hyatt King, 'Alfred Loewenberg: 1902–1949', *ML*, 31 (1950), 116–18.

before the Members of the Royal Musical Association: 1874–1944. After years of discussion and delay, it became the sixth *Proceedings* index to appear, printed finally in 1948.[97] By that time, the Association had also delegated responsibility for editing *Proceedings* to an experienced writer and scholar who'd worked with Oldman in organizing the sessions, Marion Scott: she was named the first Honorary Editor of *PMA* in July 1944, beginning with the seventy-first session.[98] The trend towards coordinating Council efforts boded well.

After Percy Buck stepped down as president, two Church of England clergymen with national scholarly reputations followed in succession, Francis W. Galpin (known as Canon Galpin) in 1938–42, and Edmund Fellowes, a minor canon at St George's Chapel, Windsor Castle, in 1942–47. Their shared connection to the Church presented strong similarities – public-school and Oxbridge backgrounds, devotion to choral, instrumental and communal music-making, and a desire to spread musical knowledge beyond academia and the world of professional music. Typifying the old style of 'amateur' yet exemplary researchers, both were also beyond seventy when they assumed the presidency: Galpin was nearly eighty, Fellowes seventy-two. Yet by virtue of their public-facing work, both were able to achieve huge strides, without chauvinism, in the wider understanding of music's place in a new national story. Galpin was a pathbreaking collector and exponent of ancient, early and global instruments, while Fellowes's editing, lecturing and practical performing did more than anyone else's to increase the appreciation of Elizabethan music as recovered treasure in Western culture. The men's differences too are instructive, and enabled each to make a distinctive contribution. Galpin remained active and forward-looking, giving a paper on music and electricity, including the Hammond organ, as late as 1938. A kind of successor to Ellis and Hipkins but engaged with fieldwork, he symbolized a refreshing alternative to the study of musical texts and ever more exacting performances of them, showing what could be learned from music's material culture, the instruments and practices of non-Western societies, local musicking in a community and new media. Despite being work-based within the Church of England, Galpin was a harbinger of new sociological and ethnographic approaches to music

---

[97] The slightly odd titling and separate issue as a 56-page pamphlet, detached from the journal itself, can be explained by the organization's name change in late 1944 to 'Royal Musical Association', with its *Proceedings* title also in process of change across 1944–45. Loewenberg compiled the classified subject index, while Erlebach did the author index. Only five copies, separately catalogued from *PMA*, appear to be extant in British libraries, at Cambridge, Leeds, Oxford, the Warburg Institute (London) and Edinburgh.

[98] Council meeting minutes, 13 July 1944, BL Add. MS 71016, fol. 18. Scott had been elected to the Council as an Ordinary Member in 1937 (with Katharine Eggar, one of the first two women elected). Her role as Honorary Editor was inadvertently omitted by Erlebach from the Council roster in vol. 71, the first she edited; it was acknowledged in vol. 72 (1945–46). Erlebach continued to compile the discussion section after each paper.

Figure 15. Edmund Horace Fellowes, photograph by Walter Stoneman, February 1944.

study. The idea that oriental influence on European music should be studied seriously was one of his key suggestions in the consultation of 1938.[99]

Fellowes's work, by contrast, began and ended with finding, editing, publishing and performing unknown or forgotten English music of the Elizabethan and Jacobean periods, especially madrigals and lute songs but also Tudor church music, including the previously unsuspected Great Service of William Byrd. Committed to making this music not just knowable but known through teaching, lecturing and demonstration, and himself 'free from the slightest arthritis of antiquarianism',[100] Fellowes was still seen by some as insular in how he viewed his special subject; he was admired for his thoroughness and industry – his editorial output was vast – but, predictably perhaps, he took little interest in other musics. In the 1938 research consultation he'd had 'nothing to

[99] See Arnold Myers, 'Galpin, Francis William', *ODNB*.
[100] From a personal reflection on his achievement and significance by Sylvia Townsend Warner, 'Edmund Fellowes as Editor', *MT*, 93 (1952), 59–61 at 60.

say' about helping students or recommending topics, and was fatalistic about any student's chances of ever finding a publisher for future music editions. His last paper to the Association, on Dowland, had been given in 1929, and his list of suggested paper topics sent to Erlebach in February 1943 consisted almost wholly of English church or sacred music themes.[101] At exactly the same time and in the same letter to Erlebach, just three months into his presidency, he admitted a sense of distance: 'The Mus. Assoc. is rather on my mind and I feel I am not doing anything to justify my position.'

It may have been this vacant feeling that led him to conceive how he might use his position to increase membership, and perhaps more, shine a light on music scholarship *tout court*. Within a year, in early January 1944, he'd become the first (and still the only) music scholar to receive the Companion of Honour (CH), awarded for service of conspicuous national importance. Council members saw this prestige as reflecting on the Association too and conveyed their enthusiasm.[102] It gave him an idea. Around the cloisters of Windsor Castle, there would probably be little difficulty in taking things further with a word here, a letter there. As Fellowes's own *Memoirs of an Amateur Musician* relates: 'In 1944 during my presidency I took certain steps which resulted in receiving the King's command that the Association should thenceforward be known as "The Royal Musical Association". This gave great satisfaction to members.' [103] In fact, RMA records show that on 23 July 1944 Fellowes wrote to the King's private secretary, Sir Alan Lascelles, 'applying for permission to use the prefix "Royal" in the name of The Musical Association'. The letter was referred to the Home Secretary, Stanley Morrison, for submission to King George VI, who then was 'graciously pleased to grant the request [...] and to command that the Association shall henceforth be known as "The Royal Musical Association"'.[104] What Fellowes said in his application is unknown, but he may have pointed to the Association's contribution to new musical discoveries fostering wider appreciation of early English music, to the group's seventieth anniversary in 1944, and maybe to a coming need for spiritual recovery from war, surely involving music, musicians and the arts. Privately of course, Fellowes was aware that royal esteem – in lieu of real cash, jobs or artistic patronage – could go a long way towards helping music scholars attract support from other sources,

---

[101] E.g. the organ in English cathedral use, S.S. Wesley, the English boy chorister, English oratorio, Elgar. His other suggestions were English opera (Purcell, Arne, Sterndale Bennett, Sullivan, Stanford) and the rise of the viola as a solo instrument. Fellowes to Erlebach, 4 Feb 1943, BL Add. MS 56236, fol. 86.

[102] Council minutes, 17 Feb 1944, BL Add. MS 71016, fol. 14. The award was conferred by HM The King. Fellowes had already been appointed MVO in 1931.

[103] Fellowes, *Memoirs of an Amateur Musician* (London: Methuen & Co., 1946), 141.

[104] J.I. Wall, Home Office, to President of the Royal Musical Association, Windsor Castle, 24 Aug 1944, BL Add. MS 71016, fols. 23, 24 (two pasted-in copies of original). Morrison, Home Secretary under Winston Churchill, 1940–45, was formerly leader of the London County Council and later Deputy Leader of the Labour Party; from 1947 he would be the prime mover behind the 1951 Festival of Britain, celebrating Britain and its achievements as part of the national recovery process.

whether publishers, charitable trusts, churches and universities, or other national and international arts organizations. He also knew the Association had important work on the horizon that would need such funding; the hope was that by lifting the distinction of the body's name, so would the whole identity of music scholarship rise in national prestige. No royal charter was required because the Association had already, by its own lights, become legally incorporated.

The official reply came to Fellowes after a month's wait. On 28 August at a Special Council Meeting called for the purpose, nine members received the news as 'a signal honour to the Association'. They then began to consider what their new name and its exchange value would entail.[105]

---

[105] Special Council meeting, 28 Aug 1944, BL Add. MS 71016, fols. 22–25. Present were Fellowes, Capt. Evelyn Broadwood, Buck, Dent, Katharine Eggar, Canon Galpin, Oldman, James Swinburne and Erlebach.

4

Towards UK Musicology, 1945–1960

If a single image could capture the Association's progress over the short period from the mid-1940s to 1960, it would have to be 'striding ahead'. Post-war restructuring provided a backdrop of increased opportunity through the Attlee Labour government's new policies in education, health care and arts provision. In the foreground stood the RMA's own determination: the group had already planted seeds of change by articulating its research priorities in the late 1930s. Together with the 'Royal' prefix joined to its name from late 1944, unexpected but sparking a careful review of the Articles of Association, these new circumstances encouraged the Council to take several steps forward. The resulting lift came through ideas and hard work contributed by experienced and younger members alike – Edmund Fellowes and Anthony Lewis, for example, separated by forty-five years in age and their distinct work environments of Church and the BBC. But for all the blended energy, progress was not a matter simply of mood change after the war, greater public recognition or confidence in the musicological concept; nor were the changes all easy or the outcomes smooth. For RMA members, the post-1945 national transition from a common culture of social-class boundaries and deference to one that increasingly valued expertise and specialization also put more distance between *ad hoc* 'amateur' approaches to research and more systematic, professionalized ones rooted in education and training. Differences and tensions remained about the methods and objects of research, even – still – about the term 'musicology', although the broad picture for music researchers became brighter and more purposeful at every level, especially in the university sector, where new posts and revised programmes began to foster music academic work. Continuity in RMA leadership attuned to both sides of the change gave leavening: the prominent *Times* journalist and RCM lecturer Frank Howes served as president for ten years, 1947–58.

Among important initiatives of this period, seven stand out for the benefits they yielded at the time and later:

- two public fundraising campaigns to memorialize deceased RMA members of international repute (Fellowes and Dent), opening the way for grant-giving and scholarly recognition at a world-leading level
- a new series of scholarly and practical editions of landmark British music otherwise commercially unavailable, supported initially by the Arts Council in preparation for the Festival of Britain, 1951 (Musica Britannica)
- practical advocacy of the value of sound recording, its scholarly potential and national preservation (British Institute of Recorded Sound)
- the concept and shaping of a new Association periodical, a 'Research Bulletin' (later *Research Chronicle*)

- a paper with full-scale appendix issued as a separate publication (Charles Cudworth's 'English Symphonists of the Eighteenth Century' with thematic index)
- financial and editorial support given to two senior external projects in difficulty (the Purcell Society and the journal *Music & Letters*)
- more public-facing activity connected with quasi-autonomous non-governmental organizations, including the Arts Council, the British Council and the BBC, as well as with the British Academy.

The implications of this fast-moving picture were certainly understood and seized. A telling moment occurred in July 1953 when the RMA Council formally converted its 'Sessional Arrangements Sub-Committee' (a legacy of the 1938 Research Committee) into its 'Proceedings Committee'. Simple but pivotal, the decision signalled better coordination of leadership and higher standards in output. Both were needed, in the Committee's words, 'to meet the changed conditions of a growing membership, more diverse activities and widened sphere of influence of the Association today'.[1] That's a fair description of the whole period and offers an outline for the discussion below.

Changed Conditions of a Growing Membership

Voluntary membership was the lifeblood of the RMA, essential to the organization's existence and continuing success. Tracking its size yearly, chasing defaulters and husbanding income from subscriptions determined what the Association could afford, from advertising and social gatherings to room hire, speaker expenses and *PRMA* production. Before the years under consideration, specifically between 1924 and 1944, the group's lists of ordinary and life members hovered variously between about 180 and 240 names. Given this small size and, amazingly, no subscription increase since 1874, the Council had rightly aimed for balance, stability and steady growth, not fireworks. Any thought of doing more than holding regular meetings for the hearing, discussing and publishing of scholarly papers would barely have occurred to anyone. That's why after seventy years of such routine, members definitely noticed a thrust from the series of *external* boosts that began in 1944 with the granting of the royal prefix, and continued apace with the ending of world war in 1945, the national purchase in 1946 of the Hirsch Collection and launch of the BBC Third Programme, the establishment of new university music posts in 1947 and the proposal in 1948, then support in 1949, for a special music edition inaugurated with public funds. Member numbers expanded under these changes, but in unpredictable spurts. Overall, the numbers rose by 74 per cent between 1945 and 1960 from 262 to 457. The biggest surge, from 307 members to 387 in the three years from 1950 to 1953, showed a spike of 26 per cent in that short but intense national celebratory span (including Elizabeth II's coronation).[2]

---

[1] Council minutes, 6 July 1953, M MS 1, pp. 57–58.

[2] Figures from members' lists in *PMA* 70 (1943–44), *PRMA* 71 (1944–45), *PRMA* 76 (1949–50), *PRMA* 79 (1952–53) and *PRMA* 86 (1959–60). Honorary Foreign Members

It was the sense of real gain in these figures, not just recovery to an earlier strength, that spurred the Council to bolder commitment in mid-1953.

A comparison of the group's make-up in 1950 and 1960, like that described in Chapter 2 above for 1875 and 1924, reveals changes that are perhaps less dramatic than one might expect when set against the earlier numbers.[3] The proportion of female members had risen slightly, for example, from 16 per cent in 1924 to 24 per cent in 1950 (21 per cent in 1960). From the little that can be known for certain about sexual orientation, both later lists also had a few more members of same-sex or bisexual orientation than before – at least ten people in 1950 (including Felix Aprahamian, Thurston Dart, Dent, Howard Ferguson, Boris Ord, Philip Radcliffe and J.B. Trend) and twelve in 1960 (including Nigel Fortune, Jeremy Noble and Andrew Porter). Although by 1960 the public listing of members' academic degrees and workplaces had already been eliminated from *PRMA*, itself suggesting greater normalization of higher education as well as a less socially self-conscious climate inside the RMA, academic qualifications published in 1950 show that some 70 per cent of RMA members worked in music or had music degrees by that time, a definite increase on the estimated 1924 figure (60 per cent); the percentage is likely to have been still higher by 1960. In geographical spread, the most obvious trend across the whole period is increased membership outside London. In both 1874 and 1924, the Association drew some 89 per cent of its members from metropolitan London; by June 1950, that proportion had fallen to 58 per cent, and by 1960 to 41 per cent. Many members resided or worked nearby in the home counties, easily commutable, but the numbers well outside London had grown too, especially in urban regions served by major universities; foreign memberships rose especially in the USA, and institutional memberships were created in 1954.

It was the name change from 'The Musical Association (Incorporated 1904)' to 'The Royal Musical Association', formally agreed by a Special Resolution of members on 2 November 1944 and approved by the Board of Trade in January 1945, which led the Council to consider ways of improving the body's governance.[4] All legal documents including the Memorandum and Articles of Association had to be reprinted with the new name; the journal's revised title, *Proceedings of the Royal Musical Association* from volume 71 (1944–45), would also need to be embedded. To review its procedures and take advantage of this opportunity, the Council appointed a subcommittee.[5] Everyone agreed that making things more transparent and democratic was essential, especially in nominating and electing members to Council and officer positions and in setting the length of Council service. The revisions aimed to manage change

---

are not included in the totals.
[3] See Chapter 2 above, pp. 50–51.
[4] See a copy of the Resolution in BL Add. MS 71016, fol. 28. The Association had been Company no. 81327 since its incorporation in 1904, and remained a limited company. See also the 'Report' of the seventy-first session in *PRMA*, 72 (1945–46), pp. xix–xxii.
[5] Council minutes, 19 Apr 1945, BL Add. MS 71016, fols. 39v–40v.

better, ensuring that Council members didn't stay in the same role for long periods or that presidents and vice-presidents didn't routinely re-circulate. Thus rotation was altered, so that two Ordinary Members would retire from Council each year and not be eligible for re-election until after one year. Candidates for election as Ordinary Members (including anyone eligible who'd rotated off) could now be nominated by the Council or, crucially, proposed and seconded by two members of the Association, in writing, seven days before the voting meeting; by contrast, nominations for president had to come from within the Council. In addition, the group's solicitors recommended raising the total membership ceiling from 500 to 600; placing 'Past Presidents' in a separate category between 'President' and 'Vice-Presidents' on the Council roster; increasing the life member subscription from 10 to 15 guineas; and if voted as necessary, increasing the annual subscription from 1 guinea to not more than 2 guineas.[6] Postal ballots were avoided at this time in an effort to revitalize physical attendance after the war.

Naturally each of these proposals was discussed and brought back to the Council for consideration, spurring further refinements or new ideas; the process wore on for many months, indeed years. The final agreed version of the revised Memorandum and Articles, presented at an Extraordinary General Meeting in January 1951, was approved on 8 February 1951.[7] Already in late 1946, changes had been made to the method of sending out Reports and Accounts for the AGM. In strict compliance with the Companies Act 1929, it was decided to send both an income and expenditure account and a separate balance sheet to all persons receiving the AGM notice (as still occurs); in turn, the 'end of financial year' date had to be moved earlier, to 30 June, ensuring time for account preparations. Yet exact details of such changes are less important than their purpose, which was to improve openness, responsibility and fairness to all members, precisely to make the best use of resources for the group's agreed purpose – the advancement of learning through the investigation and discussion of subjects connected with the art and science of music[8] – rather than for any private shareholders. This was always the basis on which

---

[6] Council minutes, 12 Feb 1946, BL Add. MS 71016, fols. 58–60. In an Extraordinary General Meeting of 12 May 1949, members voted to raise the annual subscription to 1½ guineas. The rationale was to resume printing of paper discussions, possibly to hold more meetings and to enlarge the secretary's salary (BL Add. MS 71017, fol. 20r–v. Several members resigned as a result of the increase.

[7] A typescript of the whole document (10 + 72 paragraphs) is interpolated in BL Add. MS 71017, fols. 70–90. It never appeared in full in *Proceedings*, but was available to all members by request.

[8] The formulation prioritizing 'the advancement of learning' over 'the reading of papers' had been agreed in May 1950, with a full statement of the Association's first object expanded in July, as follows: 'The advancement of learning and the reading of papers on subjects relating to the art, science, theory, practice, composition, acoustics and history of music and the use and construction of musical instruments, with discussions of these subjects and the giving of illustrations in reference to the papers read' (Council minutes, 18 July 1950, M MS 1, p. 7).

the Association operated and the source of its advantageous tax position, or charitable status. Far from reverting to some throwback of monarchical privilege or bonded servitude by taking 'Royal' into its name, the new identity of 1944 stimulated the group's sense of mission, directing its corporate capacity even more towards giving public value.

It's true that the monarchy enjoyed exceptional popularity throughout the war, which 'did much to shield the old élites'.[9] But soon afterwards, Britain also experienced a high point of class consciousness with, in 1951, the highest-ever Labour vote, a context within which the growing, mixed RMA membership gradually subdivided into recognizable interest groups. Surmised from members' lists and RMA correspondence, the five-part pattern below depicts the occupational range across which members interacted in this period, naming well-known exemplars:

- music academics, some in higher education, concerned with university or music college teaching, research and its communication, aiming for the spread of serious musical learning (Gerald Abraham, Laurence Picken, Reginald Thatcher, Jack Westrup, Hans Redlich, Thurston Dart, Denis Arnold)[10]
- music-related civil servants, librarians, broadcasting, recording or performance administrators, aiming to be methodical and fair in serving the public, concerned to enhance respect for music within a broader arts setting (C.B. Oldman, A.H. King, John Denison, Seymour Whinyates, Julian Herbage, Charles Cudworth, Earl of Harewood, Oliver Neighbour)
- independent, entrepreneurial researchers, writers or teachers, looking for opportunities to uncover, perform, translate, publish or explicate new musical information, works and practices (Edgar Hunt, Cecily Arnold, Max Hinrichsen, Emily Anderson,[11] Geoffrey Sharp, Raymond Russell, Eric Blom, Andrew Porter)
- music creatives, composers and performers, experienced practitioners interested in historical or technical exploration of music, concerned to support music study but not themselves primarily researchers (many church organists, local teachers and university tutors, besides well-known musicians such as Ruth Gipps, Myra Hess, Kathleen Long, Ralph Vaughan Williams, Arthur Bliss, Gerald Finzi, Adrian Boult)
- non-music professionals, active in business, trade, science or other humanities and civic fields, devoted to music as a private pastime or public affiliation,

---

[9] McKibbin, *Classes and Cultures*, 534.
[10] These were sometimes called the 'learned world' representatives in discussions of plans for a reception (Council minutes, 5 July 1951, M MS 1, p. 27).
[11] Anderson (1891–1962), an Irish academic, German linguist and music scholar known for her translations of the letters of Mozart and his family, and of Beethoven (some 250 of which she unearthed), worked in British intelligence for more than thirty years, receiving an OBE for her service in World War II. Her committed Beethoven research took place in the 1950s. Despite being snubbed by the German Beethoven establishment, she offered to assist O.E. Deutsch and others, passing over her own work; but internal rivalries prevented their own Beethoven letters edition and only she produced one, which remained authoritative for decades. She also contributed to Deutsch's Festschrift in 1963. See Jackie Uí Chionna, *Queen of Codes: The Secret Life of Emily Anderson, Britain's Greatest Female Codebreaker* (London: Headline, 2023), esp. 260–61.

including concert- and opera-goers, amateur performers, donors of time and considerable skill to musical causes (Eric Halfpenny, Capt. Evelyn Broadwood, Cedric Glover, Robert Mayer).

Obviously this is a simplified breakdown of a complex body whose individual members cannot all be assigned to discrete categories. But the point is clear that music study as a subject, its increasing appeal and specialization, drew a wide range of people together across formerly pronounced social divides. As research deepened and study topics diversified, so the collective group would grow in size and influence.

It goes without saying that continual revision and expansion required careful monitoring. Retaining older members and attracting new, improving communications, and generating extra value from their assets stimulated the Council's thought. At the most basic level, in March 1950 C.B. Oldman requested a speedy circulation of minutes after each Council meeting so that everyone could be reminded of agreed actions and stay abreast of developments; his request aroused new energy in Erlebach's note-taking, duplicating and mailing routines.[12] Similarly, empowering subcommittees brought more decisiveness to specific tasks. As head of the Proceedings group and Honorary Editor of *PRMA*, respectively, the two BM Library colleagues C.B. Oldman and A.H. King worked especially well together in the mid-1950s. They not only improved article styling and *PRMA* production by supplying 'Notes for Authors' and renovating the journal's design (see Fig. 16), but wove these innovations around a marketing shift begun in 1948, away from sending *gratis* copies to libraries, towards creating paid institutional memberships for libraries and other corporate bodies in 1954, raising expectations (and cash).[13] There were experiments, too, with adding a lecture meeting each session to attract wider attendance, on a Saturday; bestowing (free) life membership on the occasional retired member unable to sustain an ordinary subscription (Boris Ord, Eva

---

[12] If it was mildly surprising that no RMA Council minutes had been circulated before, the change at least shows an awareness of need. Erlebach's coverage of member meetings for lectures and AGMs continued as before in a minute book, now BL Add. MS 71017 (1949–57), while a professional reporter's typewritten record of Council and some Subcommittee meetings was produced separately from 9 March 1950. After duplication and mailing, those typewritten sheets were then pasted into additional RMA minute books now held privately in Manchester. Unexplained on the MSS themselves, the procedure is described in Erlebach's 'Summary Outline of Secretary's Duties and work for which he is responsible', n.d. (probably 1956) in BL Add. MS 71034, fols. 96–97. To gain a complete view of events, the two sources are best read together.

[13] See 'Notes for Authors of Papers to be read at Meetings', c. 1955 (BL Add. MS 71034, fols. 25–26), giving instructions under seven headings: Length, Preparation of copy, Illustrations, Discussions, Proofs, Offprints and Copyright. Further changes to the journal's layout included removal of much of the front matter and a slimmed-down presentation for the members' list, now moved to the back. The last Annual Report and Accounts to be published here appeared in *PRMA* 76 (1949–50), covering session 75 (1948–49).

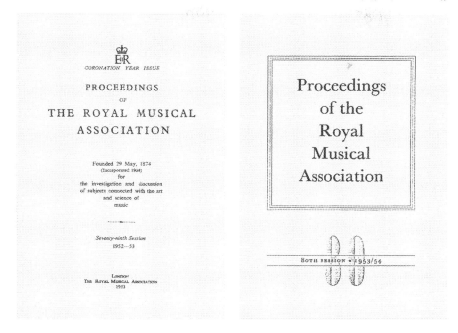

Figure 16. Cover designs for *PRMA* 79 (1952–53) and 80 (1953–54).

Morton); and shielding members from external advertising by mailshot (from Macmillan & Co. for *Grove 5*). Most impressive was the admission of past error in how the Council had deprived Egon Wellesz of his honorary status in 1938: in December 1953 Thurston Dart and Oldman proposed refunding Wellesz all his paid subscriptions and reinstating him as an Honorary Member, which everyone heartily agreed.[14] By that time, Wellesz rejoined a list that included Albert Schweitzer as the latest Honorary Foreign Member (1952).

A way to honour the Association's own distinguished scholars emerged after the death of Edmund Fellowes in December 1951. According to a letter in *The Times*, an influential group of Fellowes's friends from Oxford University, Westminster Abbey, St Paul's Cathedral, St George's Windsor, the RAM and the RMA wished to commemorate him with a memorial fund to be used 'in some practical scheme for continuing his work'.[15] Launched in April 1952 with 100 guineas from the Dean and Canons of Windsor, the Fellowes Memorial Fund grew by public subscription. The RMA gave 10 guineas in November

---

[14] Their Honorary Solicitor, Brig. H.A.F. Crewdson, had explained that the honour, once conferred, could not be withdrawn no matter where the member might be living subsequent to election (Council minutes, 17 Dec 1953, M MS 1, p. 63).

[15] 'Dr. E.H. Fellowes', *The Times* (24 Apr 1952). Three of the fourteen signatories were RMA officers (F. Howes, G. Dyson, R. Thatcher), and the committee's treasurer was Cedric Glover, the RMA Honorary Treasurer. Dyson acted as the Fund's chairman. Howes probably assisted in getting the letter placed.

1952, besides individual donations, and in June 1953 the Fund closed with £724; by mutual agreement it was transferred from the Windsor group to the Association's management for 'musical research of the type that the late Dr. Fellowes himself initiated and pursued'.[16] Accepting this responsibility opened a new branch of RMA activity, providing a model for how future individual projects might be supported. The first Fellowes beneficiary, Nigel Fortune, studied early Baroque Italian manuscripts (1954), and the second, Robert Donington, worked on the interpretation of Baroque music in performance (1957); though neither specialized in Elizabethan repertory, each used documentary or practical evidence to revealing effect.

Six years later, after E.J. Dent's death in August 1957, the instigation of the Dent Medal 'for outstanding services to musicology' followed a similar path.[17] This too involved a *Times* Letter to the Editor announcing a fundraising drive, together with an external partner, the IMS at Basel; Frank Howes, the letter's author, helped to place the announcement and arranged for its signatures.[18] But in this case, the idea came first and foremost from the RMA, recognizing, as the letter explains, Dent's multi-faceted and 'fruitful life […] spent in advancing several disparate musical causes – pure scholarship, university education which first established musicology in this country, international cooperation in both ancient and modern music, opera in English, and opera in England'. By the time the statement appeared, in early November 1958, the RMA Council had already accepted Anthony Lewis's good suggestion, in March 1958, that Dent's international stature and long IMS involvement could best be memorialized by a symbolic representation, the striking of a medal, rather than by a local cash award or grant. Funds came in, initially to be lodged with the IMS, whose Directorium would select an annual recipient.[19] Operational practicalities, however, soon moved much of the responsibility back to the RMA, with nominating power shared between the two councils. The first recipient, jointly selected, was Gilbert Reaney, a brilliant Machaut scholar from Sheffield working in California, who received his medal at the IMS Congress in New York in 1961. Before long, the list of Dent Medallists would read like a Who's Who of international musicology.

---

[16] Council minutes, 6 July 1953, M MS 1, p. 56, setting out five conditions for administering the fund, including giving the Association full discretion to make grants on its own initiative. The transfer to the RMA was made public in 'Fellowes Memorial Fund', *The Times* (29 July 1953).

[17] Purpose as expressed in the announcement letter, 'Professor E.J. Dent', *The Times* (11 Nov 1958).

[18] F. Howes to N. Fortune [RMA secretary], 5 Nov 1958 (BL Add. MS 71050, fol. 126r–v). Howes wrote the letter and asked Noel Annan, Provost of King's College, Cambridge, and Arthur Bliss, Master of the King's Music, to sign it with him.

[19] Council minutes, 17 Mar 1958, M MS 1, p. 129. The Council had already learned from J.B. Trend that Dent's will forbade the holding of a 'memorial service or commemorative ceremony of any kind whatsoever, religious or otherwise'. Lewis's suggestion circumvented that restriction and positioned the IMS as chief arbiter for what was envisioned as an annual RMA award of international standing.

Helping to organize the medal's design and execution in 1959 was none other than Nigel Fortune, already the RMA's new secretary from late 1956, replacing Rupert Erlebach. Fortune's appointment – he was chosen from a field of nine keen applicants – came at a critical moment in the organization's expansion. As a Cambridge-trained musicologist (PhD 1954) and active music librarian at Senate House, University of London, he brought a sea change to the Association's sense of professionalism, its ways of integrating old and new systems and blending academic, business and social worlds. In many ways over the next fourteen years, he would prove pivotal in lifting the RMA's reputation to a new level, from his member surveys, close consultation of the Council and measured introduction of the Annual Conference from 1966, to his highly skilled management of RMA publications, grant-writing for RMA projects, social networking and helpful advice to postgraduate musicologists.[20] In recognition of his increased workload after only three years, the Council increased his stipend to 125 guineas for 1959–60.

More Diverse Activities

The small widening in Association activity that included fundraising and later grant-giving occurred after the deaths of two senior members, both public figures; each occasion was an isolated event reflecting personal achievement. By contrast, World War II catalyzed a nationwide determination to rebuild whole structures, to make a better world by reforming fundamental systems. Education was one of these, and its role in 'social reconstruction' after the war was already in planning from 1943 under Churchill's coalition government. The Butler Education Act of 1944 stimulated expansion at secondary school level, and the Barlow Report of 1946 pushed for much greater scientific capability; together they created new demand for university places, focusing the government's attention on a large gap in provision that had long been ignored. Through this change, British academic musicology finally found the opening it needed to put down roots. More professors, serious practitioners and postgraduate students began to infuse the RMA's work, inspiring and participating in its expanded range of activities.

The historian Ross McKibbin has well described the changing educational context in his *Classes and Cultures: England, 1918–1951* (1998), noting that throughout the inter-war years, England had fewer students at university, proportionately, than any other country in Europe – even than, within Great Britain, Wales and Scotland. The total number of full-time university students in all of Great Britain was only about 50,000 in 1939, up from 40,000 in 1919; both figures represented a tiny proportion of the relevant age group in those

---

[20] For a slightly later glimpse of Fortune's work with postgraduates, showing how one Oxford student, Frank Dobbins, navigated the journey from research, paper-giving and publication (on French Renaissance poetry and secular song) to interviews and his first teaching post, see Dobbins's letters to Fortune, November 1968 to early 1969, in BL Add. MS 71045, fols. 129–31.

years.[21] McKibbin goes on to show how the English university sector's four main components in 1939 – Oxford and Cambridge, London, major 'red-brick' and minor 'red-brick' universities – grew in structure and curricula to 1951 according to their location, physical infrastructure and available private support. Since the real problem had been the narrowness of the universities' financial bases, stemming from 'the state's reluctance to fund them more extensively or to encourage more people to attend them',[22] it was obvious that redress meant accepting the University Grants Commission's proposals, during the war, for expansion. As a result, student numbers went up quickly at the civic universities, by more than 80 per cent, whereas change was slower at Oxford and Cambridge, where physical and educational limits intervened. It was the Barlow Report that led to a doubling in the number of science and technology students by 1947, while the number of arts students grew by only 50 per cent.[23] In this environment, the basis for graduate research, or any drive for organized graduate teaching, remained embryonic; only London University with its autonomous colleges, institutes, teaching hospitals and vast number of external students had a framework for developing postgraduate work in the German or American manner.

In music, academic opportunities up to the 1950s were few and the institutional shift slow. It wasn't until 1950, for example, that Oxford allowed music to become an honours course, with a new syllabus demanding a wider knowledge of musical scholarship than the old B.Mus. degree, chiefly practical; similarly, at that date the writing of a PhD thesis on a musical subject was almost unknown anywhere in Britain. Of course there had been university 'Professors of Music' for hundreds of years, even some who did more than play the organ, compose an anthem or give a few lectures; before 1945, music faculties had been most strongly established at Oxford, Cambridge, Durham, Edinburgh and Birmingham. But their function had been to train undergraduates in music techniques while supporting university performance activities, including ceremonial ones, not necessarily to pursue scholarly research or contribute to musical knowledge. Through his own initiative, E.J. Dent became an exception at Cambridge (1926–41), as did Donald Tovey at Edinburgh (1914–40) and Jack Westrup at Newcastle (1941–44; part of Durham University), then Birmingham (1944–46).

What changed noticeably in 1947 was the making of four appointments in as many university music departments, which actively encouraged scholarship. Concurrent but largely coincidental, these involved people now seen as pivotal in British academic musicology: Gerald Abraham at Liverpool (a newly created part-time post), Westrup at Oxford (after Hugh Allen's death), Anthony

---

[21] McKibbin, *Classes and Cultures*, 248. The book's subsection 'Educating Élites: The Universities', pp. 248–59, gives a fuller background. Besides the universities, McKibbin also considers educational access and social mobility, critiquing the story of English education in this period as 'a history of failure' (269).

[22] Ibid., 256.

[23] Ibid., 258.

Lewis at Birmingham (replacing Westrup) and Thurston Dart at Cambridge (a new assistant lectureship, his first post).[24] None of these scholars had followed a narrowly academic path, let alone earned a doctoral degree, though Lewis had learned from Dent at Cambridge, and Westrup had studied music as well as classics at Oxford; Abraham possessed no degree at all. Each would make an impact on their larger university communities and music training, but also shape music scholarship in their subfields through their publications, advisees and RMA work. Meanwhile, determined postgraduate students still went abroad. Dart, whose degree was in mathematics, had gone to Belgium after the war to study early music privately with Charles van den Borren; Gilbert Reaney studied medieval manuscripts in Paris with French government funding, while Denis Arnold worked on Renaissance music in Bologna on an Italian government scholarship. Initial teaching posts for advanced graduates were hard to find, often having to be split between music and extra-mural or adult education departments. For the generation after Abraham and Westrup, even improved musicological training by the mid- and later 1950s did not automatically lead to a British academic job. Journalism and publishing, broadcasting, arts management and library work still offered viable, influential careers, although for some the most promising alternative was teaching abroad, notably in the USA, where musicology had begun to flourish through the assimilation of European émigré scholars since the mid-1930s. A British brain drain was on the horizon.

In the long run, this educational transition proved a boon for the Association. More postgraduates attended RMA meetings to listen, and to present and publish their work, while some helped edit scores, catalogue material or assist with administrative tasks. Nigel Fortune was a key link, having helped Dart edit Fellowes's collection of Dowland songs for MB (1953); latterly, he extended a consistently warm welcome to students and visitors. Circles of mentoring and friendship grew among Russianists, seventeenth- and eighteenth-century English specialists, scholars of medieval chanson and Baroque opera, early instrument performers, singers, Renaissance scholars and twentieth-century serialists. Soon musicology seemed not so dull after all.

And just as academic interests began flowing in, some outward-facing opportunities arose. The Association was invited, first, to consult on a new 'London Music Centre' to be built after the war, and second, to participate in a music publication scheme for the forthcoming exhibition in 1951, the Festival of Britain. Though differing in scale, both openings showed the regard in which the Association was held.

---

[24] See, respectively, Brian Trowell, 'Gerald Ernest Heal Abraham, 1904–1988', *Proceedings of the British Academy*, 111 (2001), 339–93; Gerald Abraham, 'Jack Allan Westrup, 1904–1975', *Proceedings of the British Academy*, 63 (1977), 471–82; Michael Pope, rev., 'Lewis, Sir Anthony Carey', *ODNB*; and Allen Percival, 'Robert Thurston Dart', in *Source Materials and the Interpretation of Music: A Memorial Volume to Thurston Dart*, ed. Ian Bent (London: Stainer & Bell, 1981), 21–26.

Already in July 1944, word had come from two Life Members, Mewburn Levien and Evelyn Broadwood, that the London Society (a group of eminent Londoners concerned for planning in the capital) wished to canvass music institutions and societies about the needs of music after the war. The site and function of a possible new urban music centre were being discussed at the London County Council, which favoured the South Bank of the Thames for a cultural building with educational purpose. The city had lacked a major concert hall since the destruction of Queen's Hall by an incendiary bomb in 1941. The South Bank idea challenged RMA Council members, who instead preferred somewhere in the West End that would allow a range of performances including opera. Forming a subcommittee (Levien, Broadwood and Dent, jocularly naming themselves 'the Conspiracy'), the Council sought a paper from Patrick Abercrombie, author of the *County of London Plan* (1943), and scheduled a discussion for the first RMA meeting of 1944–45. In the event, a full members' discussion took place without Abercrombie but with written submissions from his co-author John Forshaw and their acoustic consultant Hope Bagenal. The discussion, printed in *Proceedings*, revealed fresh information and several shades of artistic and political opinion.[25]

Alongside further consultation by an enlarged London Society committee – from October 1945 it comprised nineteen senior figures, eleven of them RMA members[26] – London County Council planners moved steadily towards the concept of a large concert hall seating 3,000, with future thoughts of a medium-sized hall (1,200) and a small hall (700) attached to it, sited on the South Bank. By mid-1947, all alternative sites had been abandoned; the designing of what would open during the Festival of Britain in May 1951 as the Royal Festival Hall began in 1948, and the foundation stone was laid in October 1949. In presenting a paper touching on the hall soon after it opened, 'Musical Taste and Concert Hall Design', Bagenal extended the distinguished acoustical research tradition of John Tyndall and Lord Rayleigh, two early Association members, by adopting a historical approach.[27] His acknowledgement of contradictions, alike in musicians, listeners and architectural requirements, was illuminating and provided food for thought.[28]

---

[25] 'Discussion on a Music Centre for London', *PRMA*, 71 (1944–45), 1–17.
[26] The RMA members were Broadwood, Levien and Dent, Edric Cundell, George Dyson, E.H. Fellowes, Frank Howes, Victor Hely-Hutchinson, Maud Karpeles (soon a key founder of the International Folk Music Council), Stanley Marchant and Marion Scott. Others included Bagenal and Forshaw, Felix Cassel, Kenneth Clark, Mary Glasgow and Reginald Jacques (the last two from CEMA, Council for the Encouragement of Music and the Arts, predecessor of the Arts Council and chaired by John Maynard Keynes). See RMA Council minutes, 8 Oct 1945, BL Add. MS 71016, fol. 48.
[27] *PRMA*, 78 (1951–52), 11–29. The paper was given on 15 December 1951, chaired by Howes.
[28] The paper broaches early criticism of the hall's acoustics, generally thought too dry and later found to be partly attributable to the consultants' specifications for room surfaces being ignored. But Bagenal's paper also explained how scientists could give concert halls clarity or warmth, just not both at the same time. After inadequate correctives were

Figure 17. Festival of Britain, 1951, South Bank Exhibition, postcard photograph of an artist's impression, aerial view, Royal Festival Hall centre left.

The music publication scheme, in turn, was of a different order, originating within the Association and vesting complete authority in it for a scholarly edition of national music. Initially conceived in 1947 as a limited project, it grew to become a running series. Now approaching 110 volumes, the edition is still in progress nearly eighty years later as Musica Britannica, published by Stainer & Bell and managed by a Trust. Selecting, editing, producing and helping to market landmark pieces of music while also facilitating the music's performance and understanding, an important corollary, epitomized the Association's diversified activity in the late 1940s and 50s.

As suggested in the previous chapter, the idea of an English *Denkmäler* or monuments series had been percolating within the Association since 1938. It ultimately took shape under Anthony Lewis, back from war service, experienced in BBC Third Programme planning and just appointed to the Peyton and Barber chair at Birmingham. Lewis saw the coming Festival of Britain as a perfect opportunity to have the project financed and launched with confidence. He proceeded carefully, first getting RMA in-principle approval in October 1948, then by December, after private consultation, presenting the scheme as an invitation from the Arts Council to have the RMA 'act as technical advisers' on the project, including choice of works, negotiation for publication and financial arrangements.[29] Lewis recommended that the first few volumes, under the auspices of the 1951 Festival, whose purpose was to

---

applied in the late 1960s, a substantial renovation of 2005–07 made more successful changes to improve conditions for performers and warmth of sound for listeners.

[29] Council minutes, 14 Dec 1948 (BL Add. MS 71016, fol. 144). See also see Anthony Lewis, 'Musica Britannica: Past and Future', *Listener* (2 Feb 1956), 193, in which Frank Howes is credited with suggesting an approach to the Arts Council for financial assistance, using funds put at their disposal by Festival of Britain authorities.

show British artistic and scientific progress over time, should represent three different musical periods – pre-Elizabethan, pre-Purcell and the eighteenth century. A subcommittee of Howes, Lewis, Dent and Westrup was then appointed, and in January 1949, after exploring format and possible publishers, they presented a list of likely works for 'A comprehensive historical edition of ENGLISH MUSIC' in sixteen volumes.[30]

Lewis's original working title, 'Standard English Editions', was hardly exciting, and the plan already embraced music that wasn't English (e.g. by John Field). But titling was thought less problematic at this stage than arranging viable finance, settling the degree of member responsibility and clearing copyright for existing editions (Barclay Squire and Fuller Maitland's Fitzwilliam Virginal Book).[31] Discussions carried on for several more months. Although a firm financial commitment from the Arts Council was still lacking, members remained buoyant and proactive. They took legal advice (adjusting their Memorandum of Association), added Fellowes to the committee and, trusting that some form of government assistance would come, passed a special resolution in May 1949 to undertake the project. In July the Arts Council offer arrived – £2,000 on loan, to be repaid without interest from the profits of the publication scheme on a date not specified. In return, the RMA was to publish the first four volumes by 1 May 1951. This clarity came as a relief. More wheels started turning, with works and editors 'under review'; the Council accepted the offer in a carefully worded reply in November 1949.[32] Then began a virtual race to the Festival and beyond, with editing, production, publicity, launch, concerts, royal telegrams, receptions, BBC broadcasts and more – fireworks at last. Lewis had set a major enterprise in motion.

All this focus on the new publishing project, though, should not obscure other activities that were extensions of earlier RMA priorities in source collecting, cataloguing and international cooperation. For just as British academic life and institutional reshaping were gathering pace regionally after the war, so an urge to reconnect with research partners in other countries, and to preserve or catalogue further source materials for the benefit of international music study, came to the fore in the mid-1950s. The IMS, for example, held its Sixth International Congress in Oxford, 29 June – 4 July 1955. Jack Westrup, Heather Professor of Music and an IMS directorate member, served as organizer and

---

[30] Lewis's typed listing is pasted in at BL Add. MS 71016, fols. 149–50. Probable editors of each work were discussed at the January 1949 Council meeting, with works and editors subject to change. Ultimately only five items on the original list appeared in the first sixteen volumes.

[31] The idea's progress can be traced in Council minutes for 19 Oct 1948 (BL Add. MS 71016, fol. 135v) and 29 Jan 1949 (BL Add. MS 71016, fols. 147–48); and in minutes of the Extraordinary General Meeting on 12 May 1949, BL Add. MS 71017, fols. 18v–19v.

[32] For the offer and ensuing discussion, see Council minutes, 8 Oct 1949 (BL Add. MS 71017, fols. 32–33v; and for the draft reply, Council minutes, 17 Nov 1949 (BL Add. MS 71017, fols. 36v–37). The delay between receipt of the original offer and its positive acceptance was due partly to a postal snag and partly to recent changes in 'editorial circumstances'. In the event, the RMA would deliver three volumes, not four, by 1 May 1951.

RMA liaison. He spoke on the new blend of musicianship and music history study that now characterized several undergraduate music courses in Britain, while to close the week, the RMA gave a generous reception in London at the Arts Council Drawing Room in St James's Square.[33] More concrete work with the IMS would follow four years later, in July 1959, when a firm plan for the 'International Inventory of Musical Sources', soon known by its acronym in French as RISM, was first introduced to the RMA Council as a multinational cataloguing project for which their backing and artistic sponsorship was needed.[34] A.H. King and C.B. Oldman took the lead, seeing this effort as providing the modern replacement for Robert Eitner's *Quellen-Lexikon* (10 vols., 1900–04), widely acknowledged as a primary international goal.[35] The RMA's fundraising and scoping work to support RISM would begin in the 1960s. Even before that project came to attention, in 1956 another international initiative sought British participation through the RMA, the Joseph Haydn-Institut, Cologne, whose aim was to publish a new complete edition of Haydn's works. Friedrich Blume (founding editor of *Die Musik in Geschichte und Gegenwart* and soon to be IMS president in 1958), the Danish Haydn scholar Jens Peter Larsen and the German politician and publisher Günter Henle made up the board, with Gerald Abraham as an Institut member and Haydn's work in England a feature of the research programme.[36] In the end, Council members gave moral support and promoted the Institut's activity, notably through contact with the American Haydn scholar H.C. Robbins Landon and the conferring of RMA Honorary Foreign Membership on Blume in 1960; but they were wary of direct financial involvement.

A final angle on source materials lies in the private initiative and dedication of one man (not an RMA member, as it happened), Patrick Saul (1914–99), who from his teenage years believed that the BM should have a record archive, not

---

[33] Some 136 people attended, among them IMS visitors, RMA members and other 'representatives of English musical life', including RMA vice-president R. Vaughan Williams; the venue was provided without charge by the Arts Council. See 'End of Musicology Congress: Prof. Westrup on Music as University Study', *The Times* (6 July 1955), probably written by F. Howes to drive home for local readers the current shift in university music.

[34] Council minutes, 16 July 1959, M MS 2, fol. 6v. The idea of an international scheme to catalogue MS music sources in all countries, initiated by Friedrich Blume, had first been mentioned by Oldman seven years earlier (Council minutes, 8 Mar 1952, M MS 1, p. 39).

[35] Eitner's full title was *Biographisch-bibliographisches Quellen-Lexikon der Musiker und Musikgelehrten der christlichen Zeitrechnung bis zur Mitte des neunzehnten Jahrhunderts* (Leipzig: Breitkopf & Härtel, 1900–04). In fact the RISM project, or Répertoire International des Sources Musicales, was conceived in collaboration with the IMS as the very first goal of IAML, the International Association of Music Libraries founded in Paris in 1951. Richard S. Hill (Library of Congress) was the first IAML president, and A. Hyatt King (BM) an original vice-president; from 1955 to 1959 King was president.

[36] See F. Blume to F. Howes, 2 Aug 1956, BL Add. MS 71042, fol. 5r-v; and Council minutes, 8 Nov 1956, M MS 1, p. 111.

only of music but of speech, the spoken word and wildlife sounds.[37] Collecting on his own, badgering where he could, he was encouraged by Frank Howes and eventually the Museum Trustees, represented by Alec Hyatt King, chairman of Saul's executive committee.[38] The struggle for support was uphill, but publicity, donations and incorporation from 1951 as the British Institute of Recorded Sound (BIRS) helped raise enough money, some from Robert Mayer, to lease premises in a Museum-owned building at 38 Russell Square in 1955. Record companies and especially the public then flooded the BIRS office with 78 rpm discs as they replaced their collections with 45 rpm discs and long-playing albums. In 1966 the Institute moved to larger premises at 29 Exhibition Road, and in 1983 it became the National Sound Archive, part of the British Library; in 1997 the Archive moved to the new British Library building at St Pancras. By the time of Saul's death, it had become one of the largest sound archives in the world; now called the British Library Sound and Vision Archive, it contains more than seven million recordings on more than forty different formats from around the globe.

The Archive's relevance here lies not only in the long and direct assistance given to BIRS by individual RMA members and in the lecture series Saul created to demonstrate research potential in recordings (speakers included RMA members from William Glock and Peter Stadlen to Adrian Boult and Lord Harewood), but also in BIRS's live recording of RMA events. These included two lecture-recitals for RMA meetings – Robert Donington on 'Some Special Problems in Interpreting Baroque Music' (March 1958), and Paul Badura-Skoda on 'The Interpretation of Beethoven on Pianos Old and New' (October 1959); neither is mentioned in *Proceedings* but both have been digitized for listening at the British Library.[39] The RMA and BIRS also co-sponsored lectures by Westrup, Dean and J.P. Larsen for the London festival of June 1959 celebrating the Purcell and Handel anniversaries.[40] In addition, copies of some BBC talks relating to the RMA are held by the Sound Archive, including Ralph Vaughan Williams's recollections of C.V. Stanford as a teacher, first given extempore to the Association in 1953, then repeated and recorded by the BBC in 1956; and Gerald Abraham's talk on the origins of the Musical Association, broadcast on

---

[37] See Crispin Jewitt, 'Patrick Saul: A Life Spent Preserving Sound', *Guardian* (19 July 1999); *Playback: Bulletin of the National Sound Archive* (Spring 2000), 1–8; and Timothy Day, 'The National Sound Archive: The First Fifty Years', in *Aural History: Essays on Recorded Sound* (London: British Library, 2001), 41–64.

[38] King, 'Quodlibet', 290–92.

[39] For Donington, see BL Sound & Moving Image Catalogue, NP253; for Badura-Skoda, NP232. Donington was an RMA member living in London; Badura-Skoda lived and worked in Vienna. See P. Badura-Skoda to N. Fortune, 26 June 1959 (BL Add. MS 71038, fol. 9) and 21 July 1959 (BL Add. MS 71038, fol. 10). He was to appear in a concert series in October with the London Mozart Players; the RMA first approached him in January. Afterwards, Fortune sent a copy of the BIRS-RMA tape to Badura-Skoda in Vienna.

[40] Gerald Abraham, 'Homage to Handel and Purcell', *Listener*, 61 (28 May 1959), 961.

Radio 3 in 1974.[41] The study of sound itself would one day expand well beyond reproductions of Western music and speech as source material, towards an interdisciplinary field embracing anthropology, psychology, philosophy and much else. Imagining something of this wider potential, the creators of BIRS helped open new paths for many later RMA members, notably those contributing in the early 2000s to the work of CHARM, the AHRC Research Centre for the History and Analysis of Recorded Music.

❧ Widened Sphere of Influence: Publishing and Advocacy

The Council's perception of widened influence in 1953 undoubtedly reflected its pride in the success of MB – seven volumes by the end of 1953, with more on the way – including related performances, media coverage and a sense of new public appreciation for music and music researchers. But there were other aspects of publishing activity, too, that contributed to the Association's rising stature around this time, including some remarkable *PRMA* papers in regular meetings, the issuing of a substantial appendix to a paper a year after the paper had appeared, the RMA as a sought-after adviser for external musicological publications and the creation of a new periodical just for music-documentary material. It's important to track these before revisiting the Britannica edition in more detail, then finally considering how the RMA sought to use its newfound influence.

Research presented by its members remained the central driver behind the Association's work. While it's true that arranging an annual session's papers became slightly easier with a small committee in charge, this still didn't guarantee a rewarding presentation at every meeting. Proposals and synopses were not always articulate; opinions varied about what made for effective oral delivery as against a published essay; and papers on newer subjects, such as film music, could be insufficiently rigorous, whereas self-consciously scholarly papers, say on organ-building or multiple lute music sources, could border on the tedious. Listeners wrote in to complain, some offering suggestions.[42] To

---

[41] Vaughan Williams had first offered his comments orally after Herbert Howells's paper in December 1952, 'Charles Villiers Stanford (1852–1924): An Address at his Centenary', *PRMA*, 70 (1952–53), 19–31. Remarks so valuable, some thought, should have been captured. The secretary tried to recreate these for *PRMA* 70, but Vaughan Williams rejected them on 11 October 1953 ('Dear Erlebach, I'm afraid your screed won't do. I cannot remember saying a good deal of it, & much of it is incorrect'; BL Add. MS 71064, fol. 117). He sent his own paragraph summary instead, duly printed at the end of Howells's paper. Later A.H. King helped to arrange a fresh oral delivery, recorded by the BBC before a studio audience on 3 July 1956. Abraham's pre-recorded talk, broadcast on 5 September 1974, was similar in content to his address at the RMA Annual Conference that spring, printed as 'Our First Hundred Years' in *PRMA*, 100 (1973–74), pp. vii–xiii.

[42] Walter Emery to Honorary Editor of *PRMA* [A.H. King], 26 Nov 1956 (BL Add. MS 71046, fol. 67). Emery objected to W.L. Sumner's paper 'The Baroque Organ', given

address the problem of papers relying too heavily on reportage, or weighed down by technical source information, Alec King and Thurston Dart conceived the idea of a new kind of periodical. In March 1958 they proposed a 'Research Bulletin', an inexpensively produced publication designed for useful list material that was otherwise too slight, lengthy or diffuse for prose articles. The Proceedings Committee approved the concept in July 1958, and in 1961 the first number of *R.M.A. Research Chronicle* (*RMARC*) appeared, edited by Dart, consisting of a single 116-page 'Calendar of References to Music in Newspapers published in London and the Provinces (1660–1719)' by Michael Tilmouth.[43] Since 1961, the format has proved remarkably durable. Under the expanded name *Royal Musical Association Research Chronicle* from 1978, the periodical is still published, since 2022 exclusively as an electronic journal.

Proceedings, meanwhile, held some of the best musicological work available, drawn from papers read at RMA London meetings. 'Royal' appeared in the title from volume 71 (1944–45), which was also the first to be compiled by a designated 'Hon. Ed.', Marion Scott, a Council member and experienced musicological writer. When she fell ill in June 1952, Erlebach finished the volume for 1951–52, then A.H. King succeeded Scott for five years, editing volumes 79 (1952–53) to 83 (1956–57), followed by Frederick Sternfeld for the next five.[44] Across the whole fifteen-year period, editors experimented with pausing the Discussion section, reinstating it in tighter form, then dropping it altogether; switching from footnotes to endnotes then back again; and changing the journal's printer, in May 1949, from Whitehead & Miller, Leeds, to Barnicotts of Taunton. All in the nature of periodical management, such changes aimed to improve efficiency, save cost and gradually shape discourse in what was still a new discipline. *PRMA*'s annual print order grew from 400 in 1947 to 600 in 1953, then to 650 in 1960, each time including twenty or twenty-five (free) offprints per contributor, a feature of RMA authorship that was much appreciated and by no means universal among

---

on 11 November 1954, and to David Lumsden's, 'English Lute Music, 1540–1620 – An Introduction', on 8 November 1956, both of which he felt were not sufficiently focused on how those respective instruments related to the music written for them. He suggested that more presentations about performance be given as public lecture-recitals, with their research content published in a catalogue or list form rather than as a paper. Emery's friend H. Watkins Shaw supported him and agreed that in such cases, a printed catalogue of sources would be more valuable, and make a better contribution to scholarship, than a paper (Shaw to Honorary Editor, Nov 1956, BL Add. MS 71060, fol. 93). King handed over as *PRMA* editor to Frederick Sternfeld in May 1957, but conveyed the ideas, both of which were implemented. See Council minutes, 8 May 1957, M MS 1, p. 121, where the proposed new publication is called a 'duplicated register recording fruits of musical research'.

[43] This material had initially supported Tilmouth's paper given on 9 December 1957 as 'Some Early London Concerts and Music Clubs, 1670–1720', *PRMA*, 84 (1957–58), 13–26; Council minutes, 8 May 1957, M MS 1, p. 121.

[44] Their names were not at first credited in the journal and they did little substantive editing, but rather served as liaisons between author, Council, secretary and printers.

learned societies.⁴⁵ Still acting as its own publisher, the RMA also had to distribute copies, a process that relied on accurate addressing – by Barnicotts with help from the secretary and the latest addressograph machine – besides coordinating a network of local and foreign book agents.

Among strong *PRMA* articles that advanced knowledge, many can be seen to exhibit one of the approaches described below. As an overview, these examples show how musicological thinking developed in mid-twentieth-century Britain.

- **Revisiting and refining**. As early as 1936, Jack Westrup had looked critically at what had passed down in Purcell biography, largely through W.H. Cummings, and recommended serious revision. Others followed. In 1947 Charles van den Borren revisited Stainer's work on Bodleian MS. Canon. Misc. 213, and, while praising his unbiased approach, explored much of that source's music ignored by Stainer, its church music. In 1948 Kathleen Dale reviewed what was known of Domenico Scarlatti's keyboard music, and was able to fill in new information including from her own (modern) pianistic practice, an approach that would gain new prominence in the early 2000s.
- **Digging into new ground**. All three of Thurston Dart's RMA papers broke new ground, on Thomas Morley's consort lessons, Jacobean consort music and Purcell's chamber music, as did John Stevens on early Tudor carols and music in medieval drama, and Gilbert Reaney on the lais of Machaut. Laurence Picken uncovered an instrumental polyphonic folk music tradition in Arabic culture, Arnold Bake explored new details in Indian music, and Klaus Wachsmann, using BIRS recordings of Ghanaian music and new theorization in anthropology, revealed a division in ethnomusicological study that might yield cross-fertilization for both fields.
- **Changing the interpretative angle**. In the late 1940s, Gerald Abraham demonstrated the use of composer sketches as a valuable analytical tool for explaining Schumann's music, simultaneously validating the potential in studying nineteenth-century music more generally. In 1947 Martin Cooper took a new historiographical approach to late nineteenth-century French music. By the early 1950s, Winton Dean had critically studied the full range of Handel's oratorios rather than just the best-known or 'sacred' ones; comparing their librettos, theatrical bearings and use of the chorus led to a full reinterpretation of the composer's method, intent and achievement.
- **Taking instruments seriously**. Instead of treating instruments as museum curiosities, several scholars found ways to unlock new compositional understanding, including of Mozart and performance style, by connecting the music specifically written for each instrument to the instrument's technical resource, with implications for modern learning and teaching. Papers by A.H. King (musical glasses), Edgar Hunt and Carl Dolmetsch (recorder) and Hugh Gough (harpsichord) were particularly successful, shedding light on older repertories and efforts to revive or teach music through better appreciation of the capabilities of historical instruments.
- **Challenging a tacit judgement by amplifying the context.** Long unfairly dismissed as inferior aesthetically thus unimportant internationally, eighteenth- and nineteenth-century British music began to be studied in the 1950s as part of broader social and cultural contexts, including the Industrial Revolution, aspects of place, genre, local or regional usage, religion, commerce and social mobility, revealing

---

⁴⁵ Hope Bagenal to R. Erlebach, 10 Dec 1952: 'To receive such off-prints is something rare and is very useful. I am sending copies to various friends in different parts of the world. […] In *RIBA Journal* it is no longer done' (BL Add. MS 71038, fol. 13).

stylistic influences foreign and British as well as the social impacts of music. From 1945 and across the 1950s, pioneering articles by Reginald Nettel, Gerald Finzi, Charles Cudworth, Stanley Sadie and Nicholas Temperley opened fertile new territory for both musical and wider explorations. Scholars are still benefiting.

In fact Cudworth's paper of 7 February 1952 on English eighteenth-century symphonists offers a case study in fertilization.[46] Although his subject didn't at first seem complex – tracing the three-movement symphony-overture across the 1700s, identifying elements of an English as opposed to foreign styles – he'd hit on a rich vein of printed and manuscript material demanding more time and study than he'd first realized, both with sources and with identification of works by opening theme. The positive reception he received and his own accumulation of examples encouraged him to create an appendix for that purpose, latterly agreed by Council for *PRMA* inclusion despite the extra extent and cost.[47] In the event, the relevant *Proceedings* volume, 78 (1951–52), could not be delayed for his extended checking, so Cudworth's article went to press in 1952 without the appendix, itself finally published as a freestanding 44-page pamphlet in mid-1953, *Thematic Index of English Eighteenth-Century Overtures and Symphonies*; it included 158 handwritten incipits reproduced photographically and was named on the cover as an appendix to volume 78.[48] A composite issue of the same material, *English Eighteenth-Century Symphonies: Paper and Thematic Index* by C.L. Cudworth, was made available to non-members.[49] The whole project engrossed the author, stimulating his own and others' research, including music editorial work. In 1959, Stephen Storace's *No Song, No Supper*, a Cudworth aural illustration in 1952, appeared as volume 16 of MB, edited by Roger Fiske; by the 1970s the American scholar Jan LaRue would incorporate Cudworth's findings into his own work on the eighteenth-century symphony more broadly. A final tribute rests in LaRue's contribution to the

---

[46] 'The English Symphonists of the Eighteenth Century', *PRMA*, 78 (1951–52), 31–51. The paper was chaired by Howes, a useful discussion followed, and Cudworth's efforts to check details before article submission threw up more queries. For his extensive correspondence with Erlebach (30 Mar 1951 – 8 Dec 1953), see BL Add. MS 71043, fols. 155–78, *passim*.

[47] Council minutes, 8 Mar 1952, M MS 1, p. 39; and 8 Oct 1952, p. 46. See also C. Cudworth to R. Erlebach, 15 Dec 1952 (BL Add. MS 71043, fol. 169v): 'I've had a lot of nice things said to me about the symphonists paper, and am less ashamed of it than I was at first.' Prior music history surveys had ignored the English symphony. Cudworth's work was the first to show evidence of strength, continuity and diversity in the early English symphony, according to Jan LaRue (see n. 50 below).

[48] Now contained within BL shelfmark Ac. 5162; prefatory notes explain some differences in dating from those in the original article. At proof stage Erlebach had also introduced errors, e.g. interpreting Cudworth's 'FO' to mean Full Orchestra rather than the intended 'French Overture', 'S' to mean Strings rather than 'Symphony', and confounding some library abbreviations. Cudworth, who'd never been sent page proofs, was rightly irritated; see his sharp but polite letter to Erlebach, 8 Dec 1953 (BL Add. MS 71043, fol. 178).

[49] BL shelfmark 07903.dd.30.(2.), where part 2 is the index. The full extent is fifty-one pages. Though not directly related, this format anticipated by three decades the creation of RMA Monographs.

Cudworth memorial volume of 1983, *Music in Eighteenth-Century England* edited by Christopher Hogwood and Richard Luckett – a fully revised and updated 'Thematic Index of English Symphonies' by Cudworth and LaRue.[50] The Council's original confidence in Cudworth's findings, allowing him to expand and publish more, had been fully justified.

Support for their own members' work was one thing; appeals from external bodies, albeit with RMA connections, was something else, indicating the RMA's increased significance. Two such projects of long standing, the Purcell Society and *ML*, approached the RMA for help in the 1950s and received it. Founded in 1876, the Purcell Society produced twenty-four volumes of their projected complete edition, published by Novello & Co. between 1878 and 1926; with inadequate member funding, they'd had to leave the last six volumes undone.[51] Interest reawakened in the early 1930s. In February 1936 the Society asked the Association for advice on finance to complete the plan; in April 1936 Westrup gave his paper outlining problems in received Purcell biography.[52] After another long hiatus, fresh energy came from younger members, BBC royalties on Purcell works whose editors were dead, and small broadcast fees. In July 1953, with Anthony Lewis as Purcell secretary and Novello accepting responsibility for the remaining volumes, the Society asked to become an autonomous unit within the RMA, which was agreed.[53] The group remained self-managed but their funds were kept in a special account administered by the RMA; the Society then produced their final volumes between 1957 and 1965 with Westrup as chairman, and Lewis, Dart and Fortune as main editors; assistance with publishing costs came from the RVW Trust and the Gulbenkian Foundation.

A similar story of providing assistance when asked surrounds *ML*, an important sister journal to *PRMA* with a discursive-critical slant. From 1937 it had been owned by the London music critic Richard Capell and edited by Eric Blom.[54] When Blom left in 1950 to edit *Grove 5*, Capell continued alone but saw subscribers leave *ML*; by May 1952 the journal was bankrupt, and in June

---

[50] Jan LaRue, 'The English Symphony: Some Additions and Annotations to Charles Cudworth's Published Studies', followed by the revised 'Thematic Index', in *Music in Eighteenth-Century England: Essays in Memory of Charles Cudworth*, ed. Christopher Hogwood and Richard Luckett (Cambridge: Cambridge Univ. Press, 1983), 213–44.

[51] See 'Purcell Society, The' in *Grove 3*, including a list of the twenty-four volumes in *The Works of Henry Purcell* to 1926 with the respective editors' names.

[52] See Council minutes, 7 Feb 1936 (BL Add. MS 71015, fol. 39v); J. Westrup, 'Fact and Fiction about Purcell', *PMA*, 62 (1935–36), 93–115.

[53] Council minutes, 6 July 1953, M MS 1, p. 57. Cedric Glover, who presented the Purcell Society proposal, happened to be Honorary Treasurer of both the Purcell group and the RMA. Other Purcell committee members, with Lewis and Glover, were Dent, Vaughan Williams, Westrup, Dart, Dennis Arundell, Clive Carey, Arnold Goldsbrough and Michael Tippett.

[54] Eric Blom, 'Richard Capell (23 Mar 1885–21 June 1954)', *MT*, 95 (1954), 417–19. Financial difficulties were already present when Capell took over, but he invited Blom's help as honorary (unpaid) editor. Blom reported, 'between us we managed to save the journal' (419). Publishing services had been provided through Augener, who also issued *Monthly Musical Record*.

1954 Capell died unexpectedly.[55] Blom stepped in with an offer of £1,000 working capital and his editorial skills but asked the RMA for structural support. Unanimously, the Council agreed that *ML* must be secured. RMA members Frank Howes, Blom and Alan Frank of Oxford University Press (OUP), the proposed new publisher, set up an oversight committee, conceiving the idea of a limited company with directors, or a trust with trustees, to help manage affairs.[56] In April 1956 the Music & Letters Trust was officially registered, naming two Council members (Howes and RMA Honorary Treasurer Cedric Glover), Blom the nominal owner and Anthony Mulgan for OUP as trustees; others included the RMA Honorary Solicitor H.A.F. Crewdson and Gerald Abraham, editor of *Monthly Musical Record*. Soon afterwards, *ML*'s circulation increased.[57] In both these projects, music edition and journal, it's clear that affiliation with the RMA could open doors. For their part, the RMA saw these requests as opportunities furthering a home-grown musicology.

Before taking up MB again, it's helpful to view the series as it unfolded over its first ten or eleven years. Sixteen volumes appeared, as shown in Table 3. These were not exactly the works chosen by Anthony Lewis and his committee in 1949; changes arose from editors' availability, work dimensions, copyright issues, representativeness for each composer or period, and so on. But the project's purpose was clear, even if its name wasn't.

> The important contributions to European music made by English composers over more than six hundred years are very inadequately represented in modern publications. [...] In order that English music from Dunstable to Parry shall be available to a far wider public than can reach the few libraries in which most of it lies, the Royal Musical Association has decided to prepare a standard authoritative Edition of English music of all periods.[58]

In October 1949 three series titles were suggested – Musica Britannica, National Collection of English Music, and Musica Anglicana. By January 1950 the first had been chosen, while Stainer & Bell, keen to exploit the edition's popular pieces for separate sale to performers and the public, was selected as publisher.[59] What no one expected was a skirmish with *Encyclopaedia Britannica*, from 1944 owned by the University of Chicago, whose publisher challenged the

---

[55] R. Capell to R. Erlebach, 4 May 1952 (BL Add. MS 71056, fol. 128): 'Dear Erlebach, M.& L. is bankrupt. Cannot the RMA subscribe? Yours sincerely, Richard Capell.'

[56] Council minutes, 25 Sept 1954, M MS 1, p. 74; and 3 Feb 1955, pp. 76–78.

[57] See Howes's draft report to Council of 26 July 1956 (BL Add. MS 71050, fol. 117). Already in May 1956, OUP began sending out *ML* advertising to RMA members with Glover's permission; the rise in circulation undoubtedly benefited from new RMA subscribers.

[58] From Lewis's draft introduction to 'A comprehensive historical edition of ENGLISH MUSIC', Jan 1949 (BL Add. MS 71016, fol. 149).

[59] See Council minutes, 8 Oct 1949, BL Add. MS 71017, fol. 33r–v; and 28 Jan 1950, BL Add. MS 71017, fols. 46v–48. The Stainer & Bell contract began on 1 March 1950 with terms favourable to the RMA; a separate bank account for MB business was set up with three signatories, Cedric Glover, Lewis and Thurston Dart (Council minutes, 9 Mar 1950, M MS 1, pp. 1–2).

Table 3. Musica Britannica, 1951–61: the first sixteen volumes.

Vol. 1	The Mulliner Book	1951	ed. Denis Stevens
Vol. 2	Matthew Locke and Christopher Gibbons: *Cupid and Death*	1951	ed. Edward J. Dent
Vol. 3	Thomas Arne: *The Masque of Comus*	1951	ed. Julian Herbage
Vol. 4	Mediaeval Carols	1952, rev. 1958	ed. John Stevens
Vol. 5	Thomas Tomkins: Keyboard Music	1955	ed. Stephen Tuttle
Vol. 6	John Dowland: Ayres for Four Voices	1953	transcribed by Edmund H. Fellowes, ed. Thurston Dart and Nigel Fortune
Vol. 7	John Blow: Anthems I: Coronation and Verse Anthems	1953	ed. Anthony Lewis and H. Watkins Shaw
Vol. 8	John Dunstable: Complete Works	1953	ed. Manfred Bukofzer
Vol. 9	Jacobean Consort Music	1955	ed. William Coates and Thurston Dart
Vol. 10	The Eton Choirbook I	1956	ed. Frank Harrison
Vol. 11	The Eton Choirbook II	1958	ed. Frank Harrison
Vol. 12	The Eton Choirbook III	1961	ed. Frank Harrison
Vol. 13	William Boyce: Overtures	1957	ed. Gerald Finzi
Vol. 14	John Bull: Keyboard Music I	1960	ed. John Steele and Francis Cameron
Vol. 15	Music of Scotland, 1500–1700	1957	ed. Kenneth Elliott
Vol. 16	Stephen Storace: *No Song, No Supper*	1959	ed. Roger Fiske

RMA's use of 'Britannica' as a trade name, trying to prevent encroachment on what it claimed was its own registered property. Lawyers were consulted and letters exchanged; the *Trade Marks Journal* was perused, and feathers were finally smoothed. As things turned out, trade mark *expressions* could be protected but not the component words separately. Largely a distraction that fed English views of litigious Americans, the row soon died down.[60]

Yet it had alerted Dart to a possible need to register 'Musica Britannica' as a trade name before he arranged advertising. In May 1950 he joined the MB

---

[60] Council minutes, 11 May 1950, M MS 1, p. 5; C. Glover to R. Erlebach, 16 May 1950, BL Add. MS 71048, fol. 36 ('the very idea of an American firm claiming a copyright in the word is fantastic – they might as well try and copyright "Encyclopedia"'); and Council minutes, 30 Oct 1950, M MS 1, p. 13, confirming that Encyclopaedia Britannica Ltd would not interfere with any Association publication that was substantially a printed collection of music.

management committee as secretary and began compiling a list of 7,000 prospects who might subscribe – libraries, agents, booksellers, individuals. That was just the beginning of Dart's tireless work on behalf of the series, several of whose volumes would be edited by scholars he trained. In these early days, his concern for marketing extended from selling through the RMA first for the extra income it would yield, to using MB to generate wider interest in the RMA itself, to taking great care over typography in the series' head title, which he insisted should use Gill Perpetua Titling with the alternative 'U': 'I think it important that we should use this type since it is to a large extent our trademark' (see Fig. 18).[61] Even his notepaper heading here, giving MB as 'A National Collection of Music', showed a conceptual advance over the earlier one of March 1951, 'A National Collection of English Music'.[62]

The Royal Festival Hall was set to open on 3 May 1951 with concerts conducted by Thomas Beecham and Malcolm Sargent; the surrounding South Bank festivities began on the 4th. A mood of anticipation led up to the summer's events, generating real public excitement. Rather than any triumphalism or narrow nationalist interest, ordinary participants later recalled feeling a sense of emotional relief at the Festival, with hope for a better future through scientific advance and contemporary design. It had been in this spirit that Lewis and Howes conceived their discussions of the MB project for *Musical Times* (1 May) and *The Times* (11 May), respectively.[63] Lewis's piece, some 2,400 words, is cast historically for musical readers; it explains gaps in the conventional understanding of British music and shows exactly how the planned edition should fill them, setting out principles of quality, inclusion and intentions for musical performance. Howes, with many fewer words and a more hardened readership, focuses on the scholarship behind the edition, with results more permanent than that of a single musical performance, yet both equally proper as celebrations of the Festival. His remarks on the value of that music scholarship, and Britain's slowness to achieve it, are forthright:

> The evidence becomes plainer every day that owing to a gross dereliction of duty on the part of all the universities in this country musical studies are in arrears here compared with those in Europe and America. Music had a hard battle for recognition at the universities from the middle of the nineteenth century onwards. It won it. The victory was recognized by the establishment of faculties of music which should teach composition and stimulate practice of the art. But musicology, which is needed to unravel the many obscurities of musical history, to read old notations, to ascribe authorship on internal evidence, has only recently – and recently means in the last 10 years – obtained official recognition. The firstfruits are coming to harvest – among them the first volume of *Musica Britannica*, which is an edition of the Mulliner Book by Denis Stevens.[64]

---

[61] Dart to Erlebach, n.d. [Oct 1951], BL Add. MS 71044, fol. 30.
[62] Dart to Erlebach, 6 Mar 1951, BL Add. MS 71044, fol. 22.
[63] Anthony Lewis, 'Music Britannica', *MT*, 92 (1951), 201–04; Our Music Critic [Frank Howes], 'The Mulliner Book: "Musica Britannica"', *The Times* (11 May 1951).
[64] [Howes], 'The Mulliner Book'.

Figure 18. R.T. Dart to Rupert Erlebach [October 1951], with printing instructions for Musica Britannica titling, BL Add. MS 71044, fol. 30.

Exactly a week after Howes's article, the RMA and the Arts Council gave a reception to launch MB at the V&A in South Kensington. With its inspiring spaces dedicated to British art and design and links to the Great Exhibition of 1851, the Museum made an ideal venue for some four hundred guests celebrating 1951. Speeches in the Octagon Gallery (by the V&A Director, the Arts Council Vice-Chairman and Howes), music in the Raphael Gallery and a buffet supper in the restaurant and Quadrangle formed the programme.

Dart (harpsichord) performed from the Mulliner Book, the Peter Gibbs String Quartet played dances from *Cupid and Death* by Matthew Locke and Christopher Gibbons, and Margaret Ritchie sang four songs from Thomas Arne's *Comus*, accompanied by a mixed instrumental ensemble.[65] On the same day, 18 June 1951, Howes sent a telegram to the King's private secretary, expressing loyal greetings to George VI from the RMA president and Council on the publication of the first three MB volumes, 'dedicated to His Majesty by gracious permission', also sending a prayer for the King's return to health and strength; it was duly acknowledged by telegram the following day.[66]

Before the reception, not all RMA members had been pleased with how some of their over-zealous officers, probably Erlebach and Glover, had tried to stage-manage a show of British patriotism for the V&A event, reminding members to wear their medals. Excessive concern for social etiquette had seemingly trumped respect for the scholarly purposes behind the MB project. Certainly the music critic Stanley Bayliss was one such offended member, and resigned in protest:

16th April 1951

Dear Mr Erlebach,

[...]

While I am prepared to make monetary sacrifices towards musical research, I am not prepared to support, either out of my annual subscription or special fees, a raree show or a snob or vanity box.

I have ordered two items of the Musica Britannica, and my order can stand. But I am instructing my bankers not to renew my subscription next November.

I write as one of countless ex-servicemen who have thought it the right thing not to claim their war medals.

Believe me,

I am,

Yours sincerely,

Stanley Bayliss[67]

---

[65] Programme for Musica Britannica reception, 18 June 1951, BL Add. MS 71017, fols. 107–08. For the launch planning and potential guest list, see Howes's correspondence with Erlebach from 22 March to 12 June 1951 (BL Add. MS 71050, fols. 53–62). The aim was to use the event's prestige to gain more RMA members.

[66] See a copy of Howes's text in BL Add. MS 71017, fol. 105; and the King's reply [19 June 1951] sent by his secretary Sir Alan Lascelles, fol. 106. In December 1950 Leigh Ashton, the V&A Director, had recommended inviting a member of the royal family to the reception; it was mooted that the Queen might wish to attend. Since no one was available, Howes devised a telegram greeting to elicit a reply from the King as a substitute.

[67] S. Bayliss to R. Erlebach, 16 Apr 1951, BL Add. MS 71041, fol. 170.

In the end Howes talked Bayliss round, understanding his view completely and reiterating the RMA's important work for its own sake, regardless of national honour. Both agreed it was the music that mattered.[68]

As a postscript to the launch, it's important to add that after George VI's death in February 1952, the RMA presented to his daughter, Queen Elizabeth II, a specially bound set of the first three volumes. Howes delivered these to Buckingham Palace in July and received a note of thanks from Sir Michael Adeane, the Queen's private secretary. The Queen wished the volumes to be placed in the Royal Library at Windsor. Conveying her 'sincere thanks' to the Association for giving her 'these splendid books', she particularly wished to say 'how much she [admired] the style and finish of the bindings'.[69] Alas, she didn't hear the music. In May 1953 the RMA sent a Loyal Address on the occasion of her coronation.

Essential efforts to perform the music continued as further volumes were produced at the rate of about two a year. Sales were strong for both the RMA and Stainer & Bell, though at the RMA all income was dedicated to future MB production, not treated as profit. By agreement, the editors were at first unremunerated and the Arts Council were kept abreast of progress. With a healthy balance of more than £1,100 by November 1956 and more volumes scheduled, no demand for repayment was as yet received. Finally in May 1957 the Arts Council clarified: the RMA would not have to pay anything back before 31 December 1960; twelve months' notice would be given if anything did need to be repaid, and the Arts Council would ask for nothing if not satisfied from RMA accounts that repayment would not impair 'the Musica Britannica venture'. Additionally, Stainer & Bell's agreement was adjusted so that they'd gradually get a slightly larger commission on sales as time went by, until the RMA recovered its costs on all volumes. Clearly a success story with incentive to keep going, MB proved a benefit to the RMA as well as a model of contemporary Keynesian thinking.

Among a growing number of performances of MB music in the 1950s, several stand out relating to volumes 6 (Dowland), 7 (Blow), 8 (Dunstable), 10 (Eton Choirbook I) and 15 (Music of Scotland, 1500–1700). On 28 April 1953, at a memorial concert for E.H. Fellowes in the grand Livery Hall of the Goldsmiths' Company, some of Dowland's four- and five-part airs were performed by the Golden Age Singers, directed by Margaret Field-Hyde.[70] A few days later, on 8 May in the same hall, Blow's coronation anthem 'God spake sometime in visions' for eight-part chorus, strings and organ was heard in a concert broadcast by the BBC, with a studio repeat on 10 May.[71] In December

---

[68] S. Bayliss to R. Erlebach, 2 Aug 1951, BL Add. MS 71041, fol. 171. Howes had been a pacifist conscientious objector during World War I.
[69] M.E. Adeane to F. Howes, 16 July 1952, BL Add. MS 71017, fol. 125.
[70] https://www.semibrevity.com/2016/06/the-london-consort-of-viols-a-semi-official-bbc-team/ [accessed 1 Sept 2023]. Some of the works had been transcribed by Fellowes; Margaret Field-Hyde was an RMA life member.
[71] Council minutes, 7 Mar 1953, M MS 1, p. 50.

1953, the quincentenary of John Dunstable's death offered the chance for a reception hosted by the Worshipful Company of Musicians (Master, Evelyn Broadwood). Containing all Dunstable's known works at that time, volume 8 had been edited by the American-based Manfred Bukofzer, author of an Association paper on Dunstable in 1938 and now a renowned authority; the volume itself was a joint publication with the American Musicological Society (AMS), who paid 40 per cent of the edition's cost in return for 400 copies of the total printing of 1,000 copies, each organization having exclusive right of sale in its own area.[72] In Howes's *Times* tribute, he not only explained Dunstable's significance as 'the most notable English composer before Byrd and regarded in Europe as a leader of a school from which something could be learned', but praised the historical research 'now active, experimental and imaginative' that was bringing medieval history alive.[73]

Then in February 1956, with the publication of volume 10, Anthony Lewis devised a BBC studio concert before an invited audience of 150 MB subscribers and RMA members. With music from all ten volumes and a party at Broadcasting House, the event celebrated the whole series and looked to the future.[74] Participating musicians embraced the Golden Age Singers, Julian Bream, Dart, Lewis, the BBC Chorus and the Boyd Neel Orchestra. Composers represented were Dunstable,[75] Richard Davy ('Salve regina', Eton Choirbook), Newman ('Pavyn', Mulliner Book), Thomas Tomkins ('Toy: made at Poole Court'), Thomas Simpson (alman and ricercar, 'Bonny sweet Robin'), Locke and Gibbons (Dances from *Cupid and Death*), Blow ('And I heard a great voice') and Arne (overture to *Comus*), with two medieval carols, 'What tidings' and the Agincourt song 'Deo gracias Anglia'.[76] This broadcast was not available on the BBC Midland or Scottish services, so Dart took extra care to seek out opportunities beyond London. In August 1957 he went to the Edinburgh Festival, giving selections from the Scottish music of MB 15 with the Saltire Singers, Duncan Robertson and Desmond Dupré (lute). The music and performers were deemed attractive by a sympathetic critic, even though timing and venue had not helped the audience's appreciation.[77] Steady musical advocacy would continue.

---

[72] Ibid., 50–51.
[73] 'John Dunstable: Quincentenary', *The Times* (18 Dec 1953).
[74] Lewis, 'Musica Britannica: Past and Future', 193.
[75] In 1994 Dunstable's 'O rosa bella' was reascribed to John Bedyngham by David Fallows. See his 'Dunstable, Bedyngham and *O rosa bella*', *Journal of Musicology*, 12 (1994), 287–305. Attribution study in most medieval music is a necessary, challenging endeavour for logical reasons, as Fallows explains. Perhaps more surprising is that on this 1956 programme, the three-part chanson 'O rosa bella' was arranged for orchestra, directed from the keyboard by Dart.
[76] See the evening programme for the Home Service (London) on 10 February 1956 in *Radio Times* (3 Feb 1956), 32.
[77] M.C. [Martin Cooper], 'Recondite Music of Renaissance', *Daily Telegraph* (20 Aug 1957). The event had been programmed as the day's first morning concert in Freemasons' Hall, rather than, say, as a candlelit evening concert in Holyroodhouse.

Figure 19. *Sir Anthony Lewis*, oil on canvas by Pamela Thalben-Ball, 1976, Lewis touching the recent Sterndale Bennett volume of Musica Britannica, vol. 37.

Advocacy of a wider kind came to the fore in the late 1950s. In two important approaches, to the BBC in 1957 and the British Council in 1959, the RMA tried to lobby for change; though neither effort had precisely the result desired, they alerted those organizations, and in the second case the national press, to the RMA's voice. First, in June 1957 Howes wrote to Alexander Cadogan, chair of the BBC Board of Governors, to protest the proposed curtailment of the Third Programme that autumn. Howes's point was less a general regret about musical loss than a specific professional concern: he thought the valuable encouragement to a nascent British musicology provided by the BBC, through its bridging of academic and practical worlds, would be removed, 'and might even have the effect of stifling a young study and driving our students to America where there is great interest in every field of musicology'.[78] In reply Cadogan maintained that classical music programming, though diminished, would not disappear, and he hoped that 'musicologists will continue to help us in many ways'.[79]

---

[78] F. Howes to A. Cadogan, 20 June 1957 (BL Add. MS 71042, fols. 165–66).
[79] A. Cadogan to F. Howes, 2 July 1957 (BL Add. MS 71042, fol. 164). Third Programme output was indeed cut to twenty-four hours a week from October 1957, about three and a half hours each evening.

Second, in the national homage to Purcell and Handel of 1959, RMA members risked an outright political stand. With concerts, broadcasts, opera and oratorio performances, celebrations in Westminster Abbey, two lecture series and an exhibition at the BM, the festival would reach its peak between 8 and 27 June.[80] The RMA was even to host a formal reception at the RAM on 18 June, sponsored by the British Council. Selected foreign guests were invited, though none from East Germany, which the UK didn't officially recognize.[81] Belatedly, Lewis and Dart proposed inviting seven notable East German musicians, some involved in the Hallische Händel-Ausgabe who'd hosted Dart earlier that year, without cost or obligation to the RMA.[82] Seeking Council approval, including that of its new president Jack Westrup, yet short of time and aware of the impropriety of using the RMA's name without signed agreement, Dart forged ahead on his own: on 15 May he invited the East Germans to be his personal guests at the reception.[83] To his surprise and delight, six accepted and six arrived; but they didn't make it to the reception. The fallout later in Council, especially from a couple of members who'd felt procedure had been compromised, led to calls for tightening RMA discipline.[84] More remarkable, Dart's actions were praised publicly, though anonymously, in the Sunday *Observer* on 28 June under the editorial heading 'Out of Tune'. Calling out the Foreign Office and British Council as 'conniving in a piece of Stalinist rudeness', issuing visas grudgingly and late (too late for the reception), the paper asserted that a cold war should not 'prevent personal and cultural relations between the

---

[80] See Gerald Abraham, 'Homage to Handel and Purcell', *Listener* (28 May 1959), 961. The RMA-sponsored lectures, free and open to the public, were given by Westrup, Dean and J.P. Larsen on Wednesdays in June at Senate House, University of London.

[81] S. Whinyates to N. Fortune, 8 May 1959, BL Add. MS 71064, fols. 71–72. This letter makes clear that only one foreign visitor, Cesare Valabrega, had so far confirmed his London presence on 18 June for 'the Royal Musical Association Evening Reception'. Others had not yet replied (e.g. J.P. Larsen, Heinz Joachim) or would miss the 18th (e.g. Otto Deutsch, Suzanne Clercx-Lejeune, Walter Kolneder, Jean Jacquot, Guglielmo Barblan).

[82] Draft circular letter 'To members of the RMA Council', n.d. [5 May 1959], BL Add. MS 71044, fol. 76. 'The proposers feel that the opportunity should not be missed of permitting these musicians to hear for themselves the many different kinds of performance adopted in this country for the music of Purcell and Handel, or of discussing with English scholars their common musical problems.' The named musicians were E.H. Meyer (a longstanding RMA member), Philine Fischer, Walter Siegmund-Schultze, Konrad Sasse, Helmut Koch, Horst-Tanu Margraf and Walter Serauky.

[83] Draft letter, T. Dart to Meyer, Fischer, Siegmund-Schultze, Sasse, Koch, Margraf and Serauky, 15 May 1959, BL Add. MS 71044, fol. 75. See also Dart to Fortune, 29 May 1959, BL Add. MS 71044, fol. 77.

[84] For internal reactions, see draft minute for Council meeting, [16 July] 1959, omitted from full minutes (BL Add. MS 71048, fol. 375); J. Westrup to N. Fortune, 19 July 1959 (BL Add. MS 71064, fol. 35); and C. Glover to N. Fortune, 27–28 July 1959 (BL Add. MS 71048, fol. 377v).

Communist world and the West'. It concluded: 'Whatever the reason, this shabby behaviour does no service to the Western cause.'[85]

Clearly the *Observer* saw in music a diplomatic value the British state had missed, or overruled. But inside the RMA, a mixture of embarrassment and empathy for Dart tempered any exultant sense of holding the high ground. In the long run, regardless of procedure, national feeling or diplomatic utility, Dart's action produced the beneficial effect he sought. The recipients were able to visit London, continuing international scholarly engagement, and echoes of Lewis's 'urgent function' for MB held good too: 'giving those at home and abroad a balanced picture of English music in its many unknown aspects' and providing 'evidence of a living art', not a purely antiquarian interest.[86] Again it was the music that mattered, with renewed support for collaborative research putting it into worldwide ears.

Just six years after the East German incident, a further beneficial effect of RMA work was noted by Geoffrey Bush, this time closely touching Lewis's 'evidence of a living art'. In a paper for the 1964–65 session, Bush alluded to the invigorated picture of the nation's music achieved through recent scholarship. More than simply restoring works of neglected composers, though, he saw that research had offered a fresh source of aesthetic inspiration to modern composers.

> I wonder whether this Association fully realises how the works of research and scholarship undertaken by its members, besides being of incalculable value in themselves, have been a major factor in the revival of composition in England during this century? The links between Tippett and Purcell, Holst and Weelkes, Maxwell Davies and Taverner, are not fortuitous. A composer, in T.S. Eliot's words, needs 'a perception, not only of the pastness of the past, but of its presence'. Tippett himself says the same: 'more than anyone else, the creative artist needs a sense of continuity'. No composer can give of his best in isolation.[87]

It was a point worth making. Research as a spur to new creation, and perhaps closer association between scholars and composers of all kinds, could only be a good thing. Dent's earlier assertion that the purpose of research lay in training the imagination had found a literal manifestation.

---

[85] [Anon.], 'Comment: Out of Tune', *Observer* (28 June 1959).
[86] Lewis, 'Musica Britannica: Past and Future'.
[87] Geoffrey Bush, 'Sterndale Bennett: The Solo Piano Works', *PRMA*, 91 (1964–65), 85–97 at 89, quoting Eliot's 'Tradition and the Individual Talent' (1919) in his *Selected Prose* (London: Penguin, 1953), 25; and Tippett's contribution to *Henry Purcell, 1659–1695: Essays on his Music*, ed. Imogen Holst (London: OUP, 1959), 43.

5

Coming of Age, 1960–1980

Despite the RMA's quickened pace of achievement in the 1950s, its arrival as a mature scholarly organization is hard to pin down. Not only is such a marker impossible to define, given the group's evolution alongside that of academic musicology in the 1960s and 70s, but voices of dissent could also still be heard. Mostly vestiges of the old English distrust of an imported music discipline allegedly eschewing performance, these tended to conflate that distrust with personal feelings of rejection, misunderstanding, dread of the American influence associated with a 'take-over' in British musicology or discomfort at the Association's growing clannishness. Some freelance musicians, for instance, loved doing scholarly work and hoped to gain higher status by giving an RMA paper – 'it is an enthralling occupation', wrote the harpsichordist-researcher and viol player Cecily Arnold to Frank Howes.[1] But she and her lutenist husband Marshall Johnson were among several members in the 1950s who felt overlooked because their particular subject matter was not central to the prevailing MB thrust; they suspected collusion.[2] Others, notably a senior English critic, favoured a Eurocentric approach and claimed the Association's talks were too often parochial, tracing the life of a typical seventeenth-century English organist, for instance, rather than featuring 'real live lecturers who have something worthwhile to say on some subject directly related to real music'.[3] That view was understandable, yet the point didn't escape Nigel Fortune that this particular correspondent – the *Music Review* founder and editor Geoffrey Sharp, a life member – for all his promotion of musicological conferences abroad and his corresponding membership in the AMS from 1952, had no idea how each RMA session was devised, above all that its speakers were not commissioned for a fee but rather presented their original research freely to the group for discussion. Sharp had certainly never offered his own work, though invited by E.J. Dent, and he considered the RMA's non-payment practice 'scandalous'.[4] It was a hollow complaint. Meanwhile some more engaged members,

---

[1] C. Arnold to F. Howes, 5 Feb 1950, BL Add. MS 71037, fol. 148. See also her letter of 30 January 1950, describing her research and asking Howes's support for her membership (BL Add. MS 71037, fol. 144r–v).

[2] M. Johnson to R. Erlebach, 9 June 1951, BL Add. MS 71051, fol. 109. The couple finally gave a joint paper in November 1955, published as 'The English Fantasy Suite', *PRMA*, 82 (1955–56), 1–14.

[3] G. Sharp to N. Fortune, 25 Mar 1958, BL Add. MS 71060, fol. 85.

[4] G. Sharp to N. Fortune, 14 Apr 1958, BL Add. MS 71060, fol. 86. For the tone and content of *Music Review*, see D. Fallows, A. Whittall, J. Blacking and N. Fortune,

mostly aspirant but untrained, had in fact had their offers rejected for failing to reach expected standards (a progressive sign), while others, some living at a great distance, were more than pleased to join the RMA and receive its journal to absorb the latest research.[5] Variable responses to the Association's direction were bound to recur. The most dramatic remarks over differing American and British scholarly approaches appeared within the *Times Literary Supplement* (*TLS*) in 1973, including Howard Mayer Brown's now celebrated if intemperate comment that 'the serious musical scholar in Britain is a creature as rare as the dodo bird', an episode worth examining in detail below.[6]

For now, in charting the Association's coming of age, what matters is how the group operated and grew, what it accomplished collectively and how its individual members conceived research and published their findings over these two decades. The evidence shows solid momentum and a high level in musicological output, much of it world-leading. Clearly the RMA benefited from stable direction in its five outstanding presidents and three secretaries – Westrup, Lewis and Abraham with Nigel Fortune; then Abraham, King and Arnold with Malcolm Turner, then Hugh Cobbe. The whole period benefited from a range of occupational expertise as each successive set of officers showed measured and sustainable purpose; changeovers gave the effect of generating or continuing development along several lines at once, as in a great fugue in which every line makes sense, separately, in small groups or all together. Certainly new activities added at intervals gave depth to the texture without overwhelming the whole structure. Paper meetings, conference experiments, new publications, outreach to international scholars, occasional collaborations, regional chapters, the cultivation of students and gentle encouragement of special research interests all pointed to a mature balance between aim and achievement. I'll divide the discussion into two chronological parts, the 1960s and the 1970s, connected by a mid-section on individual papers across the whole period; this is followed by a final section on legacy funds, IMS relations and collaborative projects assisting the Association's mission – the new Music Faculty at KCL and the *New Grove* office at Macmillan Publishers.

'Musicology in Great Britain since 1945', *Acta musicologica*, 52 (1980), 38–68 at 45–46.

[5] Ernest S.E. Clark to R. Erlebach, 2 May 1954, BL Add. MS 71043, fol. 74. A surveyor working in Ahmadi, Kuwait, Clark was a musical amateur connected with the Dolmetsch Foundation. After returning to Britain and training as a parish priest in Halesowen (Clark to N. Fortune, 30 Jan 1964, BL Add. MS 71043, fol. 76), he remained a firm RMA adherent. Another loyal member, C.L.W. Fackrell, was a trained teacher whose music studies had been interrupted by war work for the Foreign Office (Fackrell to R. Erlebach, 29 Jan 1956, BL Add. MS 71047, fol. 4; Fackrell to N. Fortune, 14 Aug 1964, BL Add. MS 71047, fols. 15–16). In both cases, the RMA supported their intellectual growth and musical vocation.

[6] 'Madrigals and Motets', Letter to the Editor, *TLS* (20 July 1973), 834–35.

❧ The 1960s

In mid-1958 Frank Howes declined to stand for the Association's presidency again (he'd already tried to resign twice, but was persuaded to stay). After a split vote for a new president at the next Council meeting, a postal ballot yielded the unanimous election of Jack Westrup in November 1958. As Oxford's Heather Professor directing undergraduate music teaching, besides being a British Academy fellow and heading the multi-volume *New Oxford History of Music*, Westrup was 'the obvious and natural leader in every musicological enterprise in Britain', according to his friend Gerald Abraham;[7] by mid-1959 he'd be editing *ML* too. Westrup's industry, scholarship and practical musicianship, and the wider national and international respect he commanded, served the Association well until 1963. Council members took special pleasure in Westrup's knighthood in the New Year Honours of 1961, seeing it as a boost for their own efforts on behalf of music research; all were invited to a celebratory luncheon at Oxford, chaired by the Rt Hon. Edward Heath, Lord Privy Seal.[8] The Council were also invited to a luncheon for Frank Howes in 1961, given by the Critics' Circle in honour of his seventieth birthday.

But it was Nigel Fortune, RMA secretary, who guided the Association's mounting business and many of its innovations in this decade. Fortune's careful retention of materials, now held in the RMA Papers at the British Library, not only supports that view but brings to life many of the ordinary members and layered projects colouring the Association's larger story; no one had a stronger sense of the future historical value of the present. Of twenty-nine hefty correspondence volumes, arranged alphabetically and catalogued as BL Add. MSS 71036–64, Fortune kept or compiled the papers in twenty-eight of them; the date range for most of these is 1950–71, starting with some of Erlebach's material but consisting mainly of letters, some with enclosures, sent to Fortune between 1957 and 1970 by RMA presidents and treasurers (including Cedric Glover, David McKenna and Cedric Watkins), accountants (Bagshaw & Co., London), printers (Barnicotts of Taunton), publishers (Kraus Reprint, New York, and Blackwell of Oxford), quangos, other music bodies (AMS, IMS) and a host of members and scholars worldwide. Nothing like this richness of documentation exists for other periods in the Association's history. Fortune's professionalism unequivocally advanced the RMA's purpose as well as its member numbers, which went up fast in the 1960s, from 457 in September 1960 to 708 in September 1970, a near 55 per cent rise in a decade. Some of that growth came through international advertising in *Notes* and *Musical Quarterly*. But much also arose through RMA conference initiatives from the later 1960s,

---

[7] G. Abraham, 'Jack Allan Westrup, 1904–1975', *Proceedings of the British Academy*, 63 (1977), 471–82 at 478.

[8] Council minutes, 16 Mar 1961, M MS 2, fols. 17, 18v. As Lord Privy Seal, Heath was responsible for negotiations to secure the UK's first attempt to join the European Common Market. A former Oxford student who'd won an organ scholarship (Balliol College), he long remained interested in music.

Figure 20.
Nigel Fortune,
photograph by John
Casken, late 1990s.

encouraged by its widening university connections: the official Robbins Report advocating immediate expansion of universities had been accepted by government in October 1963. Student membership had already been introduced in 1962–63, with eligibility limited to registered undergraduates.[9] Then, over the decade from 1970 with some depletion through deaths and resignations, the rise in numbers was more moderate, reaching a total of 748 by December 1980. However they arrived, new subscriptions were welcome, offering the chance to develop RMA activity.

A steady flow of fresh members, up to seventy-seven a year, was impressive but not the only good news. In March 1961 Anthony Lewis reported that the group's £2,000 Arts Council loan, received in 1949 for the initial volumes of MB, had been converted to a grant and was not repayable. Moreover, the first issue of *R.M.A. Research Chronicle*, edited by Thurston Dart and published with the support of the Fellowes Memorial Fund and the RVW Trust, was ready for sale (600 copies, priced at 15s. to members and 20s. to others). Dart's Foreword explained its target of 'musicological raw material', including

> lists, indexes, catalogues, calendars, extracts from newspapers, new fragments of biographical information [...]. Much of this material has little or no enduring value, but some of it is of great importance. [...] The R.M.A. Research Chronicle [...] will serve to circulate some of the more worthwhile material [...], whether [the investigations] have been carried out at Universities or [...] are the result of

---

[9] 'Articles of Association of the Royal Musical Association', *PRMA*, 89 (1962–63), 99–108 at 100. The suggestion of Student Membership at a reduced rate (15s.) originated in Council in June 1961. In the first membership list showing student members (ibid., 109–24), there were only five; Michael Nyman, a student of Alan Bush's at the RAM, was one of them.

a passionate hobby, like so much of the best English musical scholarship, old and new. To print the Chronicle from moveable type would be prohibitively costly; to circulate it in microfilm would be absurdly inconvenient. The method chosen is sturdy and not too expensive.[10]

Hunting for a cheap production method using a duplicating machine was not straightforward and Fortune eventually went back to the *PRMA* printer Barnicotts for a solid result. Gathering material, agreeing layout and distributing copies became systematized gradually, whereas the extent of each issue, intended to appear yearly but in fact irregular, ranged unpredictably from about sixty pages to 150. Dart was overcommitted even before leaving Cambridge in 1964, and RMA funds were tight, so *RMARC*'s publishing schedule slipped behind almost immediately; using sequential years for each number despite actual publication year led to minor confusion.[11] Yet the *Chronicle*'s content and purpose appealed. Interest lifted especially with Paul Doe's instalments of his 'Register of Theses on Music' beginning in no. 3 (1963), reflecting a new curiosity about postgraduate music study.[12] Jeremy Noble followed Dart as *RMARC* editor in 1965, with Fortune's help on nos. 4 (1964) and 5 (1965); for no. 7 (1969) Michael Tilmouth, compiler of the first number's material, took over, editing every issue to no. 13 (1976).[13] Although the journal's 'raw material' concept prevailed, short narrative articles were also invited and began appearing in the first decade. Far from making money, the *Chronicle* struggled to pay its way in this period, even after the price was raised. Still, its value in stimulating research and, especially, drawing in more contributors than *Proceedings* could accommodate, justified its existence; ongoing support from 1966 came through annual British Academy grants, for which Fortune devised cogent applications.

Predictably, RMA legal and financial business expanded in the 1960s. To cite one instance, the cost of licensing re-recorded phonograph performances to illustrate public lectures arose in early 1961. After discussing the Association's responsibility, Fortune, the Honorary Solicitor and the Council

---

[10] 'Editor's Foreword to First Printing', *RMARC*, 1 (1961).

[11] The idea of a dissertation list, for example, first proposed by Alan Frank with Paul Doe as its compiler, was not discussed or agreed until July 1964 (Council minutes, 15 July 1964, M MS 2, fol. 38). Yet the first 'Doe List' appeared in '1963'.

[12] *RMARC* no. 3 sold particularly well, stimulating further sales of the first two numbers (Council minutes, 16 July 1966, M MS 2, fol. 52; and BL Add. MS 71055, fol. 194v, excerpt from D. McKenna's accounts). After Doe's consolidated listing in *RMARC*, 11 (1973), and a new list by Michael Dawney for Eire in *RMARC*, 13 (1976), the thesis register continued under Nick Sandon from *RMARC*, 15 (1979), with updates by Ian Bartlett to no. 21 (1988). Bartlett's work, latterly with Benedict Sarnaker, culminated in the 'Cumulative List of Accepted Dissertations and Theses to 1991' in *RMARC*, 25 (1992), 1, 3–92.

[13] For a list of each issue and its content, nos. 1–13 (1961–76), see the front matter of *RMARC*, 14 (1978). With no. 14 (1978), edited by Geoffrey Chew, the journal changed its name to the fuller *Royal Musical Association Research Chronicle*.

opted to purchase an annual licence from Phonographic Performance Ltd (now PPL), the British copyright collective for record companies; any speaker using an excerpt from a company not on their extensive list would have to make separate arrangements.[14] Conversely on the income side, a large windfall arrived that no one expected, exemplifying the RMA's participation in a global reprint bonanza. Westrup and Fortune were approached in late 1962 by a Dr B. Klopstock with a proposal from the Kraus Reprint firm of New York to reproduce and sell out-of-print *Proceedings* volumes. For months Fortune consulted legal advisers and RMA members; doubts and questions were raised, answers provided. In mid-1963 he and the Council accepted an agreement for the book and technology company to take over the Association's backstock, both *PMA* and *PRMA* (vols. 1–80, 1874–1953). Kraus would produce and sell exact photographic copies worldwide (with a 25 per cent discount to bona fide RMA members), and pay the RMA a 15 per cent royalty on net sales at agreed intervals. The contract also included future annual pickup and sale of increasingly recent *PRMA* volumes (the moving wall).[15] This fortuitous arrangement proved a boon to RMA coffers, from November 1966 yielding thousands of pounds in extra income over several years. Although Fortune and the Council had originally hesitated over copyright questions and whether each author would agree, Kraus maintained that while individual copyright remained with the authors, the right to license any reprint of a collected volume was vested in the collection's publisher, the Association, not in separate authors; many other learned societies were participating likewise. In 1969–70 the RMA clarified the position while, true to his word, Klopstock continued to send regular cheques and accounts of royalties earned.[16]

Any notion of extending the value in their own (past) intellectual property had never occurred to anyone before this. But when it happened, especially after the treasurer reported the first Kraus returns by proclaiming the Association 'rather rich at the moment',[17] Council members wondered what fresh opportunities might lie ahead and how they could use the extra income. The first idea was to acquire shared London accommodation for an RMA office (the Royal Society of Musicians in Stratford Place was tried, but it wasn't practical).

---

[14] For correspondence with Phonographic Performance and its list of covered record companies, see BL Add. MS 71058, fols. 78–90; for H.A.F. Crewdson's advice (under 'Waterhouse & Co.'), see Add. MS 71063, fols. 70–77.

[15] The full Klopstock correspondence, including Kraus Reprint brochures, terms of agreement and royalty calculations, is in BL Add. MS 71052, fols. 296 (Klopstock to Fortune, 14 Nov 1962) to 370 (Fortune to Klopstock, 19 Sept 1969). Klopstock was based in London; the periodicals branch of Kraus Reprint had been set up in Vaduz, Liechtenstein, in 1956. For a contrary view of the Kraus 'take-over' of *PRMA*, see Hermann Baron to N. Fortune, 20 Nov 1964, BL Add. MS 71041, fol. 2.

[16] For some of the cheques to 1970, see BL Add. MS 71052, fols. 371–81. The parent firm, founded by the antiquarian book dealer Hans Peter Kraus in New York City in 1939, was eventually absorbed by Thomson International in 1968 as Kraus-Thomson, which later became Thomson-Gale, then Gale-Cengage.

[17] Council minutes, 16 Nov 1966, M MS 2, fol. 54v.

COMING OF AGE, 1960–1980   177

Next was to pay their auditors a proper fee and double their IMS contribution (both were enacted).[18] Soon they'd be seeking a possible business manager, a dynamic marketing agent for RMA publications: in July 1968, with Andrew Porter's advice, Fortune identified Blackwell's in Oxford as the ideal helper.[19]

But even before the windfall, a main scholarly concern had been to revisit the structure of RMA annual sessions, with its fixed pattern of a year's London meetings yielding the sum of *Proceedings*. By 1964 several people felt this was too restrictive; more events, or a wider scope with their print offerings, ought to be explored so that the Association could grow and musicology flourish. President Anthony Lewis appointed a 'Future Development Committee' of Fortune, McKenna (Honorary Treasurer), King and Jeremy Noble. In early 1965 their chief recommendation was to try a two-day conference in London over the Easter vacation, offering the chance for regional members to join in for several papers, a shared meal and a concert; if successful, the plan could be repeated and perhaps altered or expanded. The first conference, at the RAM in early April 1966, was indeed highly successful, and Fortune started planning the second almost immediately for April 1967, followed by the third (RCM, April 1968, with a Josquin concert conducted by Noble and a tour of the RCM Collections), fourth (April 1969 also at the RCM) and so on. Agreeing a venue each time and funding the concert could present snags, but gradually additions and refinements – meeting away from London, finding external funding for concerts, and programming a few student papers – led to the firm establishment of what is now the Association's flagship annual event.[20] Integral to the annual session, all conference papers were equally open to *PRMA* publication. A closely related idea, formed in 1967 by Denis Arnold at Hull University with Fortune at Birmingham, was to hold a Research Conference for Students in the annual winter break. It too was intended to bring people together, young scholars from all UK universities, especially those who might be working in isolation, and it too was a big success.[21] With a small grant from RMA general funds to cover basic costs, the student conference proved its worth by eliciting new subscriptions; it also had the advantage of migrating healthily around the country, Hull to Birmingham, Glasgow to Cardiff and beyond.

Just before all this conferencing began, in July 1965 the Development Committee had raised a point about *PRMA* itself – specifically whether it might

---

[18] Ibid., fol. 55.
[19] Council minutes, 17 July 1968, M MS 2, fol. 64v. The Blackwell correspondence, much of it with F.J. Dymond as Oxford shop manager, is in BL Add. MS 71041, fols. 246–77 (1969–70). Blackwell's mailing list of 9,000 names attracted Fortune.
[20] For Fortune's session card of 1969–70 including the fifth conference with its three student papers (Colin Timms, Peter Ward Jones, Margaret McAllister), see BL Add. MS 71034, fol. 21r–v.
[21] D. Arnold to N. Fortune, 9 Nov 1967 (BL Add. MS 71037, fol. 166); and N. Fortune, 'Denis Midgley Arnold, 1926–1986', *Proceedings of the British Academy*, 73 (1987), 391–410 at 399–400. First held in December, the conference eventually moved to January as preferable.

be broadened into a 'journal' by accepting an occasional outside article. By 1969, some members wanted to go further and 'release the Proceedings (under a new title) from slavish commitment to the printing only of spoken papers, and increase the frequency of appearance to twice yearly, which should be possible if there is as much material awaiting publication every year as people say there is'.[22] Although attractive in theory, such ideas had to be processed carefully before the Council would alter the status quo of ninety years; discussions recurred until the modernized, two-part *Journal of the Royal Musical Association* became a reality in 1986–87. In the meantime, worries about *PRMA* and paper-giving in general ranged from (anonymous) misogynist comment around Joan Rimmer's presentation in March 1964 (see Fig. 21)[23] and management of Ian Bent's revealing but overlong text in April 1964,[24] both papers appearing in volume 90, to that same volume's cost overrun added to rising costs of the *Research Chronicle* and of the new cumulative index to *PRMA* volumes 1–90 (1874–1964), the seventh, created by Alan Smith for publication in 1966. Seemingly, RMA output was headed for a log jam just when demand was rising and the supply of good research increasing. No wonder a squeeze on resources at this moment led to a subscription rise in 1965, the first since 1949 (from 1½ guineas to 2 guineas). Its intent was to help maintain or lift standards rather than reduce them, notably to support music examples that were expensive to print but so essential to clarity in musicological texts. This feeling of squeeze all round gives another reason, if one were needed, why the Kraus royalties were so warmly welcomed in late 1966.

---

[22] N. Fortune to Cedric Watkins, 10 Feb 1969 (BL Add. MS 71047, fol. 230). For articulate member views, see Ian Bent to [Fortune], 29 June 1968 (reported to Council, 17 July 1968, M MS 2, fol. 69), and Richard Rastell to Fortune, 4 Apr 1969 (BL Add. MS 71059, fol. 21), who preferred further meetings over more print: 'the RMA is valuable precisely because it encourages personal contact'.

[23] The anonymous listener expressed disapproval not of Rimmer's paper ('Harps in the Baroque Era', *PRMA*, 90 (1963–64), 59–75) but of her cohabitation with the Irish musicologist Frank Ll. Harrison, whom she would marry in 1965. The comment probably sprang less from moral panic than from a view of cohabitation as a threat to stable marriage, itself increased since 1945 and seen as a social improvement; see Pat Thane, *Happy Families? History and Family Policy* (London: British Academy, 2010, rev. 2011). On Rimmer's wider scholarly impact, see Penny Vera-Sanso, 'Joan Rimmer (1918–2014)', *Folk Music Journal*, 11 (2016), 115–17.

[24] Bent's paper, 'The English Chapel Royal before 1300', *PRMA*, 90 (1963–64), 77–95, began as a script of 11,000 words and was reduced to 6,500 on submission, still 2,000 over length. The editor Peter le Huray consulted the Council (minutes, 5 July 1964, M MS 2, fol. 37r–v), who were swayed by Dart's plea for Bent's inexperience and his important material. The opposing view, that an author had a duty to observe the stipulated maximum, did not carry. The article was printed, but this volume's high cost raised further discussion about *PRMA* in relation to Association aims.

COMING OF AGE, 1960–1980   179

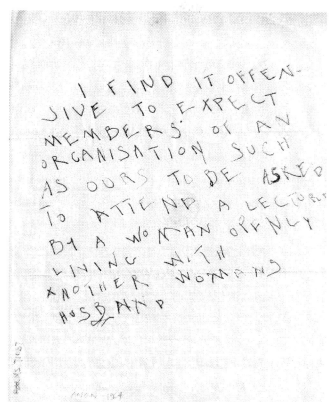

Figure 21. Anonymous correspondence to RMA [March 1964], BL Add. MS 71037, fol. 1.

❦ Individual Papers

But what of the content and direction in *PRMA* papers themselves? Were they in any sense more 'musicological', penetrating or revealing in the 1960s and 70s than articles in earlier decades? It's a tricky question because even the most impressive work of one generation stands to be validated or corrected in later ones, and current views cannot reflect all earlier reader perspectives; equally, in any humanities subject there's no guarantee that recent work will be wholly better than earlier. Value is gleaned, assimilated and revaluated continually. An important paper illustrating these contingencies was that given at the RAM on 23 October 1969 by the prominent American scholar Edward E. Lowinsky, based at the University of Chicago, whose reputation in Renaissance music preceded him.[25] Agreeing to speak on 'A Renaissance Choirbook for an English Queen', he requested his expenses from Milan to London, his own choice of

---

[25] Lowinsky's command of Renaissance music, including the theory and practice of *musica ficta*, and his ability to stimulate new scholarship were already legendary; his edition of the Medici Codex had appeared in 1968.

text editor (Fortune), a professional choral performance, and the printing of a complete musical piece (eight pages of a four-system score). Fred Sternfeld, who knew Lowinsky well and made the initial contact, warned colleagues of his friend's high demands and feisty nature.[26] To their credit, the Council obliged where they could; everything went swimmingly, listeners were charmed and Lowinsky had a wonderful time ('I was especially glad to meet so many of your young people. The meeting was a pleasure from beginning to end').[27] The published *PRMA* paper, 'MS 1070 of the Royal College of Music in London', was the first to make a detailed study of this source, outlining its physical traits and the evidence for its origin and French motet contents, offering a hypothesis about its owner and a performance of the anonymous opening piece, 'Forte si dulci'. Provocative as ever, Lowinsky made some striking claims, above all that the book's ownership could be attributed to Anne Boleyn and its editorship to Mark Smeaton.[28] Though accepted at the time, not all the assumptions behind this elegant theory turned out to be accurate; challenges to Lowinsky's ideas through fresh manuscript analysis have been made periodically since 1969, most productively by Lisa Urkevich and Joshua Rifkin in the USA, and Thomas Schmidt and David Skinner in the UK.[29]

Even apart from Lowinsky's advanced thought and star quality, the Association's high musicological standing at this time is crystal clear. Paper subjects across these two decades, in *PRMA* volumes 86–106 (1959–60 to 1979–80), move well beyond Tudor sources and genre descriptions; large walls of narrative or anecdotal text are often displaced by closely interpreted new evidence, analysis and argument; a fresh confidence shows in the more direct tone but sophisticated expectations perceptible between authors and readers; and many articles assume or directly refer to previous scholarly conversations still in play – all signs of a new maturity in the communication of British research. Certainly by 1980, *PRMA*'s pages from 1945 to the late 1970s were seen by one astute observer to 'in fact contain some of the best and most concentrated musicology Britain has to offer'.[30]

Research pathways were extended in familiar areas and opened up new ones. The following list, though incomplete, is indicative: music and eighteenth-century European print culture, dissemination networks, jazz and British popular music, medieval liturgical music, close palaeographic study of

---

[26] The Lowinsky correspondence, from January to December 1969, appears in BL Add. MS 71054, fols. 112–23; see also E. Olleson to N. Fortune, 27 Oct 1969, BL Add. MS 71057, fols. 217–18. For the performance arrangements, see Fortune's correspondence with John Hoban, director of 'Scuola di Chiesa', in BL Add. MS 71050, fols. 1–13. Among the dozen singers were James Bowman and Terry Edwards.

[27] E. Lowinsky to N. Fortune, 8 Nov 1969, BL Add. MS 71054, fol. 121.

[28] *PRMA*, 96 (1969–70), 1–28.

[29] See Jason Stoessel's review of *The Anne Boleyn Music Book (Royal College of Music MS 1070)*, a facsimile with introduction by T. Schmidt and D. Skinner, with K. Airaksinen-Monier (DIAMM Facsimiles, vol. 6, 2017), in *Notes*, 75 (2019), 697–701.

[30] Fallows et al., 'Musicology in Great Britain since 1945', 45.

music manuscripts, economic history and music, analysis of post-twelve-note music, nineteenth-century composing methods, opera production processes, analysis of early French orchestral sonority, Italian Renaissance court sources bearing on local musical cultures, opera as theatre, Slavonic music, fifteenth-century song repertories, integration of theory and aesthetics with eighteenth-century French politics, changing relations between composer and performer in contemporary music, and new American composition. The composing process remained a favoured investigation, but now Beethoven, Berlioz, Prokofiev, Bloch, Koechlin, Verdi, Wagner, Szymanowski, Elgar and Britten are added to earlier case studies, while socio-political and ethnic relevance joins some of the outcomes.[31] Similarly, the accuracy, or not, of assumptions about performing old music, though not a new question, here finds a more thoroughly technical, geographically nuanced and socio-historical set of answers than had previously been proposed, especially for Classical orchestral music. In one of the most remarkable papers of the period, Neal Zaslaw's pioneering study of early orchestras, given in April 1977, uses both text and context to offer new hypotheses about the sound of eighteenth-century performing bodies.[32]

Other papers that reported discoveries and synthesized meaning are equally impressive. Margaret Bent's focus in late 1967 on the physical make-up of the Old Hall manuscript continued her investigation of that collection's origin and purpose to reach new projections about its musical styles and date range in the early fifteenth century.[33] Daniel Heartz's study in spring 1968 of mid-eighteenth-century opera reform explores changes in theatrical production – subject, dramaturgy, characterization and acting – to suggest how European operatic innovations reflected earlier influence of 'the English taste'

---

[31] Emily Anderson, 'Beethoven's Operatic Plans', *PRMA*, 88 (1961–62), 61–71, given in March 1962, was the first RMA paper on Beethoven since 1927 and included the UK première of his *Vestas Feuer* fragment (with a substantial performers' fee covered anonymously by Anderson, Alec King acting as her intermediary; see her letters to Fortune, 2 Nov – 6 Dec 1961, BL Add. MS 71037, fols. 114–200; and Council minutes, 22 Nov 1961, M MS 2, fol. 20v). It relied in part on her recently published *The Letters of Beethoven* (London: Macmillan, 1961). Hugh Macdonald, 'Berlioz's Self-Borrowings', *PRMA*, 92 (1965–66), 27–44, grew out of his early work on the New Berlioz Edition from 1964. Alexander Knapp, 'The Jewishness of Bloch: Subconscious or Conscious?', *PRMA*, 97 (1970–71), 99–112, explored the mix of Western and Jewish influences infusing Bloch's music. Robert Orledge, 'Charles Koechlin and the Early Sound Film, 1933–38', *PRMA*, 98 (1971–72), 1–16, treated early film as a spur to Koechlin's creativity. Jim Samson's 'Szymanowski – An Interior Landscape', *PRMA*, 106 (1979–80), 69–76, looked at the composer's creative crisis from 1918, coinciding with Poland's independence.

[32] 'Toward the Revival of the Classical Orchestra', *PRMA*, 103 (1976–77), 158–87. Zaslaw later advised the Jaap Schröder/Christopher Hogwood complete recording of the Mozart symphonies for L'Oiseau Lyre, and with John Spitzer wrote *The Birth of the Orchestra: History of an Institution, 1650–1815* (Oxford: OUP, 2004).

[33] 'Sources of the Old Hall Music', *PRMA*, 94 (1967–68), 19–35. Bent would receive the Dent Medal in 1979. The Old Hall MS originally belonged to St Edmund's College, Hertfordshire; it was sold to the BL in 1973.

on C.W. Gluck, partly through David Garrick.[34] Alan Tyson's examination in late 1970 of Beethoven's composing method traces detailed evidence in his sketches and drafts, some recently available at the Pierpont Morgan Library, for one well-known piano trio, a process covering several types of sketch, possible interpretations and their bearing on how Beethoven arrived at a continuity draft.[35] Andrew Porter's detailed revelation in April 1972 of finding in Paris and restoring most of Verdi's excisions from the original autograph score of *Don Carlos* (1867), some twenty minutes of 'lost' music, resulted in four possible versions for the opera, stimulating questions about future productions, taste and value.[36] In all these papers and others besides, the signs of maturity are not in repertory or presentation *per se*, but in the nature and scope of the investigation, the research method used and the adjudged significance of the outcome. If one pair of RMA papers encapsulates a maturing from 1960 to 1980, it might be the treatments given to two well-loved if sometimes misunderstood English composers, Edward Elgar and Benjamin Britten. In 1960 Jack Westrup looked inward to explore 'Elgar's Enigma', both the famous variation set and Elgar's personality, through memoirs, letters, programme notes and personal speculation, admittedly reaching no conclusion, maintaining the enigma.[37] In 1980, after an articulate, outward-facing discussion of the uses of late twentieth-century European analysis pro and con, Arnold Whittall positively illumined Britten's musical substance in 'The Study of Britten: Triadic Harmony and Tonal Structure', showing the power of harmonic analysis to uncover distinctive purpose in the composer's subtle sense of tonal structures.[38]

An example of an RMA paper directly sparking further RMA work also deserves mention – Joseph Kerman's 'Beethoven Sketchbooks in the British Museum', given in April 1967 after his year-long research stint in the Museum collections.[39] By mid-May Kerman, from the University of California,

---

[34] 'From Garrick to Gluck: The Reform of Theatre and Opera in the Mid-Eighteenth Century', *PRMA*, 94 (1967–68), 111–27. Heartz would be awarded the Dent Medal in 1970.

[35] 'Stages in the Composition of Beethoven's Piano Trio Op. 70, No. 1', *PRMA*, 97 (1970–71), 1–19. One of Tyson's first writings on the Beethoven sketches, this work fed into others, above all his prize-winning collaboration with Douglas Johnson and Robert Winter, *The Beethoven Sketchbooks: History, Reconstruction, Inventory* (Oxford: Clarendon Press; Berkeley: Univ. of California Press, 1985).

[36] 'The Making of 'Don Carlos', *PRMA*, 98 (1971–72), 73–88. This paper was given at the Annual Conference in April 1972.

[37] 'Elgar's Enigma', *PRMA*, 86 (1959–60), 79–97. The paper embodied a plea for taking the Variations more seriously than was customary, moving beyond a frame of musical caricature and penetrating Elgar's obfuscations. It was not until the late 1970s that an Elgar sketch study had more revealing results; see Christopher Kent, 'A View of Elgar's Methods of Composition through the Sketches of the Symphony No. 2 in E♭ (op. 63)', *PRMA*, 103 (1976–77), 41–60.

[38] 'The Study of Britten: Triadic Harmony and Tonal Structure', *PRMA*, 106 (1979–80), 27–41. Whittall's now classic book *The Music of Britten and Tippett: Studies in Themes and Techniques* (Cambridge Univ. Press, 1982, rev. 2nd edn 1990) would soon follow.

[39] *PRMA*, 93 (1966–67), 77–96. The paper makes a strong case for the value of the BM's Beethoven sketch materials but also for their inadequate listing and study. Omitting

Berkeley, wanted to do more; he had conceived a major plan for a possible joint publication between the Association and the Museum of a facsimile edition of the 'Kafka Sketchbook', an autograph miscellany of primary evidence for the composer's early works that was also the most important Beethoven source in Britain. Owned by the Museum since 1875 (purchased from the collector J.N. Kafka) and much discussed since, it had never been adequately studied.[40] Kerman's idea was to celebrate the forthcoming Beethoven bicentenary in 1970 through a collaborative project between the UK's national music library and its national musicological body, facilitating international music research; the (monochrome) facsimile, proposed without transcriptions but soon amended to include them, would be introduced by him. Immediately interested, the Council formed a subcommittee of Lewis, Fortune, Dart and Kerman to investigate costs and practicalities with Museum authorities including Frank Francis, the Director.[41] In February 1968 Andrew Porter became subcommittee chair (ultimately chief editor), while the RMA treasurer, Cedric Watkins, guaranteed £1,000 towards the project, much less than the BM's share but not negligible; detailed London talks over production and marketing continued while Kerman produced his copy.[42] By early 1970 the work was done but costs had jumped: the BM now wanted £5,000, forcing the RMA to find outside funds or reduce their 'joint publication' status to a more accurate phrase such as 'in collaboration with'. Kerman advocated 'collaboration' because

> the RMA received the project in the first instance, encouraged it, appraised it, and did a great deal of spade work before presenting it to the BM. [...] Furthermore, the project would never have come up without the invitations accorded to me by the English musicological community, and by the RMA in particular. [...] RMA was front and center at almost every point [...] The suggestions of the Council are reflected importantly in the format of the final publication, which differs in a number of respects from the original plan.[43]

---

the most important, the so-called Kafka Sketchbook, already most discussed, this paper focuses on the two lesser-known sketchbooks, Egerton MS 2795 and Add. MS 31776 (containing the Sixth Symphony and the Trios, Op. 70). Kerman had undertaken his London research on a Fulbright award through Oxford, at the invitation of Westrup, Harrison and Sternfeld.

[40] Pioneering work on the miscellany had been done by Nottebohm, and especially J.S. Shedlock, an Association member, in a series of *MT* articles of 1892. The book is currently catalogued as BL Add. MS 29801 and contains 124 leaves with sketch material from the period c. 1786–99, including rudimentary sketches for known and unknown works, working autographs and fair copies.

[41] J. Kerman to A. Lewis, 17 May 1967, BL Add. MS 71051, fol. 202; Council minutes, 3 July 1967, M MS 2, fol. 58v.

[42] See especially the minutes and notes from joint meetings held in January and April 1968, BL Add. MS 71034, fols. 99–103.

[43] J. Kerman to A. Porter, 10 Feb 1970, BL Add. MS 71051, fol. 205. Here Kerman also recalls that in its original speaker's invitation, the RMA had suggested he 'not do another coals-to-Newcastle Elizabethan job' (emphasis original; Kerman was an established Byrd scholar).

In the end, 'in co-operation with' was preferred, giving the RMA intellectual credit and musicological status as the originating body who also oversaw production. Copies were sold to the public at £25, to RMA members at £20, and to BM buyers £16 13s. 4d., resulting in another gain for the Association. Moreover, the two-volume work was critically well received, notably by Alan Tyson, as likely 'the most important work of scholarship to come out of the Beethoven bicentenary year'.[44] And although the original miscellany itself is now fully digitized by the British Library for consultation online, Kerman's introduction, transcriptions, notes, inventory and 'index of works copied or sketched' still offer fruitful suggestions for appreciating Beethoven's methods in detail.

❧ The 1970s

Kerman's happy collaboration with the Association, his specialisms in Elizabethan music, opera criticism and Beethoven, and his humane approach to musicological writing generally seemed to fit him well for a longer stay in Britain. In 1971 he was invited to take up the Heather Professorship at Oxford after Westrup retired. Many UK scholars were delighted and expected fruitful engagement, particularly with students; but the Music Faculty's administrative burden didn't suit Kerman, and in 1974 he returned to his post in California, held open for him all along (unknown to Oxford). At almost the same time, another American musicologist of international stature, Howard Mayer Brown, recruited as King Edward Professor of Music at KCL following Thurston Dart's untimely death, also stayed only a short while before returning, in this case to the University of Chicago in 1974, soon succeeding Edward Lowinsky there as a distinguished professor. Like Kerman, Brown had joined the RMA in the 1970s and contributed more than one outstanding publication. Though distinct in their angles, the two Americans were viewed alike in the UK, both representing 'hard musicology' (Kerman's term), thus exerting an influence worthy or pernicious depending on one's point of view.[45]

Their conjunction in RMA annals matters partly because both men appeared in 1973, with Frank Ll. Harrison, Lewis Lockwood and 'the Svengali-like figure of Edward Lowinsky' (by oblique reference) in public journalistic combat over the nature and purposes of British and American musicology. Involving Renaissance music, *musica ficta* and the place of performance in scholarly activity, the confrontation also touched on the two cultures' differing academic structures, showing just how easily prejudice, misperception and slur can take hold. It all started in June with an anonymous book review in

---

[44] Alan Tyson, 'Beethoven's "Kafka Sketchbook"', *MT*, 111 (1970), 1194–95, 1197–98.
[45] J. Kerman, under 'American Musicology', *TLS* (19 Oct 1973), saw the attack on him in this letters exchange as vindication of his deliberate mid-Atlantic stance between the two cultures, placing him in a double bind: 'In America I am a force for soft musicology, criticism, generalism, wilfulness, urbanity, nice writing. Here I am a force for hard musicology, rigour, pedantry, deadly seriousness, slog.'

the *TLS* of H. Colin Slim's *A Gift of Madrigals* (University of Chicago Press, 1972), entitled 'Florence to Henry' (29 June 1973). Ostensibly construed along methodological lines but sharply tinged with anti-American jibes, the 1,600-word piece prompted a running correspondence over the next five months, itself typical for *TLS* readers, even editorially encouraged in this time of UK university growth, but never before seen on the subject of musicology.[46] Brown, Lockwood, Kerman and Harrison appear on one side, with Ronald Woodham (Professor of Music, University of Reading), the anonymous 'Your Reviewer' and the London bookseller John May on the other.[47] Slim, the targeted Canadian author, founder of the music department at the University of California, Irvine, never replied (he didn't have to). It was now that Brown rejected the reviewer's comparisons between British and American musicology as impossible since, he asserted, the serious musical scholar in Britain was 'as rare as the dodo bird' ('Madrigals and Motets', 20 July 1973). Another colourful image came from Lockwood (Princeton University), who described the reviewer's charge of poor musicianship in American musicologists, allegedly explaining their fixation with *ficta*, as 'the purest chauvinistic moonshine' ('Musica Ficta', 21 September 1973).

At the distance of half a century, we might take the whole affair as no more than a peevish spat, part of the traditional cut and thrust of English journalism with American wisecracks thrown in. Cynically, with a weekly sale of some 40,000 copies, this amount of free coverage in the *TLS*'s distinguished pages could even be viewed as a PR triumph, given the deep feeling the letters exude about scholarship; musicologists surely benefited from such public exposure, while the *TLS* could always use ever more interested readers. More pointedly, in addition to eliciting a degree of reflection on musicology's aims and national differences, the episode flagged future potential in more, and more open, scholarly exchanges including disagreements, which might promote cross-fertilization across Europe and the USA and further afield. Kerman's contribution indeed alluded to his own sharp interchange with Edward Lowinsky eight years earlier, in 1965, over American musicology's direction, resulting now in his admission that all sides 'have a great deal to learn from each other's strengths and weaknesses' ('American Musicology', 19

---

[46] Books in music had long been covered anonymously in the *TLS*; in this period, aggressive reviewing to stir comment was encouraged. See Deborah McVea and Jeremy Treglown, 'The *Times Literary Supplement* in the Years of Anonymous Reviewing, 1902–1974: Swinging Sixties, Slipping Seventies', *Times Literary Supplement Historical Archive* (Cengage Learning, 2012), https://www.gale.com/intl/essays/mcvea-treglown-times-literary-supplement-swinging-sixties-slipping-seventies [accessed 22 Oct 2023]. The same essay asserts that anti-Americanism was embedded, too, in English literary culture of the 1960s and 70s.

[47] Brown's letters ('Madrigals and Motets', 20 July 1973; and 'American Musicology', 19 Oct 1973) were noted in Council; see minutes, 14 Nov 1973, M MS 2, fol. 130. The rejoinders of Woodham ('American Musicology', 5 Oct 1973), Your Reviewer ('Musica Ficta', 19 Oct 1973) and May ('Anglo-American Musicology', 26 Oct 1973) were not, but must have been seen.

October 1973).[48] Harrison's letter, too, brought to bear the wider cultural sense of an ethnomusicologist, advocating the exercise of human understanding in forming conceptions and preconceptions of musical producer and recipient ('Anglo-American Musicology', 16 November 1973).

Ultimately in seeking the identity of 'Your Reviewer' – because anonymity uncovered can fundamentally alter a review's value, a *TLS* tenet from 1974[49] – we can better place this episode and understand the animus behind the 1973 piece. Denis Stevens, the English musicologist, conductor, BBC producer, editor (The Mulliner Book, MB 1, 1951), Monteverdi specialist, co-founder of the Ambrosian Singers, former RMA member and, not least, roving professor at various American universities including Columbia in New York City (1964–76), emerges as almost certainly the author of 'Florence to Henry'.[50] Thanks to new scholarship on the *TLS* archives resulting in its digitized historical index, we can quickly track Stevens as a signing contributor of some twenty-six *TLS* articles over the years 1972–97, the first of which, 'Discordant Noises in Academe' (27 October 1972), controversially sets out a personal critique of American university music departments and their musicologists, ideas reiterated almost literally in the anonymous piece of 1973. Further, the contributor identified by *TLS* researchers as the author of 'Henry to Florence', called in their scheme 'Contributor X (name withheld)', also wrote another forty-four articles over the years 1960–74, most of which treat the late medieval, Renaissance and Baroque musical subjects Stevens is known to have essayed in his other work.[51] Whether an identity was surmised by the correspondents of 1973 is unclear but probable, which may account for the campaign's vehemence: Stevens was known to be something of a loose cannon, an adroit

---

[48] See Joseph Kerman, 'A Profile for American Musicology', *JAMS*, 18 (1965), 61–69; and Edward E. Lowinsky's cogent reply, 'Character and Purposes of American Musicology', *JAMS*, 18 (1965), 222–34.

[49] D. McVea and J. Treglown, 'The *Times Literary Supplement* in the Years of Anonymous Reviewing, 1902–1974: 1948–1959: The *Times Literary Supplement* under Alan Pryce-Jones', *Times Literary Supplement Historical Archive* (Cengage Learning, 2012), https://www.gale.com/intl/essays/mcvea-treglown-times-literary-supplement-under-alan-pryce-jones [accessed 22 Oct 2023]. This essay cites F.W. Bateson's classic formulation, 'the reviewer's name is an essential part of the meaning of the review', as a key reason for *TLS*'s abandonment of anonymity in 1974.

[50] For Stevens's career and difficult personality, see Anne Pimlott Baker, 'Stevens, Denis William', *ODNB*.

[51] For 'Contributor X' and Denis Stevens, see *The Times Literary Supplement Historical Archive, 1902–2019*, published by Gale Primary Sources. For Stevens's musicological writings and editions, see the unsigned 'Stevens, Denis (William)' in *Grove Music Online*. Stevens joined the RMA in the 1950–51 session, contributing 'Pre-Reformation Organ Music in England', *PRMA*, 78 (1951–52), 1–10; but he was resistant to systems and Association rules. He left Oxford without a doctorate, refusing to make required changes in his thesis, and clashed with the RMA more than once, including over his Mulliner Book commentary; he resigned in 1959. For his correspondence with Erlebach and Fortune, see BL Add. MS 71061, fols. 121–44 (1951–59).

professional musician but not universally viewed as an authoritative musicologist. Among other regular *TLS* reviewers of music books, the most prolific was undoubtedly Wilfrid Mellers (composer and F.R. Leavis protégé), long an RMA member and founder of the University of York music department: between 1950 and 2008 he contributed more than 150 stimulating pieces on a galaxy of subjects. Meanwhile, concepts of musicology and proficient writing for general and specialist readers by British and American scholars were already permeating Macmillan's *New Grove* initiative; Brown and Lockwood became closely involved.

Back in the RMA's workaday world, new officers picked up administrative threads. The Association's Library, examined by Oliver Neighbour, had been deposited on permanent loan for members' use in the London Senate House Library in 1957, facilitated by Fortune's role there.[52] In 1967 a report from its music librarian Anthea Baird confirmed that the old IMG periodicals *SIMG* and *ZIMG*, earlier *Proceedings* volumes and *Papers of the American Musicological Society* were heavily used and required binding or boxing; a few other items had gone astray 'in the Tower'.[53] The chance of a university base for the Association came closer when Dart, professor at KCL's Music Faculty in the Strand (a mile from Senate House), interceded to establish regular RMA meetings at King's from autumn 1970, assisted by William Oxenbury. Gerald Abraham, succeeding Lewis as president in mid-1969, made pertinent suggestions, while Fortune, planning soon to relinquish his secretarial role, worked to put RMA publications on a secure footing. He monitored RMA marketing, which moved from Blackwell's to the Cambridge Music Shop in 1974, and worked with Edward Olleson, *PRMA* editor from 1967, to analyse the journal's broadening extent, music examples and rising costs: with volume 101 (1974–75), *PRMA* column width was enlarged by an inch. Changes in subscription rates became inevitable. By early 1973 the Council had raised their institutional rate, opened the 'student' category to anyone on a full-time university course and introduced a 'joint' rate for spouses; a 'retired' member category was discussed in 1974–75. Both journal editors began receiving a small stipend, while Fortune's successor from 1971, Malcolm Turner, an Assistant Keeper in the BM, brought efficiency and clarity to decision-making.

The numerical growth of the 1960s, which had largely spurred the Annual Conference and publication improvements, now prompted Abraham's encouragement of regional activity through RMA 'chapters', potentially for

---

[52] Council minutes, 6 Mar 1957, M MS 1, pp. 117–18; Nigel Fortune (for J.H.P. Pafford) to [Frank Howes], 6 Nov 1957, BL Add. MS 71054, fol. 95. Neighbour, an Assistant Keeper in the BM Music Room, was officially appointed RMA Honorary Librarian at the same meeting. His listing mentions, besides complete sets of *Proceedings* and MB, also complete sets of *ZIMG*, *SIMG* and *Die Musikforschung*, runs of other European journals, about sixty books, pamphlets and offprints, and a large pile of miscellanea.

[53] O. Neighbour to N. Fortune, 10 Nov 1967 and 29 Nov 1967 (BL Add. MS 71057, fols. 71, 75). A more recent search shows *Die Musikforschung* available through the Library's Stack Service, and the IMG periodicals accessible electronically.

northern England, Scotland and Wales.[54] Together with Fortune, in 1971 elected a vice-president, and Alec King, whose regional experience with the International Association of Music Libraries (IAML) proved helpful, the group trialled a plan for a Northern Chapter, including Scotland. Michael Tilmouth of the University of Edinburgh set up two paper meetings in 1971–72, one in Edinburgh, the other in Durham. Each was highly successful (to Londoners' surprise), with attendances of sixty to seventy and a gain in new RMA members. Fortune then produced a UK map showing the geographical distribution of members across the country (see Fig. 22).[55] On that basis, a North Midlands Chapter was mooted at Nottingham and Sheffield in autumn 1973, but nothing materialized until Michael Talbot, at the University of Liverpool in the North Western region, agreed two years later to organize it; it too succeeded.

Naturally as annual and student conferences unfolded and news of postgraduate and regional activities circulated, it was only a matter of time before the miscellany approach to RMA programming would feel truly inadequate, especially to younger scholars working on early repertories. Their need to share ideas at a sustained level of concentration inspired them, led by Stanley Boorman, to set up 'an informal Conference of Renaissance scholars'.[56] Having suggested the idea to Council in July 1971, but receiving only a £10 guarantee against loss in reply, the group pressed on, establishing what later became known independently as the 'Med-Ren' Conference, at Nottingham University in July 1972. Although their second meeting, organized by Ian Bent at KCL in July 1973, also received only a small RMA guarantee rather than a grant, this specialist Medieval-Renaissance conference flourished and has since recurred annually in international locations, reaching its fiftieth anniversary in 2022 as the 'largest academic conference on early music in Europe'.[57] A similar beginning characterized the Nineteenth-Century Music Conference, also at Nottingham, set up in 1978 by Robert Pascall and John Tyrrell and repeated two years later at Cambridge under the direction of Julian Rushton; it too continued in international locations, growing in size and influence with the explosion of work on nineteenth-century music and culture from the late

---

[54] G. Abraham to N. Fortune, 22 Oct 1970, BL Add. MS 71037, fol. 28: 'We have sniffed at this before, but run away from it. Yet I feel more and more that we are not offering enough for the people who are not within fairly easy and inexpensive train-distance from London.' See also A.H. King to G. Abraham, 19 Nov 1970, BL Add. MS 71052, fol. 265.

[55] Pasted into Council minutes, 15 Nov 1972, M MS 2, fol. 123. With a numerical count of fifty for Scotland and the North, forty for the East and West Ridings and North Midland regions, and thirty for the South West, it was decided that the Ridings and North Midlands were to be favoured over the South West. Finding a willing coordinator was also essential.

[56] Council minutes, 14 July 1971, M MS 2, fol. 97.

[57] Jack Stebbing and Francis Bertschinger, 'Medieval and Renaissance Music Conference at 50', *Early Music*, 50 (2022), 544–46.

Figure 22. 'Geographical Distribution of RMA members', c. 1972, by Nigel Fortune; redrawn from a map pasted in RMA Papers, Manchester, M MS 2, fol. 123.

1970s. While it sometimes receives an RMA contribution, this biennial conference is also run chiefly on an independent basis.[58]

For the RMA itself, an overarching focus in this decade was the Association's Centenary, celebrated with a multi-faceted set of events across 1974. Planning started in 1970, both for the regular session 1973–74, including an April Annual Conference, and for a special Centenary Celebration with more papers and two concerts on 8–9 November 1974. The Council envisioned a double issue of *Proceedings*, *PRMA* 100, as well as a concert presenting a new work, perhaps by Michael Tippett. Publicity through press and radio would attract new interest, and a further publication, potentially an anthology of *PMA* and *PRMA* articles from the journal's first hundred years selected by Andrew Porter, would be produced by a private publisher. The dual purpose of so much activity was to publicize the RMA, swelling its membership, and to make a lasting contribution to scholarship, correlating music's values through research with the wider enrichment of society.[59] RMA planners aimed high.

Invitations went out first to the great and the good, including the Dutchman Eduard Reeser, Jack Westrup, Howard Mayer Brown, the Swiss Kurt von Fischer, Alexander Goehr, Benjamin Britten and Gustave Reese (Honorary Foreign Member since 1966); all but Britten and Reese replied. Other distinguished international scholars were also approached, from Eva Badura-Skoda, François Lesure and Jens Peter Larsen to Joseph Kerman, Lewis Lockwood, Ludwig Finscher, Lázló Somfai and Rudolf Häusler (IMS secretary). Not all could attend or contribute, but many did, joined by A.H. King, D.P. Walker, Winton Dean, Daniel Heartz, Imogen Holst and Carl Dahlhaus.[60] After months of preparation and adjustment, the Council achieved its goals on five fronts: an impressive regular session, November to May, including Northern and North Midlands chapter papers; two high-calibre weekend conferences with concerts by Denis Matthews and by the Early Music Consort; a new musical work by John Joubert, 'Crabbed Age and Youth' for countertenor, recorder, viola da gamba and harpsichord, commissioned with funds from the Worshipful Company of Musicians; an enlarged edition of *Proceedings*, volume 100, with fourteen 'Centenary Essays' (four from the main session, five from the Annual Conference, five from the Centenary Celebration); and, in lieu of the anthology, a facsimile edition of another major musical source

---

[58] Rushton initially asked the Council for modest support but later withdrew the request, conscious of the RMA's perilous resources. Both conferences attracted international participation, so the Council thought it prudent to hold RMA support for fear of setting precedents it couldn't maintain (Council minutes, 6 Feb 1980, M MS 3, meeting 8001).

[59] Council minutes, 14 July 1971, M MS 2, fols. 100–01.

[60] Planning for the year's events can be followed in Council minutes from July 1970 to Nov 1974 in M MS 2, fols. 86v–143, *passim*. For a snapshot of late plans for the Centenary Celebration in November 1974, not all of them realized, see the minutes in ibid., 3 July 1974, fols.136v–137v. Dahlhaus joined as a life member in 1975, and by 1983 had been made an Honorary Foreign Member.

in the UK, *Handel's Conducting Score of Messiah*, introduced by Watkins Shaw (published by Scolar Press).[61] Attendance fluctuated, and extra costs left a small deficit after the hire of Stationers' Hall, the harpsichord and the Early Music Consort, and the printing of 1,800 copies of *PRMA* 100 (which appeared late). But the celebrations were greatly enjoyed by all who attended. Enabling solid scholarship, international goodwill and positive returns for the RMA, the Centenary was a decided success.

'Centenary Essays' indeed offered something of a model for another conference three years later, the week-long Oxford International Symposium on 'Modern Musicology and the Historical Tradition of Scholarship', held at Christ Church in September 1977 under the auspices of the Foster and Wills Scholarships and the Deutscher Akademischer Austauschdienst (DAAD).[62] Organized by Denis Arnold and Edward Olleson, both of Oxford's Music Faculty, this conference too yielded a collected volume, *Modern Musical Scholarship* (Oriel Press, 1980), edited by Olleson, who'd also edited *PRMA* 100; its contributors and their topics complemented those in the RMA centenary collection. Of its fourteen essays, half were by RMA members. In fact three contributors are common to both collections (Brown, Somfai and Walker), several senior American scholars and one key music librarian appear in each, and a senior German-born female musicologist in each discusses opera or theatre. Intersections in theory, analytical thinking, historiography and criticism, source study and iconography come to the fore in both publications. Table 4 shows a side-by-side comparison of the two contents pages. Beyond superficial resemblances, we can imagine how the Oxford symposium might have taken a lead from the RMA Centenary. Yet it also went further, focusing on methods and values in musicological investigation, questions about sources and ways of interpreting history. Self-evidently, the Oxford papers didn't celebrate an organization or its longevity, but instead examined the discipline's wider potential and future direction; and like the Centenary essays, the Oxford papers underscored the important place of British work in a widening internationalized musicology. Together the two collections made a strong statement for the health of both the RMA and British academic music study. Meanwhile another sign of the Association's international interest had been its selection in 1974 of three Honorary Foreign Members – Charles Seeger (USA), with Eduard Reeser and Kurt von Fischer. In his eighty-eighth year, Seeger couldn't contribute to the Centenary, but as the pioneer of an alternative, culturally based American musicology, he offered the RMA both

---

[61] In 1867 the Handel score came into the Library of St Michael's College, Tenbury Wells, Frederick Ouseley's private collection, of which Shaw was Honorary Librarian from 1948 (following E.H. Fellowes); when the College closed in 1985, its music MSS passed by gift to the Bodleian Library, Oxford. Shaw's publication project with Scolar Press was already in progress when RMA Centenary planning began.

[62] For a reflection on the symposium and its context, see Susan Wollenberg, 'The Development of the Faculty of Music', in *Music in Twentieth-Century Oxford: New Directions*, ed. Robin Darwall-Smith and Susan Wollenberg (Woodbridge: Boydell Press, 2023), 177–97 at 193–95.

Table 4. Comparative Contents of *PRMA* 100 (1973-74, *left*) and *Modern Musical Scholarship* (1980, *right*), both edited by Edward Olleson.

Contents

Foreword

GERALD ABRAHAM: Our First Hundred Years	vii

ALEC HYATT KING: Some Aspects of Recent Mozart Research	1
SIR JACK WESTRUP: Parodies and Parameters	19
D.P. WALKER: Some Aspects of the Musical Theory of Vincenzo Galilei and Galileo Galilei	33
HOWARD MAYER BROWN: Embellishment in early Sixteenth-Century Italian Intabulations	49
ALEXANDER GOEHR: The Theoretical Writings of Arnold Schoenberg	85
LEWIS LOCKWOOD: Aspects of the 'L'Homme armé' Tradition	97
WINTON DEAN: Donizetti's Serious Operas	123
KURT VON FISCHER: The Sacred Polyphony of the Italian Trecento	143
LÁSZLÓ SOMFAI: The London Revision of Haydn's Instrumental Style	159
DANIEL HEARTZ: Thomas Attwood's Lessons in Composition with Mozart	175
EVA BADURA-SKODA: The Influence of the Viennese Popular Comedy on Haydn and Mozart	185
IMOGEN HOLST: Holst's Music: Some Questions of Style and Performance at the Centenary of his Birth	201
CARL DAHLHAUS: Schoenberg and Schenker	209

Contents

Foreword	v
Preface	vii
Chapter 1 Denis Arnold – The Profession of Musical Scholarship	1
Chapter 2 Arthur Mendel – The Purposes and Desirable Characteristics of Text-Critical Editions	14
Chapter 3 Brian Trowell – Faburden – New Sources, New Evidence: A Preliminary Survey	28
Chapter 4 Paul Doe – The Emergence of the In Nomine: Some Notes and Queries on the Work of Tudor Church Musicians	79
Chapter 5 D.P. Walker – The Musical Theories of Giuseppe Tartini	93
Chapter 6 Howard Mayer Brown – Trecento Angels and the Instruments they Play	112
Chapter 7 Hugh MacDonald – Fantasy and Order in Beethoven's Phantasie Op. 77	141
Chapter 8 Ian Bent – Analytical Thinking in the First Half of the Nineteenth Century	151
Chapter 9 László Somfai – Self-Analysis by Twentieth-Century Composers	167
Chapter 10 Claude V. Palisca – G.B. Doni, Musicological Activist, and his 'Lyra Barberina'	180
Chapter 11 Walter Salmen – The Value of Iconographical Sources in Musical Research	206
Chapter 12 William W. Austin – Martini, Rousseau, Burney and Forkel in Twentieth-Century Perspectives	215
Chapter 13 Vincent Duckles – A French Critic's View on the State of Music in London (1829)	223
Chapter 14 Anna Amalie Abert – Opera Research: Tradition and Progress	238

distinction and balance, his name neatly sidestepping philosophical differences still brewing in transatlantic musicology.

Succeeding Abraham as president in late 1974, Alec Hyatt King brought his own interests into service, integrating his IMS and IAML links, library work, Mozart studies and publishing experience.[63] He handed over to Denis Arnold in 1978, a year after the secretaryship had passed from Malcolm Turner to Hugh Cobbe – a transition that slightly worried one or two Council members for the apparent prevalence of professional librarians now taking RMA roles when, some felt, dedicated musicologists ought to predominate.[64] But a greater practical concern came from higher printing costs and instability on the paper-planning and editorial side, including divided responsibility between the Proceedings Committee and the *PRMA* editor. Paradoxically, with more conferences and chapters yielding more papers, and more trained musicologists able to cope with editing, it became harder to get an editor's commitment. Academia made its own demands. Rising scholars naturally tended to privilege their research and departmental responsibilities over the RMA's, though some were ready to assist. Margaret Bent began editing *PRMA* 101 before leaving for Brandeis University in July 1976, one of many distinguished British musicologists finding greener pastures in Europe or North America.[65] Olleson finished volume 101, then Geoffrey Chew edited *PRMA* 102, issued two years late after difficulties with the members' list. David Greer took on *PRMA* 103, whose large extent and high cost added to the Association's deficit and led to a printer change from Barnicotts to Camelot Press. It was Fortune, finally, who picked up responsibility for sessional planning in coordination with Greer as *Proceedings* editor, both helping to rethink the RMA's yearly framework (again). Sensing real challenge from a proliferation of separate conferences, competing societies and other good outlets seeking papers, Greer adopted as a mission the renovating of *PRMA* to make it more appealing. Further positive signs in this period included the success of the first Annual Conference to be held outside London, at Cambridge in spring 1978; and the receipt of a Hinrichsen Foundation grant for exactly the amount of the RMA deficit for 1977–78, £3,838 – a minor miracle in inflationary times.[66] Reaching out but also keeping up, the Association, as ever, sought balance.

---

[63] See 'Some Aspects of Recent Mozart Research', *PRMA*, 100 (1973–74), 1–18, for King's grasp of interpretative issues, new findings, tributes to C.B. Oldman and Emily Anderson, and the values of RISM.

[64] See N. Fortune to Malcolm Turner, 5 Nov 1976, M MS 2, fol. 161. Fortune thought the secretary's duties should be re-examined before a new appointment was made. For Turner's reply and the Council decision, see ibid., fols. 158v–159.

[65] Among RMA members leaving the UK for study or employment were Gilbert Reaney, Nicholas Temperley, Andrew Hughes, Philip Brett, Stanley Boorman, Jeremy Noble, Carolyn Gianturco, Ian Bent, Hugh Macdonald, David Hiley and Davitt Moroney. Many others, including Frederick Sternfeld, Gerald Hendrie, Roger Bray and David Fallows, went for short-term or periodic appointments.

[66] Council minutes, 5 July 1978, M MS 3, meeting 7802. The Annual Conference was held at St Catharine's College, Cambridge, 7–9 April 1978, with more than a hundred

❧ Supporting and Collaborating

A flow of meetings occurs in any club or business, like turnover in officers, or ups and downs in finance. From the 1950s a particular aspect of RMA business, encouraging scholarship, was its fiduciary role as a holder and disburser of legacy funds – bequests from deceased members. After a hundred years of the group's existence, such resources naturally began to grow. In the 1970s, the Association received four memorials, from the estates of Arnold Goldsbrough, the organist-conductor and founder of what became in 1960 the English Chamber Orchestra (1973); C.B. Oldman, head of the Department of Printed Books at the BM and noted Mozart scholar (1974); Louise Dyer, the Australian music publisher and patron who contributed through MB (1974); and Thurston Dart, the brilliant performer, scholar, editor and teacher whose estate assigned half his future royalties to the RMA (1978). After considerable discussion, it was decided to keep these names attached to their funds and possibly amalgamate the money in all but the Dart bequest under the rubric 'Special Funds', with a single small-grant application for researchers requesting support, and then to find a dedicated purpose, separately, for the Dart Fund; soon highly productive (yielding £1,200 in 1977–78), it would always remain distinct. Three ideas for using it were put forward in early 1980 – a series of occasional monographs (suggested by David Fallows), enhancement of *PRMA* (A.H. King) or an annual lecture (Anthony Lewis).[67]

In a different form of fiduciary linkage, the Association's relation to MB required clarification as MB achieved greater financial success. Already in 1965, the project had begun paying a higher fee to its editors; by 1971 its surplus funds attracted the RMA's interest in 'borrowing' some. But the Association did not own MB, and its publishers Stainer & Bell were not happy to lend (they needed £3,000 working capital for each new volume); the new RMA treasurer Malcolm London thus suggested making MB a separate financial entity, a trust, with shares owned by the RMA. The decisive proposal came in 1974 from William Oxenbury, Dart's executor and secretary to the MB Editorial Committee, who wrote the Musica Britannica Trust document so that the new body could, if necessary, give financial assistance to other RMA publications.[68] Approved by the Charity Commission and discussed by Council in 1975, the Trust became operational from 1976, inevitably distancing MB affairs from

---

people participating; its success prompted further annual conferences out of London every other year. Max Hinrichsen had joined the Association in the mid-1940s and built up his London publishing business from his C.F. Peters agency, including the Hinrichsen's Musical Year Book series (1944–61). For his friendship with Alec Hyatt King, see Irene Lawford-Hinrichsen, *Music Publishing and Patronage: C.F. Peters, 1800 to the Holocaust* (Kenton, Middlesex: Edition Press, 2000), 8–16.

[67] See Council minutes, 15 Feb 1978, M MS 3, meeting 7801; and 6 Feb 1980, M MS 3, meeting 8001. The Council agreed that the Dart Fund was not to be used to sustain RMA finances.

[68] Council minutes, 13 Feb 1974, M MS 2, fol. 134; and 3 July 1974, M MS 2, fol. 140, 'Relationship between Musica Britannica and the Royal Musical Association'.

RMA accounts and communications. Stainer & Bell thenceforward became even more important to the MB enterprise, in effect its banker.[69]

Just as MB was taking off in the late 1950s, a new international music cataloguing project was proposed to the RMA by the IMS, first in 1959 and more fully in 1961. The idea was for its partner, IAML, to map and catalogue written musical sources worldwide and publish the results; editing and printing would be handled in Kassel, Germany. Called 'RISM', or in English, International Inventory of Musical Sources, this vast project required British input for the British sources and sought a sponsoring body from the nation's music research community, above all the RMA. Although cataloguing was a hard cause to sell – British enthusiasm for music documentation was never as strong as that for music editing, performing or listening – the UK RISM committee persevered. All eight were RMA members, led by C.B. Oldman and A.H. King. Like W.B. Squire before them, they saw source research as the foundation of ongoing music performance and wider understanding, so drew up a sensible five-year plan for listing seventeenth- and eighteenth-century music manuscripts in some fifty libraries across the country, using several cataloguers.[70] Pre-1801 printed sources had already been captured in Edith Schnapper's *British Union-Catalogue of English Music* (2 vols., 1957), useful as a basis for RISM updating. But because almost no UK music manuscripts had been catalogued, the new plan targeted that material, estimating a cost of £30,000 for the onsite work.

In the event, raising sufficient money even to start the project with an initial £10,000 caused disappointment and took three years.[71] In mid-1963 a British Academy grant of £750 finally came through, enabling the RMA to advertise its sponsorship of the UK RISM Committee. A *Times* notice appeared in August 1963,[72] and by summer 1964 further monies had been secured, including the BM's contribution. Thirty candidates then applied for, now, two cataloguing posts. Starting at the BM, then moving to Tenbury, Scotland, other London libraries, Cambridge, Oxford, and later York, Durham, Ireland and the rest of southern England, the cataloguers – notably Richard Andrewes, later Head

---

[69] Julian Rushton, 'Voice of Britain', *MT*, 136 (1995), 472–74 at 472. By mid-1977 Oxenbury missed the RMA's close support; Anthony Lewis reassured him that ties still ran in both directions (Council minutes, 6 July 1977, and 9 Nov 1977, M MS 3, meetings 7702 and 7703). In the period 1961–79, MB issued twenty-eight volumes (MB 17–44).

[70] See 'The International Inventory of Musical Sources', signed by C.B. Oldman, 10 Aug 1962, BL Add. MS 71051, fols. 28–30.

[71] At different times from 1960 King tried the Gulbenkian Foundation, Nuffield Foundation, Pilgrim Trust, Ford Foundation, RVW Trust, British Council and SCONUL (Society of College, National and University Libraries), seeking any external support that would trigger the BM's conditional offer of £2,600. All showed interest but no cash. King's frustration, including with the RMA Council's apathy, prompted complaint: see A.H. King to N. Fortune, 9 July 1962 (BL Add. MS 71052, fol. 145) and 4 Nov 1963 (BL Add. MS 71052, fol. 182).

[72] 'Inventory of Musical Sources', *Times* (15 Aug 1963). The notice was signed by Arthur Bliss, Jack Westrup and C.B. Oldman.

of Music at Cambridge University Library – worked from autumn 1964 to spring 1969, producing more than 50,000 record cards. Although it seemed a Herculean effort and turned out to be a relatively modest part of a larger project, this collaborative exercise proved crucial to further music cataloguing in the UK, undertaken in the 1980s by the successor RISM (UK) Trust, eventually with the British Library and Royal Holloway, University of London, all of it leading to a twenty-first-century searchable database of early music sources. The RMA made its mark at the start, thanks to King and his mentor Oldman, whose seventieth birthday was celebrated in 1964 with a luncheon given by colleagues from the BM, Bibliographical Society and RMA Council.

In the meantime, a sister project called 'RILM', or in English, International Repertory of Music Literature, was founded in New York in 1966 by Barry Brook. Promising computer-indexed abstracts of current music literature, whether books, articles or dissertations, this idea also landed in the RMA's lap as an agreed international project in which British cooperation was required, specifically the writing and gathering of abstracts. Although Brook had just received the Dent Medal in 1965, his approach met resistance from some RMA leaders, notably Fortune, exasperated by another external request to organize work unrelated (he felt) to the RMA, and also Dart, sceptical of the international systematization of anything.[73] Brook politely moderated his request, while Lewis, Westrup and King counselled cooperation and made useful practical suggestions. The concept moved forward, so that the RMA indeed helped coordinate returns of English *RILM* abstracts; by 1970, Edward Olleson was sending abstracts of all *PRMA* articles.

Underneath the cool response to both international projects, of course, lay residual tensions in how British musicologists viewed their European and American counterparts, especially in career structures and degree of state support. British scholars felt at a continual disadvantage. No episode crystallized the problem more than the IMS secretary's request, in 1977, for more RMA cash and active participation in IMS 'R-projects' (RISM, RILM and, most recently, Répertoire International d'Iconographie Musicale, or RIdIM, cataloguing initiatives). Sending his IMS budget summary for 1972–77, Dr Häusler showed that the RMA contributed a mere 6 per cent of the total received from its nine national societies and governments.[74] At a difficult moment in their

---

[73] Council minutes, 19 July 1966, M MS 2, fol. 52. Dart thought abstracts would too easily displace the reading of full articles. In spring 1967 Fortune sent some *RMARC* abstracts, but was still reluctant for the RMA to act as a national RILM committee, feeling that Brook had made unfair assumptions about British infrastructure in musicology, including staffing and funding. Brook tried to reassure him. See B. Brook to N. Fortune, 27 Mar 1967 (BL Add. MS 71059, fols. 108–09); and 5 May 1967 (BL Add. MS 71059, fols. 106–07).

[74] IMS Financial Report for 1972–77, appended to RMA Council minutes, 9 Nov 1977 (M MS 3, meeting 7703). The RMA's contribution (361 Swiss francs out of 61,347) looks very small next to those of Switzerland, Netherlands and West Germany, and even the more moderate sums from the USA, Sweden, France and Austria.

own finances, the Council felt embarrassed but not cowed by this revelation; they sought official aid but by early 1978, with none forthcoming, simply cancelled their IMS subscription. Within months they reconsidered, renewed their small contribution and asked for discretion in not publicizing it. It was a plain fact that individual UK musicologists, even collectively, could not possibly approach the state-backed sums of other countries.

In all, this range of activities shows the RMA supporting individual scholars through its legacy funds and contributing time and labour, as far as it could, to large international projects affiliated with the Association. From the mid-1960s the RMA also formed ties with two kinds of local but external organization engaged in training young scholars and bridging national traditions – university music departments, especially those introducing academic courses, and the *New Grove* initiative at Macmillan Publishers. These not only furthered the acceptance of British musicology on its own terms but enriched the intellectual depth and public communication of research results.

As discussed in Chapter 4, a group of significant music appointments came together at four universities in the late 1940s. A second wave began after the Robbins Report of 1963, recommending immediate expansion of universities and opening higher education to all who were 'qualified by ability and attainment, and who wish to attend'.[75] Because Robbins also stressed the importance of maintaining 'balance between teaching and research', and of promoting not just skills but 'the general powers of the mind [...] to produce [...] cultivated men and women', the way was clear at last for embedding musicological training in UK university education.[76] For present purposes, the most dramatic example was the new music department established at KCL in 1965 by Thurston Dart. In a thorough restructuring of its teaching and course levels, undergraduate, postgraduate and in combination with other subjects, Dart worked, by invitation, as full-time professor with three staff of his own choosing to 'educate through music rather than in it'.[77] The programme included a one-year M.Mus. in music research (including criticism), and a B.Mus. that

---

[75] Claus Moser recalled this 'golden rule' of the Robbins Committee as they documented the 'pool of ability'. See his chapter 'The Report', in *Shaping Higher Education: 50 Years after Robbins*, ed. Nicholas Barr (London: London School of Economics, 2014), 23–31 at 27. For the original report, see Lionel Robbins, *Higher Education: Report of the Committee Appointed by the Prime Minister under the Chairmanship of Lord Robbins* (London: HMSO, 1963).

[76] Both points are recalled by Craig Calhoun, 'Conclusion', in *Shaping Higher Education*, ed. Barr, 65–85 at 66, 83. Writing in early 1964, Frank Howes also confirmed that British universities, like American ones, now fully recognized musicology as a proper subject for advanced work at university level, adding that the RCM had also 'just instituted a course and a degree in musicology' ('An Art and a Science', *TLS*, 27 Feb 1964). The RCM's M.Mus., however, partly devised by Howes, was phased out in 1973; see Wright, *The Royal College of Music and its Contexts*, 270–72.

[77] T. Dart to unnamed staff at University College, London, 1 Mar 1967, quoted in Edward Breen, *Thurston Dart and the New Faculty of Music at King's College London: A 50th Anniversary Biography* (London: King's College London, 2015), 32 n.76.

embraced music history, organology, a non-European music strand, electronic music and the study of music education. By the same token, compulsory composition, fugue, orchestration and counterpoint were not included, showing Dart's commitment to differentiating KCL from music at Cambridge, where his earlier attempts to introduce similar changes had been frustrated by other faculty members. Historical performance study ran alongside ethnomusicology and sound cultures; employing lecturers from outside the UK, including, later, Howard Mayer Brown, Pierluigi Petrobelli, Reinhard Strohm and Thomas Walker, became normalized;[78] and a regular seminar series for guest lectures stimulated lively exchanges among staff and students. From the academic year 1967–68, a striking photo shows one moment of lively exchange between Dart and his colleagues, both students and lecturers (see Fig. 23). What he said to make them burst out laughing is unfortunately not recorded. Dart died prematurely in early 1971, much lamented, but the teaching and learning ethos he created, backed by London University, flourished.[79] Other universities such as those at Nottingham, Cardiff, Southampton, Manchester and ultimately Cambridge introduced similar graduate courses,[80] while KCL students often participated in RMA activity at the King's Music Faculty building, 152/3 Strand. Latterly three successive King Edward professors of music served as RMA presidents, Brian Trowell (1984–89), Curtis Price (1999–2002) and John Deathridge (2005–08). This department's dedication to musicological excellence from the 1960s onwards contributed markedly to the subject's higher standing nationally.

Finally, *The New Grove Dictionary of Music and Musicians* (20 vols., 1980) crowned all music-collaborative projects in this period. Edited by Stanley Sadie with the help of British-American advisory and editorial teams and, as calculated in 1975, nearly 2,500 contributors, themselves about 38 per cent American, 21 per cent British and 17 per cent (West) German, the project was much vaunted.[81] Macmillan took a huge risk in committing to full revision of their old property, but the idea also generated enthusiasm among a range of practising musicologists, young and old, on two continents. The risk paid off. After a decade of work at Macmillan's offices in Bedford Row, London, overseen largely by Sadie and his senior text editors Nigel Fortune and Ian Bent – three central RMA members – the project succeeded by integrating the

---

[78] The Readership of Petrobelli, who was hired by Brown in 1973, was the first position in Britain to include the word 'musicology' in its title, though positions in 'music history' had been held by Sternfeld, Tilmouth and Wellesz for some years (Fallows et al., 'Musicology in Great Britain since 1945', 56 n. 30).

[79] Dart's extraordinary activity, audacity and impact on students, also at Cambridge before arriving at KCL, are recalled in obituaries by Allen Percival (*MT*, 112 (1971), 478–79), Anthony Lewis (*ML*, 52 (1971), 236–38) and Robert Donington (*JAMS*, 24 (1971), 502–03).

[80] The Cambridge musicological MA, for instance, was designed under the friendly eye of Alexander Goehr, who, though a composer, believed in musicological professionalism. I owe this information to Julian Rushton.

[81] Stanley Sadie, 'The New Grove', *Notes*, 32 (1975), 259–68 at 266.

Figure 23. Thurston Dart and the Faculty of Music at King's College London, photograph, 1968 (*back row L to R*, Robin Bowman, Tim Daniel, Ron Powell, David Scott, Leslie East, Paul Tanton, Peter Holman; *middle row L to R*, Laurence Libin, Benedict Sarnaker, Adrienne Simpson, Pamela Dickinson, Patsy Chew, Anne Smith, Maurice Rogers, Stanley Boorman, David Fallows; *front row L to R*, William Oxenbury, Collette Harris, Jim Harding, Miriam Wilmott, Thurston Dart, Lucy Durán, John Milner, Janice Bentley, Ian Bent).

latest worldwide research within an established tradition of humane English writing about music, what Sadie fondly referred to as '*Groveheit*'.[82] The combination appealed alike to scholars and general readers.

Although known familiarly as *Grove 6*, the much-expanded book was virtually brand new rather than an updated version of *Grove 5* (9 vols., 1954; rightly criticized for its insularity); some 97 per cent of *New Grove* content was fresh, not derived from earlier editions.[83] Reimagining how to absorb new factual knowledge since the 1950s, including that in RISM and other reference sources, as well as how to represent widened musical attitudes and philosophies for the later twentieth century, planners struggled with decision-making but agreed on several points: composer entries would make up about 55 per cent of the content; material representing the forefront of research should be obligatory in all entries; consistency in treatment could be helped by using 'area editors' for setting article lengths; composer work-lists and multilingual bibliographies should be visually clear on the page, easy to navigate; entries on musical forms, concepts, style terms, acoustical and bibliographical topics, and especially national, local and popular music traditions would help set the

---

[82] Andrew Porter, 'Seeing the Stars Again: The Original Vision of George Grove and the Ever-Growing *New Grove* Revised', *TLS* (23 Nov 2001), 3–4 at 3.
[83] For the shortcomings of *Grove 5*, see D. Fallows et al., 'Musicology in Great Britain since 1945', 49, 50; and Richard S. Hill, 'Grove's Dictionary of Music and Musicians, Fifth Edition', *Notes*, 12 (1954), 85–92: 'It not only contains plenty of fallen timber [...] but also a surprising quantity of underbrush' (85).

tone of the *New Grove*; and, besides expansion in the treatment of music before 1700 and in instruments, the biggest growth area would be in non-Western coverage, embracing art and folk music traditions for every country in the world.[84] Grove himself would have been astounded at the scope Sadie and his colleagues undertook, but, appreciating the task amid changed times, would have rolled up his sleeves to help.[85]

Of course the *New Grove* was out of date on the day it appeared, as all reference works are bound to be. Research moves on, interpretations change. And the fragmented presentation of knowledge seen in its tens of thousands of headwords arranged alphabetically – the same arrangement making that information easily accessible – underscored an increasing fragmentation in musicological studies of the 1970s. But the new standard of breadth in the dictionary, embracing an immense amount of research from the previous two decades, made it, according to Denis Arnold, 'the most important reference tool of its time'.[86] Writing in *Acta musicologica* in 1982, Arnold, then RMA president, believed Macmillan's 'act of courage' in publishing the *New Grove* had been 'triumphantly vindicated'.[87] Coming only ten years after a proposed anthology of old *Proceedings* articles had been rejected by a British academic publisher, admittedly a project of much smaller ambition and appeal, the *New Grove*'s success reminds us how far the maturity and influence of British musicology leapt ahead in this one giant step. The *New Grove* was not solely British, but it did utilize the best of British musicology to date, much of it written or edited by RMA members, including senior scholars and younger ones setting new benchmarks in historical musicology, ethnomusicology, analysis and cultural studies. In that sense, the *New Grove* did not boost the RMA's reputation so much as reflect what the hundred-year-old Association already represented – a corporate body of individual music scholars from art, science, literary and public service backgrounds, pulling together with the academic sector to study and explicate music with new authority, doing so happily across class, national, political and gender differences. Acting as a huge multiplier of what the RMA had long been building, the *New Grove* served like a megaphone for a new and confident British musicology.

---

[84] All points described in Sadie, 'The New Grove'.
[85] For Grove's work in the 1870s and 80s, including the publishing context in which he began, see Langley, 'Roots of a Tradition'.
[86] Denis Arnold, 'The New Grove', *Acta musicologica*, 54 (1982), 1–6 at 6.
[87] Ibid., 2.

6

Widening Directions, Shifting Ground, 1980–2024

Anyone who's ever reached a distant goal can imagine the gratified feelings of many RMA members in the late 1970s and early 80s. With the full acceptance of music as an academic discipline, musicology hit its stride. Its stock had already gone up after the Robbins Report encouraged higher education growth, facilitating new degrees, new universities and innovative music departments. And its repute continued to rise. Professorial appointments were made in ethnomusicology (Queen's University, Belfast, 1970) and theory and analysis (KCL, 1982); the RCM and RAM taught Dart's new London degrees to selected students; and heightened student enrolment in thirty-two music departments set a new record by 1975–76 – at 1,700, more than twice the number of ten years earlier.[1] With buoyant demand for *New Grove* products across the 1980s, moreover, music scholarship was seen to sell books, lots of them, opening yet more opportunity for musicological writers, translators and critics addressing both general and specialist readers. The Association launched its own monograph series in 1985, and its redesigned *Journal* two years later; it also planned and hosted three international conferences – Handel (1985), Mozart (1991) and the Sixteenth Congress of the IMS (1997), each yielding a major publication. At the millennium the future looked bright for all kinds of musician-scholars in and beyond the academy, not least performers, programme planners and commentators in popular and traditional musics, and in early music covering everything from medieval to nineteenth-century repertories. New approaches to sound and video recording, music's role in wider geographical and political contexts, its relation to sister disciplines including philosophy, anthropology and psychology, and the use (or not) of historical evidence in making performance decisions: all these conveyed the vitality and relevance of musical research to an increasingly pluralistic society.

And yet: success often carries its own drawbacks. Strong momentum for a learned society can be difficult to maintain, whether through complacency or an endless repeat of previous strategies. With many of the Association's earliest aims met by the late 1980s, Council members began to wonder what fresh goals they should pursue and whether the centre would hold if too many

---

[1] All points cited in Ian Pace, 'Academic Music in the United Kingdom and the Dalliance with Practice', lecture, Oxford Univ. Faculty of Music, 25 April 2023; see Pace's handout with a timeline of music in UK higher education, 1945–2023, at https://ianpace.wordpress.com [accessed 5 Dec 2023].

aspects of their work changed too quickly. In addition to ever-present questions about musicology's nature, the group faced challenges to its coherence from two main directions in the 1990s – the advent of research audits by the UK government (first held in 1986), allocating and rationalizing higher education funding, and a rapid growth in research specialization, creating a maze of new subfields. Although both trends stimulated productivity and spread the benefits of research, they also tended to dilute the RMA's reason for existence. Periodic gaps in administrative continuity, experiments with paper-reading formats and meeting shapes, and marked efforts to imitate other scholarly bodies contributed to some uncertainty in the early 2000s. The result was a few years of frenetic activity but only halting progress, stimulating reassessment. Recently, signs of new purpose have emerged, drawing on RMA traditions of inclusivity in membership, advocacy for all kinds of work including composing and practice-research, and support for the broadest range of music teaching and learning at pre-tertiary as well as college and university levels. Whatever the future holds for UK academic musicology – controlled by funding from central government – the RMA will persist in creating scholars, shaping music studies and advancing research. Here I'll examine three themes: external forces affecting the Association across its most recent four decades, its internal activities in the 1980s and 90s, and its responses to change in the early twenty-first century.

❧ *External Forces, 1980–2024*

Intellectual work in music is always subject to general cultural trends as well as specific contexts affecting music study. Uniquely relevant to music scholars have been Macmillan's *New Grove* venture and Joseph Kerman's *Musicology* (London, 1985), a fierce polemic against the discipline's 'positivist' tendencies.[2] The most obvious broad processes touching research over this period have been rapid changes in information technology, and the UK government's continued scrutiny of university research. These interlinked forces deserve a closer look.

Benefits from the *New Grove* project went far beyond impressive sales of a twenty-volume music dictionary issued in 1980.[3] As David Fallows noted in 1983, through participating in the book's writing and production British scholars not only broadened their awareness of musicological activity outside the UK, but gained new confidence by contributing so substantially to the

---

[2] *Musicology* (London: Fontana Press/Collins, 1985). In the USA the book appeared as *Contemplating Music: Challenges to Musicology* (Cambridge, MA: Harvard Univ. Press, 1985). Called by Philip Brett 'a defining moment in the field' ('Kerman, Joseph', *New Grove 2*), the book's publication gave new vigour to the discipline.

[3] According to Ian Jacobs of Macmillan Reference Ltd, from 1980 to the end of 1999 the *New Grove* sold 55,000 copies (each of twenty volumes) – 25,000 in hardback and 30,000 in paper – to libraries, orchestras, music businesses and private individuals; see Langley, 'Roots of a Tradition', 199 n. 2.

enterprise. In turn, the publication 'gave a new respectability to musicology within the British intellectual community', while the Grove office provided a 'superb training' for many young scholars, including postgraduate students forging careers in academic research or publishing.[4] In fact, because Grove's senior editors had foreseen a need for grateful writing ability as well as systematic bibliographical knowledge in their team, they purposely hired a mix of British and North American music graduate students, who, given the differing strengths of those respective backgrounds, could marry the two skills in one office, sharing ideas, learning from each other and working to solve research and writing problems together. It was an astute plan that proved far more effective than teaching professional text editors how to handle complex music material.[5] It also encouraged higher writing and editorial standards for later Grove projects. Macmillan's original *New Grove* investment had been predicated partly on producing, probably, a second edition of *New Grove* in due course (known as *Grove 7*), for which corrections began pouring in almost as soon as the ink on the 1980 pages was dry. More immediately, the plan was to issue a series of spin-off composer reprints lightly updating major *New Grove* biographies and similarly, spin-off books on large subjects such as musical instruments or American music, drawing on the parent dictionary. In the event, according to Stanley Sadie, a reprint approach didn't work so well for the large subjects, where internal balance and commissioning for specialist readers had to be undertaken afresh, ultimately expanding those books into full companion dictionaries.[6] There were five to the mid-1990s, on musical instruments (1984), American music (1986), jazz (1988), opera (1992) and women composers (1994), all relying on 'live' collaboration between established experts, younger scholars and skilled in-house editorial teams.[7] In his wide-ranging interview of 1992 with the Chicago WNIB radio producer Bruce Duffie, Sadie described the planning and execution of these books, singling out

---

[4] David Fallows, 'Musicology in Great Britain, 1979–1982', *Acta musicologica*, 35 (1983), 244–53 at 244.
[5] See Richard Evidon, 'The New Grove: A Personal View', preceding 'The Grove of Academe', *19th-Century Music*, 5 (1981), 155–57.
[6] Stanley Sadie, 'The New Grove, Second Edition', *Notes*, 57 (2000), 11–20 at 19–20.
[7] *The New Grove Dictionary of Musical Instruments* (ed. Stanley Sadie, 3 vols., 1984), *The New Grove Dictionary of American Music* (ed. H. Wiley Hitchcock and Stanley Sadie, 4 vols., 1986), *The New Grove Dictionary of Jazz* (ed. Barry Kernfeld, 2 vols., 1988), *The New Grove Dictionary of Opera* (ed. Stanley Sadie, 4 vols., 1992) and *The New Grove Dictionary of Women Composers* (ed. Julie Anne Sadie and Rhian Samuel, 1994). Additionally the Grove office produced further reconfigurations of Macmillan material, including the *Grove Concise Dictionary of Music* (1988), *New Grove Handbook of Performance Practice* (ed. Howard Mayer Brown and Stanley Sadie, 2 vols.), *New Grove Handbook of Music Printing and Publishing* (ed. D.W. Krummel and Stanley Sadie, 1990) and *New Grove Book of Operas* (1996).

Figure 24. Stanley Sadie, Leanne Langley and Christina Bashford with
The New Grove Dictionary of Opera, 1992, at Macmillan Publishers,
London; photograph, *Opera* magazine, November 1992.

for its structure the *New Grove Dictionary of Opera*, 'a very exciting dictionary to work on' and 'the best of the dictionaries we've done'.[8]

Plans for *New Grove 2*, an updated print-only dictionary to be edited by Sadie, came together from the early 1990s. Some 50 per cent larger in extent than the *New Grove*, it appeared in twenty-nine volumes in 2001; though unquestionably successful as a scholarly product, the book and its completion were not without difficulties.[9] The enlargement consisted in much greater coverage of twentieth-century music (some 5,000 entries on composers including from places formerly delimited on political grounds), of popular music and jazz and of areas benefiting from expanded research after 1980 (the early Renaissance, nineteenth-century music, instruments, non-Western and traditional musics, treatments of music within societies), also adding new

---

[8] 'Musicologist Stanley Sadie: A Conversation with Bruce Duffie', 29 Oct 1992, http://www.bruceduffie.com/sadie.html [accessed 31 Dec 2023]. For detailed comment on the *Opera* dictionary, see Robert Craft, 'Dictionary of Divas', *TLS* (23 Apr 1993), 16; and Neal Zaslaw, 'The New Grove Dictionary of Opera', *MQ*, 78 (1994), 149–58.

[9] In Andrew Porter's memorable phrase, 'It is no secret that things did not go altogether smoothly at the end'. Andrew Porter and Leanne Langley, 'Two Tributes', in *Words about Mozart: Essays in Honour of Stanley Sadie*, ed. Dorothea Link with Judith Nagley (Woodbridge: Boydell & Brewer, 2005), 211–18 at 215.

coverage in areas of recent scholarly interest – gender and sexuality, women in music, postmodernism, Nazism and other cultural and political topics redolent of 'New Musicology'.[10] RMA members again contributed in all these areas through updating, fresh writing and a range of editorial roles. Because Macmillan had sold two of every three *New Grove* copies in the USA, American subjects and writers were especially well represented. Although the web-based version, *Grove Music Online*, appeared simultaneously and offered efficient basic searching, it also highlighted faults in the print version accrued through hurried production; there had been two changes of editor – John Tyrrell, a brilliant scholar of Czech music, the executive editor assisting Sadie from 1997, and then from 1999 Jane Turner, editor of the *Dictionary of Art*. Predictably, the online version revealed its own problems; like the book's later editing and proofreading, its transfer to a digital platform had been rushed.[11]

In truth, Macmillan never intended to create an online resource with *New Grove 2*, which may partly explain why the German publishing group Holtzbrinck stepped in – welcomed by Macmillan – to purchase a 70 per cent controlling share in its business in 1995, completed in 1999 when Richard Charkin became Macmillan CEO. Holtzbrinck knew the future for academic reference was electronic: witness the extensive preparations at OUP in the 1980s and 90s for revised editions of their classic *Oxford English Dictionary* and *New DNB* (later *Oxford Dictionary of National Biography*); indeed Charkin had guided the *OED*'s conversion to digital form, via CDs, as OUP's Head of Reference as early as 1981.[12] In this climate, seizing the stellar *New Grove 2* with its companion and cousin titles, including the 34-volume *Dictionary of Art* (1996), and turning them into electronic format, not to mention owning the rest of Macmillan's profitable book business, offered Holtzbrinck unrivalled opportunity. Whether they intended to complete and run a web-based *Grove* site themselves or, more likely, make a start and then sell off the music and art dictionaries, they couldn't lose; either way, speeding up the last stages of *New*

---

[10] Sadie, 'The New Grove, Second Edition'. For fair critique of the book's strengths and weaknesses, including direct comparisons with the *New Grove*, see Porter, 'Seeing the Stars Again'.

[11] Librarian-reviewers noticed. For reactions at three successive stages, see Lenore Coral, 'GroveMusic', *Notes*, 58 (2001), 406–08; Linda B. Fairtile, '*The New Grove Dictionary of Music Online*', *JAMS*, 56 (2003), 748–54; and John Wagstaff, 'Oxford Music Online', *Notes*, 66 (2009), 129–31, noting how much better the technical delivery and functionality had become. All recognized the need for more refinement, usage and feedback.

[12] Richard Charkin, 'A Very Short History of the *New Oxford English Dictionary*', *Publishing Perspectives* (26 Sept 2018). Charkin worked at OUP, 1975–88, latterly as Managing Director of the Academic Division. Having originally joined Macmillan from a digital scientific publisher, he found the company old-fashioned and out of step in 1999 ('It's a Smaller World Now', *Publishing Perspectives*, 26 Nov 2023). For Charkin and OUP, see *The History of Oxford University Press*, vol. 4: *1970–2004*, ed. Keith Robbins (OUP, 2017), *passim*. Plate 17 depicts the '*Grove Dictionaries of Art and Music*, published by OUP after acquisition from Macmillan in 2003'.

Grove 2 was essential, hence Charkin's abrupt demand to Sadie for publication in 2000. When the senior editor refused, seeking to protect *Grove*'s high scholarly standards, he was dismissed; staff morale plummeted, many old hands left, and the frantic rush to publication still took another year.[13] To its new publisher, content, functionality and usability issues were subsidiary, assumed to be correctable online later. More important to Charkin was completion. The whole publication, fronting the valuable *New Grove* name but now under a totally different regime, was available to scholars and general readers worldwide, in two formats, at the start of the twenty-first century.

Looked at in this way, the wonderful transformation of *New Grove 2* from a weighty, old-fashioned book into a light and responsive online source couldn't be faulted, especially after promised additional content, images, sound files and music examples were successfully integrated. And more, the conversion took only four years, from 1999 to 2003, plus a change of scene from London to Oxford, then New York. In January 2003 Palgrave Macmillan announced a 'de-layering' of its UK structures, including sale of 'the iconic *Grove* imprint'.[14] By February the deal was done, with OUP-USA, New York, becoming the new proprietor of all *Grove* music and art products, a landmark shift. Had OUP been in Holtzbrinck Macmillan's sights all along? It's not impossible and may have been inevitable. OUP Music Books had already been moved to New York in 1998 ('shipped off' in Meg Bent's words; Oxford made its own UK music books editor Bruce Phillips redundant).[15] With good marketing reasons for exploiting transatlantic music studies, and a good OUP fit for the *Grove* legacy given the firm's other outstanding dictionaries, such a step must have seemed obvious and logical. The rub was that, as experienced *Grove* users discovered, trust in the *Dictionary*'s accuracy (important for a reference work) would soon fall, as first Holtzbrinck Macmillan, then OUP-USA presided over errors and infelicities, gaps, misapprehensions, awkward edits, rewrites and unclear editorial directions, with few if any senior literary or university-led music professionals contracted in the New York office. In fact OUP's *Grove* operation had little in common with the *OED* and *Oxford DNB* projects affiliated with Oxford University. Moreover, since by definition *Grove Music Online* was never to be the '8th edition' or a fixed text of any kind, its severance from mature British musicology exceeded symbolic change; by 2003 the shift felt more like a rip, threatening the dictionary's scholarly integrity, careful balance of fact, opinion and style, and all who'd contributed. *Grove Music*

---

[13] Alison Latham, 'Sadie, Stanley John', *ODNB* [version of 17 Sept 2015].

[14] Steven Zeitchik and Amanda-Jane Doran, 'Palgrave Reorganizes; Will Sell Off "Grove"', *Publishers Weekly* (27 Jan 2003).

[15] Margaret Bent, 'OUP has Done it Again', *Oxford Magazine* (20 Feb 2009); see also Bent's earlier public statement criticizing the Press's closing of both poetry and academic music books, 'OUP Music and Poetry', Letter to the Editor, *The Times* (11 Feb 1999). Helpfully for the Association, Phillips became RMA secretary for three years, 1998–2001. His important work as Oxford's commissioning editor of music books is treated by Simon Wright in *The History of Oxford University Press*, vol. 4, 450–52.

Online made steady improvements in technical presentation, coding and functionality, while *Grove* sensibility in Oxford found a final UK champion in the Renaissance scholar Laura Macy as Editor-in-Chief, Grove Dictionaries of Music (2001–09). Managing well the challenges of regular updating while also developing second print editions of *American Music* and the *Instruments* dictionary, she however fell victim to the next purge, in early 2009: Macy's post, along with sixty others in New York, was abolished.[16]

When done well, big scholarly dictionaries require large amounts of human and material capital, and time. The publisher's role is to finance, cajole and manage, while the specialist editor and contributors create the best content possible. From the very beginning, Grove dictionaries experienced difficulty on both sides. Sir George's dictionary had twice been threatened with cancellation by Macmillan, the editor working nine years beyond his contract without pay to complete his four-volume book in 1889. Compromise was essential. Stanley Sadie's brinkmanship with the same firm exceeded Grove's, though the problems were strikingly similar. One big difference: Sadie was a trained musicologist – exactly what Grove was not and never wished to be. Yet both were public communicators and loyal members of the Musical Association, tracking research at home and abroad, especially in Europe and the USA as trends and new findings developed; colleagues assisted. An active Association participant since the mid-1950s, Sadie eventually served as RMA president during *New Grove 2* planning, 1989–94, and was president of the IMS during *New Grove 2*'s main editorial period, 1992–97. No one had a better grasp or more acute judgement of international music scholars and scholarship on at least four continents in the second half of the twentieth century.[17] His removal as *Grove* editor in 1999 was an incalculable loss, his achievement unlikely ever to be matched. Since that time, *Grove Music Online* has indeed evolved into a dynamic resource, stimulating thousands of new users globally to learn about music in all its guises, times and places, inspiring new questions and critical assessment. The process goes on, with music research still generating high value. Even at the price tag of $25.1 million for both Grove products in 2003, OUP New York was happy to pay: that acquisition made the company 'one of the most prestigious humanities reference publishers in the world'.[18] Meanwhile *Grove*'s distinctive origins in British intellectual, musical and literary culture stand undiminished. The first edition was printed and reprinted

---

[16] Bent, 'OUP has Done it Again'.

[17] David Fallows, 'Stanley Sadie (1992–97)', in *The History of the IMS (1927–2017)*, ed. Dorothea Baumann and Dinko Fabris (Basel: Bärenreiter, 2017), 98–101, credits Sadie's IMS presidency for advocating more direct outreach to Central and Eastern European scholars, which bore fruit in later Intercongressional Symposia in Budapest and St Petersburg, and further planning meetings in Kyiv.

[18] Henry Reece, Secretary to the Delegates and Chief Executive, OUP, quoted in Thorin Tritter, 'New York', in *The History of Oxford University Press*, vol. 4, 562.

by none other than OUP between December 1877 and October 1901;[19] the *Dictionary*'s historic connections to British musicological development will never be broken.

For all its good effects on British musicology and understanding between British and American scholars, the *New Grove* could also breezily be dismissed as 'essentially just another trophy of positivism'. That was Joseph Kerman's provocative view in his book *Musicology* (1985),[20] claiming, even after generous praise for the *Dictionary*, that at root it was a static object; it served scholars but not musicology in the sense of improving insight into heard music, encouraging imaginative responses. In fact 'positivism', or what Kerman construed disparagingly as positivistic scholarly activity, recurs as chief irritant throughout his narrative. He traces what he sees as its malign influence over the previous forty years in everything from source studies, edition-making and performance practice, to exams in American musicological training, over-emphasis on socio-contextual study and the products of dictionary-making. In remedy, he posits his own brand of 'criticism' as the proper goal of all musicological activity, by which he meant not formalist analysis (which he'd already decried five years earlier),[21] but 'meaningful', evaluative interpretations of musical works. Few could fail to empathize where the choice appeared stark – between old or new methods, boring documents or exciting interpretations, fact-grubbing labour or joyful connection of musical ends with means. But of course this fluent writer, experienced in both kinds of endeavour, knew that musicology was not so simplistic. He also knew (hoped?) his book would not be universally hailed: its main object was to goad and challenge. Among many perceptive responses in Britain, several cogent ones came from RMA members. Curtis Price and Peter Evans independently valued Kerman's call for a more delicate balance between scholastic study and critical purpose, but clarified where the author's argument seemed misjudged, too selective or unaware of British musicology's endemic differences from the American context.[22] Margaret Bent demonstrated how Kerman's narrow labelling of positivism and criticism ran roughshod over integrated critical work by a range of scholars seeking evidence precisely for new historical and musical interpretations.[23] By 2001 Andrew Porter suggested that even in the 1980s, such critique had been neither new nor as radical as many thought; rather, Kerman

---

[19] Langley, 'Roots of a Tradition', 191–94, including figure 8.1 showing print runs by fascicle in Clarendon Press Ledgers nos. 2–5 (OUP Archives, Oxford). Alexander Macmillan was 'Publisher to the Press', OUP's London agent, in 1863–80.

[20] *Musicology*, 225.

[21] Joseph Kerman, 'How We Got into Analysis, and How to Get Out', *Critical Inquiry*, 7 (1980), 311–31.

[22] Curtis Price, 'Contemplating Musicology', *MT*, 127 (1986), 26–28; and Peter Evans, review of Joseph Kerman, *Musicology* (1985), in *Music Analysis*, 5 (1986), 97–103.

[23] Margaret Bent, 'Fact and Value in Contemporary Scholarship', *MT*, 127 (1986), 85–89, arguing for 'a more generous view of musicology' (85). At the time, Bent was professor at Princeton University and president of the AMS, the second woman elected to that position (not the first, as Kerman had it).

exemplified the longstanding critic-cum-musicologist tradition of English scholarly writers from Dent to Sadie.[24] All four commentators saw something of the straw man in *Musicology*'s premise.

In hindsight, was it only drama? Kerman's idea had emerged from streams of thought already flowing in the USA and Britain. It was his thrust, his supremely confident tone, that triggered the floodgates. Whether exploding old historical narratives, demonstrating new applications of critical theory or highlighting marginalized perspectives and places, young scholars answered by expanding musicology's reach far beyond what Kerman had proposed. Much of the new work was excellent, and critical, but the shrillness in some of it, the tendency to prescribe how everyone should now think and write (notably in the 'New Musicology' camp), also intensified. Conferences, essay collections and monographs examined and re-examined the discipline's changes, focusing on what many assumed was, perhaps a little prematurely, a 'paradigm shift', as in Alastair Williams's *Constructing Musicology* (Aldershot: Ashgate, 2001).[25] More imaginative and sensitive if still Kermanesque in its convinced polemic, Christopher Page's *Discarding Images: Reflections on Music and Culture in Medieval France* (Oxford: Clarendon Press, 1993) exemplified a similar trend. Not surprisingly, this accomplished scholar-performer, a Dent medallist (1990), asserted the primacy of musical performance over traditional musicological study of medievalism, yet engaged in a degree of disparagement and confrontation that itself attracted critique, requiring explanation.[26] Gradually after 2000 a calmer consensus arrived; scholars realized that plenty of important questions remained for all to pursue without prejudice or diktat; multiple paths were possible and good work from many angles could coexist, even show complementarity, without loss of bite or independent thought.[27] Kerman's message of personal commitment had landed, but was superseded by a more sustainable diversity. The obvious next question, though, a practical one, arose from growing ethnic and gender inclusiveness in the musicological community as well as from postmodern challenges to the 'knowability' of

---

[24] Porter, 'Seeing the Stars Again', 3. For an earlier British view of the benefits of 'positivism' in Mozart research after 'artistic perception' and 'musicality' had been less fruitful, see Alec Hyatt King, 'Some Aspects of Recent Mozart Research', *PRMA*, 100 (1974), 1–18.

[25] Arnold Whittall, 'Contriving Construction', *MT*, 143 (2002), 54–57, shows how Williams's historical view is too short, forgetting the deeper history of analytical thought in early nineteenth-century writings. For a pertinent summary of the heightened tensions instigated by Kerman's manifestos, see Kofi Agawu, 'How We Got Out of Analysis, and How to Get Back In Again', *Music Analysis*, 23 (2004), 267–86.

[26] Margaret Bent, 'Reflections on Christopher Page's "Reflections"', *Early Music*, 21 (1993), 625–28, 630–33; Christopher Page, 'A Reply to Margaret Bent', *Early Music*, 22 (1994), 127–32; and Rob C. Wegman, 'Reviewing Images', *ML*, 76 (1995), 265–73.

[27] See Alan Dodson on Nicholas Cook and Mark Everist, eds., *Rethinking Music* (Oxford and New York: OUP, 1999), in *Canadian University Music Review*, 21 (2001), 135–43. The book's twenty-four chapters consider how varying approaches to musical texts and to musicology can remain valuable in a changing intellectual environment.

anything: that is, how to accommodate so much expansion. The subjects and angles of study in music research, the questions asked and the prior assumptions made by young scholars underwent a sea change over this period.[28] Its turbulence would have implications for a splintering of subdisciplines, a squeezing of teaching faculties and the unity of the RMA.

Moving to broader cultural forces, any interested observer can recognize two trends – a complete transformation in information technology and, in Britain, the state's increasing involvement in university research. In 1982 *Time* magazine chose for its 'Man of the Year' a social and mechanical object altering processes in the home, industry and world of learning, the personal computer. The *New Grove* and Kerman projects ran headlong into its influence, which, as its capabilities evolved, radically affected everyday communication as well as the way in which research is conducted and transmitted. From word-processing, score-reading, composing, on-screen editing, e-library browsing and database construction, to digital recordings and photography, sound analysis and auditory perception research,[29] online video for teaching and meeting, phone apps and social media, even discoveries about musical cultures unearthed computationally through big datasets,[30] the exciting possibilities for electronic working mushroomed from the 1980s. While these advances were welcomed by most music scholars, personal comfort zones could be stretched too, each new system posing a fresh challenge to users, including the recurring need to acquire new equipment, update software and consult colleagues. If anything, the digital age opened up almost too much information, searchable at a click, giving unlimited scope for interpreting, perhaps misinterpreting, the information retrieved. Moreover, whereas harnessing ever-newer technology animates its advocates, the same processes can raise social issues elsewhere – lack of inclusion (costs of apparatus and expertise for non-institutional users), deskilling (loss of traditional research skills and some literary ones) and the need for human discernment in interrogating digitized resources

---

[28] For personal reflections on how the field of musicology changed from the 1960s onwards, see 'Minding the GAP [IMS Guido Adler Prize]: Margaret Bent and Lewis Lockwood in Conversation with Daniel Chua', *Musicological Brainfood*, 3 (2019), https://brainfood.musicology.org/vol-3-no-2-2019/minding-the-gap/ [accessed 7 Jan 2024].

[29] See Eric Clarke and Nicholas Cook, eds., *Empirical Musicology: Aims, Methods, Prospects* (Oxford and New York: OUP, 2004).

[30] See, for example, Simon D.I. Fleming and Martin Perkins, *Dataset of Subscribers to Eighteenth-Century Music Publications in Britain and Ireland* (https://musicsubscribers.co.uk, version 1.2, Dec 2022); and the joint project between Royal Holloway, Newcastle University and nine partner organizations, 'Music, Heritage, Place: Unlocking the Musical Collections of England's County Record Offices', documenting early printed and MS music, c.1550–c.1850, in local archives. For a more established project, widely used by scholars, see Simon McVeigh, 'Rescuing a Heritage Database: Some Lessons from London Concert Life in the Eighteenth Century', *Research Data Journal for the Humanities and Social Sciences*, 5 (2020), 50–61, showing how learning and usability are continually scrutinized.

while remaining vigilant for misinformation or abuse. Human engagement is crucial. The fruitful tension between *Grove* and Kerman – disparate projects with potentially complementary outcomes – suggests that all scholars should be supported in choosing their own best ways to interact. As in scholarship, there can be more than one technological 'truth'.

Whatever technologies are involved, for many researchers physical access to a distinguished library still ranks high. In particular the national collection in London has always been central to the RMA. Oliver Neighbour, an admired Byrd scholar and Schoenberg expert, an RMA vice-president and from 1976 Music Librarian of the British Library, oversaw publication of its 62-volume *Catalogue of Printed Music in the British Library to 1980* (London: K.G. Saur, 1981–87; CD-ROM, 1993; 2nd edn, 1997), still the basis of the British Library's online music catalogue.[31] As for the RISM project, although its sponsorship passed from the RMA to the UK branch of IAML in 1982, relations among scholars and scholar-librarians remained supportive. Neighbour's colleague Malcolm Turner, Deputy Music Librarian and a former RMA secretary, masterminded the move of the British Library's Music Collections from Bloomsbury, including its newly integrated cataloguing and communication systems, to the new St Pancras building in 1997.[32] Hugh Cobbe, Turner's successor as Head of Music Collections from 1999 and also once RMA secretary, served as RMA president in 2002–05. The Library's contents and its research services in both physical and virtual forms, continually used and updated, have been invaluable to ever more music scholars. Only a criminal cyber-attack in October 2023 broke this record: taking the Library's website down and severely disrupting all internal systems for months, the incident emphasized not only the institution's importance to worldwide scholarship but also the vulnerability of every internet-based collection. Lessons are in train, and the value of physical books, microfilms and knowledgeable librarians has risen again.

A second broad force affecting scholars in all fields from the mid-1980s has been the government's systematic assessment of academic research as a means of rationalizing public funding for higher education. First called the Research Assessment Exercise, or RAE, the process was conducted in six rounds between 1986 and 2008, then replaced by the Research Excellence Framework, or REF, in two rounds of 2014 and 2021; a third exercise is set for 2029. Begun under Margaret Thatcher's administration, the programme has had both good and bad effects, with complaints leading to some reforms; the full force on many individuals and communities, however, especially in

---

[31] Richard Chesser, 'Oliver Wray "Tim" Neighbour (1923–2015)', *Fontes artis musicae*, 62 (2015), 349–51; see also Caroline Shaw, 'Remembering Tim Neighbour', BL Music blog, 23 Mar 2023, https://blogs.bl.uk/music/2023/03/remembering-tim-neighbour.html [accessed 15 Jan 2024].

[32] Hugh Cobbe, 'Music in the New British Library', *Fontes artis musicae*, 47 (2000), 27–32; see also Richard Chesser, 'Malcolm Turner, 1939–2012', *Fontes artis musicae*, 59 (2012), 389–90.

arts and humanities subjects, has long been criticized.[33] In music, where relatively small teaching units predominate, staff positions and whole courses or departments have been put at risk, some lost or closed where ratings give local university administrators ostensible reason to retrench.[34] Performing well in each round has been existential for many musicologists (concentrated in the Russell Group and mid-ranking universities), and latterly as well for further research-active music practitioners given that a lack of music provision in state secondary schools, declining progressively since the implementation of the Education Reform Act of 1988 and more sharply since the 2010s, has reduced demand for university music places. In some cases the RAE/REF process, used by department heads to mould their group's profile to government agendas, can exert pressure on a researcher's subject or method; in others, it can encourage poaching of staff from 'rival' institutions. Criteria for judging submissions and forming review panels have been much discussed, from conflicting views on 'impact', 'esteem' and 'citation' as metrics to the sometimes dubious operation of peer review. Despite tweaks, however, the underlying rationale for audit remains the same, whether couched in terms of economic management, rising educational costs, public accountability or, latterly, the need to ensure international competitiveness of UK universities.

The RMA Council expressed its concern about the RAE from the start.[35] In July 1986 the president, Brian Trowell, wrote a consultation paper for the University Grants Committee headed by Peter Swinnerton-Dyer.[36] While not presuming to speak for all British universities, Trowell asserted the RMA's role in fostering music scholarship broadly. After contrasting the older tradition of 'campus music' in UK university life against more recent research-active music

[33] Ian Pace, 'The RAE and REF: Resources and Critiques', Desiring Progress blog, 3 Apr 2018, https://ianpace.wordpress.com/2018/04/03/the-rae-and-ref-resources-and-critiques/ [accessed 17 Jan 2024].

[34] Music department closures were at first rare – St Andrew's, 1988; Leicester, 1991; Aberystwyth, 1992 – then after 2004 more common: Reading, 2004; Exeter, 2004; Roehampton, 2010; East Anglia, 2011; Lancaster, 2015; Essex, 2016; Wolverhampton, 2022; Oxford Brookes, 2024. See Ian Pace, 'Music in UK Higher Education 1: Departments and Faculties', Desiring Progress blog, 23 Apr 2023, https://ianpace.wordpress.com/2023/04/23/music-in-uk-higher-education-1-departments-and-faculties/ [accessed 17 Jan 2024].

[35] Music's future in British universities already looked bleak in 1983, with the state grant cut of c. 20 per cent in 1981–84 affecting staff teaching numbers, and research grants cut by up to 40 per cent; see Fallows, 'Musicology in Great Britain, 1979–1982', 252–53.

[36] 'The role of British Universities in musicological research: A statement by the Council of the Royal Musical Association', M MS 3, pasted-in document, pp. 1–4 at 2, after Council minutes, 9 July 1986 (meeting 8602). In October Trowell sent the final draft to nine addressees: Swinnerton-Dyer, G.A. Holley (Arts Committee), Prof. Peter Evans (Music Committee), Prof. Andrew Martindale (Arts Subcommittee), the President and the Secretary of the British Academy, the Committee of Vice-Chancellors and Presidents, the Association of University Music Professors and the National Association of University Music Staff.

faculty, he suggested how far musicology had grown, estimating that some 160 people out of a total of 220 music lecturers, spread among thirty-three British universities, were now 'substantially engaged in musicological studies'.[37] Although his succeeding list of musicology's solid achievements in Britain in fact owed little to universities, he could still pivot neatly to his conclusion that proposed cuts would damage the profession's momentum, dissuade new entrants and further delay maintenance of library facilities. Most pertinent, he offered advice about ways forward, recommending a holistic national approach with careful planning rather than *ad hoc* cuts of small departments; regional groupings for teaching and resource acquisition might help, as might the creation of specialized institutes in several universities, with fewer musicians retained elsewhere specifically to organize campus music. In the event, the RAE of 1986 took a light approach; later, some of those suggestions were indeed adopted, notably the creation of 'institutes' or centres of excellence, a global-competition strategy encouraged by government ministers after 2003.[38] More fundamental for the RMA, RAE culture contributed to a rise in the number and variety of its paper meetings from the 1990s; it also nudged the Association increasingly towards seeing itself (not altogether accurately) as a professionalized body of academic musicologists.[39]

Internal Activities, 1980–2000

By July 1984 the RMA Council under Trowell had already voted to embrace serious change, moving away from the Association's old 'learned society' image and methods. Contemplated since the early 1970s, this modernizing impulse came first from a desire to grow and change with the times, but more pointedly from a recognition that younger scholars wanted more opportunities for meeting, discussing and publishing their work; many were exploring a wider variety

---

[37] Trowell's sources are unknown, though he'd consulted Denis Arnold, Hugh Macdonald, David Fallows and Robert Pascall; his estimate of musicologically engaged staff, c. 73 per cent, may have been a little high for 1986. A more finely measured calculation of research-active staff against all employed music staff in some 100 British institutions in 2023 is suggested by Ian Pace as c. 373 out of 888, or 42 per cent ('Music in UK Higher Education 1: Departments and Faculties'). Both estimates, relatively small real numbers, show the vulnerability of UK academic musicologists among other academics, and their continuing minority status within the RMA membership. For comparison, in 2008 Prof. David Cannadine (Institute of Historical Research, Senate House, University of London) put the number of history lecturers in British universities at 3,000 ('Making History: The Discipline in Perspective', 24 July 2008, https://archives.history.ac.uk/makinghistory/resources/interviews/Cannadine_David.html [accessed 15 Jan 2024].

[38] Mike Baker, 'Dons Face Chill Winds of Change', BBC News, 11 Dec 2004, http://news.bbc.co.uk/1/hi/education/4086333.stm [accessed 23 Nov 2023].

[39] In Andrew Porter's words in the *TLS* of 2001, 'a professional union of university musicologists addressing, lighting their beacons for, one another' ('Seeing the Stars Again', 3).

of subjects in more intensive ways and sought intellectual support. This need, and the knowledge that contemporary specialist societies and sister conferences were attracting bigger numbers, sealed the Council's determination. Their central strategy was to break the rigid connection between RMA paper-reading and publication, divorcing the spoken from the published paper. In practice, this meant 'fattening out' (David Greer's term) the annual session, mostly one-hour papers given in single-paper meetings plus an annual conference, and changing the published *Proceedings* from a restricted record of papers read aloud into a fully fledged 'Journal' open to external submissions.[40] Several new ideas were recommended to achieve the expansion: more, shorter papers in a day meeting (adding round-table format and longer papers as suitable), paper selection and conference planning devolved from the Proceedings Committee to individual organizers, and the Research Students' Conference linked more formally to RMA sponsorship. Alliances with independent groups such as the 'Med-Ren', Nineteenth-Century and Analysis conferences would remain open and collaborative, potentially to grow closer, while chapter meetings were to stay on an equal footing with national ones, including submission of papers for publication. Finally, all agreed that the annual *Proceedings of the Royal Musical Association* should be retitled *Journal of the Royal Musical Association*, perhaps to appear twice yearly, have two editors and include reviews, and most definitely to include advertisements and be marketed energetically at home and abroad.[41] Opening up was considered crucial to expanding the membership.

In the event David Greer, formal proposer of many of these changes, became the *Journal*'s Editor-in-Chief. The Proceedings Committee served as Editorial Board, a second editor handled reviews, and OUP was hired as publisher – a major alteration, to improve production and widen distribution after 111 years of RMA self-publishing. Greer's announcement in the last volume of *Proceedings*, *PRMA* 111 (1984–85), stressed the imminent changes as 'just another instance' of the Association's longstanding 'adaptability'.[42] As planned, the *Journal* then appeared as *JRMA* 112 in two successive parts in 1987. Its slightly taller format and two-part issue nearly doubled the periodical's annual text area, while its

---

[40] See Greer's five-page discussion paper 'Proceedings and *Proceedings*', appended to the minutes for the Council meeting of 5 July 1984, M MS 3 (meeting 8402), the whole labelled by hand 'App. A' to the minutes, esp. 1–2. Greer had been *PRMA* editor since 1977, familiar with the system's shortcomings, and would remain *JRMA* editor until 1989 (vols. 103–15).

[41] For discussion of Greer's paper, generally affirming, see the minutes for 5 July 1984, M MS 3 (meeting 8402), also Rosemary Dooley's 'Appendix C' to Greer, 'Advertising in *Proceedings*'. Greer agreed that advertisements were desirable 'not only for the income but to banish the air of other-worldliness that lingers around *Proceedings*'. Dooley, who was RMA secretary, also suggested issuing another *PRMA* index since the last one had stopped at vol. 90 (1964), but the idea was not pursued.

[42] 'Editorial', *PRMA*, 111 (1984–85), p. v. This last *PRMA* volume, published in 1986, concluded the sessional pattern. *JRMA*, 112, parts 1–2, appeared in 1987; between August 1985 and February 1987 Greer received fifty-seven typescripts for the new *Journal*, accepting some 26 per cent for publication.

Figure 25. Cover designs for *JRMA* 112, pt 2 (1987) and 145, pt 1 (2020).

slightly altered cover, with bold red title, fronted a handsome collection of eleven articles and, for the first time, eight selective book reviews, edited by Jerome Roche. Mark Everist in 1990, then Andrew Wathey in 1995, succeeded to the editorship. In 2001 under Nicholas Cook, *JRMA* would appear in an online version for the first time. Passed to Routledge as publisher in 2009 and thence to Cambridge University Press in 2020, the *Journal* continues its distinguished record as the RMA's flagship publication, now under Freya Jarman showing more breadth in subject and interpretative angle than ever. Additionally in the mid-1980s, just before the *Journal* appeared, the Association issued its first 'RMA Monograph' under David Fallows's direction.[43] Arising from his suggestion for utilizing funds made available from Thurston Dart's estate, this series continues to publish specialized investigations of a topic, concept or repertory that are too long for most periodicals but too short for commercial

---

[43] The series title had been agreed in 1983, with maximum length as 120 pages and modest fees projected for author and subeditor; the RMA acted as publisher and Brian Jordan as agent. Ashgate took over as publisher in 2003 (absorbed by Routledge in 2016). The first volume, David Osmond-Smith's *Playing on Words: A Guide to Luciano Berio's 'Sinfonia'*, was launched at the Italian Cultural Institute, London, in January 1985.

book publishers; forty further titles have appeared to 2024, successively under Mark Everist and Simon Keefe.[44]

However grand or hope-filled, of course, modernizing visions are usually anchored in everyday procedures and good communication. The Association's growth aim was certainly met, with students central to it. A single dramatic jump from 748 RMA members in 1980 to 1,445 in 2024, a rise of 90 per cent, is one way to look at forty-odd years' development. A more nuanced view shows that for the two decades to 2000, member numbers hovered variously around 800, rising incrementally; only by enticing more students to join at much-reduced rates through a new Student Group scheme in 2000 (student numbers rising broadly across UK higher education) did RMA membership increase significantly, to c. 900 in 2017, then 1,225 in 2019 and 1,304 in 2020. Although the Group scheme numbers are always volatile, its concept has definitely widened exposure to RMA activity, bearing fruit. From grant applications, student conferences and study day organizing to submitting journal articles and utilizing social media, young researchers have eagerly taken part. Already in the mid-1980s, the Council gave official standing to the annual student conference by naming it the 'RMA Research Students' Conference', confirming the Association's tangible support and making finance for a student's attendance easier to gain.[45] In 1994 the Manchester event directed by David Fallows made a particularly strong impact.[46] Postgraduate degree completion increased, and from 1996 UK PhD listings began to be incorporated in the international *Doctoral Dissertations in Musicology* database at the University of Indiana-Bloomington, with *RMARC* retaining the list of master's theses. Aligning with the new ethos of accepting more of their own education costs, moreover, UK students sought and gained representation on the Council and its committees.[47] Other categories of RMA membership,

---

[44] With changes in the circumstances of the Dart Estate and its trustees in 1995–96, the royalties no longer went to the RMA, and alternative funding for the Monographs had to be found.

[45] David Fallows, 'Appendix A' to David Greer's paper on 'Proceedings', headed 'Suggestions by David Fallows for the Future of the Research Students' Conference', 5 July 1984, M MS 3. In mid-1995, after student maintenance grants began to be cut, Andrew Porter gave £500 to help students attend the conference; adding this to a start-up contribution from the Frank Howes estate, others joined him, including Diana McVeagh, and the fund was named as the Howes Fund (Council minutes, 20 Apr and 4 July 1996, M MS 5).

[46] With 120 delegates from thirty-five departments, the conference offered thirty papers, a workshop by the Lindsay String Quartet, study groups for the less experienced and the *Play of Daniel* organized by Fallows. Funding of £850 came from Macmillan, Littlewoods Pools and the RMA. The conference showed a lively, engaged student sector preparing for scholarly work in and beyond academia (Council minutes, 4 Feb 1995, M MS 5).

[47] Margaret Bent encouraged the Council to seek a student representative in each music department with a graduate population, letting them serve on Committees (Council minutes, 5 Oct 1994, M MS 5).

too, were adapted for changing times. Gradually the Council simplified RMA joining procedures, phased out life membership, defined joint membership more inclusively (dropping 'husband and wife'), reduced the age requirement for retired members (from sixty-five to sixty) and initiated a low-income membership offer.

In a way, students and their conference functioned like an RMA chapter working in partnership with the parent body. At the same time, apart from a new Irish Chapter founded by Hilary Bracefield in 1987 – superseded in 2003 by the Society for Musicology in Ireland – the concept of RMA regional chapters began to lose steam; faculty economies and a programming shift to study days and colloquia made the idea redundant.[48] After the premature death in 1997 of Isobel Preece, a strong RMA North leader from 1991, the merged Northern Chapter was quietly discontinued; a revitalized Scottish Chapter would be launched at Glasgow in 2002. But much-improved communications also began to encourage more independent contact among members. *PRMA*'s loss as a conduit for the members' list was addressed by issuing a separate members' booklet (1987, 1993). News and programme details were conveyed in a brightly coloured *RMA Newsletter* from 1987, then from 1998 transferred to the nascent RMA website – itself an innovation suggested by Preece, designed by Robynn Stilwell and from 2001 administered by Rachel Cowgill (followed by Andrew Earies, then Michael Byde). A monthly *RMA Bulletin* was sent electronically to all members from 2005. The first electronic members' list, converted into a database by Rachel Segal (1997), was uploaded to the site in 2007.

Meanwhile, central to the goal of 'fattening' a year's programme had been the idea of adding more, shorter papers into a day meeting, typically in November or February, with planning assigned to a specialist whether invited or self-proposed. An innovative and particularly successful example was a Research Students' Day running parallel to the main RMA day in November 1986, proposed to Council in late 1985 by two advanced postgraduates, Michael Burden and Irena Cholij. Their chosen theme, 'Study Day for Students working on Eighteenth-Century English Music', attracted a small RMA grant and was realized not through polished papers but through a mix of experienced-scholar and student presentations on research tools, methods and sources.[49] The combination answered a true need and stimulated collaboration, attracting sixty participants to the Institute of Historical Research at Senate House, London, besides requests for the material to be published. Burden and Cholij then produced a modest handbook-style publication (1987), organized several more

---

[48] Eric Cross succeeded Jerome Roche as Northern Chapter organizer while Julian Rushton succeeded Michael Talbot for the North Midlands, both in 1981 (the last became 'Midlands' in late 1987 under John Morehen). By 1991, the two groups had merged as 'RMA North' with a base at Newcastle under the leadership of Isobel Woods Preece and Ronald Woodley.

[49] Council minutes, 9 Oct 1985, M MS 3, meeting 8503; separately attached proposal for the second Study Day, with paste-down reviews of the first; also 8 July 1987, M MS 5, meeting 8702, proposing a third Study Day.

days in successive years on the same theme (two of them partially RMA-funded) and issued corresponding *Handbook*s; under different convenors, currently Colin Coleman and Katharine Hogg, these meetings and publications are still going, now at the Foundling Museum.[50] Around the same time, coincidentally, eighteenth-century British music began to feature more frequently in MB's output: Harry Diack Johnstone joined the editorial committee in 1985 and became a torch-bearer for others following this path.[51] Back in the realm of study day themes, some slightly later variations included the Rossini Day on 29 February 1992, planned by Christopher Wilson to celebrate the composer's 200th leap-day birthday; a two-day Purcell Tercentenary Conference at the Guildhall School of Music and Drama in mid-November 1995, coinciding with a Christopher Hogwood-led Purcell Festival at the Barbican; and the 'Analysis of Early Music' symposium at KCL in late January 1996, organized by John Milsom. All were timely and stimulating. By 1997 the malleable study day format had become official policy for most RMA gatherings across the year, replacing standard November and February meetings; it appealed especially to younger researchers. By 2001 a new RMA Student Liaison Officer, Susan Bagust, would be appointed to help students formulate, schedule and cost their own study day proposals for the Council's approval; it was only a matter of time before such days multiplied.

When it came to full-scale conferences of the international kind, the RMA was in its element during the *New Grove* years: Stanley Sadie played a leading role in organizing two of these devoted to his own specialisms, Handel (1985) and Mozart (1991). Stretched across seventeen days in July 1985 as part of the 1985 European Music Year celebrations, the Handel Tercentenary Festival included a plenary conference at the Royal Society of Arts involving British, German and American experts, some of them RMA members. Sadie, together with Anthony Hicks, then edited a volume of the papers, issued by Macmillan 'for the Royal Musical Association' in 1987 (yielding royalties for the RMA).[52] Although the Association itself officially contributed only a drinks reception, the wider benefits in affiliation and scholarly exchange were clear. Similarly, the international Mozart Bicentenary Conference of July–August 1991, first proposed in 1988 as a five-day companion strand to Nicholas Kenyon's 'Mozart Now' period instrument festival at the South Bank and the British Library's

[50] See, for example, Colin Coleman and Katharine Hogg, eds., *A Handbook for Studies in 18th-Century English Music*, vol. 25 (London: Gerald Coke Handel Foundation, Foundling Museum, 2021). The Research Day is now an annual conference affiliated with the Gerald Coke Handel Collection.

[51] Julian Rushton, 'Epilogue: *Musica Britannica* and the Eighteenth Century', in Peter Lynan and Julian Rushton, eds., *British Music, Musicians and Institutions, c. 1630–1800: Essays in Honour of Harry Diack Johnstone* (Woodbridge: Boydell Press, 2021), 263–74.

[52] See Bruce Wood's review of the *Handel Tercentenary Collection*, in *Early Music*, 18 (1990), 125, 127, 129. Sadie's planning papers and correspondence, besides a recording of two open forums on 'Handel's Borrowings' and 'Performing Practice in Handel', are held in the Stanley Sadie Archive at Cambridge University Library (MS Add. 10095/10/1, MS Add. 10095/19/3).

Figure 26. London blue plaque at 20 Frith Street, Soho, London, commemorating the location of a house where Mozart 'lived, played and composed' in 1764-65, placed by the RMA in 1991; photograph by Spudgun67.

'Mozart: Prodigy of Nature' exhibition in Bloomsbury (all commemorating Mozart's death in 1791), came together through Sadie. His cultivation of five honorary patrons, fifty speakers, several government officials and commercial firms – including Macmillan, who paid for the opening reception as well as a commemorative London Mozart plaque mounted at 20 Frith Street – and ultimately his work on the resulting book of essays, *Wolfgang Amadè Mozart: Essays on his Life and his Music* published by Clarendon Press in 1996, could hardly have generated better results.[53] The book, supported by a large Dart Fund subvention, included half the conference papers and earned a royalty as well as a discount for RMA members.[54] Neither of these special conferences displaced the Association's annual meeting.

Conferences naturally come in different shapes. Intertwined with proliferating study days and occasional anniversary conferences were experiments with the content of RMA annual conferences. In the 1980s these were still three-day gatherings for the whole membership, broadly themed, held in the Easter break. Themes attracting participants beyond musicology included Cyril Ehrlich's imaginative 'Music in the Market-Place' conference at Oxford

---

[53] See Sadie's Preface, 'Mozart Scholarship and the Musical World over 35 Years', pp. xiii–xvi, for a summary of advances in Mozart scholarship, 1956–91. Here he calls the conference 'the largest and most international ever held by the Association [representing eleven countries], and its first to be open to the general public' (xvi).

[54] Council minutes, 6 July 1988, M MS 5 (meeting 8802), and 15 Sept 1993; Proceedings minutes, 4 July and 26 Sept 1990, M MS 4; and also in the Manchester archive, a group of six uncatalogued folders of Collected Papers from Sadie's Mozart conference planning, assisted by Peter Owens, containing draft programmes, press releases and correspondence.

in 1988,[55] while Tim Carter's 'Music and Rhetoric' theme of 1989 stretched the Proceedings Committee's original request for a seventeenth-century emphasis to appeal to music analysts of any period.[56] By the early 1990s, following Trowell's advocacy of connecting with other music societies, itself prompted by rapid disciplinary shifts, younger planners explored the idea of joint meetings with related groups in alternate years or perhaps triennially. A series of three multi-day university meetings, for example, held in 1993 (Southampton, with the Society for Music Analysis), 1996 (KCL, adding the Critical Musicology Forum) and 1999 (Surrey, adding the British Forum for Ethnomusicology, or BFE, and the new Conference on Twentieth-Century Music), shows how this aim played out, accumulating partners and interest but not necessarily effectiveness. Organizers chose 'British Musicology Conference' as a title for the 1996 combination, then 'Third Triennial British Musicological Societies' Conference' in 1999. Any clear identity for the last two as RMA events was diluted, while all along, the potent influences from music analysis, popular music, feminism, cultural studies and post-structuralism behind these groups infused mainstream study gradually: what was 'radical' became less so,[57] while ethnomusicologists, since 1973 part of the International Folk Music Council, had already published their own newsletter and journal, becoming the highly successful BFE in 1995. From the RMA's perspective, the benefits of holding regular joint meetings with sister societies now required more thought.[58] Before consensus could be reached, another themed Annual Conference, on 'Performance', took place in April 2000 at Southampton University, and again on 'Music and Film' at the same institution in April 2001, more successfully. Surprisingly, a second Annual Conference in 2001, at KCL that October on 'The Theory and Practice of Musical Biography', stretched the meaning of 'annual', placing both the thirty-sixth and thirty-seventh conferences in 2001;

---

[55] Exploring topics from Italian opera singers in 1600 to IRCAM in Paris, Mozart to modern British composers, copyright laws to music trade sales and a round table on London orchestras in the 1930s and 1980s led by Nicholas Kenyon, the Oxford event shone a light on the value of economic analysis in studying musical culture.

[56] Proceedings minutes, 7 Oct 1987, p. 3; and 27 Sept 1988, [p. 1], both in M MS 4. The Biennial International Conference on Baroque Music, begun in 1984, had influenced Carter's idea to particularize the theme but expand its application, including to non-Western music.

[57] For helpful background on this period and its influences, see Dai Griffiths, 'What Was, or Is, Critical Musicology?', *Radical Musicology*, 5 (2010–11), http://www.radical-musicology.org.uk/2010.htm [accessed 15 Dec 2023]. The Critical Musicology Forum was active from 1992 to 2004.

[58] Already after the first joint conference, in 1993, Council members noted that too many sessions had been constructed by pre-assigned chairs rather than arising from free paper offers, hence areas such as ethnomusicology, organology or jazz had not been represented. Concern was also voiced about the need to avoid putting the RMA into the position of being seen as a clearing-house or umbrella group for other societies, rather than as a partner. The balance between parts and whole demanded care. See Proceedings minutes, 1 July 1992, M MS 4; and Council minutes, 15 Sept 1993, M MS 5.

the rationale had been to establish a new-style large event in autumn that unequivocally linked the AGM with the giving of RMA awards, placing both within the Annual Conference to attract a wider audience. The plan was only partially successful at the time; more worrying was the RAE result of 2001, in which music dropped sharply in the national subject ratings, from nineteenth to forty-eighth place.[59] By 2002, the joint-conference idea turned from experimenting with societies to joining up host institutions – a university and a music academy – specifically to explore the boundaries between research and practice, academia and the music profession, music and other disciplines. Held in Glasgow in November 2002 and organized by Warwick Edwards, 'Crossing Borders', the first RMA Annual Conference to take place in Scotland, scored an unequivocal success.[60]

Aside from involving the Society for Music Analysis, the 1993 Southampton meeting had been noted for its streamlined packaging – small groups of related papers in parallel sessions, a mix of commissioned and free papers, and a booklet of abstracts enabling session-hopping, a new idea. From 1994, the Council's decision to impose a conference fee, higher for non-members, gained new joiners on the spot; it also reflected greater RMA–academic linkage, as higher conference charges began to be levied by universities. But participation hardly wavered; RAE pressures surely pertained because now annual conferences, like study days, sparked intense networking and book-planning around hot topics. Overt strategizing by conferees may seem a world away from the background tone of earlier RMA meetings, but it was entirely characteristic for competitive academics from the 1990s onwards. Hence the special ambience of a counter-balancing experience in Maynooth, Ireland – site of a long-weekend conference in September 1995, at which no RMA members organized the meeting but many joined in with enthusiasm. According to Harry White, the event had been 'expressly designed to mark the coming of age of musicology as an intellectual discipline in Ireland', the first international musicological conference to be held there. With scholars from eleven countries, ninety-seven papers and a keynote address by Joseph Kerman, the Maynooth Conference provided musicological energy, enjoyment and reflection in equal measure.[61] Collegiality as well as a wide spectrum

---

[59] Curtis Price, 'Message from the President', RMA *Newsletter* (March 2002), 1.
[60] The University of Glasgow and Royal Scottish Academy of Music and Drama jointly sponsored the event, with the Royal Scottish National Orchestra; highlights included a lecture by Leo Treitler, new trumpet music from the Academy, the UK début of Haydn Trio Eisenstadt in a programme of Haydn's Scottish and Welsh airs edited for Henle Verlag by Marjorie Rycroft and a lively panel discussion on state support for the arts: https://www.gla.ac.uk/news/archiveofnews/2002/november/headline_29861_en.html [accessed 14 Dec 2023].
[61] Harry White, 'Conference Report: Maynooth International Musicological Conference, St Patrick's College, Maynooth, Co. Kildare (Ireland), 21–24 September, 1995', *Journal of Musicology*, 14 (1996), 579–89. In size and star power the Maynooth event eclipsed both the RMA Annual Conference in Cambridge that spring and the Purcell conference in November, but did not displace them.

of solid scholarship showed that plenty of people were still interested in the discipline as a whole. Within the Association, meanwhile, a boon to defray travel costs for distinguished RMA conference speakers, sometimes from abroad, came in the form of a considerable donation from the family of Peter le Huray (1930–92); the Le Huray Memorial Lectures began in 1999.

Already by 1995, RMA planning had begun in earnest for the Sixteenth International Congress of the IMS in London, held in August 1997 at the RCM and adjoining Imperial College, with an opening ceremony at Queen Elizabeth Hall. A similar spirit of community, a feeling for the musicological discipline as a whole, pervaded this project too, first mooted in 1991 and taking on the challenge of sister disciplines. Together with Stanley Sadie as IMS president and Julian Rushton as RMA president, Tim Carter and Andrew Wathey handled local arrangements while David Fallows organized the programme committee. Their chosen theme was modern musicology's vast scope and its relation to other fields of academic work, including philosophy and aesthetics, literary studies, art history, mathematics, computer science, historiography and sociology, alongside traditional interests in music of all forms, embracing jazz, popular music, film music and ethnic musics of every kind. To initiate finance for the week-long event, originally expected to take place at the South Bank Centre, the Association raised a guarantee fund of £15,000.[62] Even as local difficulties multiplied and solutions were found, abstracts started pouring in, reaching almost twice the number expected. Indeed in size and complexity – just over a thousand delegates and 550 speakers (200 free papers and fifty-five larger sessions), with *ten* events happening simultaneously most of the time – the Sixteenth Congress turned out to be, by Sadie's estimate, the largest IMS congress yet assembled.[63] It was a 'signal success'.[64] Its thematic threads, texts of the keynote addresses (by the mathematician Roger Penrose and the philosopher Bernard Williams) and of the round table sessions, and reports on the study sessions as well as abstracts for all other presentations, were published as *Musicology and Sister Disciplines: Past, Present, Future: Proceedings of the 16th International Congress of the International Musicological Society, London, 1997*.[65] Without doubt, IMS London 1997 revealed the health and good heart

---

[62] See Council minutes for 16 Aug and 26 Sept 1994, M MS 5. After organizers created an 'IMS Ltd' account separate from RMA funds, they gathered £5,000 in donations from commercial sponsors, including publishers, then another private £10,000, making a total of £15,000 to underwrite the Congress.

[63] The last IMS Congress in Britain had taken place at Oxford in 1955; the last one in London, as the IMG, had been more than eight decades earlier, in 1911 (see above, Chapter 2). For the 1997 Congress, see David Fallows, Helen Greenwald, Harry White, Andrew D. McCredie and Honey Meconi, 'Report from London: International Musicological Society 16th International Congress: "Music and Sister Disciplines: Past, Present and Future", 14–20 August 1997', *Current Musicology*, 63 (1997), 150–69.

[64] Fallows, 'Stanley Sadie (1992–97)', 99.

[65] Edited by David Greer, with Ian Rumbold and Jonathan King (New York: OUP, 2000). For a perceptive reaction to this near 700-page book, see Ian Cross's review in *ML*, 84 (2003), 261–65.

of international musicology, but it also embedded future challenges. Owing to the RMA's time and material investment in it, the Congress was deemed to incorporate the RMA Annual Conference for 1997, the thirty-second.

Responses to Change, 2000–2024

Strikingly, the final tranche of RMA primary source material made available for this study comes to an end in mid-1997, just before the IMS London Congress took place. These important papers, now in Manchester, include Council, Proceedings and some General minutes running variously from March 1950 to July 1997, besides related leaflets and other matter; as a group, they've been destined since 2016 for incorporation into the RMA Papers at the British Library, while later archival materials in paper and electronic format from the late 1990s onwards await future evaluation. For the historian, the terminus of 1997 prevents a close reading of the last quarter-century of RMA activity. But if we zoom in on that particular year as a kind of pause, and weave round it a broad understanding of contemporary and later events, the RMA's position, though slightly equivocal, becomes clearer and gives a hint for the future.

In fact both the Association's musicological reach and its operations were more delicately poised at the millennium than the IMS Congress might otherwise suggest with its confident outward face. Not only were various forms of inter-, cross- and multi-disciplinarity in play across music studies, but longstanding sessional arrangements were also giving way to study day and conference experiments while a run of administrative difficulties created disruption. More broadly, the nation's political temper was changing swiftly. Tony Blair and New Labour won a landslide victory in May, signalling fresh social and economic directions with spending on education paramount; by 2001 the Labour education manifesto, continuing its party emphasis from 1997, would pledge that 'the exhilaration of music' as a 'joy of life' should be learned by children in school.[66] Many people assumed that Blair's plans for more inclusiveness, more music education and university places could only bode well for all modes of musicology. Yet governments (like commercial publishers) can be fickle or unpredictable. All the while, an Association holding many subgroups and factions together over shifting ground, with aims and boundaries stretching and academic pressures rising, might find itself fraught.

Three examples illustrate RMA dilemmas in 1997. First, soon after another working group on 'The Future of the RMA' suggested ways of finding a new role for the Association, the Council agreed to retain the group's emphasis on its varied membership base, neither diluting its scholarly focus nor acting as an umbrella organization for other music societies. One or two members wanted the RMA to go further and assert itself with higher education funding authorities as the nation's primary consultative body in music scholarship. But there was pushback: too narrow an identification with higher education

---

[66] See 'Full Text of Tony Blair's Speech on Education', *Guardian* (23 May 2001).

226   THE ROYAL MUSICAL ASSOCIATION

might prejudice the RMA's connection to scholars and practitioners outside academia, including composers.[67] Moreover, the danger of seeming confined within academia was seen as a limiting factor for extending the Association's healthy diversity.

Second, on a similar issue, just as research breadth and diversity were hailed as thematic for the IMS London Congress, and the RMA continued to consider how, as (presumed) senior representative of British musicology, it might influence government, the perceptive RMA secretary Jonathan Stock demurred, politely calling out what he saw as the Association's own lack of sufficient advocacy for ethnomusicology and gender studies, rendering its claim to 'representativeness' hypocritical. He soon migrated to the BFE, but his point had been heard, and the president, Julian Rushton, concurred with him.[68]

Third, just as RMA communications were becoming more efficient across 1997 through an electronic member database, a doubling of *Newsletter* issues, UK dissertations registered internationally and plans for an RMA web presence, the actual quality of communication in RMA papers, their scholarly content and mode of address, came under scrutiny, leading in part to the creation of the Jerome Roche Award to stimulate a better standard of original paper, that is, one revealing new knowledge that was carefully researched and clearly argued so that listeners and readers could follow its claims.[69] Indeed, the Council had already received complaints from members who'd found a number of recent papers 'incomprehensible' without adequate introduction or context. Although methods of academic research and writing were certainly undergoing transformation in many fields, the RMA affirmed its support for rigour and clarity.

What all these instances show is how challenges could be addressed and adjustments made to effect improvements. In essence, the Association became more sensitive to its membership in the late 1990s, responsive to political and academic shifts yet still confident in its broad mission. Among less controversial events of 1997, Pierluigi Petrobelli had been named an RMA Honorary Foreign Member, the last one,[70] and the British Library had moved to St

---

[67] Council minutes, 14 Apr 1997, paragraph 8: 'Future of the RMA', M MS 5. The pushback came from Reinhard Strohm. The RMA is now regularly consulted by funding bodies for advice on REF panel membership, scoring and outcomes, and carefully selects cases to take up directly with university representatives when a music department is threatened with closure or an untoward funding decision appears to have been taken (as in the cases of the Institute of Musical Research in 2014–15, and of the Oxford Brookes Music Department in 2023–24).

[68] Council minutes, 7 July 1997, M MS 5. Stock is now a senior ethnomusicologist and Professor of Music at University College Cork, Ireland. The RMA's welcome of global music study advanced considerably from this period.

[69] Council minutes, 7 July 1997, M MS 5, noting that Elizabeth Roche (Jerome Roche's widow) was in the process of establishing the prize, originally 'to be awarded for a real paper, well delivered, that is of publishable quality'. The first award was given in 2001.

[70] In 1998 the honour was renamed simply 'honorary membership', and given to Winton Dean.

Pancras. Gradually a sense of optimism returned by 1999, with full voting instituted for successive RMA presidents, new committees set up to promote more efficient and democratic decision-making (such as 'Awards' to consider the Dent Medal and honorary membership) and the Council able to consider thoughtful committee recommendations rather than deciding things too casually as had largely been the case before the mid-1990s.

Looking back, those three Council dilemmas at a time of fast-paced change in 1997 had revealed particular sensitivities around RMA identity, direction and management, with few clear-cut answers to satisfy everyone.[71] Administrative officers, too, had already faced their own testing and would do so again in the future. A financial fiasco, for example, had absorbed energies in 1990–91 through the actions of an inexperienced assistant treasurer recording member subscriptions. The question of whether any 'misappropriation of funds' might be provable – a tall order – gave way to the simpler description of 'comprehensive muddle' as a statement of what had happened; certainly it offered a quicker route to settling the £6,000 loss.[72] Thanks to the RMA's Honorary Treasurer Malcolm London, half that sum was indeed recovered, and the replacement post of Membership Administrator, created in mid-1992, then opened the way for modernizing membership growth and accountability. All the more disheartening, then, was another subscriptions debacle in 2010–11, soon after *JRMA* was taken over by Routledge, whose member management through its journals department proved wholly inadequate; only with intensive work in 2012–14 by the RMA Executive Officer Jeffrey Dean, assisted by Michael Byde, was proper subscription control reclaimed through a new RMA renewal system. Dean had been appointed in mid-2001 after a decade of unprecedented turnover in RMA secretaries – seven – all competent but unable to commit for long; Dean's accumulated knowledge of RMA operations became a major asset over his twenty-one years of service.

The long search for coherence in another planning area, annual conference design, was probably inevitable. A desire to spread involvement and encourage university departments to promote their scholarly priorities, to engage with new topics and external groups, had once seemed sensible, even stimulating, as in the conferences at Manchester (2005, with IAML UK), Egham (2007, organized by CHARM: Centre for the History and Analysis of Recorded

---

[71] A point of reflection acknowledging the splintering effect of many specialist directions, inadequate representation on the Council and the competing claims of becoming more musicologically professionalized versus strengthening the traditional base of occupational diversity was raised by John Deathridge in his 'A Change of Direction for the RMA?', RMA *Newsletter* (Sept 2000), 7.

[72] The shortfall and the officer's inability to produce accurate records first came to light in February 1991. For unfolding of the affair, see the Council minutes of 15 Feb and 29 Mar 1992, M MS 5; minutes of an Extraordinary General Meeting of 15 May 1992, M MS 6, pp. 209–10; and Council minutes of 30 Sept 1992 and 26 Mar 1993, M MS 5. According to measuringworth.com, £6,000 in 1992 would amount to a sum closer to £16,000 in 2022.

Music) and Dublin (2009, with the Society for Musicology in Ireland). But on the whole, the decade of conferences from 2003, with variable calendar slots, specialist themes and uneven results for the bulk of RMA members, became fatiguing, disorientating. Adapting the ubiquitous study day format for conferences simply did not work well for three-day events meant to serve the whole RMA body. By 2013, the Council had fixed the conference as a celebratory flagship event for all, and its annual season as September: the astonishing result, according to Warwick Edwards, was a three-fold increase in participation.[73] In retrospect, the vast calendar activity showing a plethora of study days, symposia, training days and conference events may look impressive, and indeed it achieved much for many individual scholars; but in reality the density masked a splintering of musicological subdisciplines and a thinning in coherent purpose for the Association itself, except as sponsor or institutional defender in the midst of RAE/REF culture and university retrenchment. Despite strong RMA representations to London University in 2014 on behalf of the Institute of Musical Research, for example, set up in 2005 within the university's School of Advanced Study in Senate House as a hub for national music research training and seminars, the School in fact severed its support of the Institute in 2015 after only ten years. Deep disappointment at this result, and at music department closures elsewhere despite RMA efforts, could not help but darken the mood.

Around 2016, the clouds began to lift. New determination and a focus on how the Association might take on new emphases raised discussion of social purposes that could embrace and extend music research. Several areas emerged, all with a committed political component touching real-world issues – diversity and representation, immigration, music educational practices and music in schools. Ripe for musical application, these set a new tone that brought fresh expertise and creativity into the Association, enriching its membership, its output and the Council's make-up. Music composition and practice research, for example, are now significant branches of RMA work through dedicated study groups ('Music as/and Process'), conference contributions, performances and prizes (Tippett Medal, from 2020; Practice Research Prize, from 2023). Study groups drawing on wider humanities fields, as in the productive Music and Philosophy group, have also been rewarding. Adopting the best practices of Equality, Diversity and Inclusion, or EDI, has encouraged more diversity in the wider membership and on the Council, and expanded the Association's prize-giving, most recently adding books and, through the Margarita M. Hanson Award, research projects on British music before 1750. A recent scheme to help displaced Middle Eastern and European scholars echoes the efforts of earlier RMA members who assisted émigrés fleeing Nazism in the 1930s and, again, supported scholars in emerging democracies after the fall of Berlin wall in 1989. Equally important, the Association has recently added a

---

[73] 'RMA's Activities: The Challenge of Representing Every Branch of a Diverse Discipline', abstract of paper given at the KVNM Conference 2018, Utrecht, 22 Nov 2018.

completely new emphasis on music in the school curriculum, noting its rapid deterioration since 2014–15; pressing an urgent topic that earlier Association members never had to worry about nor saw as specially relevant to scholarship, this strand of work will surely be central to deepening both public and political support for the developmental values of music in education, including its feed-through of young people into future music research activity at tertiary level.

Finally, the RMA's exploration of its own history and relation to other music societies, notably in Europe, began in 2018 with a visit to a KVNM anniversary celebration in the Netherlands (see Fig. 27). The exchange continued with two panels at the highly successful RMA Annual Conference of 2019 in Manchester, which coincidentally announced the election of the RMA's first female president, Barbara Kelly. Focusing on sister organizations in Poland, Hungary and Switzerland besides the Netherlands, one of those panels launched a new venture, the Network of European Music Societies (NEMS). This group's exchange of contemporary experiences has already begun to shape better understanding of common issues in European academic networks, including the precarious position of young researchers, while also reinforcing aspects of the Association's difference from other network partners through its combined work in musicology, performance and composition, and, related to that, its members' longstanding occupational diversity, so distinctive in the RMA achievement across 150 years and championed in their presidencies by both Hugh Cobbe and John Deathridge. Now new RMA goals need to address three immediate challenges: financially supporting talented early career researchers as higher education funding decreases, already begun through a successful campaign to create three one-year fellowships; attracting, serving and representing even more diverse social and geographical interests while also seeking to become better stewards of the planet; and harnessing the contributions of scholars from a bewildering range of subfields without losing focus on music itself through its aesthetic and social values. Can all this be achieved while individual scholars still conduct and publish work of the highest quality?

Even as we look ahead to these and further challenges, theorizing and assimilating global music and musical cultures,[74] we can take inspiration from our founders, not departing from their original interests so much as moving ahead in the spirit of exploration they modelled. John Hullah was the highest official spokesman for music education in the land when he helped establish the Musical Institute, then joined the Musical Society of London and subsequently the Musical Association. John Tyndall, the Irish physicist close to William Pole who was honoured to be an original Association member and to be named a vice-president, was surely one of the most forthright investigators of his time in what we now call climate science, sound and communications research, as

---

[74] On recent musicological debates about concepts of 'global', including discomfort with continued use of national stereotypes, internationalism as a euphemism for imperialism and complacency over unjust economic and social systems, see Tamara Levitz, 'Why I Don't Teach Global Music History', *Journal of Music History Pedagogy*, 13 (2023), 118–37.

Figure 27. Simon McVeigh, Mieko Kanno, Warwick Edwards and Barbara Kelly at a conference celebrating the 150th anniversary of the Royal Society for Music History of The Netherlands, Paushuize, Utrecht, 2018; photograph, 22 November 2018.

well as being an outspoken advocate for the public understanding of practical scientific research. We can draw on their pioneering spirit and determination in our own make-up and future ambitions. The full scope of what we achieve will be up to us in concert with wider society – not universities or government alone, the media, music industry or commercial publishers alone, our students or the music profession and international colleagues alone, but all of them, all of us, together.

As for our name, 'Association' still means what it says, with 'Musical' its only, broad, qualification. 'Royal' enhanced the public benefit of our work at a crucial moment seventy years after the founding, giving music research wider currency with no strings attached. For a corporate body of such mix in pursuit of musical art and science, the name has always been, and remains, an inspired choice by the people who came before us. Time has passed again and the corporate body is still flourishing, eleven times greater in size than at the start. Still independent, self-reliant and with no shortage of ideas to explore – enough, at least, to propel us over the next 150 years – we have a lot to look forward to, and an open road ahead.

Coda

Any historical journey across 150 years of meetings, debate, published papers and special projects is well-nigh impossible to summarize. Perhaps the best approach is to recall themes in the Musical Association's chronology, at each stage fulfilling or stimulating another aspect of its mission. Seen together in a long view, not just glimpsed from the side or in partial accounts, these offer a new vista of a venerable organization: full of ingenuity and creativity despite what is sometimes perceived as its old-fashioned corporate image. Now with fresh ways of understanding who made up the Association and what its work accomplished at distinct periods, we can see why anchoring British music research in a learned society worked so well, building a path to intellectual esteem and academic status for scholars, while also encouraging deeper appreciation of musical cultures and the benefits of music research for the public – two different, related aims, equally important. This dual nature is precisely what gave the RMA its unique character from the start, and why communicating outwards about what the organization is and what its members do will always remain a challenge. As a body, the group rests on a distinctive, gloriously mixed foundation, different from that of younger, more determinedly musicological societies, and those originally rooted in academic life; yet it pursues comparable, worthy goals and encourages each coming generation to reassess the RMA's role for new times. 'What is it that you actually DO?' and 'I'm sorry, what is your organization about?' are familiar questions from well-meaning enquirers, stemming from variable perceptions of 'music', music-making, musical research and musicology in and out of academia. But the recurrence of this old conundrum also suggests that RMA members will probably always need to sharpen the group's profile from time to time, set bold goals and repeatedly emphasize a salient public message for the future. Appreciating the group's past, and the long distance travelled already, may help shape that future.

So far, the Association's development can be divided into four main phases:

- an initial search for intellectual focus on music through investigation alone, practical, theoretical and historical, without reliance on concerts, concert-giving or performances
- steady progress at setting and following scholarly protocols to help define this new 'learned' discipline in the UK, borrowing precedents from British experimental science and literate historical writing more than from Austro-German *Musikwissenschaft*, thus creating a moderated, idiosyncratic English dialect of musicology, widely scoped and embracing old and new composition, analysis, informed criticism, performance and historical cultural studies including ethnomusicological methods, all under the rubric of 'musical research'
- the gradual accumulation of a recognized group identity, moving beyond individual paper-giving and publishing to joint action, authoritative early music

editions and public advocacy, even consultancy, collaborating with or supporting, and being supported by, well-known external partners
- the building of solid relationships with universities through individual professorial appointments and teaching programmes in academic music, while also maintaining older ties with both classical and popular purveyors of public discourse on music, from book and dictionary publishers to record companies and public broadcasters.

Threaded in and around each phase, from the 1870s onwards, were three practical pursuits that aimed to further music research by all who were interested:

- promoting the collecting of musical sources – printed music and music manuscripts, and related books, journals and sound recordings of all periods – and pressing for the improvement of local and national libraries and record offices, including their cataloguing and collection accessibility
- fostering exchanges of research information, discussion and cooperation with members of other national and international music scholarly bodies, whenever and wherever possible
- revising Britain's narrative of its own music and musical cultures through new discoveries, manuscript studies, investigation of broader historical and social connections, critical editions and interpretations, performances and applied research, most recently in teaching and learning, school music education, psychology and sonic perception, health and well-being, community cohesion and individual performers' and composers' practices, as well as in historical musicology, analysis and ethnomusicology.

In essence, these two facets of the same story – a history charting identity development over a long period, and recurring practical tasks showing continued purpose – come together to support this study's underlying thesis, which is best expressed in two parts.

My main, broad, claim is that the English dialect of European musicology as it evolved through the early Musical Association was not perforce substandard or second-rate compared with the Austro-German variety, which under Guido Adler and others had its own eclectic origins.[1] The English dialect was simply different but parallel, consciously so, offering an open, alternative path into twentieth-century disciplinary developments. From the middle third of the twentieth century, both paths, or dialects, began to merge into a single wide road in Britain, a lingua franca drawing alike on experimental, observational and measurable aspects of sound as well as on text-based materials and hierarchies of musical form and genealogy. The strong English preference alike for empiricism and musical listening pleasure had already brought methods

---

[1] Alexander Wilfing has described the scholarly, political and socio-cultural setting behind the new discipline of academic musicology in nineteenth-century Austria, including the country's racist politics in the 1880s and the need to counteract myth with 'positivist' facts about cultural products in a mixed nation; see the text of his 'Guido Adler and the Eclectic Origins of Musicology', given at the Eighty-Seventh Annual Meeting of the AMS in 2021, at https://www.researchgate.net/publication/355203539_Guido_Adler_and_the_Eclectic_Origins_of_Musicology [accessed 27 June 2023].

of critical argument into music research long before Joseph Kerman's critique of what he derided as 'positivism' in the 1980s advocated more criticism; that longstanding English blend, indeed, owed much to the genuine curiosities, interests and practical music experiences of the Association's early mixed membership formed in the public domain, rather than to any rejection, on principle, of a more theoretical or doctrinaire central European system centred in universities. And in its naturally occurring form, at least in the early twentieth century, English musical research was well known by contemporary practitioners and observers (witness Sonneck in 1906) to be just as intellectually honest and musically persuasive as the products of *Musikwissenschaft*, if not necessarily seen as such by some European and American critics later, notably from the 1930s by British scholars who'd been made to feel inadequate by political propagandists in Europe and the USA.

Another, related wave of dismissiveness towards the English dialect came later from British musicologists themselves, newly elevated to the UK university sphere in the 1960s. Some were inclined to read their own musical 'arrival', or professionalization through a university appointment, as validation of the more complex, 'properly' musicological discipline they had now mastered. A corollary in sensing this progress involved, naturally, a backward glance, as if every British scholar before the age of full academic acceptance (1964) – a good ninety years from the Association's founding – could now safely be relegated to antediluvian amateur status.[2] What that dextrous conjuring left out, of course, was that an academic affiliation was not remotely available for most high-functioning British music researchers in the UK until the late 1940s.[3] For many decades, by this progressivist construction, most RMA members thus

---

[2] In 1986 Brian Trowell's consultation paper for the University Grants Committee used the increased complexity of musicology to argue that university practitioners should be protected, but also reiterated an old narrative: 'Until the foundation of so many university departments, musical research in Britain was largely undertaken by amateurs or by journalists, some of whom [...] were men of considerable distinction. In recent years musicological research has proliferated and become much more specialised, demanding a constantly widening command of a vast and ever-growing literature on music history and theory, and of more sophisticated methods of research; this has meant that the former class of part-time, semi-amateur musicologist has substantially diminished; but the concomitant increase in the number of university teachers has allowed for a considerable growth in research activity so that Great Britain has become a major international contributor to the field, on a par with Germany and the U.S.A.' ('The role of British Universities in musicological research: A statement by the Council of the Royal Musical Association', M MS 3, pasted-in document, pp. 1–2, after Council minutes, 9 July 1986 (meeting 8602). See also Chapter 6, pp. 214–15, above.

[3] By comparison, the conferring of professional status in musicology through, and only through, academic affiliation was a conscious strategy behind the AMS's founding in 1934, according to Tamara Levitz; see 'The Musicological Elite', *Current Musicology*, 102 (2018), 9–80. Such linkage might have been seen to make sense in the higher education contexts of the USA and central Europe, but would have had no purchase in

started and remained in purgatory, even if the quality, depth and value of their research, or the seniority and standing of their non-academic employment, was at a high professional level. All along, the real blame for so much sluggishness in the development of a mature British musicology, however named, defined or remunerated, lay with the British government's resistance to change, its foot-dragging and delay in advancing tertiary education *tout court*, up to and including the lack of dedicated musicological training for all but a handful of the bulk of eligible, interested students until (almost unbelievably) the 1990s.

Given this broad argument, my second, more particular claim concerns the magnitude of the Association's achievement in establishing the new discipline in its English form in the first place, then independently sustaining it and stretching its reach for some seventy years, to 1944, with little contribution from academy or government. The body's reliance on non-academic members, therefore, many of them both prestigious and productive, was essential and a great asset in keeping its interests and activities balanced. Further, the RMA went on to support closer integration of rigorous documentary and interpretative models with more critically orientated treatments through frequent interchanges with European and American scholars, and, not least, individual members' participation in new joint editing and dictionary projects, from MB and the New Berlioz Edition, for example, to the *New Grove* and its partner publications. Emphasis on performed and heard music, instrument, acoustic and sound perception studies, broad cultural investigations and meanings of music in non-European, non-classical, non-White settings, as well as understandings of historical performance and close manuscript studies, too, all served to advance a merging of the best of both approaches. RMA members participated in normalizing these conceptual exchanges.

Edward Dent, for one, was crucial not only in the early transition seeding Association meetings with exemplary visiting speakers and papers, but also in teaching singular students who would go on to become bridge builders themselves, including Frederick Sternfeld, Winton Dean and Anthony Lewis, the last another transitional figure who helped connect the media, opera and scholarly worlds and pull levers to get MB off the ground. A joining of professional music-making, opera production and scholarship continued through Egon Wellesz, Jack Westrup, Gerald Abraham, Brian Trowell and Stanley Sadie, while the blending of professional library work with music scholarship and expert management came through C.B. Oldman, Alec King and Nigel Fortune, and the fusing of professional literary work, criticism and scholarship embracing general readers was furthered by Frank Howes, Diana McVeagh, Andrew Porter, Nicholas Kenyon and, again, Sadie. These and many others passed on not only knowledge, skills and energy but wise judgement from their daily work environments; all were able to balance academic work or sensitivity to university colleagues with external music enterprises patronized

---

Britain in 1874. Moreover, as Levitz shows, the same AMS strategy was also intended to keep certain segments of the general population out of the field altogether.

directly by the British public, helping to keep an ever-widening musicological pathway open rather than narrowed down towards an ivory tower.

Ironically, it was just as the academy's welcome for an integrated British musicology showed such promise and new regard that contact with ordinary music lovers and the world of live performance seemed to recede, or break up and divide, while for many the rigours of musicology transmuted into the rigours of academic life under a state obsessed with measuring output. That shift coincided with the widening of tertiary education, new culture wars, the drawing of yet more disciplinary lines, then splintering and rearrangement again. The disruptive, unbalancing effect, necessary for positive social change, may go on for a while in repeating cycles of amalgamation, division and withdrawal. All along, individual scholars of all practices and persuasions, including modern composers and performers, students and British Academicians, librarians and philosophers, editors, broadcasters and social critics, will know that the RMA can accommodate them. Its mixed character remains distinctive among worldwide music-scholarly associations, and represents a striking achievement for a group, still with no physical office, institutional existence, royal charter, state or government grant, place of academic affiliation or source of commercial support except sale of its own publications. Tethered only to each other as individual thinkers and practitioners, RMA members remain committed to the humanizing force of music and the ethical values of music research at the highest level. Setting new goals and discovering new ways to enrich society through understanding and practice, the Association adapts and forges ahead. Beyond doubt, its collaborative, associational past augurs well for a productive future.

As a final reflection on the Association's work in recent times, I've borrowed an earlier Council's idea of consulting expert witnesses, this time for brief thoughts on what the RMA has meant to them. These are their replies, forming the last word in this story.

H. Diack Johnstone (Emeritus Reader in Music, St Anne's College, Oxford, and former General Editor, Musica Britannica)

> I became a member in 1957, I think it was, and I must be one of the oldest life members still alive. We met in the old Trinity College of Music in those days and I seem to remember asking the speaker on one occasion what he could tell us about the music of the composer he'd been telling us about. The answer was nothing: he had not looked at any of the music!! My mentor then was Walter Emery, the distinguished Bach scholar. And that's how I got into editing! I think we'd stopped printing the after-lecture discussion by then and meetings were quite different from their present-day counterparts. No prize for guessing which I enjoyed most!

Elizabeth Wells, MBE (former Curator, Royal College of Music Museum of Instruments, now Royal College of Music Museum)

Having joined the RMA as a student while Sir Jack Westrup was president, I gained immensely from RMA meetings, publications and conferences and enjoyed wonderful friendships. The rehabilitation of the RCM Collection of Instruments after a long period of neglect was challenging and exciting; generous collaboration and support of specialists within the College and from the wider world, including distinguished RMA scholars, enabled pioneering projects in the Museum (and helped avert threatened closure in the late 80s).

RMA conference participants came for a tour of the dispersed instruments in 1968 before the Museum was built, and in 1997 the RCM helped the RMA to host the IMS Congress, when there were fruitful exchanges of information throughout the week. Many good outcomes and memories: *floreat RMA*.

John Irving (Professor of Music, Guildhall School of Music and Drama, London)

The RMA Research Student Conferences were absolutely central to my development as a postgraduate in the early 1980s, giving me a sense of how my fledgling work (on the English renaissance) related to the 'bigger picture' as it was then advancing, and offering the otherwise unimaginable opportunity to network with postgrads elsewhere and (sometimes) their tutors too. I think these conferences really cemented my desire for an academic career.

Fortunately, that's how things turned out. Turning the clock forward by a few decades from those early encounters, one of the most satisfying aspects of my own academic life was being able to attend those RMA conferences as an 'oldie', hopefully passing on some wisdom to future generations!

Rachel Segal (barrister, St John's Chambers, Bristol)

As a student I learned so much from Critical Musicology, with its socio-political, broadly historicized approaches. While researching musical auteurship in golden-era Hollywood film for my PhD, especially the music of Franz Waxman, I served as RMA Membership Administrator in the 1990s and enjoyed meeting musicologists from a range of disciplines and orthodoxies. Then, after teaching at Leeds, working in music pedagogy and leading a national team in higher education policy research, I retrained as a barrister, specializing in personal injury and clinical negligence. I love my work. I'd say the analytical skills I use every day are at least partly derived from those I gained through my musicological development – seeking out and analysing evidence, focusing on close detail while also standing back to see a structure and make a coherent argument.

The RMA community 'normalized' this way of processing information, cutting across multiple contexts, with members from a variety of places exploring many different subjects. On reflection, the RMA was a lot more diverse than I appreciated at the time. The barrister's discipline of performing in court, too – being meticulously prepared, persistent and able to internalize ideas while also having strong knowledge of the Procedural Rules – is supported by my early experiences as a pianist, singer and cellist. I'm absolutely convinced that my musicological experience equipped me not only for investigating topics but also for advocating a position and building an evidence-informed case.

Fiona M. Palmer (Professor of Music, Maynooth University, Co. Kildare, Ireland)

My overall feeling is one of gratitude. It's clear to me that the RMA has been a constant – and invaluable – source of energy, networking and support for my scholarly endeavours. I well remember my first experience of an RMA event – a postgraduate conference held at Oxford University. That first conference experience allowed me to step out from within the confines of my home institution.

It was great to meet like-minded people in an external environment where ideas and methods were tested and expert suggestions made! It marked the start of a long journey throughout which the RMA has been a wellspring of intellectual stimulation and critical friendship. Developmental opportunities provided by participation in numerous conferences, and the chance to 'give back' as a Councillor, have shaped and enhanced my work. For me the RMA has been a touchstone and a springboard.

Graham Dixon (media consultant, former Head of Radio, European Broadcasting Union, and Managing Editor, BBC Radio 3)

Every area of expertise and interest needs its dedicated community. As we learned during Covid, social interaction, involving the exchange of ideas, is a deep human need. The Royal Musical Association provided this space for me at a crucial point in my personal development. Nowadays, having worked at the BBC and European Broadcasting Union, I'm more involved with media strategy and the thought world of ancient India, my more recent interest, than with musicology. But there are no regrets! The intellectual world so effectively represented by the RMA stimulated my curiosity, gave me access to expert analysis of historical data, and engendered my international outlook. All this has immeasurably enriched career, and more importantly my life experience.

John Deathridge (Emeritus Professor of Music, King's College London, and former president of the RMA)

My immediate thought is how much the RMA has developed since I first encountered it in the late 1960s, early 70s. The gentlemen scholars in command didn't exactly inspire me, though they seemed nice enough. I spent the next fourteen years living and working in Germany. I came back to the UK in 1983 to take up appointments in Cambridge (Fellow of King's and University Lecturer) and during the next thirteen years there gradually renewed my acquaintance with the RMA. It was becoming more internationally conscious and professional. But it still needed, and I certainly wasn't alone in thinking this at the time, more commitment from younger scholars.

It will doubtless raise a wry smile when I recount the following anecdote. The moment I decided to get more involved with the RMA was after I found myself on the General Board of the University of Cambridge. There I met the then Cavendish Professor of Physics. He had a famous record collection and knew *something* about music. We both sat on a central committee – gloriously named by Cambridge, as only Cambridge can, the NEEDS COMMITTEE (!) – wrestling with the economic woes of the university (still rather poor compared to the Colleges) when he suddenly stared at me and said: 'John, what is it that you actually DO?'

I realized immediately that if a fellow (musical) distinguished academic like the Cavendish professor genuinely had little idea of what musicologists actually DO, we – the musicologists – had a problem. The status of music studies at the heart of the academic establishment was not high enough obviously (there had never been a Reader in Music at Cambridge, for example, until I got the first such position in 1995), and we, the scholars in music, still had work to do to put it right. Or make it a bit better. So that was when I decided to get RMA active!

The 2000s in my view were a crucial time for the RMA when a lot of us piled in to get old moths out of the organization's cupboard. For me when I was president, it was important to put things on a more stable financial footing and to increase membership. This did actually start to happen gradually, with the astute help of Lawrence Wragg as treasurer and others.

Many of us also thought it important to broaden the RMA's interdisciplinary scope. Here the wider establishment with funding of study groups was key. Susan Bagust did a great job in increasing their number, and some of them, the Music and Philosophy group, for example, with its now biannual conferences, continue to exist to this day. This was also an important entry for popular music, listening studies, iconography, improvisation and other new adventures.

It's still the Royal Music*AL* Association. And that 'AL' may be why the RMA has had not a few members who are not academics. This strikes me as still important, and I hope people won't forget it. Since the late 60s when I first encountered it, the RMA has expanded its activities in many different fields. That hasn't pleased everybody, of course. But it is now a much improved, better-run organization, and I feel fortunate to have been able to play a small part in that process.

Natasha Loges (Professor of Music, Hochschule für Musik Freiburg, Germany)

I attended my first RMA conference when I was a doctoral student more than twenty years ago. Work and family subsequently gobbled up every minute for a stretch, so when I resumed attending RMA events, they gained a completely different meaning for me, providing essential scholarly stimulus and a respite from a hectic life. Still later, as a Council member under the leadership of Simon McVeigh and Barbara Kelly, I found the RMA a revelation for more than scholarly reasons.

It was clear that the Association needed to move forward, but the tug between past and future versions of the RMA could be conflicting and challenging. The countless open discussions around the Council table taught me much about collegiality and change. Watching wiser colleagues handle disagreement with infinite patience was an object lesson in compassionate listening and embracing multiple perspectives. So many of my subsequent decisions have been shaped by those generous, ethically driven conversations. What a debt of gratitude I owe!

Appendix I: Presidents

1874–89	The Rev. Sir Frederick A.G. Ouseley
1889–1901	Sir John Stainer
1901–08	Sir C. Hubert H. Parry
1908–15	William H. Cummings
1915–18	Sir C. Hubert H. Parry
1918–21	Sir Frederick Bridge
1921–24	Sir Hugh Allen
1924–26	Charles Wood
1926–28	Joseph C. Bridge
1928–35	Edward J. Dent
1935–38	Sir Percy C. Buck
1938–42	The Rev. Canon Francis W. Galpin
1942–47	The Rev. Dr E.H. Fellowes
1947–58	Frank Howes
1958–63	Sir Jack Westrup
1963–69	Sir Anthony Lewis
1969–74	Gerald Abraham
1974–78	A. Hyatt King
1979–84	Denis Arnold
1984–89	Brian Trowell
1989–94	Stanley Sadie
1994–99	Julian Rushton
1999–2002	Curtis Price
2002–05	Hugh Cobbe
2005–08	John Deathridge
2008–11	Philip Olleson
2011–18	Mark Everist
2018–21	Simon McVeigh
2021–24	Barbara Kelly
2024–	Simon Keefe

Appendix II: Secretaries, Treasurers, Editors, Librarian

🙚 *Secretaries*

John Stainer, Honorary Secretary *pro tem*	April–May 1874
Charles K. Salaman, Honorary Secretary	June 1874–February 1878
James Higgs, Honorary Secretary	April 1878–December 1883
Francis W. Davenport, Honorary Secretary	July 1884–October 1891
J. Percy Baker	July 1892–12 December 1930
J.B. Trend, Temp. Acting Secretary	October 1930–December 1930
Rupert Erlebach	1931–mid-1956
Nigel Fortune	late 1956–late 1970
Malcolm Turner	1971–mid-1977
Hugh Cobbe	May 1977–1982
Rosemary Dooley	1982–1987
Peter Owens	1987–1991
Chris Banks	February–July 1992
Ewan West	August 1992–September 1994
John Wagstaff	October 1994–November 1995
Geoffrey Lawrence, with Mrs Robin Anderton, Administrator	early 1996
Jonathan P.J. Stock	November 1996–September 1997
Jonathan King	November 1997–July 1998
Bruce Phillips	September 1998–August 2001
Jeffrey J. Dean, Executive Officer	September 2001–July 2022
Amanda Babington, Executive Officer	2022–

🙚 *Honorary Treasurers*

Arthur Chappell	November 1874–October 1877
Stanley Lucas	November 1877–October 1887

A.H. Littleton	October 1887–October 1893
H.C. Banister	November 1893–November 1897
A.H.D. Prendergast	December 1897–November 1901
Clifford B. Edgar	November 1901–June 1908
Arthur M. Fox	July 1908–end 1931
Theodore Holland	January 1932–October 1947
R.S. Thatcher	April 1948–mid-1949
Cedric H. Glover	October 1949–February 1962
David McKenna	February 1962–July 1967
Cedric Watkins	November 1967–1972
Kenneth Cork, with Peter Neville	1972–73
Malcolm London	November 1973–1995
Geoffrey Lawrence	1996–2004
Martin Phelen	2004–06
Lawrence Wragg	May 2006–January 2011
David Roberts-Jones	September 2012–January 2015
Valerie James	2015–

❧ Editors

PROCEEDINGS OF THE ROYAL MUSICAL ASSOCIATION

Marion Scott	July 1944–June 1952
A. Hyatt King	late 1952–March 1957
Frederick Sternfeld	May 1957–spring 1962
Peter le Huray	spring 1962–November 1966
Edward Olleson	March 1967–March 1976
Geoffrey Chew	summer 1976
David Greer	November 1976–1985

JOURNAL OF THE ROYAL MUSICAL ASSOCIATION

David Greer	1985–mid-1989
Mark Everist	1990–94
Andrew Wathey	1995–98
Nicholas Cook	1999–2003
Katharine Ellis	2004–07

Rachel Cowgill	2008–12
Laura Tunbridge	2013–18
Freya Jarman	2018–24
Deborah Mawer	2025–

R.M.A. RESEARCH CHRONICLE (TO 1976)
ROYAL MUSICAL ASSOCIATION RESEARCH CHRONICLE (FROM 1978)

Thurston Dart	1958–62
Jeremy Noble, with Nigel Fortune	1965–68
Michael Tilmouth	1968–76
Geoffrey Chew	1976–84
John Milsom	1986–91
Simon McVeigh	1991–94
Jonathan Wainwright	1994–2011
Paul Watt	2011–20
Florian Scheding and Eva Moreda Rodriguez	2020–

RMA MONOGRAPHS

David Fallows	1980–95
Mark Everist	1995–2011
Simon Keefe	2011–23
Catherine A. Bradley	2023–

Honorary Librarian

Oliver W. Neighbour	1957–2002 [collection dispersed]

Appendix III: Honorary Foreign Members and Honorary Members

❧ *Honorary Foreign Members*

1888	Hermann von Helmholtz (Berlin) François-Auguste Gevaert (Brussels) Philipp Spitta (Berlin)
1900	Hugo Riemann (Leipzig) Guido Adler (Vienna)
1909	Eugène Stradiot (Madras)
1910	Arrigo Boito (Milan) Vincent d'Indy (Paris) Hermann Kretzschmar (Berlin) Eusebius Mandyczewski (Berlin) Camille Saint-Saëns (Paris) Giovanni Sgambati (Rome)
1921	Charles van den Borren (Brussels)
1922	Oscar Sonneck (New York)
1930	Peter Wagner (Freiburg) André Pirro (Paris) Otto Kinkeldey (Ithaca, NY, then NJ)
1930–40	Johannes Wolf (Berlin)
1932–38; 1953	Egon Wellesz (Vienna, then Oxford)
1937	Alfred Einstein (Munich, then Italy, then USA)
1944	Higini Anglès (Barcelona, then Rome) Knud Jeppesen (Copenhagen, then Aarhus)
1952	Albert Schweitzer (Strasbourg, then Gunsbach)
1960	Friedrich Blume (Schlüctern, Germany)
1966	Marc Pincherle (Paris) Gustave Reese (New York City)
1968	Federico Ghisi (Florence)
1970	Oliver Strunk (USA, residing Italy)
1974	Charles Seeger (USA) Eduard Reeser (Holland) Kurt von Fischer (Switzerland)

1978	Ludwig Finscher (West Germany)
	Nino Pirrotta (Italy)
	Jean Jacquot (Paris)
1983	John M. Ward (USA)
	Jens Peter Larsen (Denmark)
	Carl Dahlhaus (Germany)
1990	François Lesure (France)
	Joseph Kerman (USA)
	Howard Mayer Brown (USA)
	Paul Henry Lang (USA)
1997	Pierluigi Petrobelli (Italy)

❧ Honorary Members

1998	Winton Dean
2004	Oliver W. Neighbour
2008	Hugh Macdonald
2009	Robert Pascall
2012	David Fallows
	Margaret Bent
2014	Arnold Whittall
	John Tyrrell
2017	Tim Carter
2019	Susan Youens
	Joshua Rifkin
	Kofi Agawu
2023	Jeffrey J. Dean
2024	John Butt

Appendix IV: Dent Medallists and Other Award Holders

❧ Recipients of the Dent Medal

1961	Gilbert Reaney	UK
1962	Solange Corbin	France
1963	Dénes Bartha	Hungary
1964	Pierre Pidoux	Switzerland
1965	Barry S. Brook	USA
1966	F. Alberto Gallo	Italy
1967	William W. Austin	USA
1968	Heinrich Hüschen	West Germany
1969	Willem Elders	Netherlands
1970	Daniel Heartz	USA
1971	Klaus Wolfgang Niemöller	West Germany
1972	Jozef Robijns	Belgium
1973	Max Lütolf	Switzerland
1974	Andrew McCredie	Australia
1975	Martin Staehelin	West Germany
1976	–	
1977	Reinhard Strohm	UK
1978	Christoph Wolff	USA
1979	Margaret Bent	UK
1980	Craig Wright	USA
1981	Anthony Newcomb	USA
1982	David Fallows	UK
1983	Lorenzo Bianconi	Italy
1984	Iain Fenlon	UK
1985	Curtis A. Price	USA
1986	Silke Leopold	West Germany
1987	Richard F. Taruskin	USA
1988	Jean-Jaques Nattiez	Canada

1989	Paolo Fabbri	Italy
1990	Christopher Page	UK
1991	Roger Parker	UK
1992	Kofi Agawu	Ghana
1993	Carolyn Abbate	USA
1994	Lorenz Welker	Germany
1995	Susan Rankin	UK
1996	Ulrich Konrad	Germany
1997	Philip V. Bohlman	USA
1998	Rob C. Wegman	USA
1999	Gianmario Borio	Italy
2000	Philippe Vendrix	Belgium
2001	Martha Feldman	USA
2002	Laurenz Lütteken	Switzerland
2003	John Butt	UK
2004	Daniel Chua	UK
2005	Julian Johnson	UK
2006	Mary Ann Smart	USA
2007	Georgina Born	UK
2008	Anselm Gerhard	Switzerland
2009	W. Dean Sutcliffe	New Zealand
2010	Martin Stokes	UK
2011	Annegret Fauser	USA
2012	Michel Duchesneau	Canada
2013	Elizabeth Eva Leach	UK
2014	Alexander Rehding	USA
2015	Marina Frolova-Walker	UK
2016	Mark Katz	USA
2017	Alejandro L. Madrid	USA
2018	Inga Mai Groote	Switzerland
2019	Gundula Kreuzer	USA
2020	Eric Drott	USA
2021	Laura Tunbridge	UK
2022	Mark Burford	USA
2023	Catherine A. Bradley	UK
2024	Sarah Collins	Australia

❧ *Peter le Huray Memorial Lecture/ The Le Huray Lecture*

1999	Timothy Rice and Arnold Whittall
2000	–
2001	Hugh Macdonald
2002	Tibor Tallián
2003	–
2004	–
2005	John Roberts
2006	Annette Richards
2007	Anthony Seeger
2008	Kofi Agawu
2009	Carolyn Abbate
2010	Jim Samson
2011	Tim Carter
2012	Martin Cloonan
2013	Gianmario Borio
2014	Alexander Rehding
2015	Georgina Born
2016	Graham Vick
2017	Andrea Lindmayr-Brandl
2018	Robert Adlington
2019	Tamara Levitz
2020	Marie Thompson
2021	Kofi Agawu
2022	George Lewis
2023	Naomi André
2024	Alex Ross

❧ *Jerome Roche Prize*

2001	Alexander Rehding
2002	Emanuele Senici
2003	Emma Dillon
2004	Benjamin Walton

2005	Sarah Hibberd
2006	Gundula Kreuzer
2007	James Quail Davies
2008	Roger Moseley
2009	Arman Schwartz
2010	David R.M. Irving
2011	Benedict Taylor
2012	Christopher Chowrimootoo
2013	Bettina Varwig
2014	Nanette Nielsen
2015	Kate Guthrie
2016	Katherine Hambridge
2017	Yvonne Liao
2018	Sean Curran
2019	Emily MacGregor
2020	Amanda Hsieh
2021	Brianne Dolce
2022	Gabrielle Messeder
2023	Shaena B. Weitz
2024	Giles Masters

Tippett Medal

2020	John Casken, *The Shackled King*
2021	Jonathan Woolgar, *Canzoni et Ricercari*
2022	Simon Knighton, *Sound Sculpture No. 5* for violin, cello, percussion, baritone and alto saxophone and electronics

Practice Research Prize

2023	Joint prize: Mine Doğantan-Dack, Edmund Hunt

Bibliography

❧ *Primary Sources*

MANUSCRIPTS

London, British Library: Music Collections, Royal Musical Association Papers, Minutes, Official Papers and Correspondence, 1874–1971, Add. MSS 71010–64

London, British Library: Music Collections, presented by the Royal Musical Association, Add. MS 56236 (1938), Add. MS 59670 (1936–51)

Manchester: Royal Musical Association Papers, *currently uncatalogued, privately held*, Minutes and Meeting records, 6 MS vols., March 1950–July 1997, M MS 1–6:

MS 1: Council minutes, 9 March 1950–21 July 1958 (paginated)

MS 2: Council minutes, 17 November 1958–16 February 1977 (foliated)

MS 3: Council minutes, 6 July 1977–7 February 1987 (no continuous pagination but some documents are individually paginated)

MS 4: Proceedings Committee minutes, 5 February 1986–7 July 1997 (no continuous pagination or foliation)

MS 5: Council minutes, 8 July 1987–7 July 1997 (no pagination or foliation; no meeting numbers after February 1993)

MS 6: Member meetings including AGMs, January 1958–June 1991 (paginated)

New York, New York Public Library for the Performing Arts, Music Division: Musical Society of London Papers, Drexel 663 (1858–64)

Windsor: Royal Archives, Windsor: RA GEO/MAIN/21589–21594, RA GEO/MAIN/21595

❧ *Selected Secondary Sources*

Abraham, Gerald. 'Musical Scholarship in the Twentieth Century'. *Studies in Music* [University of Western Australia], 1 (1967), 1–10.

——. 'Our First Hundred Years'. *Proceedings of the Royal Musical Association*, 100 (1973–74), pp. vii–xiii.

Agawu, Kofi. 'How We Got Out of Analysis, and How to Get Back In Again'. *Music Analysis*, 23 (2004), 267–86.

——. 'Lives in Musicology: My Life in Writings'. *Acta musicologica*, 93 (2021), 1–18.

Andrewes, Richard. 'Edward Francis Rimbault, 1816–1876'. *Fontes artis musicae*, 30 (1983), 30–34.

Arrandale, Karen. *Edward J. Dent: A Life of Words and Music*. Woodbridge: Boydell Press, 2023.

Baumann, Dorothea, and Dinko Fabris, eds. *The History of the IMS (1927–2017)*. Basel: Bärenreiter, 2017.

Bent, Ian, ed. *Source Materials and the Interpretation of Music: A Memorial Volume to Thurston Dart*. London: Stainer & Bell, 1981.
Bent, Margaret. 'Fact and Value in Contemporary Scholarship'. *Musical Times*, 127 (1986), 85–89.
Born, Georgina. 'For a Relational Musicology: Music and Interdisciplinarity, beyond the Practice Turn'. *Journal of the Royal Musical Association*, 135 (2010), 205–43.
Breen, Edward. *Thurston Dart and the New Faculty of Music at King's College London: A 50th Anniversary Biography*. London: King's College London, 2015.
Brett, Philip. 'Musicology and Sexuality: The Example of Edward J. Dent'. In *Queer Episodes in Music and Modern Identity*, ed. Sophie Fuller and Lloyd Whitesell, 177–88. Urbana: University of Illinois Press, 2002.
——. 'Text, Context, and the Early Music Editor'. In *Authenticity and Early Music: A Symposium*, ed. Nicholas Kenyon, 83–114. Oxford and New York: Oxford University Press, 1988.
Brown, James D., and Stephen S. Stratton. *British Musical Biography: A Dictionary of Musical Artists, Authors and Composers born in Britain and its Colonies*. Birmingham: S.S. Stratton, 1897.
Bujic, Bojan. 'Musicology and Intellectual History: A Backward Glance to the Year 1885'. *Proceedings of the Royal Musical Association*, 111 (1984–85), 139–54.
Butler, Katherine. 'Myth, Science and the Power of Music in the Early Decades of the Royal Society'. *Journal of the History of Ideas*, 76 (2015), 47–68.
Carpenter, Humphrey. *The Envy of the World: Fifty Years of the BBC Third Programme and Radio 3, 1946–1996*. London: Weidenfeld & Nicolson, 1996.
Celebrating the American Musicological Society at Seventy-Five. Brunswick, ME: American Musicological Society, 2011.
Clarke, Eric, and Nicholas Cook, eds. *Empirical Musicology: Aims, Methods, Prospects*. Oxford and New York: Oxford University Press, 2004.
Clayton, Martin, Trevor Herbert and Richard Middleton, eds. *The Cultural Study of Music: A Critical Introduction*. New York and London: Routledge, 2003; 2nd edn, 2012.
Cobbe, Hugh. 'The Royal Musical Association, 1874–1901'. *Proceedings of the Royal Musical Association*, 110 (1983–84), 111–17.
Cole, Suzanne. ''A Great National Heritage': The Early Twentieth-Century Tudor Church Music Revival'. In *Tudorism: Historical Imagination and the Appropriation of the Sixteenth Century*, ed. Tatiana C. String and Marcus Bull, 78–96. London: British Academy, 2011.
——. 'Research Report: The Early Twentieth-Century Revival of Tudor Church Music'. *Context*, 37 (2012), 130–34.
Collingwood, R.G. *The Idea of History*. Oxford: Clarendon Press, 1946.
Collins, Sarah. 'The Foundation of *Music & Letters*'. *Music & Letters*, 100 (2019), 185–91.
Cook, Nicholas. 'Between Art and Science: Music as Performance'. *Journal of the British Academy*, 2 (2014). 1–25.
—— and Mark Everist, eds. *Rethinking Music*. Oxford and New York: Oxford University Press, 1999.
Cooper, Barry. 'Musicology in Great Britain (1982–1985)'. *Acta musicologica*, 58 (1986), 1–8.

Crawford, Richard. *The American Musicological Society, 1934–1984: An Anniversary Essay, with Lists of Officers, Winners of Awards, Editors of the Journal, and Honorary and Corresponding Members*. Philadelphia: American Musicological Society, 1984.
Cudworth, Charles L. 'Ye Olde Spuriosity Shoppe, or, Put it in the Anhang'. *Notes*, 12 (1954), 25–40.
Dahlhaus, Carl. *Foundations of Music History*, trans. J.B. Robinson. Cambridge: Cambridge University Press, 1983.
Dart, Thurston. *The Interpretation of Music*. London: Hutchinson, 1964.
Day, Timothy. 'The National Sound Archive: The First Fifty Years'. In *Aural History: Essays on Recorded Sound*, 41–64. London: British Library, 2001.
Dent, Edward Joseph. 'The Historical Approach to Music'. *Musical Quarterly*, 23 (1937), 1–17.
——. 'Music and Musical Research'. *Acta musicologica*, 3 (1931), 5–8.
——. 'Music in University Education'. *Musical Quarterly*, 3 (1917), 605–19.
——. 'The Scientific Study of Music in England'. *Acta musicologica*, 2 (1930), 83–92.
Devine, Patrick F., and Harry White, eds. *The Maynooth International Musicological Conference 1995: Selected Proceedings*, 2 vols. Dublin: Four Courts Press, 1996.
Dibble, Jeremy. *John Stainer: A Life in Music*. Woodbridge: Boydell Press, 2007.
——. 'Learned Societies, Institutions, Associations, and Clubs'. In *The Oxford Handbook of Music and Intellectual Culture in the Nineteenth Century*, ed. Paul Watt, Sarah Collins and Michael Allis, 209–26. Oxford: Oxford University Press, 2020.
——. 'Parry as Historiographer'. In *Nineteenth-Century British Music Studies*, vol. 1, ed. Bennett Zon, 37–51. Aldershot: Ashgate, 1999.
Dolmetsch, Arnold. *The Interpretation of the Music of the XVII and XVIII Centuries, Revealed by Contemporary Evidence*. London: Novello; Oxford University Press, 1915, 2nd edn, 1946.
Duchesneau, Michel. 'French Musicology and the Musical Press (1900–14): The Case of *La revue musicale, Le mercure musical* and *La revue musical SIM*', trans. Kimberly White. *Journal of the Royal Musical Association*, 140 (2015), 243–72.
Fallows, David. 'Musicology in Great Britain, 1979–1982'. *Acta musicologica*, 55 (1983), 244–53.
——, ed. *Oxford, Bodleian Library MS. Canon. Misc. 213. Late Medieval and Early Renaissance Music in Facsimile*, ed. Margaret Bent and John Nádas, vol. 1. Chicago and London: University of Chicago Press, 1995.
Fallows, David, Arnold Whittall, John Blacking and Nigel Fortune. 'Musicology in Great Britain since 1945'. *Acta musicologica*, 52 (1980), 38–68.
Fauser, Annegret. 'Edward J. Dent (1932–49)'. In *The History of the IMS (1927–2017)*, ed. Dorothea Baumann and Dinko Fabris, 45–49. Basel: Bärenreiter, 2017.
——. 'Guido Adler and the Founding of the International Musicological Society (IMS): A View from the Archives'. *Vremennik Zubovskogo instituta* [Annals of the Zubov Institute], 7, no. 4 (2019), 97–113.
——. 'The Scholar behind the Medal: Edward J. Dent (1876–1957) and the Politics of Music History'. *Journal of the Royal Musical Association*, 139 (2014), 235–60.

——. 'Some Challenges for Musicological Internationalism in the 1930s'. In *The History of the IMS (1927–2017)*, ed. Dorothea Baumann and Dinko Fabris, 20–24. Basel: Bärenreiter, 2017.
Fellowes, Edmund H. *Memoirs of an Amateur Musician*. London: Methuen & Co., 1946.
Gillin, Edward John. *Sound Authorities: Scientific and Musical Knowledge in Nineteenth-Century Britain*. Chicago: University of Chicago Press, 2021.
Golding, Rosemary. *Music and Academia in Victorian Britain*. Aldershot: Ashgate, 2013.
Goldstein, Dorothy S. 'The Origins and Early Years of the *English Historical Review*'. *English Historical Review*, 101 (1986), 6–19.
Gouk, Penelope. *Music, Science and Natural Magic in Seventeenth-Century England*. New Haven: Yale University Press, 1999.
Harap, Louis. 'On the Nature of Musicology'. *Musical Quarterly*, 23 (1937), 18–25.
Harrison, Frank Llewellyn, Mantle Hood and Claude V. Palisca. *Musicology*. Englewood Cliffs, NJ: Prentice Hall, 1963.
Harris, P.R. *A History of the British Museum Library, 1753–1973*. London: British Library, 1998.
—— and O.W. Neighbour. 'Alexander Hyatt King (1911–1995)'. *British Library Journal*, 21 (1995), 155–60.
Heyck, Thomas William. 'Freelance Writers and the Changing Terrain of Intellectual Life in Britain, 1880–1980'. *Albion*, 32 (2002), 232–67.
——. 'From Men of Letters to Intellectuals: The Transformation of Intellectual Life in Nineteenth-Century England'. *Journal of British Studies*, 20 (1980), 158–83.
——. 'The Idea of a University in Britain, 1870–1970'. *History of European Ideas*, 8 (1987), 205–19.
Hoberman, Ruth. 'Women in the British Museum Reading Room during the Late Nineteenth and Early Twentieth Centuries: From Quasi- to Counterpublic'. *Feminist Studies*, 28 (2002), 489–512.
Holoman, D. Kern, and Claude V. Palisca, eds. *Musicology in the 1980s: Methods, Goals, Opportunities*. New York: Da Capo Press, 1982.
Hughes, Dom Anselm. 'Ninety Years of English Musicology'. In *Liber amicorum Charles van den Borren*, 93–97. Anvers: Imprimerie Lloyd Anversois, 1964.
Hullah, John. *Musical Institute of London: Inaugural Address, Saturday, February 14th, 1852*. London: John W. Parker & Son, 1852.
Iggers, Georg G. *Historiography in the Twentieth Century: From Scientific Objectivity to the Postmodern Challenge, with a New Epilogue by the Author*. Middletown, CT: Wesleyan University Press, 1997, rev. 2005.
Jackson, Myles W. 'Charles Wheatstone: Musical Instrument Making, Natural Philosophy, and Acoustics in Early Nineteenth-Century London'. In *Sound Knowledge: Music and Science in London, 1789–1851*, ed. James Q. Davies and Ellen Lockhart, 101–24. Chicago: University of Chicago Press, 2016.
Jackson, Roland. *The Ascent of John Tyndall: Victorian Scientist, Mountaineer, and Public Intellectual*. Oxford: Oxford University Press, 2018.
Josephson, David. '"Why Then All the Difficulties!": A Life of Kathi Meyer-Baer'. *Notes*, 65 (2008), 227–67.

Kassler, Jamie Croy. 'The Royal Institution Music Lectures, 1800-1831: A Preliminary Study'. *Royal Musical Association Research Chronicle*, 19 (1983-85), 1-30.
Kenyon, Nicholas, ed. *Authenticity and Early Music: A Symposium*. Oxford and New York: Oxford University Press, 1988.
Kerman, Joseph. *Musicology*. London: Fontana Press/Collins, 1985. Also published as *Contemplating Music: Challenges to Musicology*. Cambridge, MA: Harvard University Press, 1985.
King, Alec Hyatt. 'The Hirsch Music Library: Retrospect and Conclusion'. *Notes*, 9 (1952), 381-87.
——. 'The Music Room of the British Museum, 1753-1953: Its History and Organization'. *Proceedings of the Royal Musical Association*, 79 (1952-53), 65-79.
——. 'The Musical Institute of London and its Successors'. *Musical Times*, 117 (1976), 221-23.
——. 'Musical Research: Background and Sources'. In *The Year's Work in Music, 1948-49*, 21-29. London: British Council, 1949.
——. 'Paul Hirsch and his Music Library'. *British Library Journal*, 7 (1981), 1-11.
——. 'Quodlibet: Some Memoirs of the British Museum and its Music Room, 1934-76'. In *The Library of the British Museum: Retrospective Essays on the Department of Printed Books*, ed. P.R. Harris, 241-98. London: British Library, 1991.
——. *Some British Collectors of Music, c. 1600-1960*. Cambridge: Cambridge University Press, 1963.
——. 'The Study of Music in British Universities'. In *The Year's Work in Music, 1950-51*, ed. Alan Frank, 9-19. London: British Council, 1951.
——. 'William Barclay Squire, 1855-1927: Music Librarian'. In *Musical Pursuits: Selected Essays*, 187-99. London: British Library, 1987.
King, Richard G. 'The Fonds Schoelcher: History and Contents'. *Notes*, 53 (1997), 687-721.
——. 'New Light on Handel's Musical Library'. *Musical Quarterly*, 81 (1997), 109-38.
Kirnbauer, Martin. 'A "Prelude" to the IMS'. In *The History of the IMS (1927-2017)*, ed. Dorothea Baumann and Dinko Fabris, 11-19. Basel: Bärenreiter, 2017.
Kramer, Lawrence. *Classical Music and Postmodern Knowledge*. Berkeley: University of California Press, 1995.
——. 'Charging the Canons'. Review of *Disciplining Music: Musicology and its Canons*, ed. Katherine Bergeron and Philip V. Bohlman (Chicago: University of Chicago Press, 1992). *Journal of the Royal Musical Association*, 119 (1994), 130-40.
Langley, Leanne. 'British Music Scholarship in the Nineteenth Century'. Paper given at the 31st Annual Conference of the Royal Musical Association, with the Society for Music Analysis, King's College London, April 1996 ('British Musicology Conference'). Expanded for the IMS Intercongressional Symposium, 'The Past in the Present', Franz Liszt Academy of Music, Budapest, August 2000.
——. 'Gatekeeping, Advocacy, Reflection: Overlapping Voices in Nineteenth-Century British Music Criticism'. In *The Cambridge History of Musical*

Criticism, ed. Christopher Dingle, 147–69. Cambridge: Cambridge University Press, 2019.

——. 'A Place for Music: John Nash, Regent Street and the Philharmonic Society of London'. *Electronic British Library Journal* (2013), art. 12, pp. 1–50, http://www.bl.uk/eblj/2013 articles/article12.html.

——. 'Roots of a Tradition: The First *Dictionary of Music and Musicians*'. In *George Grove, Music and Victorian Culture*, ed. Michael Musgrave, 168–215. Basingstoke: Palgrave Macmillan, 2003.

——. 'Writing about Rhetoric: Two Views of Ancient Music from 1760'. Paper given at the RMA Annual Conference, London, April 1989; rev. as 'Burney and Hawkins: New Light on an Old Rivalry', American Musicological Society Annual Meeting, Austin, Texas, October 1989.

LaRue, Jan, ed. *Report of the Eighth Congress: New York 1961*, vol. 2: Reports. Published for the International Musicological Society by the American Musicological Society. Kassel, Basel, London and New York: Bärenreiter, 1962.

Leech-Wilkinson, Daniel. *The Modern Invention of Medieval Music: Scholarship, Ideology, Performance*. Cambridge: Cambridge University Press, 2002.

Levine, Philippa. *The Amateur and the Professional: Antiquarians, Historians and Archaeologists in Victorian England, 1838–1886*. Cambridge: Cambridge University Press, 1986.

Levitz, Tamara. 'The Musicological Elite'. *Current Musicology*, 102 (2018), 9–80.

Lonsdale, Roger. *Dr. Charles Burney: A Literary Biography*. Oxford: Oxford University Press, 1965.

Lowinsky, Edward E. 'Homage to Armen Carapetyan'. *Musica disciplina*, 37 (1983), 9–27.

Lynan, Peter, and Julian Rushton, eds. *British Music, Musicians and Institutions, c. 1630–1800: Essays in Honour of Harry Diack Johnstone*. Woodbridge: Boydell Press, 2021.

McKibbin, Ross. *Classes and Cultures: England, 1918–1951*. Oxford: Oxford University Press, 1998; paperback edn, 2000.

McKitterick, David, ed. *The Cambridge History of the Book in Britain*, vol. 6: *1830–1914*. Cambridge: Cambridge University Press, 2009.

Mandler, Peter. *The Crisis of the Meritocracy: Britain's Transition to Mass Education since the Second World War*. Oxford: Oxford University Press, 2020.

Masters, Giles. 'Performing Internationalism: The ISCM as a "Musical League of Nations"'. *Journal of the Royal Musical Association*, 147 (2022), 560–71.

Mendel, Arthur. 'Evidence and Explanation'. In *Report of the Eighth Congress: New York 1961*, vol. 2, ed. Jan LaRue, for the International Musicological Society, 3–18. Kassel, Basel, London and New York: Bärenreiter, 1962.

Morroni, June R. 'The Music Library Association'. *Fontes artis musicae*, 18 (1971), 5–18.

Mugglestone, Erica. 'Guido Adler's "The Scope, Method, and Aim of Musicology" (1885): An English Translation with an Historico-Analytical Commentary'. *Yearbook for Traditional Music*, 13 (1981), 1–21.

Olleson, Edward, ed. *Modern Musical Scholarship*. Stocksfield: Oriel Press Ltd, 1980.

Palisca, Claude V. 'American Scholarship in Western Music'. In Frank Ll. Harrison, Claude Palisca and Mantle Hood, *Musicology*, 87–213. Englewood Cliffs, NJ: Prentice Hall, 1963.

Pole, William. 'Professional Musicians and Musical Amateurs'. *Musical Times*, 24 (1883), 432–33.
Porter, Andrew. 'Seeing the Stars Again: The Original Vision of George Grove and the Ever-Growing *New Grove* Revised'. *Times Literary Supplement* (23 November 2001), 3–4.
—— and Leanne Langley. 'Two Tributes'. In *Words about Mozart: Essays in Honour of Stanley Sadie*, ed. Dorothea Link with Judith Nagley, 211–18. Woodbridge: Boydell & Brewer, 2005.
Potter, Pamela M. *Most German of the Arts: Musicology and Society from the Weimar Republic to the End of Hitler's Reich*. New Haven and London: Yale University Press, 1998.
Pratt, Waldo S. 'On Behalf of Musicology'. *Musical Quarterly*, 1 (1915), 1–16.
Scholes, Percy A. *The Mirror of Music, 1844–1944: A Century of Musical Life in Britain as Reflected in the Pages of the Musical Times*, 2 vols. London: Novello & Co. and Oxford University Press, 1947.
Searle, Richard. 'Sylvia Townsend Warner and *Tudor Church Music*'. *Journal of the Sylvia Townsend Warner Society*, 12 (2011), 69–88.
Sonneck, O.G. 'European Musical Associations'. *Papers and Proceedings of the Music Teachers' National Association*, 28 (1906), 115–37.
Stock, Jonathan P.J. 'Alexander J. Ellis and His Place in the History of Ethnomusicology'. *Ethnomusicology*, 51 (2007), 305–24.
Strohm, Reinhard. 'Postmodern Thought and the History of Music: Some Intersections'. *Revista Portuguesa de Musicologia*, 9 (1999), 7–24.
——, ed. *Studies on a Global History of Music: A Balzan Musicology Project*. London: Routledge, 2018.
——, ed. *Transcultural Music History: Global Participation and Regional Diversity in the Modern Age*. Berlin: Verlag für Wissenschaft und Bildung, 2021.
Turbet, Richard. 'Ancient Church Music published by the Motett Society: A List with the Original Sources'. *Brio*, 53 (2016), 31–41.
——. 'The Musical Antiquarian Society, 1840–48'. *Brio*, 29 (1992), 13–20.
Turner, Malcolm, and Arthur Searle. 'The Music Collections of the British Library Reference Division'. *Notes*, 38 (1982), 499–549.
Uí Chionna, Jackie. *Queen of Codes: The Secret Life of Emily Anderson, Britain's Greatest Female Codebreaker*. London: Headline, 2023.
Westrup, Jack. *An Introduction to Musical History*. London: Hutchinson's University Library, 1955.
White, Harry. 'Conference Report: Maynooth International Musicological Conference, St Patrick's College, Maybooth, Co. Kildare (Ireland), 21–24 September, 1995'. *Journal of Musicology*, 14 (1996), 579–89.
——. *The Keeper's Recital: Music and Cultural History in Ireland, 1770–1970*. Cork: Cork University Press, 1998.
Whittall, Arnold. 'Nigel Fortune: Musicologist behind a Rise in Academic Standards in Britain'. *The Guardian* (23 April 2009).
Wilfing, Alexander. 'Guido Adler and the Eclectic Origins of Musicology'. Paper given at the Annual Meeting of the American Musicological Society, Chicago (online), November 2021.
Williams, Alastair. *Constructing Musicology*. Aldershot: Ashgate, 2001.
Wright, David C.H. *The Royal College of Music and its Contexts: An Artistic and Social History*. Cambridge: Cambridge University Press, 2020.

Index

In page references the suffix *fig* indicates an illustration, and *tab* a table.

Abercrombie, Patrick   150
Abert, Anna Amalie   191, 193*tab*
Abraham, Gerald   173, 234
   academic career   143, 148
   BBC radio talks   154–55
   on composer sketches   157
   and Joseph Haydn-Institut   153
   and Music & Letters Trust   160
   'Our First Hundred Years'   34n.6, 192*tab*
   RMA president   172, 187–88
acoustics   34–35, 41, 74, 150
Acta musicologica (journal)   110, 113, 114–15, 119n.66, 130, 201
Adeane, Michael   165
Adler, Guido   49, 62*fig*, 64
Aeolian Hall, London   58, 59
Airy, George   35, 36
Alaleona, Domenico   92
Allen, Hugh   45, 95
amateurs   139
   as music researchers   4, 7–8
   in RMA membership   51, 143
American Musicological Society (AMS)   166
Anderson, Emily   143
Andersson, Otto   63*fig*
Andersson, Richard   61*fig*
Andrewes, Richard   196–97
Anglès, Higini   112, 113–14
Antcliffe, Herbert   58, 102n.17
antiquarianism   23
Aprahamian, Felix   141
Arbós, Enrique Fernándes   69
Arkwright, Godfrey   82, 98
Arne, Thomas, *The Masque of Comus*   161*tab*, 164, 166
Arnheim, Amalie   61*fig*
Arnold, Cecily   143, 171
Arnold, Denis   143, 177, 191, 193*tab*, 215n.37
   RMA president   172, 194, 201
Arrandale, Karen   99–100
Arts Council   139, 140, 152, 163, 165
Associazione dei Musicologi Italiani   93

Astley, Constance   50
Auber, Daniel   17
Audsley, George Ashdown, 'Again, What is Sound?'   84n.94
Austin, William W.   193*tab*
awards and honours
   Dent Medal   146–47, 182n.33, 183n.34, 197, 211, 247–48
   Fellowes Memorial Fund   145–46
   Howes Fund   218n.45
   Jerome Roche Prize   226, 249–50
   Le Huray Memorial Lectures   224, 249
   Margarita M. Hanson Award   228
   Practice Research Prize   228, 250
   Tippett Medal   228, 250
Ayrton, William   15

Bach, J. S.   5, 12
   B minor Mass *Credo*   7
Badura-Skoda, Eva   190, 191, 192*tab*
Badura-Skoda, Paul, 'The Interpretation of Beethoven on Pianos Old and New'   154
Bagenal, Hope   150
   'Musical Taste and Concert Hall Design'   150
Bagust, Susan   220
Baillie-Hamilton, J.   43, 76*tab*
Baird, Anthea   187
Bake, Arnold   157
Baker, J. Percy   33n.4, 49, 62*fig*, 65, 66n.63
   death   97
   Musical Association Secretary   46n.26, 49, 68–69, 95
   PMA, indexing of   74–75
Balfour, A.J.   58
Barnby, J.   37
Barnicotts (printer)   156, 157
Barrett, W. A.   40
Bashford, Christina   206*fig*
Bax, Arnold   120
Bayliss, Stanley   164–65
Baynes, T.M.   22*fig*

259

BBC (British Broadcasting
    Corporation)   140
  concert broadcasts   165, 166
  Radio 3   154–55
  talks, archive recordings of   154–55
  Third Programme   140, 167
BBC Chorus   166
Beale, Frederick   16–17, 18
Beale, Willert   20
Bedford College, London   17
Bedford Lemere & Co. (photographers),
    'Portrait of the Musical Congress
    outside the entrance to the Imperial
    Institute'   59, 60–63*fig*
Beethoven, Ludwig van   15, 92, 119, 181
  in Hirsch Library   122
  letters   143n.11
  sketchbooks   182–84
Bell, W.H.   59
Benedict, Jules   20, 50
Bennett, William Sterndale   9, 10, 17,
    36, 37
Bent, Ian   188, 193*tab*, 194n.65, 199, 200*fig*
  'The English Chapel Royal before
    1300'   178
Bent, Margaret   94, 181, 208, 210–11,
    218n.47
Berger, Francesco   20
Berlioz, Hector   16, 17, 18, 107, 181
Besseler, Heinrich   114
BFE *see* British Forum for
    Ethnomusicology
Birmingham University   149
BIRS *see* British Institute of Recorded
    Sound
Bishop, John   36, 37
Blackwell's (publisher and
    bookseller)   177, 187
Blaikley, David James   50, 76*tab*
Blair, Tony   225
Bliss, Arthur   70, 143
Blom, Eric   143, 159–60
Blow, John   161*tab*, 165, 166
Blume, Friedrich   153
Board of Trade   35, 47
Boito, Arrigo   50
Boorman, Stanley   188, 200*fig*
Borland, John, 'Orchestral and Choral
    Balance'   74, 75*fig*
Borren, Charles van den *see* Van den
    Borren, Charles
Bosanquet, R.H.M.   37, 77*tab*
Boult, Adrian   50, 51, 70, 120, 143
Boyce, William   161*tab*
Boyd Neel Orchestra   166

Bracefield, Hilary   219
Bream, Julian   166
Breitkopf & Härtel (publisher)   54, 65,
    110, 114
Bridge, Frederick   63*fig*, 81
Bridge, Joseph Cox   96–97
British Academy   175, 196
British Association for the Advancement
    of Science   35
British Broadcasting Corporation *see* BBC
British Council   140, 168–69
British Forum for Ethnomusicology
    (BFE)   222, 226
British Institute of Recorded Sound
    (BIRS)   139, 154–55
British Library (BL)   197
  'Mozart: Prodigy of Nature' (exhibition,
    1991)   220–21
  music collections   213
  Sound and Vision Archive (formerly
    National Sound Archive)   153–55
British Museum (BM)   8–9, 25*fig*, 75, 81*fig*
  Hirsch Library, acquisition of   121–22
  music collections   24, 183–85
  music library   80–81
  sound archives   153–55
British music   4, 6, 57, 58, 157–58
  see also English music
Britten, Benjamin   181, 182, 190
Broadwood, Evelyn   50, 144, 150, 166
Broadwood, Lucy E.   98
  'On the Collecting of English
    Folk-Song'   88
Broadwood & Co.   45
Brook, Barry   197
Brown, Howard Mayer   172, 184, 185, 187,
    190, 191, 192–93*tab*
Brown, James D., *British Musical
    Biography*   85
Browne, W. Denis   105
  'Modern Harmonic Tendencies'   91
Brownlow, Jane M.E.   51
Brunold, Paul   109
Buck, Percy   50, 93, 109
  Musical Association president   95,
    116–17, 124
Bukofzer, Manfred   93–94, 161*tab*, 166
Bull, John   161*tab*
Bunting, Edward   4–5, 5*tab*
  *A General Collection of the Ancient Irish
    Music*   4–5
Burden, Michael   219
Burney, Charles   15
Bush, Geoffrey   169
Butler Education Act (1944)   147

Byde, Michael   219, 227
Byrd, William   94, 135

Cadogan, Alexander   167
Calvocoressi, M.-D.   61*fig*, 64
Cambridge Music Shop   187
Cambridge University   26, 27, 105–6, 149
  Hirsch Library, hosting of   119
  St John's College   64
Cambridge University Press   217
Camelot Press (printer)   194
Cameron, Francis   161*tab*
Capell, Richard   159–60
Carillo, Julián   61*fig*
Carlyle, Thomas   6
Carnegie United Kingdom Trust   82–83
carols   161*tab*, 166
Carse, Adam   58, 125, 126
Carter, Tim   222, 224
Casken, John   174*fig*
Centre for the History and Analysis of Recorded Music (CHARM)   155, 227–28
Chappell, S. Arthur   41
Chappell, William   4, 5*tab*, 7, 9, 16–17, 20
  A Collection of National English Airs   6
  Musical Association, founding of   36, 37
Chappell & Co. (publisher)   9, 18
Charkin, Richard   207, 208
CHARM *see* Centre for the History and Analysis of Recorded Music
Chase, Gilbert   133
Chesterian (journal)   98
Chew, Geoffrey   194
Chipp, Edmund   40
choir training   64
Cholij, Irena   219
choral music   59, 74, 75*fig*, 161*tab*, 166
Chorley, Henry   17
Chrysander, Friedrich   6
Chrysander, Rudolf   63*fig*
church music   10, 135
  English   59
  Italian   5
  Tudor Church Music project   82–83, 92–93
classicism   92
Cleather, Gordon   70
Clementi, Muzio   15
Clutsam, C.H.   104
'Classicism and False Values'   92
Coates, William   161*tab*

Cobbe, Hugh   33, 43n.22, 172, 194, 213, 229
Cobbett, W.W.   46n.26, 62*fig*, 109
Coldstream Guards band   58
Coleman, Colin   220
Coleridge-Taylor, Samuel   59
collections, musical   6, 8–9, 152–55
  BM   24, 183–84
  British Library   213
Colles, H.C.   98, 108–9, 125
Collins, H.B.   125, 126
composers   143
  see also music editions
  biographies   6
  conducting by   58, 59
  performance, intentions for   15
  research focus on   xiii, 1, 4, 92, 130
  RMA connections with   143, 169, 226
  sketches and sketchbooks   157, 182, 183–84
  women   85, 205
composition   xiii, 169, 181, 228
concert halls *see* performance venues
concerts
  BBC broadcasts   165, 166
  at IMG London Congress (1911)   57–59
  of Musical Society of London   20–21
  at RMA events   177, 190
  societies focused on   13–14, 16, 19–22
conferences
  IMG 1909 Congress, Vienna   55
  IMG 1911 Congress, London   54, 55–65
    concerts   57–59
    funding of   56–57
    research papers   58
  IMG 1914 Congress, Paris   65
  IMS Sixth International Congress, Oxford (1955)   152–53
  IMS Sixteenth International Congress, London (1997)   203, 224–25
  ISMR 1930 Congress, Liège   110–11, 112
  ISMR 1933 Congress, Cambridge   109–13, 117–18
  ISMR 1936 Congress, Barcelona   113–15
  ISMR 1949 Congress, Basel   115
  Maynooth International Musicological Conference (1995)   223–24
  Medieval-Renaissance conferences   188, 216
  Mozart Bicentenary Conference (1991)   220–21
  Nineteenth-Century Music Conference   188, 190, 216

262 INDEX

conferences (cont'd)
   RMA Annual Conferences   53–54, 194,
      221–23, 227–28, 229
     'British Musicology Conference'
       (1996)   222
     'Music and Film' (2001)   222
     'Music and Rhetoric' (1989)   222
     'Music in the Market-Place'
       (1988)   221–22
     'Performance' (2000)   222
     'The Theory and Practice of Musical
       Biography' (2001)   222–23
   Society for Music Analysis joint
      conference (1993)   222, 223
   student   177, 216, 218
   'Third Triennial British Musicological
      Societies Conference' (1999)   222
consort music   109, 157, 161*tab*
Cook, Nicholas   217
Cooper, Gerald   125, 127
Cooper, Martin   157
Corder, Frederick   58
Cowen, Frederic   59, 61*fig*
Cowgill, Rachel   219
Cramer, Beale & Chappell
   (publisher)   10, 16
Cramer, J.B.   15
Creighton, Mandell   29
Crewdson, H.A.F.   160
Critical Musicology Forum   222
Critics' Circle   173
Cross, Eric   219n.48
Crotch, William   5*tab*, 10, 23
   Specimens of Various Styles of Music   5
Cudworth, Charles (C.L.)   143, 158–59
   'English Symphonists of the Eighteenth
     Century'   140, 158
   *Thematic Index of English Eighteenth-
     Century Overtures and
     Symphonies*   158
Cummings, Arthur T.   47
Cummings, William (W.H.)   58, 63*fig*,
   86, 88, 91, 157
   'The Formation of a National Musical
     Library'   80, 85
   'Music during the Queen's Reign'   53
Curwen, John   6

Dahlhaus, Carl   190, 192*tab*
Daily Telegraph, IMG London Congress
   visit to   59
Dale, Kathleen   157
Dannreuther, Edward   4, 5*tab*, 8, 28, 37,
   50

Dart, Robert Thurston   3, 141, 143, 145,
   183
   academic career   149, 198–99, 200*fig*,
     203
   Charles van den Borren, mentored
     by   94
   death   184, 199
   East German colleagues, invitation
     to   168–69
   memorial fund   195, 217, 221
   and Musica Britannica   161–62, 161*tab*,
     163*fig*, 166
   and Purcell Society   159
   research papers   157
   and RILM project   197
   RMARC editor   156, 174–75
Darwin, Charles   42–43
Dauney, William   4, 5*tab*
   Ancient Scottish Melodies   6
Davies, Mary   50
Davies, Walford   58
Davison, J.W.   20
Davy, Richard   166
Daymond, Emily   50
Dean, Jeffrey   227
Dean, Winton   105, 154, 157, 190, 192*tab*,
   226n.70, 234
Deathridge, John   199, 229, 237–38
demonstrations, musical   69–70, 85–86,
   88
Denison, John   143
Dent, Edward J.   3, 51, 61*fig*, 108*fig*, 125,
   141
   academic career   148
   death   146
   Hirsch Library, fundraising for   120–21
   at IMG Congress (1911)   58
   international work of   101–2
   'The Laudi Spirituali in the XVIth and
     XVIIth Centuries'   91–92, 103
   on library subcommittee   82
   and Musica Britannica   152, 161*tab*
   Musical Association president   95, 97,
     99–116
   papers, improved quality
     under   106–9, 234
   papers by   73, 103
   'The Romantic Spirit in Music'   107–8
   and South Bank development   150
Dent Medal   146–47, 181n.33, 182n.34, 197,
   211, 247–48
Deutscher Akademischer Austauschdienst
   (DAAD)   191
Dibble, Jeremy   86, 100

dictionaries 15
Dictionary of Music and Musicians
    (Grove) 12–13, 24, 28, 209
    see also *Grove Music Online*; *New Grove Dictionary of Music and Musicians*
    prospectus, publication of 35–36
    revisions and editions 82, 132, 200
diplomacy 101–2, 168–69
disability 50
disciplines, academic
    see also musicology
    archaeology 23
    history 3, 23–24, 26
    history of music 41, 44
    music 27–28, 148–49
    scientific 26–27, 33–35, 76–79*tab*, 148
displaced/émigré scholars 99, 112–13, 117–19, 133–34
diversity 226, 228
    academic 234
    in music culture 90–91, 134, 201, 206
    of RMA membership 50–51, 141, 228
Dixon, Graham 237
Doctoral Dissertations in Musicology
    database 218
Dodge, Janet 73–74
    'Lute Music of the XVIth and XVIIth Centuries' 71, 89
Doe, Paul 193*tab*
    'Register of Theses on Music' 175
Dolmetsch, Carl 157
Donington, Robert 146
    'Some Special Problems in Interpreting Baroque Music' 154
Dooley, Rosemary 216n.41
Dowland, John 107, 149, 161*tab*, 165
Duckles, Vincent 193*tab*
Dufay, Guillaume 86
    'C'est bien raison' 86, 87*fig*
Dunstable (Dunstaple), John 93–94, 161*tab*, 166
Dupré, Desmond 166
Dyce, William 10
Dyer, Louise 195
Dyson, George 98, 120

Earies, Andrew 219
early music 5–6
    British 93–94
    cataloguing 83
    church music 10, 59, 135
    demonstrations 69–70
    English 58, 59, 94
    key-relationships 90
    performance of 110–11, 181

    vocal 4, 86
Early Music Consort 190, 191
East Germany (German Democratic Republic) 168–69
Eastlake, Elizabeth, Lady 40
Écorcheville, Jules 58, 61*fig*
Edgar, Clifford B. 62*fig*
EDI (Equality, Diversity and Inclusion) policies 228
Edinburgh Festival 166
education 14
    see also universities
    Association members, levels of 50, 51
    of music professionals 14, 15
    policies and legislation 147, 225–26
        Butler Education Act (1944) 147
        Education Acts (1870 and 1880) 28
        Education Reform Act (1988) 214
        RAE/REF 213–15, 225–26
        Robbins Report (1963) 198
    schools 28, 214, 228–29
    teaching and training 6–7, 64
Education Acts (1870 and 1880) 28
Education Reform Act (1988) 214
Edwards, F.G. 74
Edwards, Warwick 228, 230*fig*
Ehrlich, Cyril 221–22
Einstein, Alfred 112, 113, 117, 119n.65
Eitner, Robert 3, 31, 93
    Quellen-Lexikon 153
Elgar, Edward 51, 59, 181, 182
Elizabeth II of the United Kingdom 165
Ella, John 21–22
Ellinwood, Leonard 133
Elliott, Kenneth 161*tab*
Ellis, Alexander (A.J.) 7, 33n.4, 37, 77*tab*
    'On the Sensitiveness of the Ear to Pitch and Change of Pitch in Music' 84–85
empire 57
Encyclopaedia Britannica 160–61
Engel, Carl 4, 5*tab*, 7, 36, 50
English Historical Review (journal) 26, 29
English music 57, 58–59, 109–10
    early 58, 59, 94
    folksong 88–89
    harmony 9
    song 4, 6
English Musical Gazette (journal) 15
Equality, Diversity and Inclusion (EDI) policies 228
Erlebach, Rupert 97, 124, 125*fig*, 130–31, 133–34
Ernst, Heinrich Wilhelm 17

ethnomusicology 157, 199, 203, 222, 226
Eton Choirbook 161*tab*, 166
Evans, Edwin 92, 98
Evans, Peter 210–11
Everist, Mark 217, 218
Exeter Hall, Strand, London 16
Eyre & Spottiswoode (publisher) 35

Fallows, David 180, 200*fig*, 204–5, 215n.37, 217, 218, 224
Fauser, Annegret 102
Fedeli, Vito 63*fig*
Felber, Erwin 61*fig*
Fellerer, K.G. 110
Fellowes, Edmund (E.H.) 3, 104, 107, 124, 125, 125*fig*, 139
 death 145
 'John Wilbye' 91
 memorial concert 165
 and Musica Britannica 161*tab*
 RMA president 95, 131, 132–33, 134–37, 135*fig*
Fellowes Memorial Fund 145–46
Ferguson, Howard 141
Festival of Britain (1951) 139, 150, 151–52, 151*fig*, 162–63
Field-Hyde, Margaret 165
Finscher, Ludwig 190
Finzi, Gerald 143, 158, 161*tab*
First World War 48, 65, 97
Fischer, Kurt von 190, 191, 192*tab*
Fiske, Roger 158, 161*tab*
Fleischer, Oskar 54
folksong 88–89
Folk-Song Society 88
Forshaw, John 150
Fortune, Nigel 141, 174*fig*, 194, 234
 Beethoven's sketchbook project 183
 Fellowes Memorial Fund recipient 146
 on Future Development Committee 177
 'Geographical Distribution of RMA members' 188, 189*fig*
 and Musica Britannica 159, 161*tab*
 New Grove, editorial work on 199
 professional background 147, 187
 and RILM project 197
 and RMA publications 177, 187
 RMA Secretary 132, 147, 171, 172, 173, 175–76, 187
 RMA vice-president 188
 RMARC editor 175
Foster and Wills Scholarships 191
Fox, Arthur 92

Fox, Charles 16, 18
Fox Strangways, A.H. 50, 98, 106, 113, 125
Francis, Frank 183
Frere, W.H. 58, 104
 'Key-Relationship in Early Medieval Music' 90
Friedländer, Max 61*fig*
Fuller Maitland, J.A. 58, 62*fig*, 88, 89

Galpin, Canon Francis (F.W.) 3, 58, 62*fig*, 77*tab*, 125
 RMA president 134–35
Garcia, M. 37
Geiringer, Karl 116
gender 69, 85, 205, 226
 of RMA members 40, 50, 71–72, 141
George III of England 14
George IV of England 4, 14
George V of the United Kingdom 57
George VI of the United Kingdom 136–37, 164
German, Edward 51, 59
German Democratic Republic (East Germany) 168–69
Germany 101–2, 108, 110–11, 114, 153
Gevaert, François-Auguste 49
Gibbons, Christopher, *Cupid and Death* 161*tab*, 164, 166
Gipps, Ruth 143
Gladstone, W.H. 50
Glover, Cedric 144, 145n.15, 159n.53, 160
Gluck, C.W. 182
Godfrey, Dan 59
Goehr, Alexander 190, 192*tab*
Golden Age Singers 165, 166
Goldsbrough, Arnold 195
Goldschmidt, Otto 46n.26, 50, 54
Gombosi, Otto 110, 117
Goossens, Eugene 70
Goss, John 33n.4, 37, 50
Gough, Hugh 157
Gramophone (journal) 98
Great Exhibition (1851) 7, 16
Greer, David 194, 216
 Musicology and Sister Disciplines 224
Griesbach, J.H. 33n.4, 37
Grocer's Hall, Prince's Street, London 59
Grove, George 20, 24n.30, 34, 80n.85, 81
 Dictionary of Music and Musicians 12–13, 24, 28, 82, 132, 209
 Macmillan's Magazine, editor of 28–29
 Musical Association, founding of 35–36, 37

Grove Music Online 207–10
Guildhall School of Music and
 Drama 220
Gulbenkian Foundation 159
Gurney, Edmund 28

Haas, Otto 118–19
Hadow, Henry (W.H.) 50, 58
 'The Balance of Expression and Design
 in Music' 69
Halfpenny, Eric 144
Hambourg, Mark 51
Hammerich, Angul 62*fig*
Handel, George Frideric 10, 12
 anniversary celebrations
 (1959) 168–69
 anniversary celebrations (1985) 220
 biography 6
Handel Society 10, 12
Handel's Conducting Score of Messiah
 (facsimile edition) 190–91
Handschin, Jacques 110
Harding, Rosamond 105
Harewood, George Lascelles, 7th Earl
 of 143
Harmonicon (journal) 15
harmony 9, 74, 77–79*tab*, 90, 91, 182
Harrison, Frank Ll. 161*tab*, 184, 185, 186
Harrison, May 132
Hase, Oskar von 63*fig*, 65, 66
Häusler, Rudolf 190
Haweis, R. 36, 37
Haydn, Joseph 15, 92, 116, 192*tab*
 complete works (*Gesamtausgaben*) 153
 in Hirsch Library 119, 122
Haydon, Glen 133
Heartz, Daniel 181–82, 190, 192*tab*
Heath, Edward 173
Helmholtz, Anna von 52
Helmholtz, Hermann von 34, 49, 52
 Lehre von den Tonempfindungen 7
Helmore, T. 33n.4, 37
Henle, Günter 153
Hennerberg, Carl 61*fig*
Herbage, Julian 143, 161*tab*
Hertzka, Emil 61*fig*
Heseltine, Philip (Peter Warlock) 70
Hess, Myra 59, 120, 143
Higgs, James 44n.25
higher education *see* disciplines,
 academic; universities
Hill, Richard S. 133
Hinrichsen, Max 143
Hinrichsen Foundation 194
Hipkins, Alfred (A.J.) 7, 70

'The Old Clavier' 85–86
Hirsch, Paul 82n.90, 117, 118–20
Historical Manuscripts Commission 24
Hogg, Katharine 220
Hogwood, Christopher 220
Holbrooke, Joseph 58
Holmes, Edward 5*tab*, 17
 The Life of Mozart 6
Holst, Gustav 104, 192*tab*
 'The Tercentenary of Byrd and
 Weelkes' 94
Holst, Imogen 190, 192*tab*
Holtzbrinck (publisher), *Grove Music
 Online* 207–10
Hopkins, E. J. 9, 36, 37
Hopkinson, Cecil 118
Horn, C.F. 5, 5*tab*
Horsley, C.E. 19
Horsley, William 9, 19–20
Howells, Herbert 132
Howes, Frank 125, 198n.76, 234
 BIRS, support for 154
 and Music & Letters Trust 160
 and Musica Britannica 152, 162–63,
 164–65, 166
 professional background 98, 121, 146,
 153n.33
 RMA president 139, 151n.29, 167, 173
Howes Fund 218n.45
Howsam, Leslie 29n.37
Huddersfield Choral Society 59, 64
Hueffer, Francis 4, 5*tab*, 7, 50
Hughes, Anselm 110, 125
Hughes, Margaret Watts 78*tab*
 'Voice Figures' 71–72
Hullah, John 5*tab*, 6–7, 18*fig*, 68n.68, 229
 Musical Association, founding of 36,
 37, 40
 Musical Institute, president of xxiv,
 17–18, 19
Hunt, Edgar 143, 157

IAML *see* International Association of
 Music Libraries
IGMw *see* International Society for
 Musical Research
IMG *see* Internationale Musikgesellschaft
Imperial College, University of
 London 224
Imperial Institute, University of
 London 56
imperialism 57
IMS *see* International Musicological
 Society
Indian music 90–91

Indy, Vincent d' 50
information technology 207–10, 212–13, 219
Institute of Musical Research 228
instruments
   collections of 17, 134, 236
   design and construction 4, 7, 25
   early 69–70, 85–86
   in Grove dictionaries 201, 205, 209
   keyboard 85–86
   lute 89
   non-Western 134
   research papers on 74, 76–79*tab*, 157
International Association of Music Libraries (IAML) 83, 153n.35, 188, 213, 227
International Folk Music Council 222
International Musicological Society (IMS) 66, 83, 146, 152–53
   see also Répertoire International des Sources Musicales
   Sixth International Congress (1955) 152–53
   Sixteenth International Congress (1997) 203, 224–25
International Repertory of Music Literature (Répertoire International de Littérature Musicale, RILM) 197
International Society for Contemporary Music (ISCM) 100–101, 115
   London conference (1938) 128, 130
International Society for Musical Research (ISMR; also IGMw, SIM) 66, 100–102
   1930 Congress, Liège 110–11, 112
   1933 Congress, Cambridge 109–13, 117–18
   1936 Congress, Barcelona 113–15
   1949 Congress, Basel 115
Internationale Musikgesellschaft (IMG) 32, 47, 54–66, 100
   1909 Congress, Vienna 55
   1911 Congress, London 54, 55–65
      concerts 57–59
      funding of 56–57
      research papers 58
   1914 Congress, Paris 65
   dissolution 65–66, 115–16
   English Committee 54–56
   Sammelbände der Internationalen Musikgesellschaft (SIMG) 55, 74, 93, 102, 103, 187
   Zeitschrift der Internationalen Musikgesellschaft (ZIMG) 55, 74, 187
internationalism 101–2, 111–12, 128, 199
Ireland
   IMG branch 54, 55, 66
   Maynooth International Musicological Conference (1995) 223–24
   Society for Musicology in Ireland 219, 228
Irish music 4–5
Irving, John 236
ISCM *see* International Society for Contemporary Music
ISMR *see* International Society for Musical Research
Italian music 5, 91–92, 103, 105, 192*tab*, 220

J. & W. Chester (publisher) 98
Jacobs, Ian 204n.3
Jahn, Otto 6
Jaques-Dalcroze, Emile 67
Jarman, Freya 217
Jenkins, John 109
Jeppesen, Knud 112, 113–15
Jerome Roche Prize 226, 249–50
Joachim, Joseph 17
Johnson, Marshall 171
Johnstone, Harry Diack 220, 235
Jones, Edward (Bardd y Brenin) 4, 5*tab*
   The Bardic Museum 4
   Hên ganiadau Cymru 4
   The Musical and Poetical Relicks of the Welsh Bards 4
Jones, J. Winter 80
Joseph Haydn-Institut, Cologne 153
Joubert, John, 'Crabbed Age and Youth' 190
Journal of the English Folk Dance and Song Society 98
Journal of the Royal Musical Association 178, 203, 216–17, 217*fig*, 227, 242–43
Judaism 50

Kafka, J.N. 183
Kanno, Mieko 230*fig*
Kapp, Edmond X., *Professor E.J. Dent* 108*fig*
Kastner, Alfred 70
KCL (King's College London) 6, 184, 187, 198, 200*fig*, 220
Keefe, Simon 218
Kelly, Barbara 229, 230*fig*
Kenyon, Nicholas 220, 234
Kerman, Joseph 182–86, 190
   'Beethoven Sketchbooks in the British Museum' 182–84

Musicology 204, 210–11, 233
key relationships 90
Kidson, Frank 71, 104
   'The Vitality of Melody' 88–89
King, Alec Hyatt 157, 188, 192*tab*, 197, 234
   'The Musical Institute of London and its Successors' 16n.20
   PRMA editor 144, 156
   professional background 121, 122, 132, 143
   and RILM project 197
   at RMA Centenary 190
   RMA president 172, 194
   and sound recording archives 154
   and source cataloguing 153
   on UK RISM committee 196
King's College London *see* KCL
Kinkeldey, Otto 62*fig*, 110, 112
Klopstock, B. 176
Koninklijke Vereniging voor Nederlandse Muziekgeschiedenis (KVNM) 16, 229, 230*fig*
Kraus, Baron Alexander 62*fig*
Kraus Reprint (publisher) 176
Kretzschmar, Hermann 50, 62*fig*, 64, 66
Kunst, Jaap 116
KVNM *see* Koninklijke Vereniging voor Nederlandse Muziekgeschiedenis

La Laurencie, Lionel de 61*fig*
Lacy, Michael Rophino 6n.6
Landon, H.C. Robbins 153
Langley, Leanne 206*fig*
Larsen, Jens Peter (J.P.) 153, 154, 190
LaRue, Jan 158–59
Latham, Morton 50
laudi collections 91–92
Launis, Armas 61*fig*
Lawes, William 109
Le Huray Memorial Lectures 224, 249
le Huray, Peter 224
learned societies xi, 31–32
   RMA, influence on 41–42, 49, 72
legislation
   Butler Education Act (1944) 147
   Education Acts (1870 and 1880) 28
   Education Reform Act (1988) 214
   Public Record Office Act (1838) 24
Leichtentritt, Hugo 61*fig*, 67
Lemare, Edwin 70
Leo Liepmannssohn (music and antiquarian dealer) 118
Leslie, Henry 28
Lesure, François 190
Levien, Mewburn 150

Levin & Munksgaard (publisher) 114
Lewis, Anthony 167*fig*, 168–69, 234
   Beethoven sketchbook project 183
   Dent Medal, proposed by 146
   invited to join Research Committee 131
   and Musica Britannica 126n.80, 151–52, 160, 161*tab*, 162, 166, 174
   professional background 139, 148–49
   and Purcell Society 159
   and RILM project 197
   RMA president 172, 177
libraries
   see also British Library
   access to 213
   Association's campaigns for 75–83, 85, 93
   of British Museum 80–81
   cataloguing 82–83, 122
   Hirsch Library 117–22
   of Musical Institute 17, 18
   of Musical Society of London 20
   of Musical Union Institute 22
   Pierpont Morgan Library 182
   planned 15, 23
   private 82
   of RMA 122–24, 123*fig*, 187
   Senate House Library 187
Lidgey, Charles 88
Lineff, Eugénie 62*fig*
Linnean Society 43
listening 84–85, 86, 89
Littleton, Alfred H. 45, 57, 62*fig*
Liverpool University 148
Livery Hall, Goldsmiths' Company, London 165
Locke, Matthew, *Cupid and Death* 161*tab*, 164, 166
Lockwood, Lewis 184, 185, 187, 190, 192*tab*
Lockyer, Norman 28
Loewenberg, Alfred 133–34
Loges, Natasha 238
London
   see also University of London
   Aeolian Hall 58, 59
   Beethoven Rooms, 27 Harley Street, Cavendish Square 41
   Crystal Palace 16, 17, 18
   Edwards Street, Portman Square 20, 22*fig*
   Exeter Hall, Strand 16
   Grocer's Hall, Prince's Street 59
   Guildhall School of Music and Drama 220

London (cont'd)
  Holborn Restaurant, Kingsway 53
  Houses of Parliament 59
  Livery Hall, Goldsmiths'
    Company 165
  Lyceum Club 58
  Queen Elizabeth Hall 224
  Queen's Hall 58, 59, 150
  Regent Street 17
  Royal Albert Hall 35
  Royal Festival Hall 150, 151*fig*, 162
  Sackville Street 17
  Savoy Hotel 59
  Senate House Library 187
  South Bank 150, 151*fig*, 220
  St James's Hall 18–19, 20–22
  Westminster Cathedral 59
London, Malcolm 195, 227
London Academy of Music and Dramatic
  Art (LAMDA) 19
London County Council 150
London Society 150
London Symphony Orchestra 59, 64
Long, Kathleen 143
Longman, C.J. 28
Longmans (publisher) 26, 29
Lowinsky, Edward E. 179–80, 184, 185
Lucas, Charles 9, 17
Ludwig, Friedrich 61*fig*

MacBain, Mrs J. Murray 51
MacDonald, Hugh 193*tab*, 215n.37
Macfarren, G.A. 9, 10, 20, 36, 37, 50
Macfarren, George (senior) 10
Mackenzie, Alexander (A.C.) 47n.27,
    51, 66
  and IMG London Congress (1911) 57,
    58, 62*fig*, 64, 65
Mackenzie, Compton 98
Maclean, Charles 45–46, 54, 74, 90, 93
  and IMG 55, 65–66, 115–16
  and IMG London Congress (1911) 57,
    62*fig*
  Papers Subcommittee, objects
    to 68–69
Macmillan, Alexander 28
Macmillan & Co. (publisher) 28–29,
    218n.46
  Grove's *Dictionary of Music and
    Musicians* 12–13, 24, 28, 209
    prospectus, publication of 35–36
    revisions and editions 82, 132, 200
  *New Grove Dictionary of Music and
    Musicians* 187, 199–200, 204–10
    companion dictionaries 205–6
    New Grove 2 206–10

  *New Grove Dictionary of
    Opera* 205–6, 206*fig*
Macmillan's Magazine (journal) 28–29
Macy, Laura 209
Maczewski, Alfred 12
madrigals 91, 111, 185
Maggs Bros. (antiquarian dealer) 118
Maitland, J.A. Fuller 58, 62*fig*, 88, 89
Mann, Maud (Maud MacCarthy),
  'Some Indian Conceptions of
  Music' 90–91
Marchant, Stanley 120
Margarita M. Hanson Award 228
Marshall, Julian 12
Martin, George 58
Mary, Queen consort of the United
  Kingdom 57
Masson, Paul-Marie 110
Matania, Fortunino 81*fig*
Matthew, James E. 104
  music library of 82, 118
Maxwell, James Clerk 34
May, John 185
Mayer, Robert 144
Maynooth International Musicological
  Conference (1995) 223–24
McInnes, James Campbell 88
McKenna, David 173, 177
McKibbin, Ross 143n.9, 147–48
McNaught, W.G. 57, 61*fig*, 64, 73, 78*tab*
McVeagh, Diana 218n.45, 234
McVeigh, Simon 230*fig*
Medieval-Renaissance conferences 188,
    216
Mellers, Wilfrid 187
Mellon, Alfred 19, 21
melody 88–89
Menchaca, Angel 61*fig*
Mendel, Arthur 193*tab*
Mendelssohn, Felix 10
Meyer, Ernst Hermann 110, 117, 125,
    130
Meyer, Kathi 117–18
Meyerbeer, Giacomo 17
Mills, T. Wesley 62*fig*
Milsom, John 220
misogyny 84n.94, 178, 179*fig*
ML see *Music & Letters*
Molique, Bernhard 20
Monk, W.H. 37
Morris, R.O. 124, 130
Morrison, Stanley 136
Morton, Eva 144–45
Moscheles, Ignaz 17
Moser, Claus 198n.75
Motett Society 10

Mozart, Wolfgang Amadeus   92, 107, 119, 122, 192*tab*
    biography   6
    blue plaque   221*fig*
    in Hirsch Library   122
    Mozart Bicentenary Conference (1991)   220–21
MSL *see* Musical Society of London
Muir, Percy   118
Mulgan, Anthony   160
Mulliner Book   161*tab*, 162, 164, 166
Music & Letters (*ML*, journal)   98, 103, 106, 140, 159–60, 173
music administrators   143
music clubs   13–22
    internal politics   18–19
    membership numbers   17, 19
    Musical Institute   14, 15–19, 24, 37
    Musical Society of London (MSL)   14, 19–21, 22*fig*, 37
    Musical Union Institute   14, 21–22
    Royal Academy of Music (1813)   14–15
music editions   9
    see also Musica Britannica
    complete works (*Gesamtausgaben*)   119
    Purcell   159
music profession, control of entry to   14, 15
music publishing societies   8–13
    Handel Society   10, 12
    Motett Society   10
    Musical Antiquarian Society   9–10, 11*fig*
    Percy Society   9
music research
    Association investigations into   124–31, 125*fig*
    Association's fundraising for   139
    audiences for   13, 28–29, 98–99
    British   xii–xiii, 232–35
    critique of   89–90
    culture of   117
    directions in   134–35, 179–84, 222
    funding of   145–46, 204, 213–15
    inter/multidisciplinarity in   225
    interwar   116–32
    journals publishing   98
    national approaches to   111, 115–16
    nineteenth-century   2–8, 15–19
    performance culture, connection to   13–14, 103–4, 111
    post-war   139–40, 148–49
    PRMA contributions to   157–58
    social benefits of   104–5, 127–28, 130
    specialization   204
    value of   169

music sources
    access to   3, 5, 29
    BIRS (later National Sound Archive)   153–55
    cataloguing   82–83, 153, 196–98, 213
    collections   152–55
    publication of   8–13
    referencing of   73
Music Teachers' National Association, USA   31
Musica Britannica (MB) series   160–66, 161*tab*, 163*fig*, 167*fig*, 220
    Arts Council funding and support   152, 163–64, 165, 174
    financial success of   195
    launch event (1951)   163–64
    performances   163–64, 165–66
    proposal   139, 151–52
    title   160–62
Musica Britannica Trust   195–96
Musical Antiquarian Society   9–10, 11*fig*
Musical Antiquary (journal)   98, 103
Musical Association *see* ROYAL MUSICAL ASSOCIATION
Musical Institute   14, 15–19, 24, 37
Musical Quarterly (journal)   103, 173
Musical Society of London (MSL)   14, 19–21, 22*fig*, 37
Musical Times (journal)   93, 98, 162
Musical Union Institute   14, 21–22
Musical World (journal)   16–17
musicology   1, 97, 223–25
    British   xi, xiii–xiv, 232–35
    vs. American   171, 172, 184–87, 210–11
    character of   103
    Grove/New Grove's impact on   201, 204–5, 209–10
    Hirsch Library's impact on   119–20
    importance of BBC classical music programming to   167
    interwar development of   97, 99
    post-war development of   147, 148–49, 157–58, 234
    ethnomusicology   157, 199, 203, 222, 226
    expansion of   203, 214–15
    information technology's impact on   212–13
    inter/multidisciplinarity in   225
    internationalized   191, 199–200
    vs. musical research   xii
    positivist, criticism of   210–11, 233
    PRMA contributions to   157–58
    specialization   211–12, 228, 233
    status of   200–201

Nash, John   14
nationalism   110
nationality, of RMA members   50, 51
Nature (journal)   28
Neate, Charles   17
Neighbour, Oliver   143, 187, 213
NEMS (Network of European Music Societies)   229
Nettel, Reginald   158
Network of European Music Societies (NEMS)   229
New Grove Dictionary of Music and Musicians   187, 199–200, 204–10, 206*fig*
see also *Dictionary of Music and Musicians* (Grove); *Grove Music Online*
companion dictionaries   205–6
New Grove 2   206–10
New Grove Dictionary of Opera   205–6
New Oxford History of Music   173
New Philharmonic Society (NPS)   16, 17, 18, 19
Newmarch, Rosa   51, 57n.49, 71
'The Development of National Opera in Russia'   69, 86, 88
The Russian Opera   88
Nicholson, E.W.B.   86
Niecks, F.   50
Nineteenth-Century Music Conference   188, 190, 216
Noble, Jeremy   141, 175
Norlind, Tobias   61*fig*
notation   6, 32, 74, 79*tab*, 92–93, 130
Notes (journal)   173
Nottebohm, Gustav   183n.40
Novello & Co. (publisher)   10, 45, 72, 159
IMG London Congress (1911), support for   56–57, 58
Novello, Ewer & Co. (publisher)   28
Novello, Vincent   4, 5, 5*tab*

Oakeley, H.S.   36, 37
Observer (newspaper)   168–69
Old Hall MS   181
Oldman, Cecil (C. B.)   197, 234
A.H. King nominated by   119n.66
Egon Wellesz's Honorary membership, reinstatement of   145
memorial fund   195
'Mozart and Modern Research'   107
Parry Room Library, bookcase donated to   123n.73
Proceedings Group, head of   144
professional background   143

on Research Committee   124, 130–32
and source cataloguing   153
on UK RISM committee   196
Oliphant, Thomas   24
Olleson, Edward   187, 191, 192–93*tab*, 194, 197
Modern Musical Scholarship   191, 193*tab*
opera   86, 88, 105, 181–82, 205–6
Opienski, Henryk   63*fig*
Ord, Boris   141, 144
Osborne, G.A.   20
Osmond-Smith, David   217n.43
Ouseley, Frederick A. Gore   4, 5*tab*, 20, 36, 191n.61
Musical Association president   38*fig*, 41
NPS vice-president   17
professional background   7–8, 27, 33, 50
Oxenbury, William   187, 195, 200*fig*
Oxford International Symposium, 'Modern Musicology and the Historical Tradition of Scholarship' (1977)   191, 193*tab*
Oxford University   26, 27, 112, 148–49, 184
Oxford University Press (OUP)   160, 207, 208–9, 216

Pace, Ian   215n.37
Page, Christopher   211
Palisca, Claude V.   193*tab*
Palmer, Fiona M.   237
Panizzi, Anthony   24
Parry, Hubert   86, 89, 92, 99–100
and IMG London Congress (1911)   58, 62*fig*, 64–65
Musical Association president   48, 96
Musical Association vice-president   44
Pascall, Robert   188, 215n.37
Pauer, Ernst   4, 5*tab*, 8
Pazdírek, Franz   62*fig*
Penrose, Roger   224
Percy Society   9
performance   15, 143, 211, 222
of early music   110–11, 181
historical study of   199
performance culture
music research, connection with   13–14, 103–4, 111
Musical Association's disconnection from   22–29
performance venues   58, 59, 149–50
Aeolian Hall   58, 59

INDEX

Exeter Hall, Strand   16
Grocer's Hall, Prince's Street   59
Livery Hall, Goldsmiths'
    Company   165
Queen Elizabeth Hall   224
Queen's Hall   58, 59, 150
Royal Albert Hall   35
Royal Festival Hall   150, 151*fig*, 162
St James's Hall   18–19, 20–22
Peter Gibbs String Quartet   164
Peto, Morton   16
Petrobelli, Pierluigi   226
Philharmonic Society of London   14, 40n.16
Phillips, Bruce   208n.15
Phonographic Performance Ltd (PPL)   176
Picken, Laurence   143, 157
Pierpont Morgan Library   182
Pilgrim Trust   121
Pirro, André   112
pitch
    concert   7
    human perception of   77*tab*, 78*tab*, 84–85
pitch systems   4, 7, 78*tab*, 90
Plainsong and Mediaeval Music Society   98
Pole, William   5*tab*, 43, 50, 229
    'On the graphic method of representing musical intervals'   78*tab*
    MSL member   20, 21
    Musical Association, founding of   32–37
    professional background   7, 8
political contexts   234
    Attlee Labour government (1945-51)   139
    Blair Labour government (1997)   225
    Board of Trade   35, 47
    chartism   6
    education policies   28, 147, 198, 213–15, 225–26
    international   101–2
    Nazism   108, 110–11, 114
    Thatcher Conservative government (1979-90)   213
    wartime Coalition government   147
Pontigny, Victor de   50
Poole, Mrs Reginald Lane   51
Porter, Andrew   141, 206n.9, 218n.45, 234
    professional background   143
    RMA publications, work on   177, 183, 190
    'Seeing the Stars Again',   210–11

positivism, in musicology   210–11
practice research   228
Practice Research Prize   228, 250
Pratt, Waldo Selden   52
Preece, Isobel   219
Price, Curtis   199, 210–11
Proceedings of the (Royal) Musical Association   72–75, 84–94
    abstracts   74, 197
    backstock, republication of   176–77
    Centenary issue   190
    circulation numbers   73, 156–57
    costs   178, 187, 194
    design   144, 145*fig*
    editorial processes   72–75
    editors   134, 144, 156, 194, 242
    footnotes and referencing   73
    at founding   43–44
    indexes   74–75, 123–24, 131, 133–34, 178
    marketing   144, 187
    membership records in   37
    music examples in   73–74
    music journals, compared to   98
    printing of   45
    replacement of   216
    reputation of   155
    reputational value of   72
    research direction of   179–84
    scholarship, quality of   84n.94, 98, 180–81
    subject range   32, 84
    scientific   76–79*tab*
    papers
        'Again, What is Sound?' (Audsley)   84n.94
        'Beethoven Sketchbooks in the British Museum' (Kerman)   183–84
        'Centenary Essays'   190–91, 192*tab*
        'Classicism and False Values' (Clutsam)   92
        'On the Collecting of English Folk-Song' (Broadwood)   88
        'The Development of National Opera in Russia' (Newmarch)   86, 88
        'Elgar's Enigma' (Westrup)   182
        'The English Chapel Royal before 1300' (Bent)   178
        'A Fifteenth Century MS. Book of Vocal Music in the Bodleian Library, Oxford' (Stainer)   86
        'The Formation of a National Musical Library' (Cummings)   85
        'From Garrick to Gluck' (Heartz)   182

272   INDEX

Proceedings of the (Royal) Musical Association, papers (cont'd)
'The Genius of Dunstable' (Van den Borren)   67, 93–94
'John Wilbye' (Fellowes)   91
'Key-Relationship in Early Medieval Music' (Frere)   90
'The Laudi Spirituali in the XVIth and XVIIth Centuries' (Dent)   91–92, 103
'Lute Music of the XVIth and XVIIth Centuries' (Dodge)   71, 89
'The Making of "Don Carlos"' (Porter)   182
'Modern Harmonic Tendencies' (Browne)   91
'MS 1070 of the Royal College of Music in London' (Lowinsky)   180
'Musical Libraries and Catalogues' (Squire)   82, 93
'Musical Taste and Concert Hall Design' (Bagenal)   150
'The Old Clavier' (Hipkins)   85–86
'Our First Hundred Years' (Abraham)   34n.6
'The Point of Perfection in XVI Century Notation' (Warner)   92–93
'The Reminiscences of a Quinquagenarian' (Shaw)   89–90
'On the Sensitiveness of the Ear to Pitch and Change of Pitch in Music' (Ellis)   84–85
'Some Indian Conceptions of Music' (Mann)   78*tab*, 90–91
'Sources of the Old Hall Music' (M. Bent)   181
'Stages in the Composition of Beethoven's Piano Trio Op. 70, No. 1' (Tyson)   182
'The Study of Britten' (Whittall)   182
'Toward the Revival of the Classical Orchestra' (Zaslaw)   181
'The Vitality of Melody' (Kidson)   88–89
'Women and Music' (Swinburne)   84n.94
'Women in Relation to Musical Art' (Stratton)   85
Prod'homme, J.G.   61*fig*
professionalization
 of musicology   8, 97, 139, 173, 233
 of research   23–24
Prunières, Henry   63*fig*

Public Record Office Act (1838)   24
Pulver, Jeffrey   110
Purcell, Henry   5, 157, 168–69
Purcell Society   140, 159
Purcell Tercentenary Conference (1995)   220

Queen Elizabeth Hall, London   224
Queen's College, London   17
Queen's Hall, London   58, 59, 150
Quittard, Henri   62*fig*

Radcliffe, Philip   105, 110, 141
RAM *see* Royal Academy of Music
Randegger, A.   50
Rayleigh, John William Strutt, 3rd Baron   35, 36, 37, 50, 79*tab*
RCM *see* Royal College of Music (RCM)
Reaney, Gilbert   146, 157
Redlich, Hans   143
Reese, Gustave   133, 190
Reeser, Eduard   190, 191
Répertoire International de Littérature Musicale (RILM)   197
Répertoire International des Sources Musicales (International Inventory of Musical Sources, RISM)   83, 153, 196–98, 213
Report of the Fourth Congress of the International Musical Society   56
Research Chronicle see Royal Musical Association Research Chronicle
research culture   99
Research Excellence Framework (REF, formerly Research Assessment Exercise, RAE)   213–15, 223, 225–26, 228
research methods   75, 85, 104, 106, 210–11
research papers
 see also ROYAL MUSICAL ASSOCIATION: research papers
 of Musical Institute   17
 of Musical Society of London   21
researchers, independent   143
rhythm   93, 105
Riemann, Hugo   49–50
Rifkin, Joshua   180
RILM *see* International Repertory of Music Literature
Rimbault, Edward F.   4, 5*tab*, 9–10, 19
Rimmer, Joan   178
RISM *see* Répertoire International des Sources Musicales
RISM (UK) Trust   197
Ritchie, Margaret   164

RMA *see* ROYAL MUSICAL
    ASSOCIATION
RMA Monographs   203, 217–18, 243
*RMARC see Royal Musical Association
    Research Chronicle*
Robertson, Duncan   166
Roche, Jerome   217, 219n.48
Roda, Cecilio de   61*fig*
Romano, G.   50
Romanticism   107–8
Rootham, Cyril   58, 64
Rosa, Carl   40–41
Rossini, Gioachino   17
Rossini Day (1992)   220
Routledge (publisher)   217, 227
Royal Academy of Arts   14
Royal Academy of Music (1813)   14–15
Royal Academy of Music (RAM)   14, 45, 109–10, 145–46, 203
Royal Albert Hall   35
Royal College of Music (RCM)   27, 45, 96, 203, 224
    Parry Room Library   123, 123*fig*
Royal College of Organists   45
Royal Festival Hall, London   150, 151*fig*, 162
Royal Holloway, University of London   197
Royal Institution   5, 35
Royal Musical Association Research Chronicle (RMARC)   139, 156, 174–75, 178, 243
ROYAL MUSICAL ASSOCIATION (RMA)
    see also *Journal of the Royal Musical Association*; *Proceedings of the (Royal) Musical Association*
    achievements   xii, 74, 231–38
    advocacy   83, 139, 167–69, 214–15, 225–26
    archives   xiv, 132, 173, 225, 251
    Centenary (1974)   190–91
    criticism of   171–72
    displaced scholars, support for   112–13, 117–19, 133–34, 228
    founding   xi, xii, 1–2, 32–41
    identity   xii, 41, 53, 73, 143, 227
    influence   159–60, 169, 191, 226
    Library   122–24, 123*fig*, 187, 243
    music commissioned by   190
    reputation   84, 98, 180
    Royal prefix, achievement of   136–37, 141
    administration and organization
        see also meetings; membership; officers; session planning
        committee   38*fig*
        legal incorporation   47–48
        marketing and promotion   41, 49, 99, 106, 133, 173
            by abstracts   74, 75*fig*
        Memorandum and Articles of Association   47–48, 141–42, 152
        regional chapters   187–88, 190, 219
        rules   37, 41–48
        Standing Instruction Book record book   45–47
        website   219
    awards and honours
        Dent Medal   146–47, 182n.33, 183n.34, 197, 211, 247–48
        Fellowes Memorial Fund   145–46
        Howes Fund   218n.45
        Jerome Roche Prize   226, 249–50
        Le Huray Memorial Lectures   224, 249
        Margarita M. Hanson Award   228
        Practice Research Prize   228, 250
        Tippett Medal   228, 250
    collaborations   140, 216, 229
        with British Museum   183
        on conferences   222–23
        financial support   140, 159–60
        with IMG   54–66
        with IMS   153, 197–98
        international   54–67, 109–16, 196–98
        with Joseph Haydn-Institut, Cologne   153
        with RISM   153, 196–98
    Council   40–41, 168–69, 227
        attendance at   99
        diversity of   228
        elections and appointments to   44–45, 141–42
        meeting venues   45
        Minutes   33, 37
            circulation of   144
        organization of   44–45
        subcommittees   150
            for Beethoven sketchbook project   183
            Future Development Committee   177
            libraries and catalogues   82–83
            on English music editions   152
            on music research   124–31, 125*fig*
            Papers Subcommittee   68–69, 155
            Proceedings Committee   140, 144, 194, 216
            Research Committee   117, 130–32
            working groups   225–26

ROYAL MUSICAL ASSOCIATION
(RMA) (cont'd)
  events and conferences 177, 190–91,
    203, 216, 220–25
    Annual Conferences 53–54, 194,
      221–23, 227–28, 229
      'British Musicology Conference'
        (1996) 222
      'Music and Film' (2001) 222
      'Music and Rhetoric' (1989) 222
      'Music in the Market-Place'
        (1988) 221–22
      'Performance' (2000) 222
      'The Theory and Practice
        of Musical Biography'
        (2001) 222–23
    Annual Dinners 53, 116
    concerts 190
    fees 223
    Handel Tercentenary Festival
      (1985) 220
    ISMR Congress, Cambridge (1933),
      reception for 109–10
    Medieval-Renaissance
      conferences 188, 216
    Mozart Bicentenary Conference
      (1991) 220–21
    Nineteenth-Century Music
      Conference 188, 190, 216
    number of 228
    Sixteenth International Congress of
      IMS, London (1997) 224–25
    social events 51–54
    Society for Music Analysis joint
      conference (1993) 222, 223
    student conferences 177, 216, 218
    study days 220
    'Third Triennial British
      Musicological Societies
      Conference' (1999) 222
  finances xi–xii, 48–49, 50, 175–76,
    227
    Centenary celebrations, impact
      on 191
    charitable status 143
    deficits 194
    fundraising 120–21, 139, 224
    grant funding received 194, 196
    legacy funds, disbursement of 195
    speakers' fees and expenses 70–71,
      171, 179–80
  meetings
    Annual General Meetings
      (AGMs) 44, 72, 74, 75fig,
      142–43, 144n.12, 223

    attendance at 41, 52, 71, 99, 142, 144,
      188, 191
    Extraordinary General
      Meetings 142
    lecture meetings 144
    meeting venues 40–41, 45, 187
    number of 99
    paper meetings
      attendance at 52, 71, 188
      locations 45
      number of 44, 99
      promotion of 49
      regional 188
    Research Students' Day 219–20
    revision of 216, 219
    sound recordings 154
    students, free for 105–6
  membership 31–32, 218–19
    administration of 227
    diversity of 41–44, 50–51, 141
    educational background 50–51, 141
    geographical location of 50, 51, 141,
      189fig
    Honorary Foreign Members 49–50,
      112–16, 133, 145, 153, 191, 226,
      245–46
    Honorary Members 246
    invited members 133
    Life Membership 49, 50, 142,
      144–45
    lists/databases 219, 226
    numbers
      interwar 48–49, 95, 133
      post-Second World War 140–41
      1960s 173–74
      1970s 188, 189fig
      late 20th/21st century 218
      maximum 142
    occupations 50–51, 143–44
    Original (founding) 7–8, 37,
      38–40fig
    resignations 164–65
    rules 44
    scientists 33, 50, 51
    selection of 37
    spouses 187
    students 149, 174, 177, 187, 199, 218,
      219
    women 40, 50–51, 71–72, 141
  mission 231–32
    founding 41–48
    interwar 96
    post-Second World War 139–40,
      143
    1960s 173–74

INDEX

late 20th century   203–4
21st century   225–30
officers   38*fig*, 41, 44
  continuity in   139
  elections and appointments
    to   141–42
  Membership Administrator   227
  President   239
    Abraham, Gerald   172, 187–88
    Arnold, Denis   172, 194, 201
    Buck, Percy   95, 116–17, 124
    Dent, Edward J.   95, 97, 99–116, 234
    Fellowes, Edmund (E.H.)   95, 131–33, 134–37, 135*fig*
    Galpin, Canon Francis (F.W.)   134–35
    Howes, Frank   139, 151n.29, 167, 173
    King, Alec Hyatt   172, 194
    Lewis, Anthony   172, 177
    Ouseley, Frederick A. Gore   38*fig*, 41
    Parry, Hubert   48, 96
    Rushton, Julian   224, 226
    Sadie, Stanley   209
    Stainer, John   68
    Westrup, Jack (J.A.)   168, 172, 173, 176
  Secretary   46–47, 142n.6, 241
    Baker, J. Percy   46n.26, 49, 68–69, 95
    Cobbe, Hugh   194, 213
    Dooley, Rosemary   216n.41
    Erlebach, Rupert   97, 144, 147
    Fortune, Nigel   132, 147, 171, 172, 173, 175–76, 187
    Higgs, James   44n.25
    Phillips, Bruce   208n.15
    Salaman, Charles (C.K.)   41, 68
    Stock, Jonathan   226
    Turner, Malcolm   194, 213
  Student Liaison Officer   220
  Treasurer   44, 173, 176, 241–42
    Chappell, S. Arthur   41
    Glover, Cedric   145n.15, 159n.53, 160
    London, Malcolm   195, 227
    McKenna, David   173, 177
    Watkins, Cedric   183
  turnover in   96–97
publishing   155–66, 187, 190–91
  Musica Britannica (MB) series   132, 139, 151–52
  Newsletter   219, 226

RMA Monographs   203, 217–18, 243
research papers   66–83, 84–94
  audiences for   37, 52
  feedback on   106–7
  focus on   41–44
  international contributions   66–67, 116
  languages, published in   55
  publication of   42–43, 71–75
  scholarship, quality of   67, 98–99, 106–9, 116, 226, 234–35
  selection of   68–69, 155–56, 171–72
  subject range   31–32, 41, 44, 66–67, 69, 74–75
  supply and commissioning   66–70, 105–6, 132–33
  by women   69, 71–72
  younger researchers, support for   105–6, 117
session planning   44, 45, 49, 68–69, 194
  reviews of   177, 194, 225
  subcommittees for   131, 140
subscriptions
  administration of   44, 227
  rates   42, 73n.81, 99, 140
  rates, increase of   142, 178, 187
  reliance on income from   48–49, 140
  reminders   46, 106
  types of   133, 144–45
Royal Society   25, 34, 35, 51
Rubinstein, Anton   70
Rushton, Julian   188, 219n.48, 224, 226
Russell, Raymond   143
Russian music   69, 86, 88
RVW Trust   159

Sachs, Curt   62*fig*
Sadie, Stanley   158, 206*fig*, 234
  Handel and Mozart conferences   220–21
  IMS president   224
  New Grove Dictionary of Music and Musicians   187, 199–200, 204–10
  RMA president   209
  Wolfgang Amadè Mozart   221
Saint-Saëns, Camille   50
Salaman, Charles (C.K.)   20*fig*
  MSL Secretary   19, 21
  Musical Association, founding of   33, 34n.6, 37
  Musical Association Secretary   41, 68
  and Musical Institute   17
Salmen, Walter   193*tab*

Salomon, J.P.   15
Saltire Singers   166
Sammelbände der Internationalen Musikgesellschaft (*SIMG*, journal)   55, 74, 93, 102, 103, 187
Sandberger, Adolf   61*fig*
Santley, Charles   20
Sargent, John Singer   69
Saul, Patrick   153–54
Scarlatti, Alessandro   103
Scarlatti, Domenico   157
Scheurleer, D.F.   61*fig*, 66, 102n.17
Schlesinger, Kathleen   62*fig*
Schmidt, Thomas   180
Schnapper, Edith B.   82–83, 196
Schoelcher, Victor   4, 5*tab*, 21
   The Life of Handel   6
Schoenberg, Arnold   91, 192*tab*
Scholes, Percy   110
School of Advanced Study, University of London   228
Schreck, Gustav   63*fig*
Schubert, Franz   12, 122
Schünemann, Georg   63*fig*
Schweitzer, Albert   145
science research   26–27
scientific institutions   23
Scott, Charles Kennedy   125, 127
Scott, Marion   124, 134, 156
Scottish music   161*tab*
Second World War   132–37
Seeger, Charles   191, 194
Segal, Rachel   219, 236–37
Seiffert, Max   61*fig*
Senate House Library   187
sexuality   50, 51, 141
Sharp, Geoffrey   143, 171
Shaw, Geoffrey   92
Shaw, George Bernard   70–71
   'The Reminiscences of a Quinquagenarian'   89–90
Shaw, H. Watkins   161*tab*
Shaw, Watkins, *Handel's Conducting Score of Messiah*   190–91
Shedlock, J.S.   183n.40
sheet music, market for   9–10, 12
sight-singing   6–7
SIM *see* International Society for Musical Research
SIMG see *Sammelbände der Internationalen Musikgesellschaft*
Simon, Alicja   63*fig*
Simpson, Thomas   166
Skene MS   6
Skinner, David   180
Slim, H. Colin, *A Gift of Madrigals*   185

Smart, Henry   20–21
Smeaton, Mark   180
Smijers, Albert   116
Smith, Alice Mary (Mrs Meadows White)   50
Smith, John Stafford   5*tab*
   Musica antiqua   5–6
Smyth, Ethel   59
social benefits   9–10, 51–54, 104–5, 127–28, 130
social class and status   50, 51, 97, 143–44
Société Union Musicologique   66
Society for Music Analysis   222
Society for Musicology in Ireland   228
Somfai, Lázló   190, 191, 192–93*tab*
song   4, 6, 86, 88–89
Sonneck, Oscar G.   12, 31–32, 48, 50, 61*fig*
sound   8
sound cultures   199
sound phenomena   4
sound recording   139
   BIRS (later National Sound Archive)   153–55
   licensing of   175–76
sound science   33–34
   acoustics   7, 34–35, 41, 150
sources *see* music sources
South Kensington Museum *see* Victoria & Albert Museum
Southgate, Thomas Lea   53, 62*fig*, 79*tab*, 88
Sphere (journal)   81*fig*
Spiro, Friedrich   62*fig*
Spiro-Rombro, Assia   62*fig*
Spitta, Philipp   49
Spohr, Louis   17
Spottiswoode, Hugh   45
Spottiswoode, William   33, 35–37, 43, 79*tab*
   Musical Association vice-president   38*fig*, 41
Spottiswoode & Co. (publisher)   72
Squire, William Barclay   24, 54, 58, 62*fig*, 80–82, 102n.17, 104
   'Musical Libraries and Catalogues'   82, 93
St James's Hall, London   18–19, 20–22
Stainer, Edward   50
Stainer, J.F.R.   50
Stainer, John   27, 99–100
   'A Fifteenth Century MS. Book of Vocal Music in the Bodleian Library, Oxford'   86
   MSL, member of   20
   music primers, editing of   28
   Musical Association, founding of   32–34, 36, 37

Musical Association president 68
  papers by 52, 86, 104, 157
Stainer & Bell (publisher) 151, 160, 165,
  195–96
Stanford, C.V. 27, 58, 63*fig*, 89, 154
Stanley, Albert A. 62*fig*, 64, 66
Stanley Lucas, Weber & Co. 45
Starr, Sidney 20*fig*
Stasov, Vladimir 88
Statham, H.H. 92
Steele, John 161*tab*
Stein, Fritz 62*fig*
Stephens, C.E. 37
Sternfeld, Frederick 105, 234
Stevens, Denis 161*tab*, 186–87
Stevens, John 157, 161*tab*
Stewart, R.P. 50
Stilwell, Robynn 219
Stock, Jonathan 226
Stone, W. H. 36, 37
Storace, Stephen, *No Song, No
  Supper* 158, 161*tab*
Stratton, Stephen S. 51n.35
  British Musical Biography 85
  'Women in Relation to Musical
    Art' 85
Strohm, Reinhard 226n.67
Stross, Emmy (later Wellesz) 62*fig*
students
  RMA conferences for 177, 216, 218
  RMA members 149, 174, 177, 187, 199,
    218–20
Sullivan, Arthur 36
Swinburne, James 51
  'Women and Music' 84n.94
Swinnerton-Dyer, Peter 214
Sylvester, James Joseph 50
Szymanowski, Karol 63*fig*

tablature 89
Talbot, Michael 188, 219n.48
Taylor, Sedley 36, 37, 79*tab*
teachers 143
teaching and training
  choirs 64
  sight-singing 6–7
  tonic sol-fa method 6, 64
Temperley, Nicholas 158
tempo 15, 89
Terry, Charles Sanford 73
Terry, Richard Runciman 70, 71, 82, 91,
  92, 93, 94
Tertis, Lionel 59
Thalben-Ball, Pamela 167*fig*
Thatcher, Reginald 143
Thorne, E.H. 37

Tillyard, H.J.W. 125
Tilmouth, Michael 175, 188
  'Calendar of References to Music in
    Newspapers' 156
Times, The (newspaper) 120, 121, 145–46,
  162–63, 166
Times Literary Supplement (*TLS*,
  journal) 172, 185–87
Tippett Medal 228, 250
Tomkins, Thomas 161*tab*, 166
tonality 90, 105, 182
tonic sol-fa method 6, 64
Torrefranca, Fausto 62*fig*
Tovey, D.F. 98, 148
Trend, J.B. 97, 106, 125, 141
Trowell, Brian 94, 193*tab*, 199, 214–15,
  222, 233n.2, 234
Tudor Church Music 82–83, 92–93
Turner, Malcolm 172, 187, 194, 213
Tuttle, Stephen 161*tab*
Tyndall, John 8, 34–35, 36, 37, 229–30
  Musical Association vice-
    president 38*fig*, 41
Tyrrell, John 188
Tyson, Alan 182, 184

United States of America (USA) 31, 141
universities 25–27, 147–49
  see also disciplines, academic;
    musicology
  music degrees 27, 141, 148, 153, 198–99,
    200*fig*
  music departments, closure
    of 214n.34, 228
  music posts 233
    growth of 140, 148–49, 198–99, 203
    reduction of 214
  and RMA membership 143, 194
  postgraduate study 149, 218
  RAE/REF 213–15, 223, 225–26, 228
University of Birmingham 149
University of Cambridge 26, 27, 105–6,
  149
  Hirsch Library, hosting of 119
  St John's College 64
University of Liverpool 148
University of London 26, 27, 117, 148
  Imperial College 224
  Imperial Institute 56
  KCL (King's College London) 184, 187,
    198, 200*fig*, 220
  Royal Holloway 197
  School of Advanced Study 228
  Senate House Library 187
University of Oxford 26, 27, 112, 148–49,
  184

Urkevich, Lisa   180

V&A *see* Victoria & Albert Museum
Van den Borren, Charles   50, 61*fig*, 104, 157
   'The Genius of Dunstable'   67, 93–94
Vaughan Williams, Ralph   58, 120, 143, 154
Verdi, Giuseppe   181
   Don Carlos   182
Verheyden, Prosper   67
Vernon, Philip E.   106
Victoria & Albert Museum (V&A)   7, 163–64
Victoria of the United Kingdom, Diamond Jubilee   53
Viotti, G.B.   15
Visetti, Albert   62*fig*
vocal music
   carols   161*tab*, 166
   choral   59, 74, 75*fig*, 161*tab*, 166
   folksong   88–89
   madrigals   91, 111, 185
   song   4, 6, 86
Volkmar-Arnheim, Betti   61*fig*

Wachsmann, Klaus   157
Wagner, Peter   112
Walker, D. P.   190, 191, 192–93*tab*
Walker, Ernest   125, 127
Wallace, William   59
Warlock, Peter (Philip Heseltine)   70
Warner, Sylvia Townsend   125, 127–28, 129*fig*, 130
   'The Point of Perfection in XVI Century Notation'   92–93
Wathey, Andrew   217, 224
Watkins, Cedric   183
Weber, Carl Maria von   107
Weelkes, Thomas   94
Wellesz, Egon   62*fig*, 112–13, 133, 145, 234
Wellesz, Emmy (formerly Stross)   62*fig*
Wells, Elizabeth   236
Wesley, Samuel   5, 5*tab*
Wesseley Quartet   59
Westminster Orchestral Society   58

Westrup, Jack (J.A.)   130n.85, 234
   academic career   143, 148–49, 184
   and Centenary celebration   190
   'Elgar's Enigma'   182
   and IMS Congress (1955)   152–53
   lectures and papers   154, 157, 159
   and Musica Britannica   152
   'Parodies and Parameters'   192*tab*
   on Research Committee   124
   and RILM project   197
   RMA president   168, 172, 173, 176
Wheatstone, Charles   33n.4, 36, 40
Whinyates, Seymour   120, 143
Whitehead & Miller (printer)   72, 156
Whittaker, W.G.   125
Whittall, Arnold   211n.25
   'The Study of Britten'   182
Wilbye, John   91
Williams, Alastair   211
Williams, Bernard   224
Wilson, Christopher   220
Wolf, Johannes   63*fig*, 109, 112, 114, 119n.65, 133
women
   composers   85, 205
   and music   84n.94, 85
   Musical Association members   40, 50, 71–72, 141
   Musical Association research papers by   69, 71–72
Wood, Charles   96
Wood, Henry J.   51
Woodham, Ronald   185
Woodley, Ronald   219n.48
Worshipful Company of Musicians   166, 190
Wylde, Henry   18, 19

Zaslaw, Neal   181
Zeitschrift der Internationalen Musikgesellschaft (ZIMG, journal)   55, 74, 187
Zeitschrift für Musikwissenschaft (journal)   113
Zimmermann, Agnes   40, 50

Printed in the United States
by Baker & Taylor Publisher Services